Show this
bk to Whitney.
a true 60's chronicle.

W9-CQF-831

DEEP COVER

DEEP COVER

An FBI Agent Infiltrates the Radical Underground

Cril Payne

NEWSWEEK BOOKS, New York

Printed in the United States of America

Library of Congress Cataloging in Publication Data
Payne, Cril.
    Deep cover: an FBI agent infiltrates the
radical underground.

    1. Payne, Cril. 2. U.S. Federal Bureau of
Investigation—Officials and employees—Biography.
3. Weather Underground Organization. 4. Radicalism—
United States. I. Title.
HV7911.P38A33   364.12′092′4   [B] 79-51632
ISBN 0-88225-274-7

Book Design: Mary Ann Joulwan

CONTENTS

FOR MY PARENTS

AUTHOR'S NOTE

The decision to write this book was the most difficult and prolonged decision of my life. The lengthy deliberations resulted in part from my belief that the book could have unpleasant ramifications for a number of innocent and well-meaning people—many of whom had suffered enough—as well as for the Federal Bureau of Investigation. But, of course, I was mindful of how these revelations would affect me. As I watched the events of the 1970s unfold, I realized that I had to write this book regardless of personal consequences.

I decided that certain fundamental conditions would have to be met before I started to write. First, the book had to be written by me. It was not that I viewed myself as being uniquely qualified to tell the story; rather I felt it vitally important that the story be told as accurately as possible, and without embellishment or enlargement by a professional author. Moreover, I could best ensure the protection of the identities of innocent individuals who are part of this story. Therefore, I have used many fictitious names, but all of the characters and events are true.

During my deep cover years I was not proud of many of the things I had done and I often felt that for the sake of my parents, career, and the FBI, these things were best left unsaid. But when I decided to write this book, it seemed ludicrous to attempt to make the account more palatable by omitting accounts of my unsavory behavior and distorting particular situations. How could I delete the details of sexual exploitation or drug use, which were part of the story? If the story was to be told at all it had to be told fully and truthfully.

To describe my experiences realistically without the use of profanity would have been impossible for me. Perhaps a more experienced writer could have done so—but I couldn't. While major parts of the dialogue sections are not verbatim, they are related as accurately as my memory allows.

This book is not an attempt to justify or defend the activities of the FBI, nor is it meant to serve as an apology for its actions. It describes the experiences and thoughts of one man who was intimately involved with undercover activities. Many have asked how government agents of purportedly high moral character, who had undergone thorough background investigations, could consciously violate the very laws they had sworn to uphold. I hope that this book will shed some light on the factors that influenced and motivated one particular deep cover agent.

I would like to express my gratitude to my agent, Perry Knowlton, who gave me early encouragement, and his associates, Jean Porter and J. P. Walter Reiman, who helped me in many ways. I want to thank Newsweek Books publisher Alvin Garfin and associate publisher Ann Tanenbaum for their confidence in me as a first-time author. My editors at Newsweek Books deserve a special thank you. They are Helene Mac-Lean, who has a major talent for perceptive and faithful editing, and Herbert Gilbert, managing editor, whose patience, understanding, and guidance aided me greatly. Most especially I am indebted to Valerie Hurst, an extraordinary woman, whose whole-hearted dedication throughout the work of this project was unflagging. Without her intelligent criticism—and her typing—there would have been no book. well,

1

Isla Vista

October 8, 1970 marked the third anniversary of the death of Ché Guevara, the Cuban revolutionary who was killed in Bolivia. In honor of the occasion, the Youth International Party, or "Yippies," held a news conference in New York City, where they played a tape purporting to be the voice of Weatherman fugitive Bernardine Dohrn. The voice warned that a "fall offensive of youth resistance" was about to begin that "will spread from Santa Barbara to Boston, back to Kent and Kansas." The recording went on to proclaim, "Now we are everywhere, and next week families and tribes will attack the enemy around the country. It is our job to blast away the myths of the total superiority of The Man."

Less than twenty-four hours later, at 4:10 A.M., a bomb exploded against an outside wall of the Santa Barbara National Guard Armory. Bernardine Dohrn was obviously a lady who meant what she said. But just to be certain everyone got the message, bombs were also exploded early the same morning in a San Rafael, California courtroom and at the ROTC building on the University of Washington campus in Seattle. Another bomb was disarmed before exploding inside a building at the University of California in Berkeley.

Significantly, the date also marked the first anniversary of the Weathermen "Days of Rage" when the violent demonstrations that engulfed Chicago resulted in over two hundred arrests and the bombing of a statue depicting a policeman in Haymarket Square. As the "fall offensive" began, a letter from the Weatherman underground claimed credit for the October 1969 bombing and a second bombing of the same statue: "A year ago we blew away the Haymarket pig statue at the start of a youth riot in Chicago. Last night we destroyed the pig again."

As a Special Agent assigned to the FBI's Los Angeles Field Office, I signed in as usual Friday morning and was quickly greeted by news of the bombings. The Santa Barbara bombing didn't seem overly important at that point, but then I'd never worked a bombing, knew next to nothing about the Weathermen, and had just been assigned to a "security" squad for the first time in my brief Bureau career. I did know that Santa Barbara had a Resident Agency (RA), however, that was included in the territory of the Los Angeles Division.

The agents' bullpen was buzzing with speculation about the bombing, but aside from that, it was just like any other morning. There were no cries to rally the troops or stand by for a crisis, so we went about our usual routine of a leisurely breakfast with the Los Angeles *Times*, countless cups of coffee, and a generous exchange of Bureau gossip. But when we straggled back to the office that afternoon after a hard day on the bricks, our squad area resembled a full scale mobilization.

Needless to say, the Director of the Federal Bureau of Investigation, the legendary J. Edgar Hoover, was in a rage. While he may not have been "the Man" Bernardine Dohrn was referring to, for those of us in the Bureau he was "the Director." And when the Director was tear-assed, we were all aware of his displeasure. It was bad enough for these "revolutionary-guerrillas," as the Director called them, to set off a few bombs, but to announce their intentions to the American people in advance, and then fulfill them, was unthinkable to Mr. Hoover. If this nonsense was not stopped, the public might decide the FBI had lost control of the situation. Consequently, the phones had been ringing off the wall with calls from Washington demanding a thorough and aggressive investigation with plenty of manpower.

Fred, our supervisor, who was commonly known as Fast Freddie, or the Super Chief, told me to grab a Bureau car, pack a suitcase, and meet him at the Santa Barbara RA as soon as possible.

"The RA's downtown in the Post Office Building," Fred hollered as I moved toward the elevators. "You can't miss it."

I didn't want to tell him that I wasn't even sure of how to get to Santa Barbara. I rushed out to my apartment in Marina del Ray, threw some clothes together, and headed back to the San Diego Freeway. As usual, the freeway was packed. Well, there goes the weekend, I thought, but at least it beats working Selective Service cases.

I had arrived in Los Angeles some ten months earlier with eager expectations of working in a fast, action-packed environment of the Bureau's second largest field office. Disappointingly, it had proved to be a monumental bore. I had been assigned to a Selective Service squad, where I was relegated to the position of record checker at the numerous draft boards throughout Los Angeles County.

plenty of action!

My first office of assignment after completing New Agents Training had been in Seattle, where I arrived in February 1969. Although I stayed there only nine months, the job of an FBI agent was everything I'd hoped for in the way of challenge and excitement. I was assigned to criminal fugitive squads where there was always plenty of action, little paper work, and virtually no involvement in moral judgments. Instead of developing evidence for potential prosecutions, we were concerned only with locating and arresting the fugitives so that they could be returned to the appropriate state of federal jurisdiction to stand trial. The fugitive investigations were incredibly interesting, and we were so busy, there just didn't seem to be enough time in the day to cover everything. I was so wrapped up in the job that I'd wait until Saturday morning to get my hair cut. Then one day my partner, a Bureau veteran of twenty years, inquired about my prior weekend activities.

"Goddamn!" he exclaimed. "You don't get your hair cut on your day off, son. If your hair grows on Bureau time, you oughta damn sure get it cut on Bureau time! Hell, the weekends are your time. Get out and enjoy yourself."

At the time, I was so gung-ho that I didn't always heed his advice. But once I arrived in Los Angeles, his words of wisdom were followed explicitly. In fact, the biggest problem in the LA office was trying to figure out what to do with idle time. After several months of checking records, I was replaced by another new arrival, but the situation didn't change appreciably. With more than fifty agents working on Selective Service cases was our squad supervisor, Fast Freddie, an amiable, unas-even further, I found myself unwilling to go out and harass some guy of approximately my age for not keeping in touch with his draft board. Perhaps it was because I had too many classmates who had done the same thing.

The only bright spot in the otherwise boring routine of Selective Service cases was our squad supervisor, Fast Freddie, an amiable, unassuming individual admired and respected for his fairness. Unlike many supervisors, Fred had not forgotten his lengthy career as a street agent; consequently, he recognized that many of the archaic rules and regulations were impossible to operate under if followed to the letter. In the maze of bureaucratic regulation, Fred demonstrated the ability to differentiate between the chicken salad and the chickenshit and allowed his men to function accordingly.

Fast Freddie had a lively sense of humor, but when the Inspectors descended upon the office for their annual charade, he was all business. Instead of rolling over to the Inspectors and following the exam-

typo, gup.

ple of other supervisors whose primary concern was to "cover their ass," he defended his men. He didn't offer up a youthful candidate to help fill the prearranged quota for "letters of censure;" he took the letter himself. Fred was one of the few supervisors who would stand up to the ruthless, dictatorial tyrant who served as Special Agent In Charge (SAC) of the Los Angeles Division, the notorious Wesley G. Grapp.

Since Fast Freddie and I were always able to speak candidly with each other, he was aware of my current dissatisfaction. He had offered to lobby for my transfer to the bank robbery squad, but in an office as large as Los Angeles, that was no simple matter. In the meantime, however, there was increasing speculation that a new squad would be formed to intensify the search for the Weathermen fugitives and investigate related bombings. Since Fred had worked on espionage cases for some twelve years before becoming a supervisor, he was considered both a likely and willing prospect for the new desk. The first time I questioned Fred about the rumors, he acknowledged he would like to have the squad and asked if I'd like to go with him if he were selected. My reply was an immediate "Yes."

It was a cumbersome, time-consuming procedure to obtain Bureau approval for the formation of a new squad, but the office Security Coordinator began the task of manufacturing a case load that would justify the action. Until the new squad was formally authorized, its supervisor could not be officially designated, so speculation concerning the appointment continued to circulate. But ironically, the Weathermen themselves played the most significant role in the formation of those specialized squads throughout the country.

As I would subsequently learn, the group was formed in June 1969 when the leadership faction of the Students for a Democratic Society (SDS) presented a position paper at the National Convention in Chicago titled, "You Don't Need a Weatherman to Know Which Way the Wind Blows." The phrase was derived from the lyrics of a Bob Dylan song, *Subterranean Homesick Blues*, and would eventually become the group's name. The violent, confrontation tactics advocated by the position paper caused the "Big Split" in SDS, with the Weatherman faction gaining control of the National Office.

In October 1969, the Weatherman faction put their militant, confrontation theory on the line as they battled the Chicago police in the "Days of Rage." At their last public gathering held in Flint, Michigan in December 1969, the Weatherman "War Council" decided the group would go underground. "We have to start tearing down this

14

country," Mark Rudd told the War Council. "We have to have a revolution in this country that's going to overthrow—like bombs, like guns, like firebombs, by anything and everything." Charles Manson was enshrined as a heroic symbol, and Weathermen began saluting each other with the fork sign, three fingers held up like the two-fingered peace sign but instead signifying the three-pronged serving fork left jabbed in the stomach of Robert LaBianca after his throat was brutally slashed by members of the Manson Family. It was heralded as "the year of the fork" and the criterion for revolutionary action became "the heavier the better."

Some three months after the War Council, on March 6, 1970, a violent explosion demolished a fashionable townhouse on Eleventh Street in New York City's Greenwich Village. The owner of the house, who was away on vacation at the time, was the father of Weatherman member Cathy Wilkerson. The basement had been converted into an underground bomb factory containing more than fifty sticks of dynamite, blasting caps, wiring, timing devices, and pipe. The bodies of Weatherman members Ted Gold, Terry Robbins, and Diana Oughton, a Bryn Mawr graduate and descendant of the founder of the Boy Scouts of America, were literally blow apart by the blast. The grizzly photograph of what was believed to be the remains of Terry Robbins revealed nothing but a headless torso from which arm and leg bones grotesquely protruded. There was simply too little left upon which to base a positive identification.

Apparently undaunted by the violent mishap, the Weathermen sent a communiqué from the underground in May 1970, which was purportedly a transcript of a tape. The three-page document got right to the point: "Hello. This is Bernardine Dohrn. I'm going to read a DECLARATION OF A STATE OF WAR." The text of the communication began with the following statement: "All over the world, people fighting Amerikan imperialism look to Amerika's youth to use our strategic position behind enemy lines to join forces in the destruction of the empire."

For those who may have been uncertain, the "Declaration of War" made the Weatherman position clear: "Ever since SDS became revolutionary, we've been trying to show how it is possible to overcome the frustration and impotence that comes from trying to reform this system. Kids know the lines are drawn; revolution is touching all of our lives. Tens of thousands have learned that protests and marches don't do it. Revolutionary violence is the only way.

"Freaks are revolutionaries and revolutionaries are freaks," proclaimed the Weatherman's first underground communication. "If you want to find us, this is where we are. In every tribe, commune, dormitory, farmhouse, barracks, and townhouse where kids are making love, smoking dope and loading guns—fugitives from Amerikan justice are free to go."

Quite predictably, the Director of the FBI did not take too kindly to these revolutionary exhortations. From the reports that circulated throughout the field, Mr. Hoover was outraged. The situation was rapidly progressing to the point where the group was becoming an embarrassment to the Bureau. Accordingly, drastic measures were called for to intensify the search for the fugitive revolutionaries. From all indications, the Weathermen had officially replaced the Black Panther Party as the most serious threat to internal security. The group was now the potential successor to the "Communist menace."

Any lingering doubts about the severity of the terrorist problem were dispelled on the night of August 24, 1970, when the Army Mathematics Research Center at the University of Wisconsin was bombed. The massive explosion killed a graduate student, injured four others, and caused an estimated six million dollars in damage.

Since the Director had only recently resisted attempts by the Nixon White House to implement the "Huston Plan" to broaden the permissible scope of domestic intelligence operations, I would suspect that he equated arrest of the Weathermen with vindication for his opposition. Weatherman squads now sprang up throughout the Bureau. In Los Angeles, Fast Freddie was selected to head the effort, and a number of agents from his Selective Service squad, including myself, went along with him.

Credit for the Santa Barbara bombing was immediately claimed by a group calling itself the "Perfect Park Homegrown Garden Society," but what in the hell was that? None of the resident agents had heard of a group by that name. Suspicion centered on the student community of Isla Vista where the University of California at Santa Barbara (UCSB) was located. Because of possible embarrassment to the Bureau, the Director had earlier outlawed the utilization of informants under the age of twenty-one. The effects of that decision were now painfully obvious, for there were no reliable confidential sources in Isla Vista; moreover, there was little hope of ever developing any.

A couple of days after the National Guard bombing, a UCSB student telephoned the Santa Barbara Resident Agency and offered to assist.

the FBI in its investigation. At the insistence of the agent, the caller provided personal background information for verification of his identity and a telephone number for future contact. The student claimed he was eager to meet with an agent and discuss his offer of assistance. The incident had all the earmarks of a setup, but at the time, we really had no choice but to pursue the matter.

Since I was the youngest agent in the group, had never been in Santa Barbara, and sported the longest hair—which wasn't really saying too much—I was selected to meet with the caller and determine if he was on the level. To insure my safety, Fast Freddie and the local resident agents had devised an intricate scheme in which our meeting on a pier at the Santa Barbara marina would be covered by a number of agents in radio contact with each other. The possibility of surprise was thus virtually eliminated. Our primary concern was that attempts would be made to photograph or record the meeting for the purpose of revealing my identity and causing future embarrassment.

On a beautiful autumn afternoon, I met with the student—I'll call him "Arlo"—at the far end of the pier. We were both a bit apprehensive at first, but in no time at all, our uneasiness passed. Arlo was a rugged, athletic-looking kid who had obviously given considerable thought to working for the FBI. He impressed me right away with his straightforward analysis of the situation and seemed genuinely disturbed by what was taking place in Isla Vista. Like so many of his age, Arlo was against the war in Vietnam but equally opposed to the use of violence to focus attention on the issue. In Arlo's opinion, the militant, highly vocal minority of activists who employed violence in order to raise the public consciousness were actually more concerned with starting a revolution than ending the war.

I obtained some additional background information from Arlo, established a communications system using code names, and advised him I'd be back in touch after some further checking. Although I didn't realize it at the time, our meeting marked the beginning of a lengthy relationship that would prove to be personally enlightening and professionally rewarding.

Isla Vista, or I.V. as the locals called it, was located a short distance north of Santa Barbara and was unlike any community I had ever seen. Its limited commercial district was adjacent to the campus, and the housing, most of which stretched north along the coastline, consisted of apartments, duplexes, and older houses which were rented to students or those of similar age. A few single-family dwellings were

17

owned by professors or university employees, but for the most part, Isla Vista was pure youth culture.

From what I was told, the Santa Barbara campus was once considered a fun-loving party school where academics were secondary to having a good time. It was jokingly referred to as the University by the Sea, since both the school and Isla Vista were built on cliffs next to the Pacific Ocean, providing a panoramic view of the Channel Islands looming on the horizon. With a university environment that provided miles of isolated beaches and a community composed almost entirely of students, it's not difficult to understand why fun in the sun might take precedence over learning. After all, there aren't many institutions of higher education where you can surf between classes, play volleyball, or just lie on the beach and pretend to study.

By the time I arrived in Isla Vista, there was little evidence of the carefree party days of old. On the contrary, I.V. looked like a militant, revolutionary community whose inhabitants appeared hostile, suspicious, and defiantly radical. It seemed as though everyone had long hair, dressed shabbily, resented authority, and despised the Establishment. Illegal drugs were used openly and in apparent disregard for potential arrest. It wasn't at all uncommon to see kids nonchalantly smoking marijuana as they walked to class, and the "Smoothie" stand, which sold a blended concoction of fruit, yogurt, honey, and ice cream, featured a Peyote Smoothie with the price determined by the number of buttons requested. Vacant lots had been converted into communal people's gardens where organic vegetables were grown. The walls of just about every commercial building in town were covered with brightly colored psychedelic murals and revolutionary slogans. Even the streets were painted with replicas of Viet Cong flags and antiwar graffiti. I don't recall a stop sign in I.V. that hadn't been altered to read "STOP the War" or "STOP the Pigs." In the revolutionary vernacular of the day, Isla Vista was a "liberated Zone" for the youth of the counter-culture.

While I wasn't actually present during the violent turmoil that had earlier rocked Isla Vista and produced the dramatic change in attitudes, I did have the opportunity to speak with a number of students, as well as law enforcement officers, who were involved in the confrontations. As best I could tell, the situation was a prime example of revolutionary philosophy at work. A small group of dedicated, militant activists decided to raise the "revolutionary consciousness" of the student population by conducting demonstrations protesting the Vietnam War and the draft. They also threw in a few local issues that were

18

of far greater concern to the average student, such as rent gouging by absentee landlords, overpricing by local businessmen, and the absence of any participation in the county political process. But the primary issue would become "exploitation" by the Bank of America which was located in the very heart of I.V.

Initially, the only people concerned with the demonstrations against the bank were the activists who put them on, many of whom were non-students. But as the disruptions continued to escalate, county law enforcement decided it was time to put an end to the foolishness. From all indications, the officer selected to supervise the problem was less than competent, and his conduct, not to mention his inflammatory appearance, only intensified an already volatile situation. According to the version I heard, the contingent of law enforcement officers rolled into Isla Vista and brazenly waded into the demonstrators only to discover that the activists were armed with rocks, bottles, and projectiles. What was anticipated as a show of force to restore law and order reportedly turned out to be just the opposite. In short, law enforcement suffered a resounding kick in the ass during the initial confrontation, and a number of police officers were seriously injured.

But the humiliation suffered by the police was probably the worst thing that could have happened. The anger and frustration of the police were an essential ingredient for the success of the revolutionary formula. If a small group of radicals could create enough violence to provoke the police into overreacting, then the subsequent police repression would involve *everyone* in the student community. Once an innocent student was hassled, arrested, or subjected to curfews, it was believed that his "revolutionary consciousness" was raised because he had become personally involved in the struggle; therefore, such students would join forces with the radicals in justifiable opposition to police repression. The purpose of the original demonstrations would then become irrelevant. According to the theory, violence committed by a small minority results in police repression of the majority, producing more popular support for the radical minority.

Law enforcement unwittingly played its role to perfection by calling for emergency assistance from departments as far away as Los Angeles. With only two roads leading to the campus and Isla Vista, the entire area was effectively sealed off and turned into a war zone. The boys from the big city's tactical squads had come to teach those dirty hippies a lesson. With officers from a number of departments rampaging and out of control, there was little regard for individual rights. Anyone with long hair was fair game.

By the time order was restored, the Bank of America had been burned to the ground, and a well-meaning student who was pleading with the crowd to refrain from violence had been shot to death on the steps of the bank. The shooting was initially attributed to unidentified demonstrators, but it was later revealed, after what could only be explained as an attempted cover-up, that the fatal bullet came from a police officer's weapon which had accidentally misfired. Hundreds of innocent students had been arrested, beaten, and harassed. Apartments had been raided, doors kicked in, and indiscriminate searches conducted. Numerous injuries were sustained by both students and police.

It was almost as though a handful of radical activists and county law enforcement had worked in concert to radicalize the community of Isla Vista. Instead of a hundred militant protestors, there were now literally thousands. Virtually no one in the student community had gone untouched by the incident, and regardless of the original issues, the residents of I.V. had become united in their hatred for the "pigs."

The beer and marijuana once stockpiled in I.V. residences were replaced by weapons. Dynamite, blasting caps, and automatic weapons became fashionable. Fraternity and sorority members, jocks, surfers, independents, politicos—the entire spectrum of university life—began to look, dress, and act like dedicated revolutionaries. But paradoxically, the great majority of our informants would ultimately come from these same groups. Like Arlo, many had been arrested and beaten for nothing more than standing in their own front yards and watching the show, or for missing curfew. Now they had a criminal record they would have to explain to friends, parents, and prospective employers for the rest of their lives. While most despised the local authorities, many were astute enough to realize that the incident had been precipitated by a small minority of militants who were trying to destroy the system through violence.

And what had the militant activists really accomplished? The bank had been rebuilt, the war hadn't been stopped, a student was dead, a number of innocent people had police records, and Isla Vista had become an armed camp where paranoia, suspicion, and hatred of "the pig" reigned supreme. Students like Arlo realized that it was only a matter of time until the community erupted in violence once again.

The pressure from Bureau Headquarters to solve the Santa Barbara bombing was unrelenting. But as usual, when a situation appears so grim that it can't get any worse—it does. Shortly after the bombing of the National Guard Armory, someone tried to blow up the entire fleet of vehicles at the Army Reserve Center! A large number of jeeps and trucks were positioned in precise military fashion against the chain link fence that encloses the facility. After scaling the fence late one evening, someone had opened all the gas tanks and poured a trail of gasoline that connected each vehicle in the line. Luckily, the gasoline was not ignited by the crude timing device and there was no damage. Nevertheless, the heat was on, and Washington wanted results.

We were working seven days a week covering every possible lead, and a daily teletype had to be submitted to the Bureau each evening detailing the day's progress. In reality, our progress was slight, especially since the investigation had centered on individuals living in Isla Vista, and it was impossible for regular agents to operate in the area. A clean-cut FBI agent couldn't even drive through I.V. in a Bureau car without half the street people hollering "pig" and following along on bicycles. And on more than one occasion, unmarked police cars left unattended mysteriously ended up with flat tires or broken windows. It was a situation the FBI was unprepared to deal with.

Many blocks in the community were organized into tenants' groups whose members were assigned specific times for "pig watch." Once the police were spotted, the entire block could be systematically alerted in a matter of minutes. In practice, the limited access which allowed the police to seal off I.V. quickly, also effectively prohibited them from entering unnoticed. This was just one of the many features which made Isla Vista a haven for fugitives.

I arranged with Fast Freddie to have another agent sent up from Los Angeles to help cover my contacts with Arlo. We had been meeting nearly every day, and Arlo just didn't have the time or an excuse to be traveling into Santa Barbara regularly. Since it was essential that we begin meeting in Isla Vista, the Crane arrived to give me a hand.

The Crane and I had been in the same class in law school, although we weren't close friends until we entered the Bureau. He was a few months ahead of me in New Agents Training and was leaving for his first Field Office about the time I arrived in Washington. He did manage to give me the big picture on Bureau training however, as well as a thorough introduction to the bars in Georgetown.

Crane had been transferred to Los Angeles a couple of months before I arrived, and like me was bored with the routine of being a gofer. He had come over to the Weatherman squad when it was formed, and I was damn happy to have him in Isla Vista. At the time, I'm sure neither of us realized it would be Christmas before we returned to Los Angeles.

Crane and I had both been raised in conservative Texas families and had attended high school, college, and law school in the state. We were the same age, were nonsmokers, and shared the distinction of being an only child. I suppose we had exactly the type of conservative, patriotic background the FBI wanted in an agent. But it was a background that left us unprepared for the life-style we encountered in Isla Vista.

Demonstrations, drugs, and free love were things I'd never even heard of when I was in college. If a woman had attended classes at Texas Tech during the early sixties without a bra, she would have probably been asked to leave. In Isla Vista some five years later, bras were about as common as whalebone corsets. Things were beginning to change when I started law school in 1965, but we were so isolated from the undergraduate campus at the University of Texas that it wasn't really noticeable.

I was naturally aware there was a war going on in Vietnam, but in all honesty, at the time it wasn't of paramount importance. It seemed real only when I learned that friends from college had been killed. Between working, studying, and attending law classes, my days were well-occupied. And I always figured that once I graduated from law school and passed the bar exam, I'd actually be in Vietnam with plenty of time to learn about the issues. I never even *considered* any other course of action. If the draft board said go, which they surely would, I'd go. It was my duty as an American, and never once did I stop to think that perhaps the war was illegal, immoral, or unnecessary.

Shortly after graduating from law school in June of '68, everything suddenly changed. I had applied for Officer Candidate programs in the navy, air force, marines, and army and unexpectedly failed every physical test because of hypertension. The army had been my last attempt, and when I was rejected for the Officer's Program, they changed my draft classification to 1-Y. Now I didn't even have to go! But since I'd always planned on entering the service, I hadn't interviewed a single law firm during my three years of school. While I should have been overjoyed at my good fortune with the draft, I couldn't help feeling a little guilty at not serving my country. Perhaps I was still enthralled by Kennedy's Camelot and his challenge to "ask what you can do for your country." But whatever the reason, I immediately applied to the FBI, and by mid-October received an appointment as a Special Agent.

While I had an opportunity to study the Vietnam issue after becoming an FBI agent, my underlying opinion regarding the propriety of the war remained unchanged. Had it not been for the profound experiences of Isla Vista, my life might have remained unchanged as well.

With the help of Arlo and other sources we had developed, investigation into the armory bombing began to focus on a Weatherman-oriented collective that published an underground newspaper in Isla Vista. Many of those involved in the group were former UCSB students with a lengthy history in the antiwar movement. Several of the group's leaders were found to have been associated with the missing Weatherman fugitives, and there was substantial evidence that certain Weathermen had recently visited the area.

Crane and I began to scrutinize the activities of collective members, often with the aid of surveillance teams from Los Angeles. Fast Freddie had obtained an aging Volkswagen bus for our use in I.V. and was in the process of leasing more undercover vehicles for the new Weatherman squad. Without the proper vehicles, surveillance was an impossibility in Isla Vista since the inhabitants could spot a "pig" car blocks away. But due to the layout of the community, it was often easier to follow a subject on foot or bicycle. We soon learned, however, that vans were ideal for photographic surveillance. I would drive up to a location with an unobstructed view, park the van, lock the door, and casually walk away. Crane would be sitting in back with the curtain behind the front seats partially separated. As our subjects would enter or leave the location, he would photograph them with a telephoto lens. On one particular occasion, we had a thousand millimeter lens about the size of a bazooka mounted on tripods in the back of the van. With a telephoto lens that size, we could park a block away and still obtain full face photos. But since people were constantly walking within inches of the van, the photographer had to be exceedingly quiet and possess a well-trained bladder.

As the weeks passed, I slowly realized that my appearance wasn't all that different from many of those in Isla Vista. For the first time in my life, I sported a mustache, and my hair was longer than I ever thought possible. My appearance wasn't that of a dedicated freak, but I certainly didn't look like any FBI agent I'd ever seen. I began spending more time rapping with street people, learning a new vocabulary, and building self-confidence.

The first major function that Crane and I attended with our new hippy look was the Tenth Anniversary Celebration of the National Liberation Front (N.L.F.). The festivities were conducted in the park, which was centrally located in the heart of Isla Vista. The park, which was actually just vacant land, had been the scene of earlier disturbances, and one corner of the adjoining property was occupied by the newly constructed Bank of America. I suppose it was a matter of corporate pride—and defiance—to build another bank, but from a practical standpoint, it couldn't have been in a worse location. Just about every rally or demonstration would begin in the park, and since the nearby bank was viewed as a symbol of corporate exploitation and a grim reminder of a tragic death, it was the frequent target of angry protestors.

The organizers of the celebration, a number of whom were suspects in the earlier bombing, had worked for weeks making Viet Cong flags for the event. Flags were flying everywhere in the park, and even the street in front had a Viet Cong flag with the slogan "NLF Will Win" painted on its surface. The celebration had been well-publicized and was attended by a bizarre conglomeration of people from around the state. By far the largest and most militant delegation was the group from Berkeley. It was soon apparent that they had come prepared for a revolutionary action.

As the festival got under way, it was like many of the others we would attend over the next several months. A local band played rock music to attract attention, freaks milled around the park, dogs and children ran wild while frisbees and marijuana smoke filled the air. I'll never forget seeing one little boy, not more than five years old, who was parading through the park carrying a large Viet Cong flag. Another kid of approximately the same age playfully pushed the boy from behind and sent him tumbling down a slight incline. The little boy jumped up and verbally assaulted the kid by calling him a "fascist asshole!"

The featured speaker for the event was Chicago Seven defendant Rennie Davis. For some reason, the United States Attorney in Chicago had requested that all public statements made by the seven defendants, as well as by attorneys William Kunstler and Leonard Weinglass, who had been sentenced for contempt, be recorded by FBI agents using concealed recorders. Since both the antiriot convictions and contempt charges were under appeal, the Chicago Seven defendants and their attorneys had been released on bail pending the outcome of the appeal.

In order to record the speech of Rennie Davis, an agent had been dispatched from Los Angeles with a briefcase recorder. Crane and I called the guy "Chop" and jokingly referred to him as the Bureau's "token oriental." Some higher-up had apparently decided that he could pose as a foreign graduate student and nonchalantly sit on the grass with his briefcase amidst hundreds of freaks. He did his best, but no sooner had he sat down than a couple of heavy-looking dudes pounced on him and succinctly outlined the alternatives: either leave immediately or have his ass stomped. Chop's protestations went unheard and he wisely chose to leave.

The recording incident was both ridiculous and unnecessary. It seemed highly unlikely that one of the convicted defendants who was out on bail would publicly urge a large group to violence. And when Davis made his brief talk, his remarks were innocuous and noticeably lacking in revolutionary fervor.

Later that evening, Crane and I got up enough courage to talk with Rennie Davis. Surprisingly, the guy seemed friendly and eager to answer our questions about the war. He certainly talked as though he knew what was going on in Vietnam. After a lengthy conversation, I walked away wondering whether Rennie Davis was really the dangerous radical he was made out to be. Much to my surprise, I would have a number of future opportunities to find out.

When darkness descended upon the park, drug use became the major pastime. Clouds of marijuana smoke filled the air as joints were passed from every direction. As we gathered around a roaring bonfire, half-gallon jugs of cheap wine began making the rounds. Within a short time the crowd was in high spirits. But the main topic of conversation was the same one I'd heard discussed over and over again in Isla Vista: how to destroy the Bank of America.

Opposition to law enforcement and the Bank of America seemed to be the overriding issues that galvanized the diverse community. The residents were outraged at the audacity of a giant corporation that would immediately rebuild after the violent demonstrations and tragic death of a student. It was almost like a game among those who were constantly trying to figure out how to "destroy the monster." But the folks in San Francisco had anticipated those games when they designed and constructed their new banking facility. Isla Vista residents bitterly referred to the bank as "The Alamo" since the structure resembled an impregnable fortress.

The thick walls were reportedly constructed of reinforced concrete, and the few windows were protected against breakage by a decorative metal lattice. Concrete planter boxes around the exterior walls provided a further margin of safety against ramming or explosives. The building's tile-surfaced roof featured an exaggerated overhang and slope. It would take a mighty heave to throw objects onto the flat portion of the roof, and those that didn't make it would slide off a good distance away

from the walls. The parking lot was well-lighted, separated from the park by a chain link fence and guarded nightly by security officers who remained outside in the lot. And according to local rumor, the bank possessed a sophisticated alarm and sprinkler system that would make another fire an impossibility.

As the crowd in the park grew more surly, rocks and wine bottles began flying over the fence and smashing against the bank. One freak ran up to the fence and scored a direct hit with a wine bottle against the drive-in window. The bullet-proof glass remained unbroken as the bottle shattered. The security guards quietly dodged the flying missiles and made a diligent effort to keep from provoking the attack. The group began taunting the guards from outside the fence and eventually succeeded in pulling down a small section of the barrier.

Several times during the day's events, I'd heard activists from Berkeley comment that they wouldn't try to tell Isla Vista residents what form of revolutionary action they should employ, since that was a decision properly made by members of the community. Unfortunately, a few members of the Berkeley contingent strayed from their stated position.

There were a number of people milling around the bank on a subsequent evening, and Crane and I had been among the crowd for hours. We had been observing the Berkeley group, many of whom were in and out of their converted school bus, and we were intrigued by the activities of one particular freak who wore a beret and sported a beard and mustache that resembled Ché Guevara's.

It was a bit chilly, and after walking the area for hours, we decided to head over to the Taco Bell for a late dinner. Just as we were crossing the street, we heard a tremendous explosion, followed shortly by cheers from the crowd.

Holy shit! I thought. Some bastard's really done it! Crane and I looked at each other in stunned, silent disbelief, then went running back toward the bank. It seemed that our friend from Berkeley had casually lofted a military hand grenade on top of the Bank of America, blowing a good-size hole in the roof! But the hole was a minor problem compared to the chaos that followed. The bank's sophisticated sprinkler proceeded to dump several feet of water on the interior, causing considerable damage to the contents. The hand grenade didn't destroy the bank, but it certainly produced one gigantic mess.

As we would later discover, the various radical organizations along the West Coast possessed an abundance of military weapons and explosives. Most of those armaments were provided by individuals of similar persuasion who had been drafted and were systematically ripping them off from the military. (Fort Ord seemed to be the local favorite.) An entire truckload of explosives seemed mild when compared to the plans of another I.V. group: they claimed to have obtained an army field bazooka for their assault on The Alamo!

In December 1970, Weatherman leader Bernardine Dohrn issued another communication from the underground, entitled "New Morning: Changing Weather." The statement began by reflecting on the earlier "townhouse explosion" where three Weathermen were accidentally killed while manufacturing "anti-personnel bombs" to be used in a "large scale, almost random bombing offensive." The projected offensive was designed "to hurt the pigs materially" because it was believed that the earlier bombings of buildings had failed to do so.

Significantly, the townhouse explosion had changed the direction of Weatherman philosophy. According to the communiqué:

"The townhouse forever destroyed our belief that armed struggle is the only revolutionary struggle. It is time for the movement to go out into the air, to organize, risk calling rallies and demonstrations, to convince that mass actions against the war in support of rebellions do make a difference." The tendency to consider "only bombings or picking up the gun as revolutionary" was described as a "military error."

While the communication did not repudiate violence altogether, it seemed to indicate a new strategy that was not based entirely on armed struggle and certainly not on politics, but more along the lines of the youth culture. In an apparent attempt to encourage Weathermen to achieve a leadership position among youth, the document states:

"People have been experimenting with everything about their lives, fierce against the ways of the White man. They have learned how to survive together in the poisoned cities and on the road and the land. They have moved to the country and found new ways to bring up free wild children. People have purified themselves with organic food, fought for sexual liberation, grown long hair. People have reached out for each other and learned that grass and organic consciousness-expanding drugs are weapons of the revolution. While we sing of drugs, the enemy knows how great a threat our youth culture is to their rule. Thus, the free style of the commune will transform them from bourgeoisie to revolutionary radicals."

It now appeared that the Weathermen had begun to focus their efforts on the hippies and street people whose amorphous subculture was a major segment of the highly individualistic, unstructured coalition called the "Movement." Of particular interest to me was the following statement:

"It is our closeness and the integration of our personal lives with our revolutionary work that will make it hard for undercover pigs to infiltrate our collectives. It's one thing for pigs to go to a few meetings, even meetings of a secret cell. It's much harder for them to live in a family for long without being detected."

2

Undercover (Unofficially)

While Crane and I were in Isla Vista, the efforts of the Weatherman squad in Los Angeles had been directed toward the Venice area, where a number of known Weatherman associates lived. Of particular interest were a group of activists who would later become known as the "Tucson Five" after their refusal to cooperate with a federal grand jury investigating the alleged interstate transportation of dynamite and firearms by Weathermen John Fuerst and Roberta Smith.

When I first viewed our squad's Venice operation early in 1971, I was astounded. To get money out of the Bureau for special projects had never been a simple matter, but from all indications, that was no longer the case where the Weathermen were concerned. An apartment had been rented next to a house occupied by members of a Weatherman collective, and every individual who visited the house was photographed along with his vehicle. A portable communications system in the apartment alerted a surveillance team parked several blocks away, whenever unidentified subjects left the house and drove off. Provided with the license number and description of the vehicle, the surveillance team followed them.

The Bureau had authorized the purchase of two radio-equipped Honda "750" motorcycles, perfect for maneuvering in the bumper-to-bumper traffic on the Los Angeles freeways. But while motorcycles were highly effective, they were also highly dangerous. Being a motorcycle enthusiast myself, I owned a Triumph Bonneville which I used on undercover assignments and surveillances. Riding the freeways was dangerous enough, but on those rare instances when it rained, the oil-slicked pavement was almost like ice. And since a surprising number of motorists had little regard for motorcycles, particularly those ridden by freaks, many drivers seemed to delight in seeing just how close they could come to hitting you as they passed by. In short, you had to be a little looney to be a biker on the surveillance team's "chain gang." The other team members used leased Volkswagen vans and sedans or older Bureau cars that had been altered to look inconspicuous. Their radios were hidden under the seats or in the glove compartment to avoid detection.

Crane and I would occasionally work with the surveillance team, but since we were the only two agents who didn't look like agents, our undercover activities in Isla Vista took precedence over the L.A. operation. When we did work in L.A., we were primarily utilized to check out residents or addresses in areas where regular agents would attract attention.

There were a great number of people who still believed the FBI had no "hippy" agents. While many of those involved in the antiwar movement had become justifiably suspicious, it was doubtful they would associate us with FBI agents. For example, Crane and I would sometimes be sent on late night "trash patrols" in Los Angeles. Since J. Edgar Hoover had previously used his testimony before the Senate Appropriations Committee to declare publicly that Fathers Daniel and Philip Berrigan were guilty of an "incipient plot" to kidnap Henry Kissinger, the field was placed in the unenviable position of investigating groups of militant, antiwar Catholics in order to substantiate the Director's charges. I often wondered if any of the former priests and nuns involved in those activist groups ever saw a couple of freaks loading their garbage into a VW van in the middle of the night. After we made our "trash patrol" rounds, we left the garbage in the Bureau garage so that other agents could go through it the following day in search of evidence.

We discovered that working undercover in Los Angeles required a whole new approach to the problem of concealed weapons. An informant had advised us that Mark Rudd would visit a bar on the Sunset Strip to complete a transaction for the purchase of dynamite. Regular agents were positioned around the area to make the arrest if we spotted Rudd. Crane and I had cut down an alley in back of the bar to check out the rear door in case a foot race was necessary. We looked like most of the other freaks on the Strip with our long hair, jeans, boots, and army surplus fatigue jackets. As we walked down the alley, two cops came out of the shadows.

"Hold it!" one officer commanded. "What are you doing?"

"Nothin'," I said. "Just takin' a short cut to our car."

"What's in your pockets?"

"Nothing," Crane answered.

"Pull your hands out real slow," he ordered. "Both of you!"

The officers moved over to search us and first reached into Crane's coat pocket. The cop turned white when he pulled out a snub-nosed .38 special! They ordered us to lie face down on the pavement with our arms and legs spread-eagled. The cop gingerly reached into Crane's opposite pocket and pulled out a blackjack. He stepped over toward me and immediately hit the jackpot, locating a .38 snubby in my right pocket. From my position on the ground, I glanced over to my right toward the rear entrance of the bar. Three freaks were standing outside on the landing watching the show. Then I looked back at the younger officer who was covering us. His eyes were as big as saucers, and the .357 combat magnum in his hand was shaking. I suppose it wasn't every day that he collared two freaks in an alley packing heat.

After being handcuffed and walked out of sight, the matter was resolved when we showed our Bureau credentials. Needless to say, we were through for the night. Since people from inside the bar had seen the bust, we couldn't possibly return. It didn't really matter, however, for Mark Rudd never showed up.

Although I continued to maintain an apartment in the Marina, about the only time I would see it was on the weekends, since most of our undercover work was conducted in Isla Vista and Santa Barbara. It got to the point where Crane and I could almost drive Highway 101 blindfolded after traveling it so often. I doubt there was a single demonstration, rally, conference, or workshop held in I.V. or Santa Barbara during 1971 that we didn't attend. In addition, we made frequent trips to talk with Arlo and other student sources. The situation progressed to the point where Santa Barbara was almost like home.

The first statewide meeting we attended in Isla Vista was the Peoples Peace Treaty Convention. The purpose of the convention was to "ratify" a peace treaty negotiated by a group of American antiwar activists with representatives of North Vietnam. It was hoped that overwhelming support from students could ultimately force the United States government to accept the treaty. A noble though highly impractical idea.

After attending dozens of conferences, conventions, meetings and workshops, we observed that the only factor common to every gathering was that the participants could never reach agreement on anything. The various political groups were fiercely dogmatic over their ideologies and fought constantly for influence. At times there seemed a much greater concern for political theory than for the war in Viet-

nam. Participants would argue for hours over whether the students or the workers would bring the revolution. I had a difficult time understanding why the Bureau was so concerned over the threat from the so-called "New Left."

The smaller discussion groups were no better. Political groups would attempt to take over the meeting, dominate discussion, or change topics by asking for a consensus of the majority present. Even worse were the endless hours of "criticism—self-criticism" sessions. In one discussion group I attended, the participants argued violently for over an hour about whether self-criticism should come before criticism, or vice versa!

Occasionally, there were some intelligent, articulate speakers who possessed a wealth of knowledge on a particular subject. At the Peoples Peace Treaty Convention, for example, there was Bob Scheer from *Ramparts* magazine, who impressed me immensely. He said some disturbing things about the conduct of the war, especially about the secret bombings of neighboring countries in Southeast Asia. He seemed to have so much detailed, factual knowledge on the subject that his speech had to be taken seriously. While some of his claims sounded outlandish at the time, they were later proved to be correct. Crane and I talked with Bob Scheer after his presentation and posed a number of questions about the war. He provided thorough, concise answers, and though I'm sure he didn't realize it, his remarks raised serious doubts in the minds of two FBI agents regarding the conduct of the war.

Another individual who impressed me with his seemingly unlimited knowledge of the war and Southeast Asia was Tom Hayden. I must have talked with him on at least a dozen different occasions, and each time came away feeling enlightened but overwhelmed. He could expound on a subject as though he were reading the text from an encyclopedia. He seemed more like a thinker or political theoretician than a violent revolutionary. Somehow, I had the feeling that Hayden was just too smart to believe that things could be changed by fighting in the streets. He attended many of the conferences in Isla Vista, and since I lived only a few blocks away from his apartment in Venice, I'd run into him from time to time.

In a way, I couldn't help feeling sorry for Tom Hayden. From all indications, he was still paying heavy dues for his commitment to what were perceived by some as radical political beliefs. His car was vandalized a number of times while parked near his apartment building in

Venice. Once a surveillance team agent was sitting in the rear of a truck late one night when a car pulled up, two men jumped out, and proceeded to smash windows and flatten the tires of Hayden's car. The agent got the license number, but an inquiry on the plate came back with a report "not in file," a not unusual practice for undercover vehicles. According to the agent, it was later learned that the vehicle belonged to the Intelligence Unit of a local law-enforcement agency.

Since most of those who attended conferences in Isla Vista and Santa Barbara were noticeably short on funds, lodging accommodations were always a major problem. Many of the religious student centers in I.V. often provided floor space for sleeping bags, and the local organizers generally tried to locate space in area residences. But by far the most luxurious accommodations were provided through the courtesy of the Santa Barbara YMCA.

One of the student organizers for another conference we attended worked part-time at the "Y" and persuaded YMCA officials to allow the male delegates to sleep on the gym floor. Naturally, the student didn't reveal that the "delegates" were predominantly freaks or that the "conference" involved radical politics. From what I was told, YMCA officials, under the impression that it was a religious conference, agreed to provide use of the gym floor with the understanding that none of the other facilities be used.

The episode that followed was probably unrivaled in the annals of Young Men's Christian Association, for it could best be described as "Drug and Perversion Night at the Y"! Word of the unusual accommodations had spread like wildfire through the conference, and when the student organizer unlocked the building late that evening, he was followed by a crowd of both men and women. The group wasted little time removing their clothes, smoking dope, and drinking beer. But the party really got under way as the nude "delegates" began cavorting between the pool, steam room, and sauna. In revolutionary terms, the "Y" had been "liberated." As might be expected, many couples wandered through the building in search of more privacy.

The only guy that seemed to give a damn about the unscheduled orgy was the student employee. He managed to clean up the building before morning, but a more significant problem remained: the frolicking delegates had gone through dozens of towels during the evening's festivities. During the next day's session, the poor guy made a frantic plea for donations to the laundry fund so it would appear the towels were used by authentic "Y" members.

One of the most fascinating conversations I had in Isla Vista was with Jennifer Dohrn, the younger sister of Bernardine. Dohrn described how the Weathermen had arranged for the escape of Dr. Timothy Leary from the California Men's Colony located some four miles west of San Luis Obispo, in September 1970. After Leary scaled the twelve-foot-high fence, he entered a waiting car and was driven to San Francisco. Jennifer noted that Leary was concerned about being recognized in San Francisco, and when the occupants of an oncoming car waved frantically, he thought sure he'd been spotted. According to Jennifer, Leary was told to relax because all of the individuals who had just passed them were Weatherman fugitives!

Leary was hidden in San Francisco for a short while, and when he finally surfaced publicly, it was in Algiers in the company of fugitive Black Panther leader Eldridge Cleaver.

According to Jennifer, the group rode camels out into the desert shortly after their arrival in Algiers where Dr. Leary took a massive amount of acid, reportedly enough for both him and the camel. When last seen by his companions, the good Doctor was galloping off into the desert in search of the pyramids.

On March 1, 1971, the Weathermen commemorated the tragic Manhattan townhouse explosion by bombing the United States Capitol in Washington. There was no doubt among those of us assigned to Weatherman investigations that the pressure to locate the fugitives would become even more severe. The investigation of the bombing, code named CAPBOMB, would be thorough and exhaustive. But unlike most bombing cases, this one would eventually be resolved.

While the dramatic bombing of the Capitol received widespread media coverage, the consequences within the Bureau were insignificant compared to those that followed the incident that occurred one week later. On the night of March 8, 1971, a secret group of antiwar activists known as the "Citizens Commission to Investigate the FBI" broke into the Bureau's Resident Agency in Media, Pennsylvania and removed more than a thousand documents. Some two weeks later, the group began mailing individual documents to members of Congress and newspapers. For the first time in history, actual FBI documents describing the Bureau's domestic intelligence activities against campus organizations, peace groups, and black activist movements were made public. What had once been only suspected was now officially confirmed.

J. Edgar Hoover was enraged. He followed the time-honored Bureau tradition of designating a scapegoat, in this instance the Senior Resident Agent in the Media RA. In his infinite wisdom, Director Hoover gave the unfortunate agent a month on the beach, or suspension without pay, and a disciplinary transfer to Atlanta. And just to spread a little misery around the field, Hoover continued to overreact by closing more than one hundred RA's, about twenty percent of the Resident Agencies. A crash program was then instituted to equip the remaining RA's with sophisticated burglar alarm systems.

We participated in just about every demonstration held in Isla Vista or Santa Barbara that year, and I quickly learned what it was like to be a protestor in the streets. At times it wasn't all that good. The activities would usually start with a rally in the city park; then a marching, clapping, chanting throng of antiwar demonstrators would move through the streets of downtown Santa Barbara. Most of the marches were peaceful, but confrontations with the police were not uncommon.

In one instance, a group I was with sat down in the middle of Santa Barbara's main street and refused to move. The police arrived in force, issued a warning to move or be arrested, then charged into us like the horse cavalry from the Old West. We beat a hasty retreat, but when a nightstick whistled past my head from an officer in hot pursuit, I threw in the afterburner and ran like hell.

This sit-down incident was repeated over and over again. A peaceful, well-meaning antiwar march that was a legitimate expression of public dissent could suddenly erupt into violence through the efforts of a handful of radical activists. And invariably, the entire antiwar movement would be blamed for the disorder. Since the participants were on their home turf, demonstrations in Isla Vista were bolder and more militant. Crane and I once attended a rally in the I.V. park that dragged on for hours without generating any enthusiasm or popular support. When the rally broke up, we headed back to Los Angeles, only to discover that a small group of radical crazies had attacked the ROTC building on the adjacent campus and attempted to burn it to the ground.

After seeing law enforcement officers come roaring into Isla Vista like a military armored division, I could more readily understand why they were held in such contempt by the local residents. Heavily armed cops were loaded into dump trucks which menacingly circled the park in convoy. Others packed into squad cars and patrolled the area with the doors held open so they could instantly jump out and pursue the unwary. There were times when it was difficult to understand exactly who was provoking who.

The morning of Monday, May 3, 1971 marked the beginning of the "May Day" demonstrations in Washington when Rennie Davis and friends hoped to "close down the government." Thousands of antiwar protestors descended on Washington with plans of blocking bridges, traffic intersections, and government buildings in retaliation for Nixon's earlier military "incursion" into Laos. At the same time, I was with demonstrators near Isla Vista who were attempting to block entrances to a number of corporations that specialized in government defense contracts. While the group succeeded in disrupting business operations, it didn't begin to compare with the situation in Washington.

In a chilling example of White House paranoia, the Justice Department authorized massive arrests by Washington's Metropolitan Police Department. Some ten thousand people were arrested, many of whom just happened to be in the wrong place at the wrong time. Federal courts subsequently ruled the mass arrests unlawful since they denied citizens the right of free speech and assembly.

In my own mind, the Justice Department's response to the May Day demonstrations was another disquieting policy decision that seemed lacking in legal justification. It seemed to me that Assistant Attorney General Robert Mardian, head of the department's Internal Security Division, and his chief prosecutor Guy Goodwin, had already managed to undermine the grand jury system. Subpoenas were being used for fishing expeditions and to harass activists who were not even allowed to have an attorney present in the grand jury room. While there were valid arguments on both sides of the immunity issue, there was something disturbing about sending youthful activists to jail for as long as eighteen months for refusing to testify about their friends. Granted, something had to be done, but surely there was a better way. If not, every citizen of the United States was in trouble.

When Robert Mardian traveled to Isla Vista, he decided to address a group of student activists in a lecture hall on the U.C. Santa Barbara campus. Since Crane and I knew many of the activists fairly well, we were instructed to attend the meeting to assure Mardian's safety. I never understood why he agreed to address the students, but his appearance was a disaster. I don't think I've ever heard a more prejudiced, inflammatory, and narrow-minded speaker. The guy seemed to go out of his way to ridicule the group's questions. With all the problems that had already arisen in I.V., was it really necessary to provoke the students any more? By the time he abruptly terminated the discussion and stormed out of the room, I had become one of his more persistent hecklers.

In view of the intensified search for the Weatherman fugitives, Fast Freddie decided to place two additional agents from one squad undercover "unofficially" to work with Crane and me. Consequently, we were soon joined by KK, the Florida Flash, and Joe, the Bionic Freak. With four undercover agents sporting long hair, beards, and mustaches, it was anticipated that we would have an all-freak surveillance team capable of both infiltration and discreet observation. In time the group would become collectively known around the office as "The Beards."

We were a competitive, tight-knit group who shared each other's respect and a unique sense of camaraderie. There were no ideological zealots or macho heavies who wanted to teach the "communist hippy subversives" a lesson. If anything, the group was open-minded, receptive to change, and somewhat skeptical of the dogmatic pronouncements of Bureau Headquarters. Since we were all attorneys, none of us viewed our employment with the FBI as absolutely essential for our economic survival. But more importantly, I think our legal training allowed us to see both sides of any issue objectively and to listen, consider, and evaluate the arguments before forming an opinion.

One thing that was a little shocking, however, was the surprising number of affluent professionals such as doctors, lawyers, and professors who provided invaluable assistance to the Weathermen fugitives. It was difficult to understand why those individuals would actively support an organization which espoused revolutionary violence as a political tactic. Without that assistance, especially during the formative stage of the underground, I seriously doubt the Weathermen would have eluded capture for such a lengthy period.

Regardless of our efforts, it seemed as though we were always one step behind the Weathermen fugitives. By the time we uncovered their false identification, they would have already changed again; when we located their residences, they would have recently moved; and as soon as we identified their vehicles and the phony registration information, the cars would be resold to another Weatherman. It became frustrating always to be so close, yet never close enough.

While we were often requested for other assignments, the SAC of the Los Angeles Division continued his refusal to acknowledge our existence officially. At the time, he made it abundantly clear to Fast Freddie that in the event Mr. Hoover should learn of our unusual appearance, he would deny any knowledge of the matter and throw us to the wolves. In short, if we made a mistake and were publicly exposed, it would be our ass.

Although several of the larger Bureau Field Offices had their own "mod squad," it was never known just how high up in the Bureau hierarchy the knowledge of our existence went. From all indications, it went to the very highest levels, for we were never present during the annual office inspections. And since the Inspectors were appraised of the situation, the decision had to have been made near the very top. Oddly enough, we never learned whether J. Edgar Hoover actually knew that his organization had "hippy" agents.

In late 1971, my friend Crane resigned from the Bureau in order to return to Texas and practice law. We had been through a lot together, and I was sorry to see him go, but at the same time I was happy he was returning home to enter the profession he had trained for. I think we were fortunate to have experienced a life-style in which values, opinions, and ideals were completely different from our own. Nevertheless, I could understand the almost mystical magnetism of the Lone Star State which only native Texans can truly appreciate.

Fast Freddie had designated an agent who was aptly called the Rodent to fill Crane's spot with The Beards. Rodent had only recently arrived in Los Angeles, and like the rest of us, he was an attorney. In commemoration of Crane's "retirement," we thought it only fitting, and perhaps prudent, to enter the FBI office late one evening for the purpose of obtaining a group photograph in the lavish office of SAC Wesley G. Grapp. Not only would it provide Crane with a fond reminder of his freak days with The Beards; it might also help cover our ass in the event Grapp decided to screw us. It was with a great sense of satisfaction that I leaned back in Grapp's overstuffed chair and propped my sandals up on his desk in preparation for the photo session.

3

The November Committee

Early in 1972, we developed information concerning an upcoming conference in Santa Barbara which would be attended by activists from throughout the West. The stated purpose of the conference was to organize the San Diego Convention Coalition (SDCC) in preparation for the Republican National Convention scheduled for the following summer in San Diego. As originally conceived, the SDCC would function as an overall umbrella group that would channel the resources and energies of the various political organizations on the West Coast into an effective, unified front. The organizations that comprised the SDCC would each have representatives that would assist in the planning of protest demonstrations for the Republican Convention.

As one might expect, the Bureau was vitally interested in the plans of the SDCC. With an incumbent Republican president seeking reelection, it was imperative that the FBI have the situation well under control. Moreover, memories of the violent confrontations that marred the '68 Democratic Convention in Chicago remained vividly clear. And to make matters worse, the Weatherman fugitives might surface during the convention to set off explosives or promote disruptions.

Merely to attend the Santa Barbara conference would be relatively simple, but to penetrate the SDCC effectively would require membership in a movement-oriented organization. What was needed was a "front" organization that we controlled as officers and members and that emphasized a flexible, vaguely-defined ideology with broad appeal. It was out of this need that the "November Committee" was born.

By the time the conference got under way, it was virtually impossible for anyone to enter or leave the building where the meetings took place without being photographed. The attic windows of a nearby church provided an unobstructed view for a wide assortment of telephoto lenses and a video tape camera. Every license number in the parking lot was recorded for subsequent investigation. A surveillance team was positioned in the area to determine where and with whom certain activists were staying.

Inside the building, there were group representatives from as far away as Seattle and Austin. Not only were the usual large contingents from Berkeley and the Bay Area present, but just about every major city along the West Coast was represented. The activists from San Diego who provided the major leadership for the SDCC, had already begun negotiations with the city regarding camping facilities for the thousands of demonstrators who were expected to attend. The group had a slide presentation which showed the layout of the city, convention facilities, and the various areas under consideration for camping. Most of the discussion centered around selecting a location that could not be effectively sealed off by the police. According to the SDCC representatives, city officials had initially offered a camping location that was a peninsula with only a single access road.

Also discussed at the conference were the various types of protest demonstrations which might be staged in San Diego. The general consensus seemed to be that it was imperative to plan protests that would attract as much media attention as possible. Most of those in attendance believed it was essential that Nixon be publicly embarrassed in his home state in order to demonstrate his vulnerability.

We became acquainted with the leadership of the SDCC during the conference and advised them that the purpose of the newly formed November Committee was to provide housing and arrange transportation for the numerous protestors who would be traveling south through Los Angeles. The idea was enthusiastically received by the San Diego activists since Los Angeles would be a logical stopping point before traveling on to the convention. They were told that we planned to place advertisements in underground newspapers requesting that protestors call or write the November Committee office in Venice if they desired housing or transportation from L.A.

Naturally, the SDCC leadership didn't realize that the highly praised efforts of the November Committee would provide the FBI with names, location, and vehicle identification of activists who stopped in Los Angeles, as well as a realistic estimate of the approximate number of demonstrators traveling to San Diego. By the time the conference had ended, we had established channels of communication with the San Diego organizers, and the November Committee was well on its way to becoming a significant factor in planning for the Republican Convention.

In early spring, The Beards lost another outstanding member when my friend KK announced his resignation from the FBI. Much like Crane, KK had decided it was time to return to Florida and begin practicing law.

Although The Beards seemed to be steadily losing members to the legal profession, Fast Freddie selected two other agent-attorneys to join us. Shortly thereafter, Panda and Jay became charter members of the November Committee.

Following a long-standing tradition, we had scheduled a going-away luncheon for KK on his last day in the Bureau. It was to be held in the private dining room of a modest restaurant and was a final opportunity for his friends in the office to say good-bye. But on the morning of the luncheon, we heard the startling news that J. Edgar Hoover had died. After forty-eight years as Director of the FBI, the living legend was no more.

My initial reaction to the news was concern for KK. I felt certain that attendance at the luncheon would be sparse, especially among the older agents who had worked under Mr. Hoover for decades. But somehow, it just didn't seem right. KK had done a tremendous job, and it was only fitting that he be honored by his associates on his last day as an agent.

I arrived at the luncheon in hopes that at least the younger agents would show up. It no longer seemed like such a festive occasion, but we'd try to make the best of it. When I walked into the dining room, I couldn't believe my eyes. The place was packed! The older agents had shown up in record numbers. The noise level in the room was almost deafening as the boisterous crowd competed for the attention of the lone cocktail waitress. Had a stranger wandered into the room, he might have thought it was the office Christmas party! Instead of the somber gathering I had envisioned, the luncheon became a time for joyous celebration.

While J. Edgar Hoover enjoyed the respect of most agents, it would be a mistake to assume that they liked him personally. If the truth were known, I think the great majority of agents felt an overwhelming sense of relief upon hearing of his passing. Few agents wanted to see Hoover humiliated or disgraced by being forced to resign after a lifetime of service. But at the same time they were aware that he had outlived his usefulness, and many of his actions during the past few years had done nothing but discredit the man and the organization. One veteran agent speculated that Mr. Hoover's demise had prevented the self-destruction of his own legend. At the same time, virtually everyone looked forward to the future with new hope for meaningful change.

Ironically, the day after J. Edgar Hoover's death was far more shocking to the great majority of Bureau employees. On May 3, 1972 President Richard Nixon appointed L. Patrick Gray III as Acting Director of the FBI. The announcement was completely unexpected and caused total bewilderment within the Bureau. Everyone asked the same question: "Who the hell is L. Patrick Gray III?"

On May 5, 1972 the GOP officially voted to hold their convention in Miami rather than in San Diego. After our efforts with the SDCC and November Committee, it was disappointing to learn the convention would be held in Florida. We had all been looking forward to the trip to San Diego and the challenge of undercover work that was certain to produce dramatic confrontations. But all was not lost. At the next conference we attended in Isla Vista, I announced that the November Committee was now planning to coordinate transportation for activists desiring to attend the Republican National Convention in Miami. Once again the idea was supported by those in the SDCC. Thus we would still have a good idea of the relative strength of protestors traveling from California, and in addition, we now had an excuse for asking leading activists if they planned to attend the convention and how they planned to get there.

Since summer was just around the corner and I wouldn't be going to the convention, I decided to get a haircut. Looking like a freak had been an interesting, enlightening experience, for it was amazing how differently I was treated. While it had been a gradual change, each particular stage had brought about a discernibly different reaction. For some reason, the most dramatic response occurred when my hair began creeping below my shoulders, and out of necessity I started wearing a headband. I could never really understand the significance of a headband, but it seemed to strike fear and loathing in the hearts of the "silent majority." Although I didn't plan to cut off all my hair, a return to a more moderate shoulder length style seemed in order. A few days later, I sat down in a barber's chair for the first time in more than twenty months.

4

MIDEM

"Mornin', C."

"Mornin', Boss," I instinctively replied, trying to sound at least partially awake after a long, hard night in the streets of Venice. I lay motionless in the waterbed, holding the telephone receiver firmly and hoping to prevent the inevitable sloshing sound which would surely tell my supervisor he had caught me in the sack again. "How's everything in the world of crime?" I asked.

"Not too bad so far, but it's still early. Got a teletype this morning from the Bureau. They want you and the Rodent to take a little trip."

"Yeah? Like to where?" I inquired cautiously.

"Would you believe MIDEM?" Fred cryptically suggested, knowing full well I didn't know what he was talking about.

"How can I believe it when I don't know what it is?" I asked.

"Well how does the Democratic National Convention in Miami Beach sound to you?" he asked with obvious delight.

"Not that bad, Boss, not bad at all! When do we leave?"

"Won't be for a week or so, but you may be there all summer with those damn conventions going on. Looks like they'll keep you through the Republican Convention in August."

"Fun in the sun, Boss, fun in the sun! Say, you got any spare phone numbers down there a man might use?" My head was feeling better already.

"Not for you, C. I'm sure you won't need them anyway. Say, I got another call holding. Get together with Rodent and the other guys and see how long it will take you to wind up your work here, then call me back this afternoon."

"Okay, Boss, talk to you later."

"Oh yeah, C," he interjected, "you guys also figure out a cover story for the November Committee operation. Call me later."

"Right, Boss,' I said, slowly hanging up the phone.

I lay back on the waterbed and tried to visualize the sparkling white beaches and luxurious high-rise hotels. It sounded like a great opportunity for a free summer vacation and was certain to include some excitement in the streets.

As I crawled out of bed and stumbled into the bathroom, I was greeted by the reflection of that long-haired freak I had come to know as myself. Suddenly the significance of my conversation with Fred dawned on me. The Bureau was actually sending freaks to Miami on official business. After working in an undercover capacity for almost two years without official sanction or the apparent knowledge of J. Edgar Hoover, we were now officially recognized and our help was being requested. It would certainly be interesting to see what effect we would have on veteran agents in the Miami office, many of whom had never even talked with a freak, much less worked with one who was on their side.

Although I had been in the Bureau less than four years, it was amazing how the entire tone of the organization had changed since Pat Gray had become Acting Director. Agents were now allowed to sport mustaches, sideburns, and longer hair. White shirts and conservative dark suits were no longer de rigueur. Women were finally being accepted for Special Agent positions. Virtually all the archaic rules and regulations were being reevaluated, and long-overdue changes were being instituted daily. It was almost as though the Bureau was finally coming to grips with the contemporary problems of effective law enforcement, rather than concentrating on protecting our image with the public.

I was not looking forward to our meeting that morning since I would be the one to deliver the news to the Beards about the convention trip, while also revealing that three of my friends were not included. They would naturally be disappointed, for an opportunity like this had never existed before. I felt certain, however, that with their resourcefulness, they would end up in Miami before the summer was over.

As we discussed the conventions over breakfast at the Brown Bagger, it was obvious that there was disappointment among our group, but we were all excited over the fact we had been officially recognized. If this was any indication, we would be doing more and more traveling in the future. Under Mr. Hoover, there had been very little travel by agents between the various field divisions except for Bureau Specials, which were investigations that attracted an unusual amount of publicity. It now appeared that agents with particular areas of expertise would be flying anywhere in the country that Bureau Head-quarters (FBIHQ) deemed necessary. Perhaps in a few short months we would be collectively known within the Bureau as The Flying Freak Brothers, making weekly trips to the major demonstrations and rock concerts from coast to coast.

We finally decided that Rodent and I should put out the word that we were traveling to Miami to coordinate convention activities for the November Committee and to assist our friends from the San Diego Convention Coalition (SDCC) with planning. Several of the SDCC people had merged forces with the Miami Convention Coalition (MCC) whose principal leader was former "Chicago Seven" defendant Rennie Davis. I wondered if Davis would remember me from our conversations in Isla Vista during the Tenth Anniversary Celebration of the National Liberation Front.

While Joe, Panda, and Jay were running the Los Angeles offices of the November Committee, Rodent and I would contact our acquaintances in Miami under the pretext of informing our members about what they could expect in the way of demonstration activities during the convention. We reasoned that it would lend credibility to both operations while also facilitating our overall goal of determining exactly which individuals from the West Coast were traveling to Miami, and what the leadership of the MCC was planning in the way of confrontations. When I ran the scenario past Fast Freddie later that afternoon, he was so enthusiastic that he assured me he could ultimately sell a program to the Bureau which would result in travel authorization for the remainder of our group.

After enjoying the usual Fourth of July celebration on Venice Beach, accompanied by beer, dope, and fireworks, I began preparing in earnest for our departure. We were given a rousing send-off on the morning of July 6, when Joe, Panda, and Jay drove us to L.A. International in the Volkswagen bus.

We received the usual contemptuous looks as we waited to board the plane, but were more intrigued by the fact that not a single metal detector was in evidence at the National Airlines gates. We located seats near the rear of the large cabin, and I immediately began my search for the best-looking flight attendant. After a few minutes of observation, it was evident there was an easy winner.

"Excuse me, Miss," I said in a hushed voice as the young lady passed down the aisle. "Federal law requires us to identify ourselves to you upon boarding. I'm Special Agent Payne and this is Special Agent

45

Bloom, FBI. Would you please notify the captain we're on board and armed."

"Er, ah, yes," she replied incredulously, staring at our FBI credentials in shocked disbelief. "May I take your identification up to the captain?"

"No, I'm sorry, but we're not allowed to let these credentials out of our sight," I answered.

With that, our vivacious young flight attendant turned and attempted to make her way back to the cockpit. To say that she was skeptical of our alleged employment would have been the understatement of the year. I could just imagine her coming off a long night on the town, dragging out of bed for a five-hour flight, then having two doped-up hippy freaks identify themselves as FBI agents carrying concealed weapons. To add insult to injury, she was also expected to believe that the clean-shaven young agents pictured on the credentials were identical with the two scruffy, long-haired passengers in the rear of the plane.

Since Bureau headquarters had never officially recognized our existence or the unique nature of our assignment, we still carried FBI identification credentials with photographs taken when we entered the Bureau. In my particular situation, the photo was made in 1968. Ordinarily, agent photographs were periodically updated to eliminate identity problems, but in our case, the Field Office would always provide some nebulous excuse for our official absence during the photo session. This procedure protected officials at both Bureau headquarters and Field Offices, since neither wanted to go on record as having official knowledge of our activities. All credential photographs had to be approved by the Administrative Division in Washington, and if the pictures did not depict the proper Bureau image of short hair, conservative dress, and serious expression, they were rejected and sent back to the field for another attempt.

Officials of the Domestic Intelligence Division, who had authorized our travel to Miami, were aware of our hippy appearance. Nevertheless, no one seemed the least bit concerned about these travel problems. The entire world was going bonkers over terrorist hijackings, and I was flying to Miami with faded jeans, workshirt, head band, shoulder-length hair, body odor, and a loaded .380 Walther PPK tucked away inside my boot!

Another furtive glance toward the forward area and I knew we were not even close to passing the test. Out marched our stewardess, who, I later discovered, had the unbelievable name of Mary Smith, followed closely by our smartly dressed captain. It was immediately obvious that he neither liked nor believed what he was seeing.

"This is Captain Johnson," Mary said, as she quickly moved beyond our seats and headed toward the more peaceful confines of the rear galley.

"Hello, captain." I warmly greeted him with my most authoritative but conciliatory voice. "I'm Special Agent Payne and this is Special Agent Bloom. Here's our identification."

"Thank you," he replied without a smile while closely examining our credentials. His eyes darted speedily from our photographs to our faces, then back to the photographs. "How do I know this is really you? I mean, they don't look anything like either one of you. And besides, I don't like the idea of weapons on my aircraft."

"Yes sir, captain," I began. "I realize we don't look much like our pictures, but we've been on special assignment and haven't been able to get them updated. Here, I also have a badge in my wallet if you would like to see that."

As I reached back for my wallet, I could sense that the captain seemed rather uneasy. He probably expected to see me whisk out a .44 magnum that would come to rest against the shining brass buttons of his uniform. He appeared to breathe a sigh of relief when he noticed that my hand contained only a harmless wallet. I reluctantly opened the wallet to display the badge pinned inside, which I was certain would prove about as impressive as the production of a Captain Marvel ring.

We were often told while undergoing New Agents training that the FBI had the "big laws and the little badge," while state and local police had the "big badge and little laws." This was one way of justifying the inescapable fact that although a wide variety of federal statutes provided us with law enforcement jurisdiction throughout the country, our meager little badge looked like something Dick Tracy would have rejected on sight. It was a miniature shield of lightweight metal, devoid of an engraved badge number or other noteworthy details. It was reported to have undergone a brass plating, but this mysterious finish generally departed shortly after issuance. This was the first time in four years I had displayed it to anyone.

The captain made only a cursory inspection of the badge, which apparently added little to our credibility. "Anyone could buy one of these things," he observed. "What else do you have?"

I was about to reply that it would be impossible to purchase a badge like ours, since no respectable pawnshop would even consider carrying such unsalable merchandise. Fortunately, the Rodent realized that I was running out of tricks and came to my rescue.

"Look at our tickets, captain," Rodent chimed in, passing his ticket over for inspection at the same time. "Notice that they have the designation 'GTR' and a number written in on the bottom portion. That means we paid for our round trip tickets with an official 'Government Travel Request' instead of cash or credit cards. If we weren't employees of the United States government, we wouldn't have access to their travel requests."

Sounded like a cogent argument to me, but Captain Johnson remained unimpressed. "I don't know the first thing about these GTR's, or whatever you call them," he said. "All I do is fly the airplane, and I'm not going to do that until I'm sure of your identity. Don't you have any other identification?"

I had already begun digging through the wide assortment of cards, notes, and receipts that always seemed to collect in the back of my wallet. "Well sir, Here's my FBIRA card, and oh yes, here's my SAMBA card also."

"SAMBA card?" the captain asked, looking at it carefully.

"Yes sir, that's the Special Agents Mutual Benefit Association. It's for hospitalization benefits, and see, here's my name and Social Security number on the back. The FBIRA card represents membership in the FBI Recreation Association, for like ah, office activities. My name and office are also on that one."

It was these two innocuous documents that caused our captain to relent. I suppose he reasoned that if you had FBI health insurance and could go to their parties, you had to be an agent.

"Okay, okay," the captain said. "It's just that I've already been hijacked to Algeria once, and that was enough. Why doesn't the goddamned FBI give you some identification with your pictures on it? I mean, all that hair and beard, Jesus, you might as well not even carry these things."

Captain Johnson walked briskly back to the cockpit, and in a matter of minutes, the mammoth jetliner was pulling away from the terminal. The remainder of the flight was uneventful, with the exception of some lengthy conversation with Mary Smith. Mary was naturally intrigued by our government employment and strange appearance. She was full of questions concerning my background, education, life-style,

48

and assignments. I courteously tried to answer as many as possible without going into detail.

Mary was a long-time resident of Miami and seemed to know the area like a book. She recommended several restaurants and local bars that were popular watering spots, but cautioned that our appearance would not be regarded as an asset.

We walked out of the airport into the blazing afternoon sun, into what I soon discovered was a typical summer day. We were met by a blast of intense heat, the likes of which I will not soon forget.

After hailing a cab, we headed into the city for our scheduled meeting at the Miami FBI office. It was difficult to understand why undercover agents would be briefed in the office rather than at a more secure location, but perhaps Bureau officials were still too naive about covert operations. They were aware, however, that photographic surveillance of the Chicago FBI offices had been conducted by various demonstrators during the 1968 Democratic convention in hopes of identifying informants who had infiltrated their ranks. Those of us who were experienced in these matters had learned that you can never underestimate the capabilities of your adversaries.

The Miami office was not unlike every Bureau Field Office I had visited. The usual Spartan furnishings of "government gray" metal desks and chairs were crammed together in large bull pens or squad areas where agents shared telephones and dictating equipment. Squad supervisors were provided with a small cubicle from which they assigned cases, but only the Special Agent In Charge (SAC) and his assistant (ASAC) were entitled to the luxury of carpeting and wooden furniture.

Our meeting began with brief introductions to the supervisors and agents who would be coordinating intelligence coverage of demonstration activities during the convention. Separate channels of communication, each with different phone numbers, had been established to receive intelligence gathered on various organizations known to be in attendance. Several additional telephone lines had been installed so that regular informants as well as undercover agents could immediately relay information to open lines manned twenty-four hours a day. We were provided with intelligence briefings on planned activities of the Miami Convention Coalition (MCC), along with current informant reports concerning possible street actions.

While the briefings continued in the open squad room, nearly every secretary, stenographer, and clerk paraded through the room in order to catch a glimpse of the bizarre visitors claiming to be members of their organization. Since there had previously been little Weatherman activity in Miami, most of the office employees had no idea that the FBI actually had agents who looked like freaks.

I overheard one old-timer mutter to a colleague, "Son of a bitch, just like I always thought. The minute J. Edgar Hoover dies and this goddamned Gray takes over, everything goes to shit. No order or discipline in this outfit anymore! Got a bunch of damn hippies carrying FBI credentials!"

The few younger agents assigned to the Miami office did not seem to share the opinion that the Bureau was suffering from moral decay, although they did retain a perceptible amount of skepticism. But the impressionable young ladies of the office were much more receptive, apparently sensing that we must be involved in an exciting and highly dangerous assignment.

While trying to keep one ear open to the briefing and also monitor the young ladies moving through the room, I began to assess the undercover agents I would be working with. Several among the eleven-member undercover group gave me immediate cause for concern. In any Bureau "special," the ultimate recipient of the assignment may well be the agent with the most influence in the local office power structure. If the Bureau requested that the names of two agents experienced in Weatherman cases be submitted by selected offices, a large amount of political maneuvering could come into play before the final decision was reached.

As I observed my colleagues, I was at a loss to explain why some had been selected over more qualified agents on the West Coast. Almost half had hair no longer than the average Miami agents, sported beards or mustaches of only a week's duration, and were dressed in exactly the same manner as an off-duty FBI agent. I was soon to discover that several of these agents knew absolutely nothing about revolutionary politics or alternative life-styles. Many had never even participated in antiwar demonstrations. The summer vacation I had envisioned would certainly have its drawbacks if things got tough.

If any of these inexperienced undercover agents attempted to join a street action with some of my radical friends from Santa Barbara or Berkeley, they would be identified as "pigs" in about two seconds and confronted with the very real possibility of having their asses stomped. When the militant hard-core activists were in attendance, peaceful demonstrations could erupt into violent confrontation with the slightest provocation. Many of these agents would be walking liabilities with whom we could never associate publicly for fear of jeopardizing our cover stories in Los Angeles. If our movement friends saw us associating with obvious "pigs," we would receive the same designation, and two years of undercover work would be wasted. This unfortunate situation was bound to create friction, because you did not insult a fellow agent by openly questioning his ability to carry out an assignment. You simply hoped for the best.

Also scheduled to arrive for the opening of the Democratic Convention was a group of about twenty agents from across the country whose previous experience in surveillance or interviews would help them identify the Weatherman fugitives. These agents would not actually participate in protest demonstrations or planning sessions but would be used only in the event that an undercover agent ran into someone who resembled a fugitive.

Perhaps these initial problems of security and personnel selection were attributable to the relative inexperience of the Bureau in conducting covert operations with undercover agents as opposed to informants. Since we had only recently received official sanction, it could justifiably be argued that the leadership of the Domestic Intelligence Division, or Division Five as it was commonly known, was forced to rely solely upon personnel selections by field supervisors who were familiar with an agent's experience and ability. But after being briefed on communications requirements and the transportation to be made available, I seriously doubted that the Bureau hierarchy had the slightest understanding of the nature of our assignment.

We would be required to call our contacting agent at least once every hour while demonstrations were in progress. A precise synopsis of intelligence information gathered from infiltration of planning sessions was to be telephoned in each morning and afternoon. Our reports would be incorporated into twelve-hour summaries prepared by agents in the Miami office, which were to be submitted by coded teletype to Division Five. A constant flow of current information was to be provided to the Bureau at all times so that they could disseminate information about changing developments to the appropriate agencies.

But why would a long-haired freak, committed to the politics of confrontation and a revolutionary life-style, suddenly leave a marching, chanting throng of twenty thousand demonstrators to search for a pay phone? My earlier experience had taught me that this was the surest way to arouse suspicion. On more than one occasion, I witnessed leaders of radical organizations in Isla Vista designate members to observe area telephone booths for just such activity. During one of the many assaults on the local Bank of America, I watched helplessly as rocks and bottles shattered telephone booths where unsuspecting individuals, quite possibly informants, were thought to be relaying information to law enforcement authorities.

It was suggested that we hide small two-way radios in our cars. But this equipment had a limited range, and transmissions were never totally secure. In addition, we often found ourselves miles from our vehicles after marching in demonstrations. To attempt to conceal radios in our clothing, as proposed by one veteran agent, and rely on an earplug and the FBI "Chap-Stick" microphone for communications, was totally absurd.

Even more ludicrous were the vehicles we were given: four- to five-year-old Bureau cars stripped of all communications equipment and awaiting sale by auction to the public. I knew of very few freaks who drove four-door Ford sedans with gaping holes created by the removal of antennas and radio equipment. The cars might just as well have had the FBI seal painted on each side. After vehement objections, we managed to wrangle a commitment for three rental cars of a subcompact variety, but we remained far short of suitable vehicles.

It was as though no one in the Miami office had anticipated the logistical requirements for an undercover operation of this type, and no one in authority seemed inclined to request further Bureau authorization for needed expenditures. There was general uncertainty as to whether we were a blessing in disguise that could lend invaluable assistance in demonstration coverage, or a problem looking for a place to happen that would become an administrative responsibility.

After settling into our accommodations, most of the undercover group got together that evening to discuss coverage of protest activities. The Bureau had selected agents from the offices of Chicago, New York City, Washington, Cleveland, San Francisco, and Los Angeles—all considered active Weatherman areas. Although some agents were noticeably lacking in proper appearance and experience, the rest were eminently qualified. I would have no reservations whatsoever about introducing them to my counterculture acquaintances.

Our capabilities increased significantly the following day with the unexpected arrival of the Panda from Los Angeles. The Bureau had originally scheduled twelve undercover agents to work the conventions, but when one was unable to come at the last minute because of an ongoing investigation, Panda was selected to take his place. I was overjoyed, though surprised, to see my L.A. friend, since he was an extremely competent undercover agent. If Fast Freddie could just get our two other associates to Miami, the entire membership of the November Committee would be in attendance.

During the next few days, I began making contact with former leaders of the San Diego Convention Coalition (SDCC) who were now living in Miami and assisting the Miami Convention Coalition (MCC) with plans for demonstrations. Several of them recalled my participation in the Santa Barbara planning sessions prior to the change in convention sites, and were eager to provide details of the upcoming activities. These organizers indicated they favored peaceful and legitimate forms of protest during the Democratic Convention, with primary emphasis placed on high visibility and meaningful attempts to raise the political consciousness of the American viewing public. Most of the organizers openly supported or sympathetically endorsed the nomination of Sen. George McGovern, which they believed was virtually assured. They strongly felt that a recurrence of the violent confrontations which marred the 1968 Chicago Democratic Convention would severely damage McGovern's chances for election. But regardless of their differences over the propriety of supporting any candidate, they were united in one thing: they despised Richard M. Nixon and everything he stood for. If they were to have their way, things would not be so easy for the Republicans and old "Tricky Dick" come August.

The center of activity for the youthful nondelegates from throughout the country was Flamingo Park, a thirty-three-acre plot located in a residential area some three blocks south of Miami Beach Convention Center. After lengthy discussions between Police Chief "Rocky" Pomerance, Miami Beach officials, and representative of the MCC, the city reluctantly agreed that the park could be used as the campsite and meeting area. From the demonstrators' point of view, it was an ideal location because it provided all essential facilities and was close to the convention hall itself. The abundant shrubbery, foliage, and massive hibiscus trees surrounding the park permitted limited access to the main camping area and created a feeling of privacy.

Life in Flamingo Park, now referred to as "People's Park," became a circus during the days preceeding the convention opening. The great majority of the campers were kids under twenty-one who seemed most concerned with smoking dope, drinking wine, and enjoying themselves. They didn't mind raising a little hell in the park, but few appeared politically dedicated enough to risk having their heads busted in the streets. Weekend activities centered around rock music, futile attempts at political speaking, nude swimming, and availability of outstanding "Jamaican Red" grass. It was a dealer's holiday, with every popular drug available in unlimited quantities at competitive prices. As the sun went down, dealers openly hawked their wares like hot-dog men in the Cotton Bowl on New Year's Day. Signs were often posted outside tents advertising the "goodies" available inside and their current prices. The illegal drug business attained a character similar to the commodities market, with prices fluctuating from day to day.

There was little concern over the likelihood of arrest, since most believed that local authorities considered the park a "liberated zone"—in revolutionary vernacular—for both drug use and sale. This impression was apparently correct and represented sound judgment on the part of Miami Beach police. We were frequently questioned by agents in the Miami office over the possibility of narcotics arrests by police in the park. This concern stemmed in part from increasing media criticism of local police for ignoring open drug violations. I pointed out that, if necessary, major suppliers could be followed out of the park and arrested away from volatile crowds. Any attempt to make arrests inside the park would surely prove disastrous.

A wide variety of organizations inhabited the small camping area. The most desirable acreage was occupied by rows of identical army surplus tents laid out with military precision. There were larger headquarters-type tents for meetings and dining facilities. The overall appearance was that of an infantry field exercise. This tent city was reverently referred to as "Resurrection City II" by the Reverend Ralph Abernathy and his followers in the Southern Christian Leadership Conference. During daylight hours, a large crowd of "residents" could be seen milling around the "city" engaged in maintenance projects, political meetings, group singing, and cooking over open fires.

I was to see Rev. Abernathy depart from an air-conditioned limousine into the scorching afternoon sun, remove his coat, make a grand entrance into the park, and then conduct television interviews in front of Resurrection City II. But when the cameras left, Rev. Abernathy left. And after the sun went down and darkness enveloped the park, Resurrection City became a ghost town. Only two or three tents in the entire complex were actually occupied at night. While television cameras were around, there was nonstop activity within the "city," but during evening hours, the area was virtually deserted in favor of air-conditioned motels. These actions generated considerable friction among other inhabitants of the park, since the Resurrection City II tents, unoccupied at night, took up at least three times as much camping space as that of any other group.

There was also obvious antagonism between members of the "Yippies," or Youth International Party, and the "Zippies," a more militant faction who had left the party after disputes over tactics and leadership. The Zippies were upset over the "elitist attitude" displayed by early Yippy leaders Abbie Hoffman and Jerry Rubin. They felt Hoffman and Rubin had become "tools of the establishment" who had exploited the antiwar movement by profiting from books and lectures. They also criticized the fact that Hoffman would be allowed inside the convention hall as a reporter for *Popular Mechanics*, rather than joining his "brothers and sisters" outside in the streets.

"Rubin and Hoffman are nothin' but elitist pigs, man," one disgruntled Zippy told me. "Now that they're hot-shit celebrities, they think they're too fuckin' good to sleep in the park with the people. They gotta have a nice cool room at the Albion so they won't fuckin' sweat at night. Fuck that shit man, they can both kiss my ass!"

I spoke briefly with Abbie one morning and sensed that he was aware of the unrest among the Zippies. It was the only time I was to see him in the park, and he seemed quite reserved with his rhetoric, being content to offer innocuous comments and social niceties. Perhaps his experiences in 1968 and the subsequent trial of the Chicago Seven had convinced him it was wiser to risk unpopularity than to advocate violent confrontations. His presence went almost unnoticed in the park, and he acted much more like a reporter than a protest leader. Although the national media still considered him a spokesman for the demonstrators, his influence among those in the park appeared minimal at best.

Although such diverse political groups as the Students for a Democratic Society (SDS), Vietnam Veterans Against The War (VVAW), Young Socialist Alliance (YSA), Progressive Labor Party (PLP), Yippies, Zippies, and countless others occupied the park in virtual harmony, they all seemed to share a common contempt for the small delegation of the National Coalition of Gay Organizations (NCGO). The gay representatives were victims of continuous harassment, and scarcely a night would pass when their tent was not slashed, robbed, or vandalized.

As they passed out Gay Power buttons and proudly displayed the organization's clenched fist flag, I couldn't help but admire their perseverance and dedication, even though I was unable to rationalize their sexual preferences. It was almost as though they were totally oblivious to this belligerent environment, for they seldom displayed anger. Perhaps this was due in part to their previous experiences as members of a grossly misunderstood, intimidated, and persecuted minority, but it appeared more readily attributable to their deep commitment to equal rights.

Over the past two years, I had listened to hundreds of speakers expound upon how we were "all brothers and sisters in the revolutionary struggle against imperialism," only to find out that this apparently did not include gay people.

While the various political groups were actively vying for support among the inhabitants of People's Park, a wide assortment of religious organizations were busily engaged in spreading the gospel. Some held daily revival meetings, while others read Bibles by candlelight or offered hourly meditation counseling for what they referred to as the "troubled generation." Their presence was generally disregarded by most of those in the park, although the persistence displayed by many of these evangelists was often hard to ignore.

Most demonstrators had previously become accustomed to the chantings of the robed Hare Krishna sect, as well as to the fervent "One Way" shouts from the legions of Jesus Freaks who regularly attended major demonstrations. While members of these groups appeared most concerned with soliciting donations, they were easy to ignore. But the more zealous lay missionaries from local fundamentalist groups simply refused to take "no" for an answer. The more verbal abuse they received, the more they seemed to enjoy it. They had come to save lost souls, and with their modern public address system, they were able to expose everyone in the park to the gospel of salvation.

Of all the religious organizations in the park, none aroused such heated passion and bitter controversy as the Jews For Jesus. This group consisted of a handful of young Jewish men, all under the age of thirty, who had converted to Christianity. They were always dressed neatly in dark slacks, white shirt, and the traditional Jewish yarmelke. Nearly all of the group sported long beards and appeared to have been of the Orthodox faith at one time. They were a studious-looking group whose only unusual characteristic was the fact that they were never without a copy of the King James version of the Bible.

The Jews For Jesus were initially ignored by the inhabitants of the park, as were many of the other religious groups. But as the days leading up to the opening of the convention passed without incident, the predominantly elderly Jewish population of Miami Beach began to venture into the park. This evening walk seemed to be the primary social occasion of the day for most of the local populace. As word of the excitement of a walk through the park began to spread, more and more residents ventured through the gates to gawk and point. More and more elderly Jewish people discovered the Jews For Jesus. And were they ever upset!

I have seldom witnessed such impassioned hostility as was directed at the Jews For Jesus. The most serene, amiable-looking ladies—typical Jewish grandmothers—would almost resort to physical violence after being urged to convert to Christianity, especially if the urging came from a young man wearing a yarmelke and reading verses from the Bible to justify this decision.

"You're no Jew," one elderly woman shouted. "You gave up your belief. You have no right to call yourself a Jew. No right! You don't even know what it means to be a Jew. You should be ashamed of yourself."

The controversy seemed to grow as the news spread throughout the Jewish community. The converted Jewish-Christians never seemed to lose their temper, but many of the week's most potentially violent confrontations were to occur in front of the Jews For Jesus tent.

Upon leaving the relatively secure confines of Flamingo Park, one immediately confronted the harsh realities of Miami Beach. Although freaks were distinctly a minority among the crowds now roaming the sidewalks and beaches of the city, it was evident that they were an unwelcome minority. The citizens of Miami Beach had been preparing for the Democratic Convention for many months and looked forward to increased summer revenues from the delegates. They did not, however, look forward to the prospect of a violent confrontation similar to the one that occurred during the 1968 Chicago convention. Long-haired hippy invaders, whose very presence was at best only tolerated, were greeted with contemptuous looks by members of the local business community. We were viewed by many as outside troublemakers who had traveled to Miami Beach for the avowed purpose of destroying the city.

Perhaps a significant amount of this animosity was attributable to the nature of the Miami Beach population. The city appeared to be composed primarily of elderly, retired Jewish residents who existed on fixed incomes. They were dependent upon the city or synagogue for whatever social and recreational opportunities they might enjoy in their seemingly unlimited leisure.

The typical senior citizens of Miami Beach, like their counterparts throughout the country, were simply unable to comprehend this new, liberated life-style where nothing was considered sacred and everything, even government and religion, was subjected to intense criticism. Nor could they begin to understand the long hair, drugs, abusive language, or complete disregard for personal appearance.

Many of the restaurants, delicatessens, and cafeterias in Miami Beach attempted a strict enforcement of dress codes in order to limit the number of demonstrators allowed in their establishments. If they did not care for your appearance, you had to be prepared for an extended wait before a table became available. Instead of the usual cheery greeting from the hostess, we were nearly always met with, "You boys got shoes on, you boys got on shoes?" No shoes, no service. It was also not uncommon to have the proprietor inquire in advance about our ability to pay the check. Even if we passed all the requisite tests, we received little, if anything, in the way of service, since everyone was aware that hippies never tipped. It should be pointed out, however, that a small minority of establishments treated us like human beings.

By early Sunday afternoon, July 8, Flamingo Park finally began to resemble a People's Park. The Boston chapter of the Students for a Democratic Society (SDS), along with other SDS chapters from around the country, and the Miami Women's Coalition, had scheduled a demonstration to be held that evening in front of the Miami Beach Playboy Club. This was the site selected for the 1972 Democratic Sponsors Club Dinner, a formal Sunday evening affair with all the major Democratic contributors in attendance. The demonstration was to begin at seven-fifteen in order to provide an appropriate greeting for the sponsoring fat cats as they drove up the long circular driveway into the Playboy Plaza entrance.

Since this was to be the first planned confrontation of the convention week, the sultry atmosphere was filled with expectation as the various speakers, nearly all of whom were women, tried to generate enthusiasm for the demonstration. Rivers of perspiration flowed down their faces as they struggled to hold the cumbersome bullhorn aloft. Impassioned pleas for participation and solidarity filled the park. As one speaker so aptly stated, "It's time to get off your ass and into the streets!"

The Playboy Clubs had long been an object of intense criticism by the women's liberation groups because of the Playboy "exploitation" of women in the clubs and the magazine. Given this long-standing animosity and the rebellious nature of the crowd, it was certainly not difficult to obtain support for an evening visit to the Playboy Club.

The Playboy Plaza complex was located on Collins Avenue, in the heart of the luxurious "hotel row" area. During the lengthy walk from People's Park, we passed the row of massive hotels that lined the avenue and looked out on the Atlantic Ocean. Familiar names such as the Fontainebleau, Doral, and Eden Roc had always produced a mental picture of wealthy guests basking in oceanfront sunshine, while their less affluent friends and relatives remained marooned in the dismal snows of the Northeast.

We arrived at the Playboy Plaza to find that a small crowd had already gathered near the entrance to the long circular drive. A large number of signs and banners were in evidence. The usual antiwar chants began emanating from the demonstrators, but most of their efforts were directed at intimidating the occupants of the limousines that filed into the driveway. As their chauffeurs were forced to slow down for the sharp turn into the drive, fenders were kicked, windows were pounded, and several antennas were broken off. But once the limousines passed through the congestion at the base of the drive and reached the canopied entrance of the complex, their passengers could enter the building in relative safety.

Since the demonstrators were unable to block access to the entrance drive, many began throwing rocks from various vantage points at the limousines waiting to discharge their guests. But because no skirmish lines had been established, rocks flying from several different directions occasionally missed limousines and hit demonstrators across the way.

As the crowd became increasingly frustrated, an SDS spokesman suggested we march up the drive and block the entrance to the building. No sooner had the crowd begun to press forward toward the building when hundreds of Florida Highway Patrol officers suddenly appeared from the underground parking garage. They were a most imposing site in their full-dress riot gear, complete with helmet, shield, and gas mask.

The crowd hastily retreated back to Collins Avenue to analyze the situation from a safer distance. As soon as we returned to our original position, the police filed back into the garage in an orderly fashion. Each time we attempted to move forward, out they would come to establish a perimeter around the entrance. This organized yet restrained show of force was to be reenacted several times throughout the coming week.

When word spread that all guests had arrived and dinner was under way, the demonstration started breaking up and the various groups began straggling back to the park. While the demonstration had not resulted in a militant confrontation, it did provide a good indication of what could be expected from local law enforcement.

I was amazed to observe several members of our undercover team standing at a distance from the crowd outside the Playboy Plaza, looking as though they were spectators rather than participants. They would frequently walk down the street in search of a telephone booth while the demonstrators were actively engaged in taunting the police. I couldn't help but laugh to myself as I noticed a line at one nearby phone booth. It was obvious to me that there were almost as many plainclothes police officers in attendance as demonstrators. Another classic example of overkill, I thought, and one which would not go unnoticed by the more militant groups.

This lack of concern about security precautions was underscored the following day when we received word that two members of our undercover team had already been compromised. For some unknown reason, they had tried to attend a meeting of the Vietnam Veterans Against the War (VVAW) which was being conducted in a remote area of the park. Since several law enforcement agencies, including the FBI, had previously penetrated the leadership of the VVAW through informants, most of the organization's plans were known well in advance.

The VVAW activists were naturally suspicious of any strangers who attempted to approach them and were no doubt aware their organization had been infiltrated. They publicly stated that subpoenas ordering their immediate appearance before a federal grand jury in a distant city were issued solely to prevent their attendance at the Democratic Convention. This argument apparently contained substantial merit, for on the final evening of the convention, delegates passed a resolution condemning the Nixon administration for attempting to "intimidate and discredit" the VVAW. Nevertheless, six members were indicted by the federal grand jury at Tallahassee the following day on charges of conspiring to cause riots at the upcoming Republican National Convention with firebombs, automatic weapons, and slingshot-propelled fireworks.

When the two undercover agents approached the group in the park, one VVAW member claimed he recognized them as "narcs" who had arrested him in Gainesville, Florida. The entire group then confronted the agents and accused them of being "pigs." After a prolonged shouting match that nearly erupted in physical violence, the agents felt it would be far wiser, and much safer, to leave the park rather than continue their futile denials. When their usefulness as undercover operatives came to an abrupt halt, they were content to spend the remainder of the week on local golf courses.

This unfortunate incident seemed to produce a sobering effect on all of us. Those who had little undercover experience were now more reluctant to approach protest leaders. They realized only too well that their chances of success were minimal at best, especially since they possessed no fictitious identification. On the other hand, we could always refer to our acquaintances from the SDCC who knew us under assumed identities, for verification of our lengthy involvement in radical politics. At least we would have ample opportunity to bullshit our way out of a close situation.

On Monday, July 10, 1972, the Democratic National Convention was formally called to order. There was little activity in the park until around noon, when continuous daily showings began of films revealing the devastation caused by U.S. Air Force bombings. This project was called the "Air War Exposé" and was sponsored by the Miami Convention Coalition. The films were often accompanied by comments from former Vietnam veterans who claimed to have personal knowledge of the atrocities committed by the American military command.

Most of the MCC organizers I spoke with that day seemed resigned to the fact that only a small fraction of the anticipated demonstrators would actually arrive; nevertheless, they remained confident that the situation would change dramatically in August.

The major action of the day was to be a late afternoon march from People's Park to the convention hall, where an outdoor rally would be held. The demonstration, referred to as a Poor Peoples March, was sponsored by a number of groups, including the National Welfare Rights Oranization (NWRO), the Southern Christian Leadership Conference (SCLC), the People's Coalition for Peace and Justice (PCPJ), and the National Tenants Organization (NTO). Since it was to be the first organized march through the streets of Miami Beach, it would provide the first real test of convention security precautions.

The march was scheduled to leave the park at five-thirty and once we began lining up, it was apparent that nearly everyone would join in. Signs, banners, balloons, and a multitude of Viet Cong flags were carried by the demonstrators. When we filed out of the park, filling the narrow street from curb to curb, several groups began chanting their favorite slogans:

Ho, Ho, Ho Chi Minh,
N.L.F. is going to win!
Ho, Ho, Ho Chi Minh,
N.L.F. is going to win!

One, two, three, four,
We don't want your fucking war!
Five, six, seven, eight,
Stop the war before it's too late!

As we passed through the residential section and the business area, the sidewalks were packed with neighborhood residents and shopkeepers who had actually been waiting in line to see the show.

Many of the elderly residents were visibly shaken by what they saw. I could just imagine them asking themselves, "Can this really be happening in the good old U.S.A.?" The outrageous contingent of Zippies marching directly in front of me, seized this opportunity to offend the sensibilities of middle America:

The Pope smokes dope,
The Pope smokes dope,
The Pope smokes dope and
He likes it in the ass!

And if that chant didn't get the attention of the audience, many of whom appeared to be of Latin-American descent, then perhaps a nearby group of elderly Jewish residents would understand the Zippies' Nazi salutes and accompanying chants of "Seig Heil, Seig Heil, Seig Heil," or individual shouts of "Vote for Eichmann, the burner with a brain."

For those who had somehow missed the Zippy message, there was the more direct approach:

Fuck Nixon,
Fuck Nixon,
Fuck Nixon,
Fuck Nixon!

The visible reaction of shocked disbelief followed closely by outrage could arguably be interpreted as the highest tribute to the fine art of Zippy guerrilla theater. By the end of the summer, after meeting and observing many of their number, I reached the conclusion that their only ideological commitment was to what can best be described as the politics of absurdity.

When the convention hall finally came into view, there was an even larger crowd of elderly spectators lining the sidewalks. I recall thinking that these people must have absolutely no conception of the potential violence that could erupt at a gathering like this.

After chanting for several minutes in front of the Convention Center, we took seats on the street, sidewalks, and curbs to listen to a large number of rally speakers. They included Dr. George Wiley, executive director of the National Welfare Rights Organization, Ralph Abernathy from the Southern Christian Leadership Conference, Dr. Benjamin Spock, who was later to become the People's Party candidate for president of the United States, and feminist Gloria Steinem.

Ms. Steinem was clearly the easy winner with the audience. Dr. Spock was a distant second. Many of the speakers who espoused the cause of "oppressed minorities" generated little enthusiasm among the predominantely white, well-educated middle class group of antiwar protestors. We must undergo fundamental social change in our country, the antiwar protestors agreed, but first the Vietnam War must be stopped.

After the speeches had ended, the four streets surrounding the Convention Center became a surging sea of humanity. The carnival atmosphere of People's Park pervaded the large crowd that wandered aimlessly through the streets. Nearly everyone wanted to walk around the sprawling complex, both to see and be seen. For those few who looked upon this confusion as a discreet opportunity to reconnoiter the enemy, there must have been an awakening of awesome proportions, for the Convention Center resembled an impregnable fortress.

The entire structure was enclosed by a six-foot-high, chain-link fence topped with strands of barbed wire. The fence, which had been specially erected for the conventions, prevented access to the grounds and the hall except through one of four heavily manned gates. Should demonstrators attempt to storm the hall, the gates would be closed immediately, leaving the invaders some forty yards shy of the building entrance. And if things really got out of hand, there was an abundant supply of aging city transit busses available for positioning along the street as a barricade in front of the convention hall.

The area of enclosed land around the hall was occupied by legions of police dressed for action against rioters. In our earlier briefing at the local FBI office, we had been told that approximately one thousand local and state law enforcement officers were on duty, along with three thousand National Guard troops who were housed in local high school gymnasiums. The Guard would be called only if necessary, and if the situation deteriorated even further, there were two thousand paratroopers from the 82nd Airborne Division and five hundred marines at Homestead Air Force Base ready for immediate deployment.

Also in attendance were countless numbers of federal law-enforcement personnel, including agents from the FBI, Secret Service, CIA, U.S. marshalls, and various branches of Military Intelligence. There must have been at least two law-enforcement officers for every demonstrator who had come to Miami Beach.

As the evening wore on, groups of demonstrators would suddenly push closer to unmanned sections of the fence, sending police reinforcements scurrying from one side of the enclosed compound to the other like mice trapped in a giant maze. Officers stationed at large intervals inside the fence would dodge an occasional rock or bottle, but demonstrators seemed primarily concerned with forcing the police to redeploy their forces. When taunting, jeering protestors leaned on the fence, to direct verbal abuse at the officers a few feet away, the police would often respond by firing a powerful stream of Mace into the face of the protestor. The victim would then be observed groping blindly in anguished pain, screaming for assistance from the People's Medics, who provided first aid.

In this chaotic situation, I casually passed among the crowd to determine if any individual or group was advocating the use of violence. Most of our FBI superiors had never been able to understand that most violent acts that occurred in demonstrations were the result of spontaneous behavior by individuals rather than of advance planning by radical organizations. People caught up in the excitement and emotion of the moment simply felt compelled to attract attention by committing some brazen act under the cover of a large crowd.

Scarcely any of the spontaneous demonstrators outside the hall were identifiable as militant political activists. While many of those present shouted "Liberate the hall," I was fairly certain nearly everyone realized it would be ridiculous to make such an attempt. Even those few shouting "Down with the fence" must have been aware that the end result would be a busted head and a lengthy stay in jail. This anticipation became a reality later that evening in the most serious incident of the convention week. I had noticed two older, experienced-looking demonstrators surveying the situation from a safe distance and discussing the reactions of the police to the various moves of the crowd. I watched them walk along the front of the crowd, occasionally engaging in brief conversations with some of the more vocal protestors. I moved well ahead of them and joined a chanting group positioned a few yards away from the fence. In less than five minutes, they had worked their way over to my location and began sizing me up.

"Wanna get in the hall, man, maybe raise a little shit?" one asked.

"Well sure, brother," I replied, flashing a warm smile, "but how you plan on gettin' in?"

"We gonna take out the fence, man," his partner answered. He spoke in a serious, yet strangely confident manner, acting as though this were an everyday occurrence. "Once the fence goes down, everybody can rush in behind."

"Okay brother, but look, even if you do get the fence down, have you got anybody to help rush the hall? I mean like ah, those pigs gonna fuckin' kill us less we got lots of folks rushin' in for confusion." I was struggling for a plausible method of discouraging these idiots, without sounding fearful of some heavy action with "the man." If these guys were really serious, I certainly wanted to know them better.

"No sweat, man," the first protestor replied. "We got all these people around here ready to move on the hall, but try to get some more help, huh?"

Without waiting for my reply, the two organizers continued on through the crowd. I began drifting back nonchalantly toward the area where I had last seen Rodent to advise him of the situation. I lost sight of the two protestors when the surging crowd erupted with excitment as police rushed toward a distant gate apparently being threatened by another group, leaving several yards of fence directly in front of me unguarded.

In seconds, the two protestors darted from the crowd and lunged forward toward the unprotected fence. As they clung tightly to the top links, they instinctively lifted their feet, allowing all of their body weight to pull against the small-gauge wire attaching the fence to the posts. When one section of fence began sagging toward the ground, it was obvious they knew exactly what they were doing. They were hastily attacking sections on either side when three other demonstrators bolted from the crowd to lend assistance. The wire holding the fence began to snap like dried twigs as the five audacious protestors strained and pulled in unison. A frenzied cry rose up from the crowd as larger sections of the fence fell to the sidewalk. In a matter of minutes, five freaks had toppled almost fifty feet of the chain-link fence which earlier had seemed such a formidable barrier.

The police, reacting to the cry that rang out from the crowd, came running back at full gallop but nearly stopped in their tracks when they saw the gaping hole in their defenses. They called for reinforcements while cautiously maintaining a safe distance between the selves and the crowd. The two leaders paused in front of the droopi fence to look back at their fellow-demonstrators, not one of whom moved, then briefly tried to urge them on to the hall. Had the crowd been of the same determination as the two leaders, literally hundreds could have made their way into the convention grounds and on toward the building entrance. The demonstrators faced absolutely no resistance for several minutes, and then for the brief moments that followed, they encountered only a handful of confused and badly outnumbered officers.

When not a single protestor inched forward toward the expansive opening, not even the three who had fearlessly offered assistance, the two leaders wisely retreated into the security of the crowd. They had provided the golden opportunity the demonstrators had been shouting for, but once it was offered, no one took advantage of it. Perhaps they feared that once through the fence, they were in enemy territory, and when the spacious breach in security was contained, they would be sealed off among hundreds of angry and humiliated police officers.

Once the police regained control of the situation, they began moving en masse through the length of fallen fence and into the street. The crowd readily sensed it was time to return to the park. It had been a long night but they had proved in stunning fashion that the menacing fence was only an illusory symbol of security.

I stuck close to the two protestors who led the assault on the fence, talking with them again on our walk back to the park. We briefly discussed returning to the hall later that evening, but they soon decided it would be too risky without the cover of a large crowd. The only identifying information I could obtain was that one was named "John," and both claimed to be from the New York City area. While they voiced displeasure over the demonstrators' reluctance to follow their example, they really didn't seem at all surprised or upset. I had hoped to observe them entering an automobile, which could have provided assistance in determining their identity, but after returning to the park, they were lost in the confusion. It was the last time I would ever see them.

Shortly after midnight, I telephoned the office to report our activities, only to find that they were already preparing communications regarding the damaged fence. They were somewhat disgruntled over the fact that I had been unable to identify the leaders of the incident, but seemed pleased that at least we had seen what happened. We estimated the march participation at around two thousand demonstrators, although these figures generally varied widely between organizers, media, and police officials. I was surprised to read a news report the following day which stated that the fence had been leveled after it was stormed by five hundred protestors.

Tuesday's schedule of activities for nondelegates consisted of a wide variety of events including the "First Annual Fone Freak Convention," sponsored by the Yippies, a VVAW Conference on Drugs, a parade for Abortion and Prison Reform, sponsored by the Zippies, and the National Coalition of Gay Organizations March and Kiss-In. In addition, the Miami Convention Coalition was busily hauling sand for the construction of a sixty-foot "dike" near the Convention Center, to focus attention on the massive bombing campaign being waged in North Vietnam. Every organization had planned some type of activity which would result in media coverage and exposure for their cause.

By the previous evening's "fence toppling" standard, the Tuesday night march was relatively uneventful.

During the Monday night rally, I had noticed several regular FBI agents who had been brought in to provide physical identification of any suspected Weatherman fugitives we might locate during the convention. Most were casually dressed, making no pretense of being anything other than a plainclothes law-enforcement officer. They certainly did not blend in with the local residents, and they attempted to do nothing more than stand in the background and observe the crowd. Their only function was to remain available in the immediate area and lend assistance if requested.

When we had approached the Convention Center earlier, I was amazed when one of these agents abruptly joined our marching throng and began to mingle with the demonstrators. I discreetly pointed this out to Panda, who was equally bewildered. The agent who had apparently decided to go "undercover" was about my age. He was clean-shaven, wore expensive metal frame glasses, and had his short hair greased down in the archaic manner of a wethead. He wore a white short-sleeved dress shirt open at the collar, plaid Bermuda shorts, black nylon stretch socks, and black wing-tip oxford shoes. The absurdity of this attire was matched by his ghostly-white legs. The final touch was the black ball-point pen clipped to his shirt pocket. That pen most assuredly bore the stamped inscription "U.S. Government."

As the rally began in front of the hall, Panda and I positioned our-selves amidst our friends in the Zippies. While we traded jokes with the Zips, I caught a glimpse of our new "undercover" agent out of the corner of my eye. I silently motioned to Panda, who instantly got the message as our colleague moved closer and closer.

"The son of a bitch is crazy," I muttered to Panda. We were hemmed in, and this village idiot, who might as well have been wear-ing a badge and uniform, was about to approach us. I was afraid if we tried to thread our way through the crowd, he would follow us the en-tire way, attracting even more attention. I turned to face him with a scowl that I hoped would tell him to stay the hell away, but it had abso-lutely no effect. I turned back around.

"Here he comes, C," Panda warned. "Hang on!"

Yeah, I'll hang on, I thought. And if I get out of this one, I personally am going to hang that bastard up by his balls! He was about three feet behind me now and slightly to my right. We said nothing, not daring to acknowledge him for fear he would act like an old friend. Then it hap-pened.

"Would you guys follow me," he stage-whispered. "I've spotted a subject that looks exactly like Jeff Jones."

Panda and I remained silent, hoping he would get the picture and go away.

"Say listen," he started again, edging even closer, "I've found this —"

"Split!" I replied tersely.

"What?"

"Get the fuck out of here before you heat us up." I spoke slowly and deliberately through clenched teeth, never once turning to look in his direction.

"I just need you to take a look at —"

"Shut up, you stupid son of a bitch!" I interrupted. After glancing around quickly, I turned partially so that I could see him out of the corner of my eye. Casually stroking my mustache to cover my mouth, I opened up with both barrels. "If you ever approach us again like this, I swear to God I'm gonna start yellin' you're a fucking pig. These freaks 'll stomp the livin' shit out of you, and I might just help 'em. Now get your ass away from here!"

My colleague apparently got the message, because he soon disappeared through the crowd. It was inconceivable that a conventionally dressed FBI agent would approach us in front of the Convention Center, as we stood in the middle of several thousand protestors, and expect us to accompany him through the crowd to view a suspected Weatherman fugitive. Inconceivable, but it had just happened.

When the rally broke up, most of the crowd moved toward the area where the fence had collapsed the night before. The fence was completely repaired, and police were positioned every three to four yards inside the enclosed area. They now directed streams of Mace toward those who ventured too close. This form of law enforcement made the rock concert, scheduled for later that evening, much more attractive. In less than an hour, the crowd had forsaken politics in favor of grass, beer, and music.

On the following day, shortly after lunch, approximately one hundred demonstrators attempted to gain entry to the Doral Beach Hotel, convention headquarters for Sen. George McGovern. The entrance to the hotel was immediately sealed off by the Florida Highway Patrol, but members of Senator McGovern's campaign staff persuaded the officers to allow the demonstrators to enter the lobby. The protestors, who displayed Viet Cong flags and a large poster of Lyndon B. Johnson, apparently left over from the morning's Zippy parade, enjoyed the plush surroundings of the Doral so much that they occupied its lobby for the next six hours.

They had come to confront Senator McGovern, soon to become the official presidential candidate of the Democratic Party, and compel him to clarify his position publicly on immediate withdrawal from Vietnam. The group was advised that Senator McGovern was not available, but that ranking members of his staff would discuss his position on the issue and answer questions. As might be expected, this was not acceptable to the group.

I'm sure the protestors realized that once they occupied the lobby, they were in control of the situation. Most of them had appeared astonished when allowed to enter, knowing that McGovern would not dare risk the adverse publicity resulting from a violent confrontation in his own convention headquarters. The only way these demonstrators would leave, short of actually talking with the candidate, was after they were arrested, handcuffed, and dragged from the hotel in full view of the network television cameras. McGovern's staff had committed a tactical blunder that could be corrected only by the candidate himself.

Even before his belated appearance, McGovern probably knew he had been placed in a difficult position. He must have been aware of the increasing dissatisfaction among antiwar groups over his position on withdrawal from Vietnam and legalization of marijuana. The majority of those in attendance, several of whom claimed to have campaigned actively for McGovern, seemed to believe he had sold them out after clinching the nomination, and was now softening his controversial positions in hopes of winning broader support among moderate and conservative party workers.

After viewing the treatment given his spokesmen by this clapping, shouting, chanting group, he certainly could not have been laboring under the illusion he was appearing before a friendly audience of campaign workers. Although he was one of the first politicians to speak out publicly against the war, in the minds of many activists he had become nothing more than a tool of the establishment.

Considering the situation he faced, I suppose Senator McGovern did his best in trying to reason with an unreasonable audience. The group was predictably unhappy with his statements concerning withdrawal from Vietnam and had no qualms about exhibiting its displeasure. Nevertheless, he did placate the demonstrators with his appearance, and they ultimately left the hotel of their own accord.

Many law enforcement authorities had predicted that if any violent confrontations were to take place during the Democratic Convention, they would most likely occur on Thursday, the final day of the convention. I had continued to report that there appeared little likelihood of substantial violence, since few of the more militant, hard-core activists had been observed, and the atmosphere in People's Park continued to be tranquil, though outrageous. Poet Allen Ginsberg could be seen peacefully engaged in trancelike chanting while the Zippies were busily rolling the "world's largest joint," in preparation for their afternoon "smoke-in."

One older individual who required absolutely no assistance in relating to the younger generation was Dr. Benjamin Spock. He was a frequent visitor to the park, and unlike other national celebrities, seemed neither to expect nor require special treatment. He attended every march and rally, often lining up in the middle or the back of the group like anyone else.

I spoke with Dr. Spock on several occasions throughout the week and each time came away impressed. He was a tall, imposing figure who always stood out in a crowd. Although well over twice the age of most demonstrators, he seemed in perfect physical condition. He was consistently friendly, informative, and interesting, but more importantly, he always had time to answer questions. Perhaps this can be attributed to Spock's interest in the People's Party, and his attempts to generate attendance for their nominating convention at the end of the week. Along with many others in the antiwar movement, Spock viewed the People's Party as a viable alternative to the two major parties. He seemed as dedicated to his beliefs as anyone I had ever met. One might question *why* a man of his professional stature and apparent financial success would become so deeply committed to such an unpopular cause, but the sincerity of his commitment was unquestionable.

The final day's march in support of political prisoners and the Seven Point Peace Proposal for Vietnam was anticlimactic. There had been little excitement since the opening night of the convention, and most organizers were now talking of August and the Republicans. The majority of the marchers appeared uninterested in staying around for MCC planning sessions or the People's Party convention. Since the park would soon be closed to campers, the primary concern now became transportation out of the city.

Our undercover contingent assembled at the FBI office the following day for debriefing sessions and to assist with final paperwork. There was a perceptible feeling of relief among the employees of the Miami office, for they had made it half way through the summer without any significant problems. The entire office staff had worked long, hard hours, and the coverage of convention activities was the product of a total team effort.

While demonstrating our effectiveness, we had also managed to make our presence appear indispensable. The group of "identification" agents would be allowed to return home until shortly before the Republican Convention began on August 21, but our undercover team would be required to remain in Miami during the interim period. We were expected to maintain contact with our acquaintances in the MCC in order to gather intelligence information on disruptive activities being planned for the Republicans.

Several members of our group were elated over the prospect of a

five-week paid vacation in Miami Beach. But after more than a week
of virtual inactivity, it became apparent that the rest of the summer
would be a gigantic bore. Nearly all our acquaintances in the movement had left the city, and there was simply no one left to contact. In
addition, since we had neither suitable housing nor a cover story for
credibility, it was impossible to approach MCC organizers we didn't already know.

The vacation I had envisioned turned into a boring routine. Even
sleeping late had become tiresome, and the anticipated fun-in-the-sun
failed to materialize. After living on the beach in southern California
for a couple years, I had become a devout sun-worshipper and occasional body-surfer. But Miami Beach was a completely disappointing
experience. In many areas, the beach was relatively nonexistent.
Where it was more extensive, including the private areas owned by
hotels, cigarette butts protruded in profusion from the surface of the
sand which the merciless sun heated to such an extent that it was often
impossible to walk on it with bare feet.

Perhaps I had become spoiled by the wide expanse of sand along the
Marina Peninsula, cleaned daily by the Los Angeles Park Department,
and by the refreshing breeze that always seemed to offset the warm
rays of the sun. Or maybe it was the fact that freaks were easily accepted in Los Angeles. Whatever the reasons, I was more than ready to return to California.

Panda, Rodent, and I had managed to maintain close contact with
Fast Freddie, our supervisor in Los Angeles. Since he was staying at
my apartment on the beach, we could usually locate him at night if we
were unable to call during the day. Based on our collective conversations with Fred, it appeared that our colleagues who remained had
done an outstanding job in running the November Committee.

According to Fred, Joe and Jay had made contact with leaders of the
VVAW, who requested that the November Committee participate in a
cross-country caravan traveling to Miami for the Republican Convention. It was an unexpected opportunity for undercover agents to infiltrate the West Coast leadership of the VVAW, determine the extent of
their plans for convention demonstrations, and also to develop credibility for the November Committee operation. The situation also provided the three of us with ammunition to support the argument that
our assistance was temporarily needed in Los Angeles.

After we discussed our current predicament with Fred, he called
several of his friends in Division Five and convinced them that we

were now essential back in L.A. Since the entire membership of the November Committee consisted of only five FBI agents, three of whom were presently in Miami, it was not too difficult to sell the Bureau on the idea of our return. After conferring with Miami supervisors, who were somewhat reluctant to let us leave, the Bureau officially concurred with Fred's proposal but insisted that we get back to Miami at least two weeks before the opening of the Republican Convention.

Before any of the various parties involved in the decision had an opportunity to change their minds, we packed our bags and headed for the Miami airport.

5

MIREP

Little had changed in Los Angeles during our brief absence. The seaside ghetto of Venice, with its dilapidated tenements, deserted buildings, and multiracial population, remained as timeless as ever. It was a city of individualists, although many of the elderly citizens stayed because of economic necessity rather than choice. While the beatnik era of the fifties had given way to the flower children of the late sixties, representatives of both periods remained highly visible. The different ethnic, cultural, social, and political factions of Venice retained the ability to pull together and save the area from the changes envisioned by land developers who wanted to transform the area into a luxurious extension of neighboring Marina Del Rey. "Keep Venice Funky" encouraged the bumper stickers, and somehow, the population always managed to do just that.

From our small headquarters in the heart of the Venice canal district, the November Committee continued to function as a clearinghouse for information about transportation to the upcoming Republican Convention. Joe and Jay had done a magnificent job of establishing credibility with the Vietnam Veterans Against the War (VVAW) and were busily preparing for the cross-country caravan. According to the local VVAW leadership, caravans were being organized in Los Angeles, San Francisco, and Portland on the West Coast as well as in several East Coast and Midwestern cities. All three regional caravans would meet in Jacksonville, Florida on August 19, then proceed to Miami Beach together as "The Last Patrol." VVAW organizers were predicting six thousand vehicles for the final procession into the city.

The Bureau was overjoyed by the opportunity to infiltrate the caravans, but since Division Five viewed the VVAW as the most potentially violent organization traveling to the conventions, the office steadfastly refused to allow undercover agents to work alone. If we had to

74

travel in pairs, this posed an immediate problem, since there were only five of us, and our "organization" had already committed two Volkswagen vans for the trip. The situation was later solved when Panda agreed to return with the caravan, and Fast Freddie recruited Leroy, who was also a Vietnam veteran, to lend assistance.

Rodent and I would return by air some two weeks before the convention started, concentrating our efforts on West Coast activities, while Joe, Jay, Leroy, and Panda would accompany the caravan to Miami Beach and cover VVAW activities.

We also began to receive information from Fred regarding a new undercover program at the Bureau. Division Five had apparently been impressed with our performance during MIDEM, and was reportedly formulating plans to establish an *official* undercover program designed to penetrate the Weather Underground. Little was known about the basic structure of the plan, but unusual requests were emanating from the Domestic Intelligence Division. Sensitive information, which was once only whispered about, was now being requested in writing by the Bureau.

A coded teletype dated July 24, 1972 from the Acting Director, FBI, to the SAC's of seventeen Bureau field offices and marked "PERSONAL ATTENTION," signaled an end to the unofficial program of the Hoover era. The significant portion of the lengthy communication contained the following:

BY IMMEDIATE TELETYPE REPLY ADVISE IDENTITY OF
AGENTS HANDLING WEATHERMAN AND OTHER NEW LEFT
EXTREMISTS CASES, BOTH FUGITIVE AND INTELLIGENCE.
INCLUDE THEIR AGES, THEIR EXACT ASSIGNMENT INCLUDING
THOSE WHO HANDLE WEATHERMAN AND THOSE WHO
HANDLE OTHER EXTREMIST CASES; THEIR CASE LOAD: AND IF
BEING UTILIZED ON THE STREET DOES THEIR PERSONAL
APPEARANCE MAKE THEM READILY AVAILABLE TO CONTACT
WITH MOVEMENT INDIVIDUALS, AS WELL AS ACCEPTANCE BY
THEM. ALSO INCLUDE IF AGENT CAN PERSONALLY
RECOGNIZE FROM PAST EXPERIENCE ANY WEATHERMAN
UNDERGROUND MEMBERS, BOTH FUGITIVE AND
NONFUGITIVE, AND SET FORTH IDENTITY OF SUCH MEMBERS
AFTER AGENT'S NAME.
    IDENTIFY AGENTS BEING USED IN UNDERCOVER
ASSIGNMENT AT THIS TIME AS DISTINGUISHED FROM THOSE

WHO CAN READILY MOVE AMONG MOVEMENT PEOPLE
BECAUSE OF THEIR APPEARANCE. SET FORTH AGE OF THESE
AGENTS, CURRENT TARGETS OR ASSIGMENTS AND POTENTIAL
FOR PENETRATION INTO WEATHERMAN OR SIMILAR-TYPE
UNDERGROUND OPERATIONS.

FURTHERMORE ADVISE IDENTITY OF OTHER AGENTS WHO
COULD BE UTILIZED IN UNDERGROUND ASSIGNMENTS. SET
FORTH BACKGROUND OF THESE AGENTS INCLUDING AGE AND
MARITAL STATUS, AVAILABILITY AND KNOWLEDGE OF
WEATHERMAN IDEOLOGY. ADVISE IF USE OF SUCH
PERSONNEL IS WARRANTED IN YOUR OFFICE AND INDICATE
WHAT DEGREE THESE AGENTS CAN BE UTILIZED, WHAT
THEIR TARGETS WILL BE AND ANY RECOMMENDATIONS FOR
SUITABLE COVER.

FURNISH YOUR PERSONAL EVALUATION AS TO WHICH OF
THE AGENTS PRESENTLY BEING UTILIZED IN UNDERCOVER
CAPACITY AND THOSE RECOMMENDED FOR SUCH ASSIGNMENT
YOU CONSIDER TO BE BEST PHYSICALLY AND
PSYCHOLOGICALLY QUALIFIED FOR UNDERCOVER
ASSIGNMENT.

I WANT TO IMPRESS ON EACH SAC THE EXTREME
IMPORTANCE OF THESE INVESTIGATIONS AND THAT I EXPECT
WEATHERMAN AND SIMILAR GROUPS TO BE HUNTED TO
EXHAUSTION. THIS CAN ONLY BE DONE BY UTILIZATION OF
SUFFICIENT MANPOWER AND PENETRATION INTO THE
UNDERGROUND BY INFORMANTS AND AGENTS WHERE
WARRANTED. YOU ARE REMINDED OF THE TWO OBJECTIVES
TO BE ACHIEVED IN THESE CASES: ONE. SHORT-RANGE, THE
IMMEDIATE APPREHENSION OF THE FUGITIVES AND TWO,
LONG-RANGE, PENETRATION AND NEUTRALIZATION OF THE
UNDERGROUND APPARATUS.

THIS TELETYPE HAS BEEN SENT YOU MARKED PERSONAL.
IT IS ABSOLUTELY NECESSARY THAT THE INFORMATION
CONTAINED HEREIN BE HANDLED ON A STRICT NEED-TO-
KNOW BASIS. YOU WILL RECEIVE FURTHER INSTRUCTIONS AS
THEY ARE FORMULATED. HANDLE THIS MATTER
IMMEDIATELY AND SUTEL INFORMATION REQESTED
ATTENTION DOMESTIC INTELLIGENCE DIVISION.

This was a momentous occasion. It was the first time that a written
communication from FBIHQ officially recognized the existence of un-

dercover agents, requested detailed information concerning their activities, and authorized their future deployment.

The information from Fred's Washington sources indicated that Acting Director Pat Gray was highly in favor of establishing an undercover capability to penetrate the so-called "underground" and had given the project his blessing and encouragement. There were even rumors of an upcoming "In-Service" for undercover agents which would explan the new program.

Most of the local groups I contacted during the following week were generally noncommittal about their plans for the Republican Convention. Nearly everyone indicated they would attend, but many were strangely tight-lipped about when they would leave, how they would travel, or where they expected to stay in Miami. I was beginning to wonder if the thousands of demonstrators predicted by MCC organizers would actually arrive. I was not overly enthusiastic about returning myself. The only redeeming feature was the prospect of some exciting street action, for we all anticipated a totally different group of protestors for the Republican Convention.

On the morning of August 10, 1972, it was back to Los Angeles International for our return trip to Miami. Rodent seemed to share my noticeable lack of enthusiasm, and it was apparent that his wife, who provided transportation to the airport, was even less excited about the event. Having made two previous flights on National Airlines, we saw little reason to change, especially since the absence of metal detectors at their boarding gate meant we didn't have to advise half the terminal of our identity. In our "native dress," we looked for all the world as though we could scarcely afford a ticket.

Upon boarding the plane, we were pleasantly surprised to be greeted by none other than Ms. Mary Smith, the helpful flight attendant from our maiden voyage to Miami. Mary was equally astonished by our arrival, probably recalling the furor surrounding our earlier trip, but she acted warm and friendly. We headed for the back of the aircraft, grabbing a plentiful supply of magazines on our way. I suggested Rodent try his luck at selecting the stewardess this time, since my track record with National wasn't exactly the best. I wasn't looking forward to another hassle over identification. It was only a matter of minutes before his vivacious young selection bustled toward the cockpit. We had previously remarked how fortunate it would be to have the captain from the first flight as our pilot. Since Mary was again one of the crew members, we felt this was a possiblity. That faint hope was dashed as the captain came out for a personal inspection.

"Well, here we go again, Rodent," I mumbled. "Better get those 'creds' out and have your best bullshit ready."

This captain was somewhat older and more officious-looking than the first. After producing our credentials, Rodent began the usual spiel about being on special assignment, inability to update credential photographs, use of Government Travel Requests, and concealed weapons—all to no avail.

"Do you have a badge?" the captain curtly inquired.

Not knowing whether Rodent was carrying his badge, and figuring that it must mean something to the guy or he wouldn't be asking, I immediately answered while reaching for my wallet. "Yes sir, captain, right here."

The pilot had a curious look on his face as I produced the small shield for his inspection. He examined it carefully while I prepared myself for the typical response which follows the display of our seldom-used badge. The captain straightened noticeably, looked us over from head to toe, then continued as though he had made a startling discovery.

"Gentlemen," he began, "I have been told by reliable authorities that FBI agents are not issued badges because the FBI does not even have badges, only identification cards. How do you explain the fact that you have a badge?"

"Sure they do, Captain," I began. "All FBI agents are issued badges when they enter the Bureau. We don't ordinarily use them, but we all have them for use in raids or situations where visible identification is required. Not everybody carries them, but we all have them. Where did you hear we didn't use them?"

"A customs man I know in Miami positively assured me that the FBI does not have badges, only identification cards. But you don't look anything like those cards anyway, and besides, the guy said the FBI doesn't issue badges."

"Well, I'm sorry, captain, but the customs man was mistaken. If you'd like, you can have the tower contact our office to verify our identity. Ask for the Squad Nineteen supervisor."

I didn't mind being nice to the captain and trying to explain our unusual assignment, but this was getting ridiculous. Then I glanced toward the front of the aircraft and noticed that Mary was staying clear of the controversy this time but finding the whole situation amusing.

"By the way, captain," I continued, "we flew on this airline several weeks ago to the Democratic Convention and had a similar problem.

One of your flight attendants, Mary Smith, was on that flight and is aware of our identity. She might be able to put your mind at ease about our employment."

"You know Mary Smith?" the Captain asked increduously.

"Yes sir," Rodent immediately replied, "she helped us last trip."

The captain headed forward and spoke briefly with Mary, then entered the cockpit and closed the door. As we moved away from the boarding ramp, a smiling Mary Smith came walking back, shaking her head from side to side. She leaned over the seat in front of us to speak in a softer tone.

"Nobody seems to believe you two are FBI agents," she jokingly said. "Come to think of it, I'm not sure I do either! But the captain seems to think if you flew with us a few weeks ago, you must be who you say you are. Anyway, we're taking off."

Mary flashed a broad grin and went about her duties.

"Well Rodent, do you feel like maybe somebody up there is tryin' to tell us somethin', and we're just not gettin' the message?"

"Could very well be, C, could very well be."

One of the few advantages of our early return to Miami was the opportunity to socialize with the undercover agents we had worked with during MIDEM. I looked forward to seeing several of the guys and finding out what had taken place during our absence. After a few drinks with our associates, it was evident that absolutely nothing of importance had occurred. Our friends who had remained in Miami all summer were well-tanned, claimed to have become scratch golfers, and had visited nearly all of the popular night spots in the area.

I was instructed to recontact my friends in the MCC during the two weeks before the Republican Convention was to begin and obtain current information on their plans. This was really not an assignment that required two weeks, since other than procuring a tentative schedule of activities, the leadership either didn't know exactly what would take place or wouldn't say. It again underscored the fact that Bureau officials were incapable of understanding that the organizers could speak only for themselves with any degree of certainty. The typical activist detested rigid organizational structure and centralized authority. In short, it was of little consequence what Rennie Davis, David Dellinger, or other MCC leaders said, did, planned, or promised; once protestors arrived in Miami, most of them would do exactly as they pleased.

The fact that we were required to return to Miami nearly two weeks before the convention opened indicated the significant difference in administrative priorities given the two conventions. We had arrived only three days before the opening of the Democratic Convention, generally unacquainted with each other and totally lacking in equipment and documentation necessary for a successful covert operation. But for the Republican Convention, the internal situation within the Bureau had changed dramatically.

In one of our frequent office planning sessions before MIREP, we again emphasized the need for more suitable transportation. Various types of cars were immediately rented under fictitious rental agreements by local agents. We had pointed out the problems in reporting up-to-the-minute information during violent confrontations, when streets were blocked or clogged with demonstrators, and had suggested using motorcycles as we had in Los Angeles. Two Honda "750" motorcycles were rented and placed at our disposal. Several of the inexperienced agents voiced reluctance over approaching protest leaders without the benefit of fictitious identification after the unfortunate incident with the VVAW. Names and identifying data were solicited and a Miami agent was dispatched to procure phony drivers' licenses through his contacts at the local CIA office. It was almost as though money, time, and effort were no longer of concern.

There was also increased pressure for up-to-the-minute reporting from the Bureau. The supervisors and convention coordinators were desperately scratching for any information, material or immaterial, relevant or irrelevant, to include in their daily communications to Washington. It was considered essential to convey the impression that the Miami situation was entirely under control, and that we were privy to every convention activity that might occur.

Impressions were not only conveyed to top Bureau officials in Washington. In what had to rank as the height of the ridiculous, we were required to gather at the Miami office during regular business hours and in our finest freak attire, so that the Special Agent in Charge (SAC) could parade us in front of high-ranking members of the Republican administration. The purpose of this show was to convince the Republican officials that the FBI really could infiltrate radical organizations and determine the extent of their convention plans.

We had previously been advised that top officials from the Justice Department had rented an apartment in a high-rise building across from the Convention Center in order to have an observation post. As best I can recall, at least one of the officials who questioned us that day was from the Justice Department, possibly the Internal Security Section. At any rate, it was obvious that the questions, which were almost as foolish as our presence, were intended primarily to determine the degree of political embarrassment which could result from various protest activities.

It might be argued that the increased administrative preparation for the Republican Convention was directly attributable to the anticipated escalation in protest activities. But I would strongly suggest that the more realistic reason for increased concern was basically political.

Pat Gray was a Republican appointee who owed his bureaucratic existence to President Nixon. Although he was only *Acting* Director, it was evident that he enjoyed the position and, barring some unforeseen controversy with the President or Congress, would soon become the Director. It seems only natural that Gray would be intensely concerned with showing the President and his friends in the Republican Party that the right man had been chosen to head the FBI.

Among the Bureau hierarchy in Washington, uncertainty and insecurity were rampant. After spending their entire Bureau careers under J. Edgar Hoover, senior officials did not know what to expect from their new leader. Not only was Gray an unknown quantity; he was an "outsider" as well. Many officials did not privately support his views or innovative changes, but since it appeared to be a foregone conclusion that Gray would become a permanent fixture, most old-timers seemed content not to rock the boat while concentrating on protecting their own position and power base. In any event, they were all astute enough to realize that although the Bureau had consistently publicized its image of independence from partisan politics, that had never been the case and was certainly not so now. It is safe to say that none of the Assistant Directors wanted to drop the ball during the Republican Convention and become the first test case for Gray's anger.

By the weekend before the convention opening, it was evident that predictions of increased attendance were correct. Demonstrators from all over the country were streaming into the park to set up campsites. They were an older, more serious group who seemed to associate only with trusted friends. While the bulk of demonstrators attending the Democratic Convention activities were young, gregarious and intent on having a good time, this group was characterized by the secretive and somewhat paranoid behavior of experienced protestors. They had not traveled great distances to make new friends; instead, they had come to show the country exactly how they felt about Richard Nixon and his policies.

One common denominator of both conventions, however, was the continuation of outrageous antics by the Zippies. On Saturday morning, two women Zippies paraded topless through Flamingo Park, accompanied by a small group of cheering male Zips and a drummer. Perhaps this was considered a "liberated" version of the *Spirit of '76*.

By Saturday afternoon, the park was packed with demonstrators, many of whom were staying in other locations throughout the city. They had turned out to welcome the arrival of "The Last Patrol," the VVAW caravans traveling from the East and West Coasts. Rodent and I were just as eager as the crowd, for we had speculated for days about the condition of our four associates from the November Committee. We had been advised that they had left Los Angeles on August 15 in a caravan of eighteen vehicles, but we had received little information on their progress since that time.

The Bureau had naturally been receiving up-to-the-minute information from agents stationed throughout the country on the progress of both caravans. These agents were provided with the license numbers and descriptions of the vans used by undercover agents, and were instructed to be on the alert for a prearranged signal that would indicate they were in danger or needed to make contact. A more sophisticated warning device had been arranged for the two agents traveling from Boston in the east coast caravan. The lab had installed a small transmitter that continually broadcast a slow, intermittent beep on Channel Four, the common frequency among all FBI offices. As the van passed through various Bureau field divisions on its way South, agents could pick up the beep on their car radios and determine the relative location of the caravan. If the undercover agents encountered any problems, the driver could reach under the seat and flip the transmitter's toggle switch which would then broadcast a much faster beep, indicating they needed assistance.

The arrival of the caravan was one of the most dramatic events of the summer. The park was virtually deserted as nearly everyone moved into the surrounding streets to welcome "The Last Patrol." The screaming throng of demonstrators was wildly enthusiastic as the strange assortment of vehicles, all decorated with signs, flags, and banners came rolling into the city with horns blaring. As the caravan circled and recircled the park, demonstrators jumped on hoods, fenders, and trunks. The cars then drove into the camping area which had been reserved for them.

The new arrivals to the park had the look of a small, poorly-equipped, revolutionary army. Bits and pieces of military clothing, gear, and rations were in evidence everywhere. It seemed as though every member of the caravan wore some type of military attire. The jubilant demonstrators were more than happy to offer a warm, personal welcome, although no one seemed to notice that the caravan was about 5,950 vehicles short of orginal estimates. Even as the tumultuous celebration began to wind down, I had the distinct impression that most of the demonstrators had a profound respect for the Vietnam vets, and now that they had arrived, the week's activities could go forward.

It is difficult to describe the feelings I experienced upon seeing my four colleagues from Los Angeles. We had become close personal friends through our work, but even beyond friendship and employment, there seemed to exist an unspoken feeling of exultation over their successful operation. Every member of the November Committee had finally arrived in Miami Beach, and now it was time for our own celebration. In a brief moment away from the crowd, I suggested to my colleagues that as soon as they could get away from their VVAW friends, they accompany me to a distant motel room for a hot shower, a stiff drink, several joints of "Jamaican Red," and then to a restaurant for the largest steak we could locate in the city.

It was almost mind-boggling to think that in vehicles leased by the government, undercover FBI agents had traveled thousands of miles with VVAW members supposedly bent upon violent confrontation at the Republican Convention. As I learned later, the West Coast caravan had progressed in strict military fashion, maintaining a constant speed well below the legal limit through the use of communications equipment in the front and rear vehicles. Rest and fuel stops were made only as a group at specified times. Since VVAW organizers had anticipated harassment by local authorities along the way, they had stated in advance that absolutely no illegal drugs, alcohol, or weapons would be allowed in any of the vehicles. This seemed like a wise decision, although I never really thought it would be enforced; however, prior to leaving, and on several other unannounced occasions during the trip, each vehicle was thoroughly searched.

My friends had traveled from Los Angeles to Miami with VVAW members, camping out each night, surviving on meager amounts of bread, baloney, peanut butter, and C-rations. The caravan underwent frequent harassment by various law enforcement agencies in the form of identification checks and searches for contraband, and was even fired upon by a hidden sniper along a remote stretch of highway in Louisiana. In another unplanned occurrence, one of our vans was used to transport the cameras and technical equipment of a female French photographer who, with the assistance of a New York City production company, was filming a documentary of the caravan and convention activities. How shocked they would have been to discover that four of their stars were FBI agents!

After eating, sleeping, rapping, and traveling with these veterans, what was my colleagues collective impression? It was not what I expected. According to the agents, whose opinions I highly respected, the VVAW members they had traveled with had no intention of promoting violent confrontations. My friends had reached the conclusion, based on their personal experiences, that the Bureau was totally wrong in its assessment of this group.

My colleagues seemed to believe that the veterans were genuinely interested in bringing about an end to the war in Vietnam. While we had only read and seen news accounts of the war, these men had actually experienced the gross inhumanities of daily combat. They had had a first-hand look at the mindless hypocrisy that governed this war of attrition, which they now viewed as a needless, senseless waste of human life. According to the agents, the veterans stressed that their peace efforts at home should be nonviolent, for they had already experienced enough violence abroad.

I must confess to an initial skepticism about this appraisal of VVAW intentions, due primarily to my conditioning to the contrary by the Bureau. I suppose these doubts also resulted from my belief that if any group had the knowledge, training, resources, and motivation to employ violence, it was the VVAW. Because these men had experienced the strange exhilaration of combat, the stress of constant fear, and the emotions of death, it seemed likely that they would have the balls to commit acts of violence. While many of the more revolutionary activists espoused violence or terrorism as tactics from time to time, there were few who impressed me as actually having the courage to carry out such threats. By the end of the week, after observing countless VVAW members risking their own personal safety to prevent violence, I was in complete agreement with my colleagues' conclusions.

On Sunday afternoon, Flamingo Park, once again known as People's Park, was the scene of one of the most bizarre events imaginable. The park was packed with demonstrators, reporters, photographers, and the ever-increasing number of elderly Jewish residents who had come to take in the show. For most campers, it had been a late, lazy morning after an extended evening of smoking, drinking, and nude swimming. Frisbees floated gently through scattered clouds of marijuana smoke, while groups of demonstrators sat in small circles engaged in animated conversation.

A flatbed truck-trailer had been moved into the park for use as a stage, and while most of the demonstrators went about their business or lolled in the warm sunlight, leaders of the MCC began to make announcements of scheduled activities. Suddenly, from out of nowhere, there appeared twenty members of the American Nazi Party, dressed in their finest Nazi uniforms with bold swastika armbands. Before anyone realized what was happening, they had forcibly taken over the stage and began yelling "White Power" while giving the "Heil Hitler" salute.

I thought I had been exposed to some real crazies during my Bureau career, but these Nazi idiots easily won the award. I had believed that no organization could evoke more intense emotional reactions among the local Jewish population than the Jews For Jesus, but once again I was mistaken. The senior citizens in the park went absolutely berserk when they saw the uniformed Nazis giving their salutes. One had to look no further than the terrified faces of the elderly to understand the fear that the hated swastika emblem produced in the minds of those who had endured the Holocaust.

After the inhabitants of the park were able to grasp the reality of the situation, all hell broke loose. Scattered groups of demonstrators began rushing the trailer with whatever weapons they could find, but the Nazis held the high ground and used their heavy boots to kick anyone who approached the stage. At this point about one hundred VVAW members linked arms and circled the stage. Thirty veterans then broke from the circle, and attacked the Nazis with chairs, clubs, hammers, and tent spikes. Within minutes the stage had been reclaimed, and the screaming, kicking intruders were dragged from the park.

After the dramatic events of the afternoon, one simply didn't know what to expect from the evening's activities. SDS began a concerted effort to generate support for their later march on the Fountainbleau Hotel, where a gala affair honoring Mrs. Nixon was being held. SDS members had already engaged in verbal confrontations with MCC leaders Rennie Davis and David Dellinger over the use of violence in their demonstrations. SDS as well as the Zippies had consistently refused to endorse the MCC pledge of nonviolence, and it appeared certain that their relationships would deteriorate even further over the coming days. I could see the friction mounting as the respective groups childishly argued over the use of the public address system and stage. When all was said and done, each protestor would act exactly as he wished, for this fragile coalition of individuals was incapable of accepting the authority of leadership in a disciplined manner.

I had spoken with Rennie Davis about this leadership dilemma several days earlier and received the impression that he was not deluding himself into believing he had any real authority. I think he viewed his role with the MCC mainly as that of a recognized spokesman of the antiwar movement who possessed sufficient credibility to negotiate with Miami Beach officials and obtain several significant concessions. He was an intelligent, articulate spokesman of a large and growing segment of American society, but I doubt Rennie was ever naive enough to believe he had the power to control the thousands of demonstrators expected to descend upon the city. He probably realized that the city and state officials would negotiate only with an individual they perceived as a recognized leader of the antiwar movement; if not Rennie, then someone else of similar statute.

The SDS march on the Fontainebleau was not widely supported by those in the park, even though it was the first major street action of the Republican Convention. While less than five hundred protestors participated, they were so well organized that they succeeded in snarling traffic along Collins Avenue for more than two hours. The demonstration started shortly after seven as guests began to arrive for the preconvention dinner. Automobiles were kicked, scratched, and dented, and several guests were pummeled about by the noisy crowd as they tried to enter the hotel.

Shouts of "Stop the War" and "Keep The Rich Out" punctuated the evening air, although SDS organizers had prepared a number of chants for their highly vocal followers:

> Nixon, Agnew, you can't hide,
> We charge you with genocide!
> Run Nixon, run Nixon, run, run, run,
> People of the world are picking up the gun!

Rocks, bottles, cans, and occasional eggs came flying through the air, but a major confrontation failed to develop since authorities maintained a relatively low profile. No arrests were made, and the demonstrators quickly lost interest and returned to the park.

On Monday, August 21, 1972 the Republican National Convention officially opened. In slightly more than a month, I had experienced both gatherings of our major political parties, each conducted in the same hall and city, but under entirely different circumstances. The number, experience, dedication, and organization of the protestors had changed substantially, as had the emphasis, intensity, and interest of the FBI. While the Democrats sought to regain power, the Republicans were going to have to justify their past actions in order to retain power. Another distinction between the two conventions was the marked contrast between the official delegates. For the most part, the Republican delegates were substantially older and of a higher income level than their Democratic counterparts. They had a serious, businesslike attitude, and many gave the impression of being old-time politicos.

Perhaps these perceptible differences played some role in the way they were treated by demonstrators. The bulk of animosity and discontent within the country was predictably aimed at the Republican Party and its leadership; thus many of those who were unhappy with Richard Nixon's policies were attracted by the innovative approach of Senator McGovern. But the main difference was the inclusion of young, inexperienced, nonprofessional delegates into the nominating process of the Democratic Party. Anyone who attended both conventions could not help but notice that representation among the Democratic delegates seemed to transcend barriers of age, sex, race, or income. The demonstrators appeared to display an affinity for these delegates even though they might not condone their politics. I think many demonstrators were compelled to ask themselves whether politics had come out of the smoke-filled rooms and into the hands of common people.

The Monday night march from People's Park to the Convention Center produced a turnout almost twice as large as any during the Democratic Convention. The massive rally, held in front of the hall, was in commemoration of "Soledad Brother" George Jackson, the black activist who had been shot to death one year earlier by guards in San Quentin prison during an escape attempt. The organizers had scheduled the usual number of prominent speakers, but for effectiveness, none could come within light years of the speech delivered by Jane Fonda.

I had seen Jane Fonda frequently around the Santa Monica-Venice-Marina Del Rey area, for she lived only a few minutes from my place on the beach. For a Hollywood celebrity, she was totally unpretentious in her dress, appearance, and life-style. Jane must have shared my cravings for fresh donuts because I would often see her at the outdoor service window of the Boys Market bakery, looking for all the world like any other early morning donut freak. Although I never spoke to her beyond the usual "hello," I had talked with her future husband, Tom Hayden, dozens of times at various meetings and conferences.

I never pretended to understand what caused Jane Fonda to conduct herself in such an unpopular manner, but I was curious, as I had been in Dr. Spock's case, about the forces that motivated such behavior. I always questioned why a talented, attractive young lady seemed to go out of her way to offend the sensibilities of the public who had made her a celebrity. At one point, she was even being compared to Tokyo Rose, while many of our elected representatives were demanding that the government prosecute her for acts of treason or sedition. Fonda had jeopardized her livelihood, not to mention her freedom, at the height of her career in order to speak out against the war. In hindsight, I suspect there are few individuals of such prominence who would have been able to withstand the massive public criticism she received.

Fonda was the only rally speaker I have ever witnessed who had the ability to gain the complete attention of the audience. Conversations stopped as the group listened intently to her every word. It was not so much the content of her remarks, although that was well organized, but rather the delivery. It was a moving, compassionate presentation that completely mesmerized the audience.

Since there was no question Fonda was an accomplished actress, I wondered whether her speech had merely been another example of her professional talents. My emotions told me I had listened to a sincere, dedicated, and courageous woman, but if I was mistaken in that judgment, then she most assuredly deserved another Academy Award for her performance that evening.

On Tuesday morning, the activity within the park began much earlier than usual, with demonstrators busily engaged in preparing costumes and signs for the evening activities. The MCC planned to stage the "Street Without Joy," a spectacle in which demonstrators in Vietnamese costumes would line the streets to the Convention Center when delegates converged on the hall to nominate Richard Nixon. The protest was designed to depict the suffering and death inflicted on innocent Vietnamese civilians by American bombing attacks.

When the delegates began to arrive at the Convention Center late Tuesday afternoon, they were forced to pass through the ghoulish surroundings of the "Street Without Joy." There were hundreds of demonstrators dressed in the black, pajama-like clothing of the Viet Cong and the pointed straw hats favored by Vietnamese peasants. Most of the demonstrators wore white grease paint on their faces, their features highlighted in black to simulate death's heads. The gruesome portrayal of human suffering was accentuated even further by painted red tears flowing down the stark white faces of several women. Demonstrators silently lined both sides of the streets, many holding large poster-size photographs of screaming children in flames and dead infants strewn about devastated villages like discarded garbage. A small elephant, accompanied by a group of "mourners," pulled a coffin through the street, symbolizing the death of Vietnamese life.

The "Street Without Joy" had been staged to dramatize the "crimes" of the Republican regime, and judging by the reactions of the entering delegates, the spectacle was at the least a cause of personal embarrassment. Delegates accustomed to the loud, obscene shouts of protestors were caught off guard by the eerie silence. As they strode purposefully toward the hall, many with heads down and eyes fixed to the pavement, they looked more confused than angry. Their muted conversations were amplified by the strange stillness, causing them to feel self-conscious and uneasy. I think it safe to say that most were totally unprepared for an emotional experience of this magnitude. Even the most callous delegate would find it difficult to engage in jovial conversation while viewing the anguished terror on the faces of dying children. Regardless of who was ultimately responsible for these inhumanities, every delegate who passed through the demonstration must have felt some degree of sympathy for the innocent victims of the Vietnam War.

As Rodent, Walrus, and I walked near the Convention Center, we were approached by a bright-eyed young lady with a portable tape recorder and notebook. This freshly scrubbed young woman identified herself as a reporter for a campus newspaper at a large southern university. She was covering the convention activities and asked if we would consent to an interview. Having little better to do at the time, we replied that we would talk with her if she would first explain why she had picked us. She advised that it was our long hair and overall freaky appearance.

When we said we were from California in response to her opening question, her eyes lit up with delight over the aptness of her selection. She apparently subscribed to the widespread belief that all of the country's crazies lived in California.

We must have provided the reporter with thirty minutes of collective "information" about the November Committee and the unfortunate plight of its leader, Ritchie Rosen. Our main purpose in traveling to Miami, we told her, was not to engage in violent demonstrations, for our organization did not condone the use of violence, but rather to generate publicity for Rosen, a West Coast activist who was presently incarcerated in San Francisco on trumped-up charges of subversion. "Free Ritchie Rosen," we shouted into the microphone, "Free all political prisoners." We described the solicitation efforts of the "Ritchie Rosen Defense Fund" in great detail, assuring the reporter that once the country was aware of Ritchie's treatment by insensitive government officials, his name would become a rallying cry for the antiwar movement.

The young lady thanked us profusely and promised faithfully that she would do everything in her power to publicize the unfortunate plight of our leader. During the following months, we often speculated about whether Ritchie became a campus celebrity, for Ritchie Rosen was none other than the fictitious identity used by the Rodent.

As darkness descended on the Convention Center, crowds of demonstrators began to fill the surrounding streets. The senior citizens of Miami Beach once again turned out in record numbers. Spectators of all ages lined the sidewalks and curbs, chatting amiably while waiting for the show to begin. On this particular evening, they would not be dissappointed.

6

All Hell Breaks Loose
(And I Get Worked Over)

While demonstrators milled about the streets surrounding the heavily fortified hall, riot-dressed police stood shoulder-to-shoulder along the inside of the chain-link fence. The conciliatory, low profile approach to law enforcement had vanished, and both sides were abundantly aware of the change. The tension built as the crowd taunted the police, only this time, many of them were answering back.

"Hey, you pig-fucker," one protestor hollered through the fence, "bet you'd really like to hit someone with your stick, wouldn't you? You're a big brave son of a bitch, aren't you, you fascist asshole."

"Well come on over the fence, puke," the cop responded, steadily beating his menacing nightstick into his open palm. "You're such a big, tough talker. Just get your ass on over here, boy, and I'll knock your goddammed head off!"

After about an hour of mutual heckling, many of the police took the initiative, occasionally luring the inexperienced demonstrators close enough to the fence to fire powerful streams of Mace into their eyes. The police, obviously frustrated after weeks of nonretaliation, had now become the aggressors. I realized that when the fence no longer separated the two forces, all hell would break loose. Any FBI agent who had ever attended a major demonstration as an undercover participant, knew only too well that the greatest threat to his personal safety came not from the protest groups he had infiltrated, but from the angry, frustrated police, rampaging and uncontrolled.

These officers had trained for months in the latest riot control methods and techniques. Federal grants had equipped them with the most efficient equipment available. They had waited all summer for the confrontation in which they would demonstrate the effectiveness of their training, but had been forced to maintain a low profile, contain demonstrators, and overlook flagrant drug violations. They had endured weeks of verbal obscenities while constantly dodging bottles and bricks. In short, they were fed up with taking shit from long-haired, dope-crazed hippies who were unhappy about the war.

I believe that any law-enforcement officer who evaluates his colleagues as well as himself objectively would have to conclude that many men have entered the profession for the sense of power the job confers—power in the sense that the ethnic background, economic status, or educational level of the officer is of absolutely no consequence in determining the scope of his authority. The average citizen will obey his commands and respect his profession, and in the event that his authority is disregarded, he need reach no farther than his hip to express his power. Among younger officers, there is also a strong desire to impress one's associates. It is a mental state which is often referred to as the "Wyatt Earp Syndrome." In the macho world of law enforcement, every officer or FBI agent wants the professional respect of his peers, always hoping to be included when the office heavies are assembled for a dangerous arrest. There is a unique sense of camaraderie among police officers, stemming in part from the inherent danger of their occupation and the common awareness that their very existence may depend on the actions of a fellow officer. Unfortunately, this same esprit de corps often seems to produce an us-against-them attitude.

With these factors in mind, it becomes somewhat easier to understand the actions of the police in Miami Beach. Many of them were confronted for the first time with adversaries who had absolutely no respect for their authority, adversaries who even went out of their way to ridicule them. Many of them, frustrated by weeks of inactivity, perceived this blatant affront to their official authority as a personal affront. If the protestors were not taught a lesson, the public might also lose respect for their authority, and they would ultimately lose their sense of power.

Outside the Convention Center, both sides continued to bombard one another with verbal abuse. Out of nowhere, a shiny black limousine appeared and tried to force its way through the hundreds of demonstrators clogging the street. As the limousine's horn blared incessantly, the crowd descended on the vehicle, kicking the fenders and banging on the doors. The driver panicked, stepped on the gas, and headed into the crowd. After only a few yards, the limousine collided with an unsuspecting demonstrator, sending his body hurtling through the air. The vehicle continued on with demonstrators running in hot pursuit until it sped out of sight.

By the time an ambulance arrived for the injured victim, the crowd had become increasingly hostile. It was at this point that the police decided the situation was getting out of control. Without warning and in unison, they began to loft tear gas canisters over the fence and into the unsuspecting crowds. Thousands of angry, screaming demonstrators retreated as ominous gray clouds of tear gas billowed up in every direction.

Mass confusion prevailed. I ran toward a group of senior citizens, pausing briefly to warn them of the impending danger. They looked at me as though I were crazy and gave little indication of following my advice to take cover. They didn't seem to understand that tear gas was in the air and probably moving in their direction. I heard a chorus of wailing sirens as I circled back toward the other side of the Convention Center. Three ambulances had stopped in the street near a grassy knoll, their emergency lights flashing as attendants held oxygen masks to the faces of several fallen victims. One elderly gentleman being carried into the ambulance had reportedly suffered a heart attack after inhaling the gas.

The police moved into the streets, arresting anyone they could grab in the immediate area of the Convention Center. Subsequent news reports estimated that over two hundred demonstrators were arrested.

I have no idea why the police suddenly began to use tear gas without first warning the crowd to disperse. Perhaps they believed that the immediate situation was out of control, or maybe they anticipated massive confrontations the following day and wanted to warn the demonstrators that they meant business. At any rate, their aggressive behavior took the demonstrators completely by surprise, for few, if any, were ready for a violent confrontation at the Convention Center.

Wednesday, August 23, 1972, was the final day of the Republican National Convention. It had been termed a "Day of Unacceptance" by protest organizers, for it was to be the first time that President Nixon would enter the Convention Center to deliver his acceptance speech. It would also be one of the longest, most tiring, and most unforgettable days of my life.

The crowds formed early in People's Park, preparing for the confrontation which would surely occur. Demonstrators huddled in groups of four and five, speaking softly of their plans for the day. There was an atmosphere of cautious determination, and while there were cordial greetings among friends, everyone seemed deadly serious about their tasks. It became increasingly obvious as I walked through the park that my predictions had materialized. The experienced, militant, hard-core element of radical activism had arrived, almost equally divided between women and men. One look at their dress and you knew they had come prepared for business. Both men and women wore hair nets to prevent their long hair from flowing out of their motorcycle helmets. Clothing was worn in layers so that outer portions could be removed after saturation with tear gas. Army field jackets were favored because their tight cuffs and high collars provided additional protection from gas. Jeans were tucked into combat or hunting boots. Gloves, goggles, and bandannas provided additional protection; nearly everyone carried a surplus gas mask. The standard uniform of earlier demonstrations—cut-off jeans, T-shirt, and sandals or tennis shoes—was nowhere to be seen.

While I had never placed much faith in the theory that the elusive Weatherman fugitives would surface during the demonstrations, I was not at all surprised to see those of similar beliefs in attendance. Anyone familiar with Weatherman tactics would be aware that the small meetings of four or five protestors were last-minute planning sessions of "affinity groups."

The Weathermen had pioneered the concept of affinity groups. They were first used in October 1969, during the violent Days of Rage demonstrations on Chicago's near North Side. Four or five trusted friends would walk down the street as a unit, then suddenly run in different directions, breaking windows, hurling rocks, and attacking police. The group would be armed with clubs, chains, pipes, and rocks.

Weathermen apparently considered affinity groups their most potent guerrilla tactic. The usual targets were the police, government buildings, and offices of private companies having defense contracts. Police vehicles were considered fair game and would be trashed by the group whenever the opportunity presented itself.

I saw several familiar faces from the West Coast in the park. When I noticed the constituents of some of the affinity groups, I realized I had underestimated the extent of the relationship between the activists from San Diego and from Santa Barbara. I was invited to join two of these groups, but I had decided in advance that it would be better to compose a group made up entirely of undercover agents if we wanted to retain our mobility. If we had our own group, we could more easily deal with the perplexing problem of being considered agent provocateurs. If I were to join an affinity group, I would certainly be expected to participate in the group's activities. I would then be adding to the overall law-enforcement problem in order to build credibility among group members. Simply stated, you could not obtain the trust of militant, violence-oriented extremists unless you appeared to be of similar persuasion.

While talking with an affinity group from Santa Barbara whose members had seen me at numerous street actions over the past year, one member mentioned that they would be harassing chartered busses carrying delegates to the Convention Center. As I was about to leave, a demonstrator unknown to me approached us.

"You fellows need sand?" he inquired. "We brought in two sacks over near the gate."

"We ain't got no sand, brother," my friend answered, "but we got everything else! What the fuck we need sand for?"

"You know man, like if a pig grabs ya. Put some sand in each pocket of your jacket, then if you get busted, throw a handful in the pig's eyes and run like hell."

"Right on, brother, outta sight!"

As my friend from Santa Barbara rushed over to the sand bags, I went in search of my undercover colleagues. The friction that had been building for days between the MCC, SDS, and other organizations over tactics and ideology had now erupted into heated arguments. MCC leaders continued to urge nonviolent protests. SDS argued that every individual should make his own decision about what form the protests would take. But the tear gas and mass arrests of the previous evening, as well as the oppressive heat and lack of sleep, seemed to override these factional arguments. Virtually all of the demonstrators were preparing for a violent confrontation.

I soon located Rodent, accompanied by Walrus and Pigeon, two other members of our undercover contingent. We decided to head for the rental car Walrus had parked nearby. It was almost noon by the time we called the office to report on the current situation in the park. Walrus then suggested that we drive out Collins Avenue to a distant restaurant he had discovered that served home-cooked meals. As the car sped out of Miami Beach toward the restaurant, I sensed that we shared the same conflicting emotions. We were decidedly apprehensive about the prospects for the day, realizing only too well that the shit was about to hit the fan. But we were also elated by the anticipation of a tough, challenging assignment of unknown proportions. Like the police, we wanted to prove ourselves, although I suspect we were much more intent on proving our ability to the Bureau than to each other. I fired up a joint in anticipation of an enormous meal that Pigeon jokingly referred to as The Last Supper. This was the final day of our undercover work together. In a short time we would all be going our separate ways.

About one-thirty, we stumbled out into the scorching midday sun, completely stuffed, uncomfortable, and still a bit stoned. We piled into the stifling car, and as we approached the hotel area of the city, we discovered that traffic was being diverted because of a chanting group of about four hundred demonstrators who had gathered on a nearby side street. We parked the car and our undercover affinity group reluctantly went into action.

Unlike the affinity groups in the park, we had no helmets or gas masks. The only masks available from the local Bureau office were of a design not yet available to the public and would therefore have attracted too much attention. I wore a headband to keep my shoulder-length hair out of my eyes; several layers of workshirts; a tight-fitting knit shirt, and jeans. I had decided to wear cross-country running shoes rather than heavier boots because I anticipated we would be running most of the day. None of us carried any weapons or FBI identification. We were strictly on our own, relying on our experience, ability, and ingenuity to bring us safely through the day.

In a short time, we had caught up with the demonstrators, few of whom I recognized, and joined their march. As the scorching sun began to fry my somewhat scrambled brain, I wondered why I had gorged myself at lunch. The demonstrators were chanting the usual antiwar slogans as the group marched steadily and peacefully through the streets.

The four of us were positioned in the back quarter of the march as we rounded a corner and started down a narrow side street composed of two- and three-story buildings. Suddenly, without any warning, six to eight deafening shotgun blasts went off overhead. My heart jumped to my throat as that bolt of electrical energy called fear shot through my body. Any lingering effects of marijuana were instantly wiped out by the first burst of adrenalin. The screaming, terrified demonstrators didn't know how to react, and for a brief moment, the entire crowd seemed frozen.

"Incoming! Incoming rounds!" someone yelled, apparently a veteran.

Glancing forward, I could see several tear gas canisters spinning crazily in the street, spewing their contents in every direction. Four more blasts ruptured the air. I looked up to see police crouched along the rooftops of several buildings, pointing their sawed-off riot guns equipped with tear gas launchers toward the crowd below.

"The sons of bitches are crazy!" I yelled toward my colleagues who, like me, were instinctively searching for cover.

Screaming, panic-stricken demonstrators were running past us, trying to escape the tear gas fired into the front of the march. We joined them after another glance forward revealed about one hundred police in full battle gear, in hot pursuit. With gas masks tightly in place, they looked like invaders from a distant planet.

To this day I don't understand what precipitated the massive tear gas attack. It was shortly after two o'clock, and we were already running for our lives. We ran several blocks toward the beach, scrambling over and around parked cars, lawn furniture, and startled pedestrians. The police were close behind, their riot batons in the ready position. The stampeding crowd crossed Collins Avenue, ran down the street for a couple of blocks, then darted through a vacant lot toward the ocean. The police were still coming, charging like cavalry officers in an old Western. The few unfortunate protestors who stumbled in the sand were swiftly spread-eagled, faces buried in the sand, and handcuffed.

We ran at least a half mile down the beach, passing through private beachfront areas, luxurious hotel cabanas, snack bars, and shrubbery, often moving out into the surf to cross the barriers between hotels. Some demonstrators tried to escape into the rear entrances of hotels, but these were hastily locked after several glass doors were shattered. I thought we could eventually outrun the police because they were loaded down with riot equipment, and I knew from experience they would have a difficult time breathing in the gas masks. On the other hand, the tear gas they were using not only affected the eyes, it also adhered to clothing and skin, producing a burning sensation followed by nausea. As often happens in such situations, we had escaped most of the initial tear gas clouds, but as demonstrators who had passed through the clouds came running past us, we would be overcome by the fumes on their clothing. It was an extremely effective form of crowd control. Quite simply, it made you sick as hell.

Rodent and I paused briefly to catch our breath, having long since lost Pigeon and Walrus in the confusion. There were bodies scattered up and down the shoreline, but it looked as though the police had run out of gas. I heard a plaintive "aw shit" from my colleague, then looked ahead to see another group of police running toward us from the opposite direction. Reinforcements had arrived and were attacking from both sides.

"Hope you're a good swimmer," I cracked, knowing full well that Rodent hated the ocean with a passion.

Off we ran, over the same stretch of beach we had just covered. Since it looked like a choice between a swim in the Atlantic Ocean or arrest, we ran toward the back of the next hotel we passed. There were several black women in starched white uniforms standing near the rear service entrance of the hotel, watching the race. Rodent and I streaked right past them, through the service entrance and into the basement area, past the linen room, laundry and dish rooms, then out a side door to a small parking area. We were back on Collins Avenue, and no one was breathing down our necks.

As we cautiously made our way toward the area of the Convention Center, we encountered an unbelievable sight: Miami Beach looked like a city at war. Huey Cobras, the military helicopters used in Vietnam, were screaming across the sky, darting between the luxurious high-rise hotels along the beachfront, hovering over crowds of demonstrators, then swooping down over Collins Avenue with a deafening roar. You could actually see the crew in their helmets and flight suits. One crew member was standing in the open doorway as if he were sighting his fifty-caliber machine gun in the Mekong Delta. There was a continuous wail of sirens. Clouds of tear gas floated up in every direction. On virtually every side street, some type of police skirmish was in progress. Instead of defending the Convention Center itself, the authorities were forced to defend the entire city from hit-and-run attacks of affinity groups. And no one, not even the protestors, knew where they would strike next.

Near the central business area of Collins Avenue, just a few blocks away from the Convention Center, it was utter chaos. Rodent and I stood on the sidewalk, staring in disbelief, not knowing what to do next. Demonstrators were beginning to take over the street. They stopped traffic by blocking vehicles with their bodies or by pushing trash cans and newspaper vending machines into the street. Within minutes, we stumbled on Walrus and Pigeon who had successfully eluded police along the beach. Now at least our affinity group was back together. As we stood on the corner talking, I noticed my acquaintances from Santa Barbara and San Diego moving toward us from a side street. They were in three groups marching five abreast with arms locked together. We fell in a few yards behind them as they turned onto Collins Avenue. What followed was a classic example of a highly disciplined, well-organized affinity group at work.

Dozens of chartered busses along the avenue were trying desperately to push their way through the jammed streets. Nearly all were filled with well-dressed Republican delegates who were being transported from their hotels to the Convention Center for President Nixon's acceptance speech. Although several of the busses were being bombarded with rocks and bottles, most of the delegates inside tried to remain cool and unconcerned.

From about ten yards away, I watched as my West Coast friends attacked their first chartered bus. The first affinity group, composed entirely of women, stopped abruptly in front of the bus, and three of the members lay down in the street, blocking its path. While the bus was prevented from edging forward, a second affinity group attacked from the rear. Two men ran to the driver's side and one opened the side panel to the engine. The second man, the "mechanic," stuck his head, shoulders, and arms inside the compartment and quickly ripped out spark plug wires and distributor cap. In seconds there was a tangle of black wires lying on the pavement like week-old spaghetti. The coughing, sputtering bus belched one final cloud of dark gray smoke and died.

While two men attacked the engine, two more members were at work on the other side of the bus. As they knelt together on the pavement, one man used a pair of long, needle-nose pliers to reach into the massive tire rim for the valve stem. Once it was located and pulled into the open, the other member snipped off the base of the stem with surgical precision, using a pair of metal snips from the tool kit. "Wooosh" went the tire as the stale air rushed out, causing the bus to sink rapidly to the metal tire rim. The two men scrambled on to the next tire, then on to the other side for the rest. The fifth member of the team acted as a rear guard, assigned to provide protection or early warning of attempted interference. In less than five minutes, the affinity group had immobilized the bus.

The delegates inside, who had been trying to convey an image of confidence and optimism, were now visibly terrified. The street was swarming with screaming demonstrators, many beating violently on the bus windows to intimidate the occupants. There was not a police officer in sight. The demonstrators controlled the streets. During the next hour, this same affinity group disabled at least ten more busses. After all traffic was stopped, assistance from the women's group was no longer needed. By an hour before the convention was scheduled to begin, traffic had been stopped for fifteen blocks along Collins Avenue.

After the majority of chartered busses had been disabled, the affinity groups began to concentrate on taxicabs. Since all of the delegates displayed their convention credentials, ribbons, and buttons on their suits and dresses, they were easy to identify. Some of the smaller cabs navigated through the cluttered portions of Collins Avenue and turned off onto side streets. But if a cab could be stopped or slowed down by throwing large nails under a tire, the affinity group would spray the windshield with black paint, while other members attacked tires on both sides with knives and ice picks. Collins Avenue was beginning to resemble a battlefield with disabled vehicles strewn everywhere.

The delegates then foolishly decided to leave the safety of their stranded buses and walk several blocks through the tear gas and riotous crowd to the hall. Perhaps they had lost all hope of receiving assistance from the police and reasoned that if they didn't begin walking, they would miss the President's acceptance speech. Or maybe they could no longer stand the suffocating atmosphere of the busses which were now no longer air-conditioned. At any rate, it was a fateful decision for many, because this was exactly what the affinity groups had wanted.

Within minutes after the first delegates ventured into the streets, the three groups we had been following stopped attacking vehicles and began terrorizing delegates. Since they were drastically outnumbered, the delegates were easily separated into smaller groups of two and three as they struggled along the sidewalks. They were immediately surrounded by the screaming mob who shoved, kicked, and spat at them as they swept them along. The female protestors were the most vicious, facing the delegates and delivering insulting obscenities. They were determined to provoke a physical confrontation, usually concentrating on the woman in hopes of inciting her male companion. While one protestor might rip the delegate's dress, another would be breaking an egg over the shoulder of her husband's suit.

I was right behind the female affinity group from California as they surrounded a horrified woman delegate from the South. We were trying desperately to get through the crowd because it looked as if the group was going to tear the woman apart.

"You smell pretty, you blond bitch!" one female protestor screamed in the lady's terror-stricken face. "You're nothing but a rich fascist cunt! Fuck you and pig Nixon both!"

100

"Eat the rich, eat the rich!" another taunted.

"Death to the imperialists!" shouted a third member.

We managed to move several yards ahead of the group, abruptly stopping on the sidewalk and effectively screening off several of the protestors who were harassing the delegates. We were joined by three other demonstrators, dressed as though they might be VVAW members, and escorted the delegates down a side street to safety. I could not understand what had happened to the police, but assumed that if these few blocks of Collins Avenue were any indication, they had their hands full throughout the city.

A short time later, two motorcycle officers came roaring down Collins Avenue, lights flashing and sirens wailing. I remember thinking that they were two of the most fearless cops I had ever seen, or two of the most stupid. The streets were in shambles and demonstrators lined both sides, hurling rocks, bottles, eggs, and bags of excrement at anyone who ventured past. The officers barely moved as they maneuvered between disabled vehicles, newspaper vending machines, lawn furniture, and trash cans which had been set ablaze. One officer was suddenly toppled by a length of lead pipe thrown from the crowd. His partner hurriedly parked his machine and ran to help him. Another motorcycle officer soon joined the group and radioed for assistance.

While the officers were being bombarded in the middle of the street, their shiny new Harley Davidson motorcycles were parked a few yards away at a corner intersection. They proved to be an inviting target, for their gas tanks were opened and the heavy machines were pushed over on their sides. In seconds the motorcycles were engulfed in flames.

Two plainclothesmen, making no pretense of dressing like the demonstrators, unexpectedly bolted from the crowd, dragging two long-haired demonstrators into the street. One protestor was restrained with a hammerlock while the other was dragged by his hair. All hell was breaking loose on both sides of the street, but the plainclothes officers fearlessly stood in the middle of the intersection and frisked their prisoners. One protestor was quickly handcuffed, but I noticed the other one cautiously moving his hand toward his coat pocket as the officer reached back to pull out his cuffs. An instantaneous flick of the wrist and the officer was blinded by an enormous fistful of sand. As he dropped to his knees, the protestor was off like a flash, running wildly through the crowd along the sidewalk.

The officer's partner took off in hot pursuit, leaving the startled, handcuffed protestor standing alone over the blinded officer. The scene was almost comical until the pursuing officer pulled out his forty-five automatic and began shouting.

"Halt! Halt! Stop, you son of a bitch, or I'll shoot! Stop! Stop, you mother-fucker or I'll shoot! Stop, goddammit!"

I thought for sure the officer would start firing, but fortunately, his better judgment prevailed. Had he fired into the turmoil along Collins Avenue, he would probably have killed someone, but not the offender. He came walking back to his injured partner a short time later, out of breath, dejected, and without his man, only to discover that the handcuffed prisoner had also escaped into the crowd.

By nightfall, most of the roving bands of protestors had regrouped along the maze of small streets between the Convention Center and Collins Avenue. While random trashing continued in the downtown area, most groups were beginning to concentrate on the attack on the Convention Center itself. Law-enforcement authorities had already towed a large number of aging transit busses to the front of the Convention Center, where they were lined up bumper to bumper to provide additional protection for the hall. Squads of police officers who ventured out from this barricade were met by a barrage of rocks and bottles. Hundreds of rounds of tear gas had been fired during the day, leaving the entire area around the hall saturated with noxious fumes. It was reported later that gas had drifted into the convention hall through the ventilation system.

Police officers fired tear gas into the mob near the hall, then quickly advanced, hoping to arrest those who had been overcome. But many of the demonstrators who were wearing gas masks would run into the streets, pick up the spewing gas canisters, and hurl them right back into the middle of advancing police officers, sending them into hasty retreat. I had become so accustomed to breathing gas fumes by this point that I was feeling almost immune. That impression vanished when one of a barrage of gas canisters hit my leg as I was running away. Stopping momentarily to inspect the injury, I was engulfed by a giant cloud of gas that burst directly in front of me. It was a direct hit. I wanted to claw my eyes out, they burned so badly, while my lungs seemed to have collapsed from the fire raging inside. It was a terrifying experience, not being able to see, walk, run, or breathe.

The Rodent soon came to my rescue, leading me back into the security of the crowd. In seconds, one of the People's Medics was by my side, a calm young woman, wearing a construction-worker's hat with a large red cross painted on the front. As I cried out in pain, she grasped my long hair with one hand, pulling my head back slightly to check my eyes for contact lens. Most experienced demonstrators were aware that if tear gas was trapped behind contacts, the results could be disastrous. The lady then flushed my eyes with cod-liver oil from a large squeeze bottle. My vision was quickly restored, although slightly blurred, and the pain began to subside. I thanked her profusely as she moved on to help others.

It was strange to see the large number of senior citizens, many sitting nonchalantly in lawn chairs on spacious porches of retirement apartments, who were calmly holding moistened handkerchiefs to their noses so they could watch the confrontation. Many had turned on their garden hoses so that protestors could soak themselves and rid their clothing of gas fumes. I had done this several times during the day, but after suffering the direct hit, I stopped at a small fountain in front of an apartment and submerged my entire head, much to the delight of the elderly onlookers.

It was almost nine o'clock and we had been running, breathing tear gas, and dodging various missiles for seven hours. The sirens were still wailing, small fires were burning from trash heaped in the streets, and the air in Miami Beach would probably be polluted for days. We had wandered into Walrus, who, like us, was trying to decide what to do next. We were a few blocks away from Collins when we realized that police reinforcements had been sent into the area. They had regained control of Collins Avenue and were beginning a systematic sweep of the many side streets and alleys between Collins and the Convention Center. A squad of ten to twelve men marched up a side street from their staging area along Collins, and as the scattered protestors ran back toward the hall, out would come another squad from the next intersection, sealing off the side street. Unless you could make it to one of the alleys, many of which were also crawling with police, you were under arrest. We played this cat-and-mouse game for almost an hour, hoping that eventually we could work our way back to the park.

After running through a maze of alleys and back streets, I had become totally confused. We were with a group of six other protestors when I moved out of the shadows of an alley to peer up and down the deserted side street. I could see the lights of Collins Avenue a block off to my left as I eased out into the darkened street. I was about halfway across when a squad of police officers rounded the corner and rushed up a slight incline after me. I instinctively made a hard right and sprinted for the next intersection, hoping to outrun them. I hadn't taken three full strides when another squad of officers rushed out from behind a building about ten yards in front of me.

"Look out, C!" I heard Walrus yell from his position behind me.

Twelve police officers wearing jumpsuits and riot helmets, and wielding nightsticks, had snared me. I gave the nearest cop my best left head fake, cut sharply to the right curb through a small flower bed along the sidewalk and on toward the porch of an apartment house. I tried another fake on the last officer, spun around, and jumped over the porch steps to move back into the alley. I felt the wind from the nightstick whistling past my head as the officer took a mighty swing when I leaped over the steps. I stumbled slightly and when I looked up, there was another officer crouched about three feet in front of me with his riot baton held over his head, ready to lay me out. I didn't have to think long about my next move.

"Okay, okay, you got me," I shouted, raising my hands high above my head and standing up straight.

"Don't move, asshole!" the officer shouted as he pulled my arm down, grabbed it tightly, and walked me toward the middle of the dark street.

"You're a real wise-ass, ain't you, boy," one of the officers hollered.

"Think you're real fast on your fucking feet, huh, puke," commented another.

"Get them hands up behind your head, get 'em up, goddammit!" A sharp jab to the ribs from a nightstick offered encouragement.

I was standing in the middle of the dark, narrow street. The flashing blue lights on police cars and the street lights along Collins Avenue, a half-block away, provided the only illumination. About ten officers from the squad who had cut off my escape were standing shoulder to shoulder directly behind me, while the two officers who had cornered me were off to my left. I stood with my hands clasped behind my head, watching the squad of officers some twenty yards in front of me handcuff the other unfortunate demonstrator. The arresting officer hastily frisked me while the jawing started from the squad behind me.

"This puke here must think he's a real bad-ass hippy, being such a big, tall, old boy. That right, puke, you a bad-ass mother-fucker?"

"That's right, pig!" I instinctively retorted.

I couldn't believe that that inflammatory statement had come out of my mouth, for I had been making a conscious effort to keep it shut. Maybe I had just been playing the radical role too long. I had always been able to deal with pressure in a detached, unemotional way and even seemed to function more efficiently under stress. Now I could feel all ten of the officers moving in closer behind me after my impulsive remark.

"Hey boys," one officer said, "we got us a real wise-ass hippy here, a real loudmouth cocksucker!"

"Ain't got no respect for the law, do you, asshole?" another yelled in my ear.

An officer from the squad below walked up the slight hill, stopping about a foot in front of me. He reached for a set of "flexa-cuffs" which were frequently used in mass arrests since they were cheap and eventually disposable. They were constructed of tough plastic, supposedly unbreakable, and once fastened to a prisoner's wrists, they could be removed only by cutting.

"Okay, gimme your hands," the officer in front commanded.

As I brought my hands down from my head and extended them toward the cuffs, *whack*, a riot baton came crashing down on my right forearm. I grimaced with pain as my brain told me the forearm had to be broken. My right arm fell limp at my side and I instinctively reached for it with my left hand.

"Nobody told you to put your hands down, asshole!" an angry voice screamed from behind.

"Goddammit, he told me to put 'em down!" I shouted, turning my head slightly to see who had smashed my forearm. *Whomp* came another blow to my right shoulder, almost driving me to my knees. *Whomp, whomp*, two more stunning blows to my right biceps and shoulder blade followed in rapid succession.

"He told me to put 'em down," I yelled. "I'm not resistin', gimme a break!" My mind was telling me to shut up and stay cool before they smashed every bone in my body, but unfortunately, my emotions were not listening. I was supposed to be on the same side as these guys, and they were going their best to cripple me for life. I could barely straighten up from the blows to the shoulder as the smiling officer who had ordered me to put my hands down moved around to handcuff my wrists in back, rather than in front like the other prisoners'.

"Cuff that cocksucker real good and tight," an officer advised from behind.

"Tighten 'em down so he'll remember what a swell time he had in Miami Beach, right, puke?" another cop offered.

"Don't worry, this big ol' hippy boy ain't goin' nowhere when I get through with him," replied the officer, groaning mightily as he put all his weight into tightening the plastic handcuffs.

I was trying to keep my wrists spread slightly to provide for circulation, for I knew that these restraining devices were most harmful when they were fastened too tightly. But the officer sensed what I was doing.

"Get them hands together, boy!" one commanded, adding a painful jab to the kidney to get my cooperation.

My wrists felt glued together behind my back as I straightened up slightly. *Whomp* came another blow to the same spot on my right shoulder. I slumped over, writhing in pain. The individual who had always been confident that his cool composure could overcome any adversity, was now operating solely on emotion. To be more precise, unmitigated rage.

"You guys are really tough, aren't you," I shouted. "You get your kicks out of beatin' a handcuffed prisoner with your fuckin' sticks. Big bad pigs! Big bad piggies!"

Before I had even finished my brief tirade, I felt two arms reaching around my head from behind, pulling my bandanna headband down over my eyes. With my restricted vision, I could see six or seven arms flailing wildly as the nightsticks smashed into the the tops of my feet and ankles. New arms would occasionally pop into view, as the sticks began concentrating on my shins, each agonizing blow falling with a sickening thud. As I stood helplessly handcuffed and blindfolded for what seemed like an eternity, all I could see were arms with nightsticks, each frantically vying for striking room like the tentacles of an octopus gone mad.

For the first time in my life, I experienced the overwhelming anger that can cause human beings to take the life of another. Never had I been overcome by such violent rage. I strained against the handcuffs with every ounce of strength I could muster, for I was determined to kill every last one of those bastards. Had I been able to reach one of my attacker's guns, there is not the slightest doubt in my mind that I would have emptied it into the officers, knowing full well that I would have died in the process. The only thought in my mind was to break free and kill them. I had never truly understood how humans could become so enraged that they were compelled to commit murder in total disregard of their own safety or freedom. I understood perfectly now. The officers continued beating my feet and shins while they screamed unintelligible words of encouragement to each other. I remained bent

106

over at the waist and another blow across my back sent me drooping still further, but I struggled frantically to keep from falling to the pavement. I recall hearing someone shout "here puke," as one of the officers took full advantage of my vulnerable position and gave his nightstick an excruciating upward jab into my rectum. It surely would have sent me sprawling except another officer had stepped in front to push my head even lower, while his friend behind me continued his driving upward thrusts into my asshole. I thought for a second I would pass out, but I suppose I was too infuriated to go down. Something told me that my only chance was to keep yelling in the hope of attracting some attention.

"Help me! Help me!" I shouted, fighting to hold back the tears. "The pigs are beatin' me and I'm handcuffed! I'm handcuffed, goddammit! You stupid sons of bitches! You're just a bunch of fuckin' cowards! Why don't you take off the cuffs and fight like a man." Bone-cracking blows were still landing on my ankles and feet, but I had managed to straighten up and was trying to use my shackled hands to ward off the thrusts to my ass. I struggled to keep my legs together as one cop tried an upward swat at my balls.

"Get these fuckin' pigs off me before I'm killed! Help me! Help me!" I screamed as loud as I could. Maybe a member of the news media would hear me and come to investigate. I was beginning to be overcome by the hopelessness of my situation. I suppose I had been too enraged and intent upon revenge to be frightened earlier, but now I was coming to my senses, and I was scared shitless.

"Okay men, that's enough," I heard a voice say. "I said that's enough, dammit!"

The beating stopped. I tried to tilt my head back to look forward from under the bandanna, but all I could see were the feet of the man in front of me. Someone pulled my headband up slightly, and I met the eyes of a grizzled, sun-baked, veteran sergeant who looked like he had been walking a beat for thirty years. At that point he was the most beautiful guy in the world.

"Come on, boy," he said, grabbing me by the arm and leading me down toward the lights on Collins Avenue. He paused after a few steps and turned back to the group. "I want the arresting officer to come with me and book this man."

The three of us headed slowly down the street. Each step was an agonizing ordeal, but I wanted out of there so bad that it didn't seem to matter. "You're not going to get away with this shit," I told the officer on my left. He was the one who ordered me to put my hands down, and I was certain he had taken several swings with his nightstick. "Did you get enough licks in?" I inquired as calmly as possible. "You and your buddies might think it's open season on freaks, but I guarantee you it'll cost you your badge. Does it make you feel tough beating a handcuffed prisoner?"

"Shut up!" the officer snapped back.

I could tell I was getting to him and knew he wasn't too happy that the sergeant was hearing the story. "I'm sure your chief would really be proud of you. It takes a lot of guts to beat a handcuffed prisoner, huh pal? I'd like to run across you without all your pig buddies, then we'd see how fuckin' tough you are."

"That's enough!" the sergeant interjected. "For someone who damn near got killed back there, you didn't learn much, did you? Get this prisoner photographed and in the truck," he barked to the officer.

The officer walked me over to the processing area that had been set up in the middle of Collins Avenue. The authorities were using a new system in which a Polaroid photograph is taken of the arresting officer and his prisoner, and all relevant information concerning the offense is filled in on the back. The photograph is then given to the officer transporting the prisoners so that the arresting officer is free to rejoin his squad.

After the photograph was taken, I was moved over to the Miami Police Department's truck to await transfer to the temporary stockade. I pleaded with the officer to loosen my cuffs since I had lost all feeling in my fingers, but he ignored my request. Although the mobile jail could hold at least thirty prisoners, the only other occupant was the protestor who was arrested with me. He was a short, wiry kid of about nineteen who appeared less than enthusiastic over his predicament. As soon as I was pushed into the truck, he came to my assistance, helping me to my feet.

"Are you all right, man?" he asked. "The pigs beat the livin' shit outta you, man. Jesus Christ! I thought they were gonna kill you."

"I was beginning to wonder myself," I commented.

"You really stood up to 'em though. You ragged the shit out of 'em. After I saw what they did to you, I wasn't about to open my mouth. You sure you're okay?"

"Well, I'm not exactly brand new, brother," I replied, "but I think I'm gonna make it."

I began to examine the situation in detail now that I had time to think. One side of the wire mesh door in the rear of the truck was wide open, and I could see only one officer about five yards away with his back to us. There were high ventilation slits near the ceiling of the compartment, and by standing on the metal benches that lined the walls, I could see out. The police officers were apparently continuing their sweeps up the side streets, for I could see little movement near the truck.

Strangely enough, I actually spent about five minutes seriously considering the possibility of escape. One leap and I would be out of the mobile jail with only a thirty-yard sprint separating me from the darkness of the beach. The only guard I could see was a heavyset officer who didn't look like a runner.

"Say man," I whispered to my cellmate, "you wanna make a break for it? There's only one old guard out there, and we can make it to the beach before he knows what's happening."

My young friend stared at me in disbelief as he sat dejectedly on the metal bench. "Man, you gotta be fuckin' crazy," he answered, shaking his head slowly. "The pigs nearly kill you, and now you wanna go back for more. No way, José. It's suicide, man. You'll never make it. I'm staying right here."

"Well, I guess you're right, brother, but I can't even feel my fingers, these cuffs are so damn tight. If I don't get 'em off soon, I'm gonna loose some fingers."

"Turn around and I'll take a look," my young friend instructed. "Shit, you're right, man, they're already turnin' blue. You got anything we can cut 'em off with?"

"Not a thing, man, not a thing."

We both started searching the compartment for a sharp metal edge to rub the cuffs against. I was getting desperate when I suddenly remembered my money clip. The only thing I had carried that day was an old, inexpensive, money clip with ten dollars for emergency purchases. The police had failed to discover it when they frisked me. It had a small penknife on one side and a nail file on the other, although neither blade was more than two inches in length.

After a little maneuvering, my friend pulled the money clip out of my front pocket, opened the small knife blade, and began trying to saw through the plastic cuffs. It certainly wasn't the simplest trick in the world, since he was handcuffed too. The blade kept bending and heating up, causing it to slip and slash into my wrists.

"Keep going, man," I encouraged. "Don't worry about the wrists, just get the damn things off!"

"Okay, they're your wrists," he replied. "If I could just get my cuffs off, I could pull your arms away from your back. Just a second; let me try to pull mine off."

"Forget it, man, it can't be done," I said.

"You never seen my wrists," my young friend shot back. "I already got a lotta play in 'em cause they didn't tighten 'em up."

I sat down on the metal bench to watch my frail little friend attack the cuffs. I watched in amusement as he pulled up his pants leg to rub perspiration on his hands and then spat on his wrists for additional lubrication. He was right about one thing though. He had the smallest arms, wrists, and hands I had ever seen. He grunted, groaned, pulled, and strained.

"You're just wearin' yourself out, man," I offered. "They won't come off."

"Man, I'm makin' progress. They're comin'."

Like hell they are, I thought. The only way those things will come off is with a knife. My friend was now bent over in a violent contortion. He let out another mighty groan, straightened his body, then held up the plastic loop with one hand as he broke into a triumphant smile.

"Son of a bitch," I muttered. "You're incredible, absolutely fucking incredible!" It was now my turn to be amazed.

My friend was quickly back at work, trying to saw through the thick plastic while I kept watch on the guard. We heard voices discussing moving us to the stockade, and we returned to the bench just as the driver came around back and bolted the door. Since we were unable to work while the truck was moving, my friend replaced the money clip in my pocket, advising that he would begin sawing again as soon as we stopped.

As we drove through the streets of Miami Beach, I got my first glimpse of the magnitude of the disorders. The entire city seemed to have been trashed. Scattered groups of demonstrators still lined many of the side streets shouting words of encouragement as we passed by in the police truck.

"Fight back, brother, fight back!" they yelled.

"Right on," I shouted halfheartedly, wondering when this day would come to an end. Had I only known what was in store for us, I would have been even more depressed over my failure to escape.

We soon entered a remote area occupied by hundreds of officers and vehicles, which served as a command center and temporary stockade for arrested demonstrators bound for the Dade County jail in Miami. We were pulled out of the police truck, my companion acting as though he were still handcuffed, and immediately moved to one of several trucks parked alongside each other. These were clearly not Police Department vehicles, for they looked exactly like commercial moving vans.

Conditions inside the truck were a nightmare. There were twenty-five to thirty demonstrators packed inside in total darkness. There was no ventilation, and since tear gas clung to our clothes, our eyes and lungs began to burn again. The smell of vomit, urine, and perspiration permeated the darkness, competing with the tear gas. The occasional flicker of a match or lighter provided a brief glimpse of the other silent faces entombed in the airtight metal box, but the flame only burned up what little oxygen was available.

My friend from the police truck had stuck close by and was soon back at work on the cuffs. After what seemed like a lifetime but was actually about thirty minutes, he managed to cut through the plastic. I rubbed my hands and fingers to get the blood circulating, wondering if my wrists would ever feel normal again. But at the moment, nothing mattered except thanking my friend for his assistance. By the time we arrived at the jail, the two of us had freed another six demonstrators with the tiny blade.

We stood in the darkness well over an hour, hoping for the moment when the doors would be opened and we could get a quick breath of fresh air. Many of the demonstrators talked softly with one another, occasionally shouting at the officers outside and banging on the metal walls. Amazingly enough, someone lit a joint, causing the polluted atmosphere to be saturated with the sweet smell of marijuana smoke.

"Put the fuckin' joint out, man, we can't breathe in here as it is," yelled one prisoner.

"Hey, come on, man, put it out," said another.

Before any action could be taken, one of the men began vomiting. Another demonstrator was overcome by the sickening smell and joined him. Within seconds, a third prisoner began freaking out, beating and kicking on the metal doors, thrashing his arms wildly about the enclosure, literally trying to climb the walls.

"Let me out, let me out! Please, please let me out!" he screamed before slumping down to the floor.

As I stood there in the dark, my body throbbing in pain and my senses revolted by the sickening odors, I tried to concentrate on mental pictures of better times and better places, although my brain would have none of it. The thought which kept recurring was—What in hell am I doing here? I'm supposed to be one of the "good guys." Work hard all your life, go to college, law school, land an exciting job with the government, settle back and enjoy, enjoy. But the more I thought about it, the more I realized that what really concerned me was not my current situation, but the uncertainty and confusion caused by the day's experiences.

I shared some of the goals of the antiwar movement, but could never condone the violence of the affinity groups I had watched that day. The constitutional freedoms that protected them had been denied many of the delegates trying to attend the convention. But were the actions of the police any better? Was it necessary to vent their personal frustrations on defenseless protestors or to confine them in inhuman conditions? I was not surprised at the behavior of the police, but I *was* disappointed. When you analyzed the situation, there were no "good guys." Neither side was totally blameless, because both were equally guilty of excesses. After having experienced the behavior of both sides and from what I considered a fairly objective viewpoint, I began to have substantial difficulty in rationalizing the behavior of either group. I had heretofore been content in the belief that I was doing the right thing, taking the appropriate action, and giving my best efforts to help the country. Now, I was no longer certain.

After an eternity of darkness, more prisoners began to arrive, bringing a fleeting gasp of fresh air. The doors opened briefly as bodies were literally crammed into the truck. It finally pulled out of the stockade and headed for the Dade County jail several miles away. The heat within the metal compartment was unbearable. Each time the truck turned a corner, we would fall like dominoes against each other, often slipping painfully to the floor which was covered with hundreds of small carpet tacks. We arrived at the jail shortly after midnight, and when the doors to the aluminum compartment were thrown open, we were met by a dense, eerie fog that shrouded the faint glow of distant spotlights. It was a scene right out of a science fiction movie. As we emerged from the truck, we discovered that the "fog" was created by the steam escaping from the sweltering compartment and colliding with the warm night air. The spotlights turned out to be floodlights set up by television cameramen to film our arrival. A subsequent news account stated that a reporter entered one of the truck compartments with a thermometer and found the temperature inside to be in excess of 140 degrees!

We were herded into a large holding-tank facility in the jail which seemed like heaven after hours of suffocating darkness. After everyone in the tank had been processed and moved into cells, I began to have strong suspicions of what was about to take place. When a booking officer approached me, asking my name, where I had been arrested, and the charges against me, all of the pieces began to fit together. I could identify none of the officers who had beaten me earlier because my eyes had been covered. Even the arresting officer had been scarcely visible because he had been wearing a riot helmet with plastic faceshield. I was hoping that the Polaroid arrest photo would include a witness in addition to the picture of the arresting officer with his name and badge number on the reverse side. But the arresting officer knew they had worked me over pretty thoroughly, and that if I made a police brutality complaint, he might have to identify his fellow-officers. The arrest photograph and booking information had probably remained in the officer's pocket, for I was told that there was no record of my arrest. My photograph had been "lost."

There was now some confusion among the booking officers over what to do with me. They hurriedly took another photograph, scribbled minimal arrest information on the back, then directed me into a hallway to be escorted to a cell. The jailer who unlocked the metal gate leading to the elevator was the epitome of the Southern redneck deputy sheriff. He was about forty years old, over six feet tall, and so obese that he had trouble seeing his shoes because of the enormous roll of fat that hung over his belt. He wore his hair in a flattop cut, with the sides and back shaved in military fashion.

He looked me over carefully for several minutes without saying a word. I countered with an icy stare, although I soon sensed that his looks were more inquisitive than disdainful.

"Say," the jailer finally said, staring into my eyes with a sincere expression on his pudgy face. "What's an ol' boy like you doin' in jail with all these young kids? Ain't you a little old for all this long hair and protestin'?"

There were other demonstrators within earshot, not to mention several officers, and since I had gone this far with the role, I decided I might just as well finish.

"I just hope I never get so old," I began, "that I'm afraid to exercise my consititutional rights by speaking out against the ridiculous policies of our government and Richard Nixon. Because if I do, I'll end up exactly like you, following along in blind obedience like the rest of the silent majority."

The jailer did not reply as he opened the door for a waiting deputy who escorted me to the elevator. As I entered the elevator, I wondered if it was the militant, long-haired West Coast radical who had spoken or the Special Agent of the FBI who had undergone a thorough education during the day.

I was placed in a large cell with approximately fifty other demonstrators, some of whom were my friends from the West Coast, but when I approached them I immediately sensed hostility and a reluctance to talk. The only reason I could come up with was the fact that I had been alone downstairs with booking officers for nearly an hour, while the rest of our group had been taken to cells. Perhaps they believed I was an informant who hadn't really been arrested at all.

I located a bunk bed and quickly discovered why so many were vacant. There were no mattresses, only bare metal to lie on in wet clothing. After spending hours in the darkened, sweat-box compartment of the truck and exiting wringing wet, it was strange to find oneself in an air-conditioned cell. The holding tank had been cool but refreshing. The cell area was cold enough to cause uncontrollable shivers. My body ached, I was soaked with sweat, vomit, and tear gas, and now I was freezing.

Miami officials had anticipated a mass arrest. Over one thousand demonstrators had been arrested on the final day, and officials had provided courts and public defenders for round-the-clock arraignments. When the guard called out names, usually in groups of five, the prisoners would meet with a public defender and briefly discuss their case, plea, and ability to make bail. The entire group of demonstrators I arrived with had been called; then a second group, booked even later, was called. I kept asking the guards to try to find my arrest record, explaining that I had been there for hours without being called, and that I had been rephotographed at the jail. After another hour or so, they called my fictitious name, and I left the freezing cell.

I met with four other demonstrators and a young public defender in the hallway just outside the courtroom. The attorney had all of our arrest photos and questioned us briefly on our ability to post bond. When he inquired about my case, I described what had occurred and told him about the missing photograph. He glanced at the photo he was holding, both front and back.

"You've got no problems," he said. "You're home free. There's no arresting officer, no location of arrest, and no charges are filled in. The judge will dismiss this right away."

He was right. Shortly after five in the morning of August 24,

1972, I walked out into the streets of Miami an exhausted but free man. The sun was about to come up as I walked in the general direction of the FBI office. I tried to hail a cab, but none would even slow down for a passenger of my appearance. I had walked several blocks when I noticed a car following me, passing several times, circling the block, then reappearing from another direction.

First I thought it might be the police out to hassle a long-haired freak or wondering why a freak was walking the streets at this hour. Either way I would lose, for I had no identification. The vehicle finally stopped in a crosswalk near the curb some ten yards in front of me. I cautiously approached it, trying to see who the two occupants were while thinking about which way I would run if necessary. As I moved closer, I was relieved to see a police-type radio under the dash and two guys who looked like agents.

"You need a lift?" the man on the passenger side inquired.

I leaned over and stuck my head in the window. "Which way you headed?"

"Over to Biscayne Boulevard," the driver replied. "Say, aren't you Bill from L.A.?"

"Right, you guys from the Bu?"

"At your service! Jump in."

I experienced little difficulty falling asleep that morning. The officer interrupted my slumber a few times that afternoon with requests to come in and assist with paper work concerning my arrest, but I merely babbled an unintelligible reply into the receiver, rolled over, and went back to sleep.

I was amazed to learn on the following day that I was not the only FBI agent among the more than twelve hundred demonstrators arrested during the Republican Convention. Rodent and Walrus were also included in the select group. They had made their way back to the rental car shortly after midnight when they were passed by a long procession of approximately fifteen police cars, lights flashing and sirens screaming. Thinking the cars were responding to another confrontation, they followed the speeding procession, ending up on a dead-end street which took them directly into a staging area for the Miami Police Department! The officers had merely been in a hurry to get home. They were immediately arrested, charged with "Loitering by Prowling," and taken to the Miami City jail. A few hours later, the charges were dismissed, and they were released.

All three of us went to the office Friday afternoon to report the circumstances surrounding our arrest and assist in preparing a communication to the Bureau. The SAC had scheduled a victory celebration for all the agents who had worked on the conventions. One of his Bureau contacts, a senior official at the nearby Bacardi Rum Company, had graciously agreed to provide the company's luxurious private bar, along with plenty of their powerful rum, for our final get-together.

A few hours before the party was to begin, we visited with the local security supervisor, convention coordinators, and other office officials. They were perplexed over the unusual turn of events because none of them had ever had to advise the Bureau that an FBI agent had been arrested, especially three FBI agents with long hair! The fact that we had been following instructions seemed to have little bearing on the matter. None of the officials knew how the Bureau would react to this news, and none wanted to take the responsibility of reporting it. They were sympathetic about my "unfortunate" incident with the police but were unanimous in their opinion that nothing further should be said about it.

I did voice concern over the fact that I would probably need medical attention, especially if my legs did not improve, and that for my own protection, it seemed wise at least to advise the Bureau of the beating so they would know it had occurred while on official duty. I would thus not have to lie to the insurance company about when, where, and how the injury actually occurred. None of the officials were swayed by my reasoning, however, and they insisted that no mention of the incident be made to the Bureau. When one agent remarked that other complaints of police brutality had been officially submitted, a couple of which were made by news reporters, I began to wonder. Perhaps it was time someone got the attention of local law enforcement and put a stop to this madness.

After a discreet but firm suggestion that a local agent handle the communication, I thought "What the hell, one more day and I'll be out of this place. *They're* the people that have to live in this community, and if they're not concerned, why should I be?"

Several months later, when I finally saw the teletype describing the arrest, I wondered if they were talking about the incident that I had experienced.

LA SEVEN EIGHT FIVE TWOS (EXTREMIST) ON THE EVENING
OF AUGUST TWENTYTHREE, SEVENTYTWO, WAS ARRESTED BY

Collins Ave!

THE MIAMI POLICE DEPARTMENT NEAR COLLINS AVENUE, MIAMI BEACH, FLORIDA. AT THE TIME OF ARREST, THE SOURCE WAS OBSERVING "TRASHING" ACTIVITIES BEING CONDUCTED BY WEATHERMAN SUPPORT PERSONNEL FROM THE SANTA BARBARA, CALIFORNIA, AREA. WHEN ARRESTED, THE SOURCE WAS ADVISED HE WAS BEING CHARGED WITH DISORDERLY CONDUCT AND RESISTING ARREST. HE WAS FINGERPRINTED AND PHOTOGRAPHED AND PLACED IN A HOLDING FACILITY ON MIAMI BEACH.

APPROXIMATELY ONE AND ONE HALF HOURS LATER, HE WAS TRANSPORTED TO THE DADE COUNTY JAIL WITH FORTY OTHER DEMONSTRATORS, SEVERAL OF WHOM WERE FROM THE WEST COAST AREA. ON ARRIVAL, IT WAS DETERMINED HIS PHOTOGRAPH AND BOOKING SHEET HAD BEEN MISPLACED, AND HE WAS RE-BOOKED AT THIS TIME. HE REMAINED CONFINED FOR APPROXIMATELY THREE AND A HALF HOURS, AT WHICH TIME HE WAS TRANSPORTED TO CRIMINAL COURT NO. ONE FOR A BAIL HEARING. THIS SOURCE WAS REPRESENTED BY A PUBLIC DEFENDER, WHO MOVED THAT THE CASE AGAINST HIM BE DISMISSED IN VIEW OF THE FACT THAT NO ARRESTING OFFICER OR SPECIFIED PENAL CODE VIOLATION WAS NOTED ON THE SECOND BOOKING PHOTOGRAPH. HE WAS RELEASED FROM CUSTODY AT APPROXIMATELY FIVE AM, AUGUST TWENTYFOUR, SEVENTYTWO.

THIS SOURCE WAS ARRESTED UNDER THE NAME WILLIAM LANE.

THE IDENTITIES OF THE ABOVE SOURCES WERE NOT JEOPARDIZED BY THESE ARRESTS.

7

Weatherman In-Service: The Drug Scene

On the morning of August 28, I dragged my bruised body down the long corridor of the Miami Airport toward the departure gate. I was becoming more and more concerned over the increase in the dark bruises that covered both my legs and the tops of my feet. My entire right side listed to starboard because of the blows to my shoulder and forearm. It was becoming increasingly difficult to walk in an upright position, but the thought of sitting on my injured posterior during the flight to Dallas seemed even more unbearable. As we soared over the city and viewed the sparkling beaches behind the plush hotels of Miami Beach, I recall thinking it would be a long time before the good ol' boys of Miami got another swing at me with their lethal wooden weapons.

When we landed in Dallas, I was met by my parents, whom I hadn't seen in several months. It was a long-overdue visit, and I felt certain that after a few days' vacation in Denton, with Mom's home cooking, I would be greatly improved. This was my first summer visit in years, and during the brief ride home, I was reminded of how beautiful the Texas countryside looked when green.

My parents were naturally inquisitive about my Miami assignment. I'm sure they had often recalled the brutal confrontations between police and demonstrators during the 1968 Democratic Convention in Chicago. The three of us had watched in silence as television cameras captured the savage beatings of protestors by the Chicago police, transmitting each succeeding blow into the tranquil atmosphere of our living room. I had recently graduated from law school, and I was living at home during this time, awaiting orders to depart for Washington to enter the FBI Academy. I remember expressing my intense outrage over the senseless beatings, and for the first time in my life feeling that perhaps the police, rather than the demonstrators, were at fault.

Since I had seen very few newspaper accounts of the conventions during the summer, I didn't know what impressions the public had received about demonstration activities. We had been told during our initial briefing sessions that the major networks were concentrating on the actual nominating process rather than on the street activities. Although arrests on the last day of the Republican Convention had exceeded those in Chicago, it appeared that many people in other parts of the country were unaware of the full extent of the disruptive activities.

It was difficult to provide adequate answers to my parents' questions without giving them the history of the antiwar movement and explaining the unique life-style of the demonstrators. I'm sure they sensed that I was physically exhausted and didn't want to discuss my experiences in detail. In response to inquiries from my father, I acknowledged that I had been beaten by the police, but I minimized the incident, saying only that I had been in jail for a brief period after my arrest.

Most of my time was spent sleeping, reading, and relaxing, and within a few days, my legs and my overall condition showed marked improvement, although the deep black bruises remained.

At the same time, however, the condition of my posterior was getting worse. With each bowel movement I experienced increasing discomfort and was soon shocked to discover I was passing blood. When the situation deteriorated to the point that I was bleeding even without a bowel movement, I decided it was time to return to Los Angeles and see my physician.

I was greeted by the fantastic weather enjoyed by southern California during early September: crisp cool days, cloudless skies, and an abundance of sunlight. My apartment, located on the sands of the Marina Peninsula, faced west and provided unbelievable views of the sunsets. Returning to the apartment and hearing the crashing of the waves gave me an immediate lift. Several neighbors dropped by to fill me in on the latest news. My only reminder of Miami was the irregular bleeding which refused to subside.

After a physical examination the following morning, my worst fears were realized. I was suffering from a rectal fissure and would have to undergo corrective surgery in two days. The operation presented no problems, and I was released three days later. Everyone on the hospital staff was extremely thoughtful and courteous during my stay. I have often wondered since then if the nurses ever figured out how a long-haired, hippy freak was able to obtain group hospitalization insurance through the FBI.

After a week spent cautiously sitting on top of pillows and praying unsuccessfully that my first postsurgical bowel movement would never occur, I was able to return to work. The chief topic of conversation among our small undercover group was the upcoming trip to Washington. We were to attend a one-week Specialized Weatherman In-Service, to be conducted at the new FBI Academy in Quantico, Virginia. These seminars were a new trend which had almost completely replaced the Bureau's traditional General Criminal In-Service. The new format had proved very popular with agents in the field since it allowed them to receive specialized instruction on cases they actually handled, and to return home in half the time.

When Joe and Panda explained the unprecedented travel and security instructions ordered for the in-service, I thought they were putting me on. The six of us who had worked in Miami during the conventions were each instructed to attend, but we were advised that all travel and hotel reservations were to be made under our assumed identities. We were further instructed that no more than two of us could fly on any one airline flight, that we were to stay in a "secure" hotel in Washington, D.C. prior to departing for the Academy, and that under no circumstances were we to bring firearms. In addition, we were told to wear our "usual undercover clothing" for travel and for our week of classroom instruction. In my entire Bureau experience, these were the strangest, most detailed security precautions I had ever heard of.

We immediately voiced vehement objections on the phone with our supervisor, Fast Freddie. Why different planes when we always flew together to save taxi fares? Had we not recently completed no less than four flights to Miami on the same plane? And what in the hell is a "secure" hotel? Why, for the first time in the history of the Bureau, were FBI agents not allowed to carry firearms?

In order to quell the potential rebellion, Fred reluctantly agreed to telephone the Domestic Intelligence Division, or Division Five, as it was commonly referred to, and seek clarification of the instructions. He then advised us that these explicit security precautions were being taken as part of the new undercover program which would be explained to us during our week at the Academy. Now that there was an *official* program, it appeared that officials of Division Five were beginning to cover their ass, in case the exposure of an agent resulted in publicity embarrassing to the Bureau.

We were to travel on separate flights to avoid suspicion or identification of the entire group. In the event that we ran into any of our movement associates during the trip, we should be dressed as we "normal-ly" would and not in business attire. Before making hotel reservations, Fred was to consult with his counterpart in the Washington field office to determine a "secure" hotel which did not employ any known activ-ists and was located in a "straight" area of town.

Fred was told that there would be no necessity for firearms since, for some unexplained reason, we would not undergo the usual day of fire-arms training on the Academy ranges. Until this time, I had never heard of the FBI instructing agents on official business not to carry their firearms on airline flights. In fact, during the height of the sky-jacking rage, every agent was ordered to carry firearms on all com-mercial flights.

It was encouraging to see the Bureau sanction the establishment of an official undercover program and show some concern over the safe-ty and well-being of its participants. Perhaps they were going over-board with instructions as they generally tended to do when imple-menting fundamental changes, but at least they were trying to do something positive. However, we were discouraged by some of the glaring defects in the preliminary planning.

In view of the fact that over four hundred police officers from every part of the United States were attending National Academy classes, and that several New Agents Training classes and numerous In-Service sessions had also been scheduled, why were our highly sensitive imple-mentation meetings to be held at the FBI Academy? What about the maintenance force, cafeteria workers, and contract employees, not to mention the various military personnel who often visited the Acade-my? From the beginning of my "freak" career, I felt that our greatest asset was Hoover's constant public pronouncement that the FBI had no long-haired hippies, and that it never would. Most police officers, as well as the majority of the public, seemed to have no inkling of the ex-istence of our undercover activities. Should the word get out, we would lose our limited ability to infiltrate terrorist organizations.

There was also justifiable concern over the directive to bring only our "usual undercover clothes." This was to be my first visit to the new Academy, but I doubted there had been any significant change in dress requirements. Conservative slacks and sport shirts had always been acceptable for classroom instruction and dining, although coat and tie were required for the Wednesday night dinner and most social occasions. The standard gray range uniforms required for all firearms training were allowed in the cafeteria when we were engaged in firearms instruction, but gym attire or other casual sports clothing was strictly forbidden.

It was simply beyond my comprehension that they wanted us to come to the new Academy looking like freaks. I finally decided that the only explanation was that Bureau officials had no conception of how we dressed on undercover assignments. I felt reasonably certain, however, that it wouldn't take them long to realize the error of their ways.

There were lengthy discussions among the six of us concerning our travel to "The Great Freak In-Service," as it was now called. Our repeated appeals to Fast Freddie and the Bureau over the firearms restrictions had fallen on deaf ears. Fred privately advised us that if we were discovered ignoring specific Bureau orders, we would be on our own.

While packing for the trip the following morning, I decided that it was ridiculous to worry about a gun being found in a suitcase that would also be full of grass. With that rationalization out of the way, I carefully packed my Walther automatic and a lid of Columbian for the journey to Washington.

Since our in-service class was not to start until Monday, we decided to leave on Saturday and enjoy a holiday weekend in Washington. After the long ride from Dulles International Airport we got to our "secure" hotel located near the heart of the District and registered under our fictitious names. I had previously called Linda, an old friend from my New Agents Training days, and she had graciously agreed to drive in from Maryland that evening to act as our chauffeur and tour guide. She and I had dated for a couple of months while I was living in Washington and had corresponded occasionally over the intervening years.

Linda was a genuine, all-American girl who loved the outdoors, but was equally at ease in the city. She continued to be employed as a computer programmer for another federal agency. Although I hadn't seen her in nearly four years, I felt certain that her exposure to radical political thought, alternative life-styles, and the drug scene was minimal at best. I was eagerly anticipating our reunion, but I was worried that my freaky personal appearance might prove too much of a shock for her.

By the time Linda called from the lobby, Panda, Rodent and I had smoked a couple of the Columbian joints and were finishing off a six-pack of beer. As we stumbled into the elevator, I prepared them for the upcoming introductions. When the elevator doors opened, I noticed Linda standing across the lobby, anxiously observing each departing guest. Although we had fleeting eye contact, I could tell she was unaware of my identity; so I purposely avoided any sign of recognition until the three of us had almost walked past her. Not until I gave her a hearty greeting and familiar smile did she realize that the three dope-crazed freaks standing in front of her were to be her escorts for the evening.

Linda was visibly stunned. Like so many other friends from my conservative past, she simply could not bring herself to believe that this was the same man she had known four years earlier. Unable to speak, she merely shook her head from side to side with questioning amusement before joining the three of us in uncontrollable laughter.

After I introduced her to Rodent and Panda, we walked out into the crisp fall evening. As we piled into her car and headed in the general direction of Georgetown, I sensed that Linda was still somewhat perplexed over this completely unexpected turn of events. We fielded her questions about our appearance and assignment as deftly as possible and, as always, she was discreet enough not to press for additional information.

As we passed the brilliantly illuminated Washington Monument and drove toward the Potomac, I noticed that Panda was holding up a joint in the back seat, silently questioning whether it was permissible to fire up. Since I was half loaded at this point anyway and had serious intentions of becoming completely loaded before the evening was over, I matter-of-factly asked Linda if she had any objections to our smoking a joint. She was quick to reply that she did not mind, and Panda was equally quick with his lighter.

In a matter of seconds, the pungent smell of marijuana smoke had thoroughly saturated the interior of the small car. The partial illumination provided by oncoming headlights revealed a nervous look on our driver's face. While I never seriously considered that Linda would have become involved with hard drugs, I did assume that after spending her entire life in the Washington metropolitan area, she had probably tried marijuana, or at least had been exposed to it. But this appeared to be an erroneous assumption. She politely declined each pass of the joint, and I could sense her increasing apprehension. As I rolled down the window and threw out the roach, I felt embarrassed at causing such an unwarranted imposition on an old friend.

After my associations with the liberal-minded individuals in the antiwar movement, the use of marijuana seemed no more unusual to me than the use of alcohol or tobacco. At the University of California at Santa Barbara, it had replaced beer, the mainstay of my college experience, as the most popular campus diversion, and was as integral a part of the so-called hippy life-style as long hair and jeans. The altered state of awareness brought on by the use of marijuana was one that I found both pleasurable and relaxing. When compared to the other popular drugs of the period, such as acid, speed, or downers, marijuana seemed about as potent as beer.

I have never been able to rationalize how our government can provide us with incontrovertible clinical evidence that regular use of tobacco can result in lung cancer, while continuing to allow its sale and use by anyone who can afford it. Alcohol remains the number one drug problem in the United States, with both its physical and psychological effects well documented, yet it continues to be readily available in most areas of the country. I recall hearing older agents lecture about the evils of marijuana, at the same time that they were taking ten milligrams of Valium each morning for "nerves" and stopping off for a few martinis on the way home from work. But were it not for my unique opportunity to live on both sides of the issue, I am sure my views would have remained exactly the same as those of the great majority of agents today.

My undercover experiences brought me to the point where I considered marijuana use a normal social occurrence. It was a social habit which all of my new associates practiced in a fairly open manner, although I'm sure they knew that it remained an illegal act with potentially severe penalties.

I was later to experience paranoid reactions from other conservative friends of the past who, like Linda, were suddenly confronted by my new life-style. Although I was certain many of these people had smoked marijuana, I seemed unable to understand that their obvious nervousness stemmed not from the fact that a formerly conservative friend was smoking, but that their friend also happened to be an FBI agent. Perhaps the real reason for my failure to discern this important distinction was that after several years of functioning in an undercover capacity and making a consistent effort to avoid looking, acting, or even thinking like an agent, I no longer consciously visualized myself as an employee of the FBI.

We soon discovered that Georgetown looked the same as it had four years ago, but our altered appearance made a considerable difference in how we were received. We were denied entrance to many of our former watering holes since we were not properly attired in coat and tie, and several doormen took a dim view of the length of our hair. Linda ultimately suggested that we try some of the livelier clubs and discos that catered to a younger, more liberated clientele.

After closing down Georgetown and enjoying an early breakfast, Linda drove us through the darkened, near-deserted streets of Washington and dropped us at our "secure" hotel.

We spent most of Sunday in bed, recovering from our night on the town. The rest of the day was spent in front of the television, watching the Redskins win yet another football game. Since Monday morning would require an early departure from the hotel, we discussed our travel plans in detail to avoid confusion in checking out and obtaining cabs. We were astounded to discover that in spite of the efforts to install us in a "secure" hotel, we would be expected to take the regular Bureau transportation, the BuBus, from Washington to Quantico.

Agents who traveled to Washington for in-service training were usually required to assemble on the corner of Eighth Street and Pennsylvania Avenue, near the side of the Justice Building, to wait for chartered busses to transport them and their luggage to Quantico. Every Monday and occasionally on other weekdays, anywhere from fifty to two hundred clean-cut, conservatively dressed men with luggage—obviously G-men—faithfully assembled at the side of the Justice Building, come rain, shine, sleet, or snow, to await the arrival of chartered busses. Given those circumstances, why would long-haired hippy freaks, in native dress no less, be instructed to assemble on the very same corner, at the very same time, to board the very same busses as the FBI agents? Once again, convenience and penny-pinching was taking precedence over security.

We had decided that the best way to board the BuBus was to take separate cabs that would drop us off individually one block either side of our meeting point. We would then walk to positions where we could survey the situation and also check for any antiwar associates. After years of undercover work, I had developed a high regard for the mobility of those involved in the antiwar movement. It was not at all uncommon to see familiar faces from Los Angeles involved in street actions in San Diego, Santa Barbara, San Francisco, or Seattle. Although most of these people had little money, they always seemed to find ways to travel, even if it meant using their thumbs. While the possibility of being seen by a movement acquaintance was remote, we wanted to take no unnecessary chances.

Our simple plan worked to perfection. After watching the group complete the preliminary paper work and board the bus, we crossed the street and got right on. We were met on the top step by a conservative-looking Bureau official, clipboard in hand, who appeared rather perplexed by our appearance, but equally uncertain whether to acknowledge us or not. It was obvious he was going to let me make the first move. I glanced into the bus and noticed the beaming face of the Walrus, who was sitting near the front.

"The L.A. Connection has arrived! C-C-C," Walrus sang out, much to the amusement of the others on the bus.

"Hey Walrus, what's happenin'?" I yelled back.

"Panda! Panda!" boomed the familar voice of the Pigeon from somewhere near the rear of the bus, bringing more laughter from the group. By this time our Bureau official had apparently concluded that we were the right freaks.

"Hello, I'm Bill Preusse, Division Five," he said. "You must be our friends from Los Angeles?"

He greeted me with a firm handshake and warm smile.

"Yes sir," I replied, vigorously pumping his hand, "I'm Cril Payne. Nice to meet you."

As the rest of our group boarded and introduced themselves, I moved toward the back, greeting several of the undercover agents from the Miami conventions who were scattered thoughout the bus. I also noticed a couple of agents I had worked with in Seattle, now apparently assigned to Weatherman cases, and a number of younger agents sporting week-old beards in preparation for undercover assignments. I located a seat by the Pigeon and in a short time the BuBus began rolling out of Washington.

During our hour-long ride to Quantico, the Pigeon brought me up to date on recent Weatherman activities on the East Coast. The two of us enjoyed a long laugh as we anticipated our reception at the Academy, for we both knew that they could not possibly be prepared for our arrival. Of the forty-five agents on the bus, at least ten would qualify as hard-core freaks, capable of provoking a confrontation with any red-blooded police officer merely on the basis of personal appearance. And if our hair length was offensive, our usual undercover clothing could only be described as outrageous: ragged, faded jeans with countless patches; workshirts with embroidered peace symbols and marijuana leaves; headbands, cowboy hats, caps, leather visors, army surplus field jackets, aging boots or sandals, not to mention T-shirts whose graphic distortions of the American flag were certain to produce negative reactions.

After turning off the Interstate Highway and entering the Quantico Marine Base, we traveled briefly through the dense Virginia forest. At first glance, the new Academy looked like a small university set in a remote and beautiful campus. We located our luggage and filed into the Administration Building, where we signed in and received our room assignments, keys, and identification badges. We were instructed to store our luggage and report back to the auditorium for orientation and a tour of the new facilities.

When we arrived in the auditorium, it became obvious that the supervisory agents assigned to the Academy staff were less than enthusiastic over our presence. In all probability, they and the Division Five officials had expected undercover agents with slight sideburns, trimmed mustaches, and collar-length hair, wearing new jeans and starched shirts. Whatever the case, our hosts were visibly perturbed by our outlandish appearance.

We were given a detailed list of rules and regulations along with materials to be used in our classroom discussions. No direct mention of our clothing was made, but the orientation supervisor did point out that the "hippies" in our class would not be allowed access to the post exchange, package store, or enjoy other Marine base privileges during our stay, and we were not to leave the Academy grounds without official permission.

During our guided tour, we were greeted by reactions of shocked disbelief. Most of our colleagues made no attempt to disguise their indignation at the fact that long-haired freaks were violating the sanctity of "Hoover University." Scornful looks, offhand comments, and public speculation about our gender seemed to be the primary response, although many just gawked in openmouthed astonishment. Our first noontime visit to the dining hall was a memorable experience. Conversation stopped when we entered the spacious dining room with our trays. A thousand eyes were riveted to our every move as we made our way toward two vacant tables in the far corner. The spectacle of ten freaks enjoying a light lunch at the FBI dining facility was apparently too much for many of those in attendance.

Our in-service class began shortly after lunch with the introduction of various Domestic Intelligence Division officials and the particular areas of responsibility handled by those assigned to the Revolutionary Activities Section. Each of the forty-five participants was requested to stand, introduce himself to the group, and tell what office he represented. We were given the week's schedule of classes and the topics to be discussed. We then listened to a general review of the nationwide Weatherman investigation to date.

After classes adjourned for the day, we gathered in the suite assigned to Panda and Buddha. There was a firm rule prohibiting alcohol in any of the dormitory rooms at the Academy; however, this rule had been disregarded by virtually every agent who ever attended in-service classes. A brief tour through the area occupied by police officers attending National Academy classes was certain to reveal an even greater disregard for this restriction. It should not be difficult to understand why veteran police officers, separated from their wives and families for four months, restricted by nightly curfews like college freshmen, and suddenly thrust into the forgotten world of academia, were not inclined to forego the pleasures of alcohol merely because it was against the rules. The rules were simply not enforced. In addition, the bargain prices at the marine base package store made drinking an even more attractive pastime.

Perhaps the largest problem confronting the social drinker at the Academy was that of ice. It had to be surreptitiously "appropriated" from the dining hall after evening closing hours. This was accomplished by entering the kitchen through the cafeteria serving areas and filling plastic trash bags at the two large ice machines. Since these were the only ice machines in the entire Academy complex, this appropriation had become a nightly ritual for many agents.

When we attended the original FBI Academy located near the heart of the marine base, we could walk into the town of Quantico after classes for dinner and drinks. In the new Academy, some twelve miles from the city of Quantico, we were virtual prisoners in isolation unless we were fortunate enough to have access to a car. The situation improved when the Bureau installed a beer hall next to the main dining room. It was small and constantly crowded, providing only the amenities of a snack bar, television, and ice cold beer by the pitcher or mug. The beer hall was often pointed to as one of the progressive changes of the new Bureau and was viewed by most agents as a step in the right direction. Many of the more serious beer drinkers made it their second home, while the martini and highball crowd adjourned to their dormitory rooms. Nevertheless, the beer hall did serve as a central meeting place for renewing old acquaintances, making new friends, and learning about law enforcement problems throughout the country.

The first cocktail hour of the "Great Freak In-Service" was conducted with only the bare essentials of scotch, bourbon, and tap water. After a couple of drinks, we headed over to the dining hall for another barrage of hostile looks. Later that evening, we returned to Panda's room and resumed our bull session. The conversation turned to our summer in Miami and then inevitably shifted to grass. We all recalled with amusement the Jamaican Red I had scored in Flamingo Park and the enlightened perspectives it had provided. With the encouragement of Panda, I immediately began touting my latest purchase of Columbian.

Armed with artistically rolled joints, roach clip, and matches, the five of us, in finest freak attire, made our way out of the dormitory and over toward the auditorium where nightly movies were shown. We ventured behind the auditorium into the dense Virginia woods adjacent to the building. As we stood in near-darkness amidst towering oaks, toking on that fine Columbian, it brought to mind the nightly rap sessions in Flamingo Park and the many tense situations we had experienced together. Sharing a joint with an old and trusted friend seemed as much a part of the movement life-style as the universal abhorrence of the Vietnam War. We all realized that if an FBI agent intended to infiltrate the more radical elements of the movement, he would certainly be expected to share a joint regularly. The problem was how to convince Division Five officials of the necessity of preparing for this type of activity without admitting to familiarity with drug use.

While working on our second joint, we were startled by the direct glare of bright lights. A bolt of fear shot through my brain when I realized they were the headlights of a Bureau patrol car. In our haste to fire up, we had failed to notice a service road to nowhere. When the Security Patrol Clerk had made a U-turn at the dead end, his headlights framed our images against the darkness. I felt certain our intruder would immediately smell the marijuana if he left the patrol car for a closer inspection. But as luck would have it, he failed to spot us. After what seemed like an eternity, the security clerk completed his U-turn and drove off.

We hastily returned to the dormitory where we agreed that the woods had not been declared a liberated zone for marijuana use. We had all experienced tense moments before, often while stoned, and had always managed to come out on top. It was part of the game we had played for years, only this time our adversary also happened to be our employer.

Since my first day in the FBI as a member of New Agents Class Number Six, the Training Division Supervisor in charge of enforcing dress regulations was Sy The Spy Tullai. Sy had reportedly been assigned to espionage investigations in the New York City office before receiving a promotion to the Training Division for his outstanding security work. He was the epitome of the properly dressed agent of the Hoover era. During my four months of New Agents Training, I never saw him wear anything other than white dress shirts, nondescript ties, and conservative dark business suits with oxford or wing-tip shoes. If Sy spotted a new agent in class wearing a sport coat, colored shirt, slip-on loafers or loud tie, he would immediately admonish the culprit for his "dereliction of duty," then launch into his usual sermon on maintaining the proper Bureau image.

Besides being the Training Division's relentless crusader against improper dress, Sy was also the final authority on personal grooming. He seemed to have the uncanny ability to survey a group of new agents standing some fifty yards away and spot sideburns one-eighth of an inch beyond the proper length. He had no qualms about accosting a new agent between classes if the offender's hair appeared to be touching the collar, or was not properly styled. Sy had never been an advocate of the natural look, preferring instead that each hair be firmly in place at all times. He himself was virtually bald, and the few lonely sprigs on the sides and back of his head were shaved to their shortest possible length.

I had noticed Sy's contemptuous looks when we entered the Administration Building on Monday. We had jokingly speculated in Los Angeles that our presence at the Academy might well push Sy over the edge. He did not speak to us when we arrived, probably intending to ignore the problem. When he realized its magnitude, what he failed to understand was that we were doing exactly as we had been instructed.

Lectures at the Academy generally ran for fifty minutes with a ten-minute break each hour. Those of us in the back of the class had noticed Sy looking in from the hallway during the first hour. We were therefore not surprised to see him storm into the room as we left for out first break. We returned to find that Sy was filling the blackboard with Academy dress regulations. Outlawed for wear in classrooms and the dining hall were: jeans, T-shirts, work shirts, tennis shoes, sandals, cut-offs, and hats. We were also specifically instructed to wear shoes at all times. As Sy continued to list items of unacceptable attire, it was apparent that the freaks in the class had nothing suitable to wear. After dismissing objections from several members of the class, he dropped the bombshell which sent me into orbit.

"You gentlemen who do not have white shirts and ties will be allowed to leave a few minutes early for lunch," he said. "I want you to go to the Academy store, located next to the dining hall, and purchase a white shirt and a tie. As you know, ties are required for the Wednesday evening meal. You may also purchase slacks if needed."

My blood began to boil. After all the indignities we had endured as unsanctioned undercover agents, this was too much.

"Mr. Tullai," I shouted from the back of the room, not waiting to be recognized, "we're doing exactly what we were told to do. The Bureau instructed us to wear our usual undercover clothing for security reasons. We even had our supervisor call the Bureau to be sure that's what they wanted. The only clothes we brought are the ones you say are prohibited. Now you tell us to go over to the Academy store and buy a white shirt and a tie. We could have brought those with us if we had been told to do so. You're crazy if you think I'm going over there and spend one goddammed cent on a shirt and tie!"

I could see the blood rushing up Sy's face until the top of his shiny dome was crimson. I'm sure he had never been addressed in that tone, especially by a freak, and the silence in the room only served to heighten the tension. Within seconds, my classmates recovered from their shock and began backing me up with shouts of "right on" and "damn right." Sy must have sensed that we would not be intimidated, for he quickly stormed out of the room.

Our next instructor, who had been patiently waiting to begin his lecture, appeared totally dumbfounded. I'm sure he was upset over having heard the conversation, realizing he would probably have to write a memo explaining the incident. He struggled through his remaining time as best he could, then quickly escaped to the security of the faculty offices.

When we returned from our break, Assistant Director Thomas J. Jenkins, who was in charge of the Training Division and the Academy complex, was waiting at the rostrum. He was a tall, dignified-looking man who projected the exact image one would expect of a top Bureau official. It certainly didn't look good for the visiting freak team.

"Gentlemen," Jenkins began, "I can understand your concern over the misunderstanding about your dress. I realize that you men who have been working undercover are following the instructions that you were given. I have a high respect for the job you men are doing and the sacrifices you have made. I want you to enjoy your stay here at the Academy. Don't worry about not having dress shirts or ties; just wear the clothing you brought."

Assistant Director Jenkins flashed a smile and walked out of the classroom. The freaks had won the first battle, but the war was far from over. We all realized that Tullai would be mad as hell after being overruled by his superior. In fact, several of the new agents we met later in the week told us of Sy's diatribes to their classes over our appearance and disrespectful behavior.

After the last class of the day, we adjourned to Buddha's suite for the evening cocktail hour, complete with ice this time. The primary topic of conversation was our confrontation with Tullai. The more we talked about the incident with Sy The Spy and about our experience in the woods, the more appropriate it seemed to roll up a few. My colleagues locked the doors, placed towels under each, and prepared to fire up.

Within thirty minutes all six of us were higher than the balls on a giraffe. Absolutely stoned, incredibly ripped, and well on our way to the outer cosmic regions. There was general agreement that the Columbian was indeed some fine grass. The FBI Academy had finally been "liberated," as our revolutionary friends would have proclaimed.

When we realized that we had only about ten minutes before the dining hall closed, Buddha went to work with the deodorant spray. After cracking a window and restoring the room to some semblance of order, we cautiously checked the hallway before exiting. We were definitely a happy group as we floated over to the dining hall. Just as we had suspected, the food did taste much better, especially the second helpings.

After dinner, we walked downstairs to the recreation hall, where Leroy and Rodent made a futile attempt at stoned ping-pong. There were several National Academy members shooting pool at nearby tables, and it was obvious they were taking in the whole show. Rodent would attempt a mighty smash and end up sprawled over the net, watching helplessly as the ball sailed across the room. Leroy would then experience severe balance problems as he tried to bend over and retrieve it. The game was finally discontinued due to lack of interest and energy.

My observations of the National Academy men in the rec hall led me to believe that many of them knew exactly what we had been doing. For the most part, they were street-wise police officers, many of whom had worked their way up through the ranks. Marijuana was a social problem which they were confronted with on a daily basis in many of the larger metropolitan areas. Their experience was in marked contrast to that of the typical FBI agent. I would venture to say that no more than five percent of the veteran FBI agents knew what marijuana looked or smelled like. Since the Bureau had no drug jurisdiction, we received no drug training. Many of the younger agents had no doubt been exposed to marijuana on college campuses, but would be reluctant to acknowledge the fact.

The next day's activities included a two-hour morning lecture entitled "Drugs of Abuse," and I was eager to see if the Bureau had actually located an instructor with some detailed knowledge of the subject. We had facetiously discussed getting loaded in honor of the drug lecture but dismissed the idea as impractical. One of the Division Five supervisors had mentioned the previous day that participants at the first Weatherman In-Service, held in August while we were in Miami, had complained that the lecturer concentrated too much on heroin production and use, rather than on drugs popular among revolutionary types. He suggested that if this were again the case, we recommend to the instructor that he focus more directly on information we could use in our assignment.

Just as predicted, our lecturer started with slide shows on poppy growth in Turkey, followed by the harvesting of raw opium, its conversion into morphine base, and on to the final transformation into street heroin. The initial presentation was interesting but essentially useless. The agent who would soon be involved in the life-style of revolutionary politics would seldom, if ever, come in contact with heroin. When several class members suggested that he provide more information on drugs popular in the movement, he responded by reading the remainder of his material on heroin.

Our instructor had been kind enough to bring along samples of many of the common drugs of abuse and meticulously spread his collection over the front row of desks. In addition to heroin of both the white and brown variety, and several different types of shooting kits, he had also brought some large, professionally mounted displays of commercially produced barbiturates and amphetamines—almost every commonly abused prescription drug. I noted with amusement several familiar brands of amphetamines directly responsible for getting the majority of my law-school class through exams each semester.

There was also an abundant supply of hashish in assorted forms and colors, along with a substantial amount of marijuana in kilos, bricks, lids, and bottles. Our instructor had also made a trip to the local head shop, for he displayed numerous types of smoking paraphernalia, including roach clips, hash pipes, carburetors, bhongs, and rolling papers. Most of the freaks were quick to note that all of the hash and most of the grass had simply been thrown out on tables in a variety of unsealed containers.

After the lengthy lecture on heroin, he briefly touched on opium and cocaine. Once again our lecturer wandered off into the growth, production, and chemical composition rather than concentrating on how they were commonly used and the effects that each produced. He provided limited information on cocaine, which was rapidly increasing in popularity on the West Coast, advising only that the drug was always sniffed, that its use resulted in violent behavior, and that psychological addiction was not uncommon. His understanding of the effects of cocaine was in marked contrast to what my experience indicated.

During our first break, a crowd gathered around the three front tables where the drug samples were displayed. Many of the freaks in our class were exhibiting more than a passing interest in them. The large test tube of cocaine contained twelve to fourteen ounces and had a street value of about fifteen thousand dollars, even in those days. I recall thinking that it was a good thing the tube was sealed. But that was not the case with the endless varieties of hashish which could be closely examined. In fact, they were examined so closely that I noticed that several large chunks were diminishing in size with each inspection. When our instructor left the classroom for a short break, the interest in the display noticeably increased.

The second and final hour began with a textbook presentation on barbiturates and amphetamines. Although our instructor explained the contrasting effects produced by depressants and stimulants on the central nervous system, he possessed little knowledge of their street names. With a vocabulary limited to "uppers" and "downers," how would the new undercover agent react when approached on the street by a "bean freak" offering to sell "red devils," "Christmas trees," "black mollies," or "ludes"? Our Bureau expert was unable to provide even the slightest information about relative street prices for these drugs. He was also unable to shed any light on the potentially fatal interaction between depressants and alcohol.

Our lecturer devoted less than ten minutes to his presentation on psychedelics. LSD, mescaline, DMA, MDA, and STP enjoyed widespread popularity in the late sixties and were still being used occasionally by revolutionary groups to test suspected infiltrators. I had always felt that this was one of the most dangerous aspects of our undercover assignment. Bureau officials were aware of the problem, but were unable to understand that in a communal situation, it was not unusual for the entire group to be given acid without warning, even though none of the residents were under suspicion. Many of the people I met viewed LSD as a highly prized commodity—often obtained at substantial risk—to be shared with close friends.

The most difficult situations occurred at larger communes and outdoor festivals, or after street actions, when large groups would gather for rap sessions where the inevitable half-gallon of red wine would be passed around. Since it was generally believed that "pigs" were afraid to drink from these bottles for fear of contracting a disease or of being drugged, many of the more security-conscious groups carefully noted who consistently refused to participate. As the evening wore on, some well-meaning freak would decide to liven things up by surreptitiously adding ten hits of acid to the wine bottle. It was not unlike the behavior of an otherwise conservative teenager who slips a pint of vodka into the punch bowl at the Senior Prom so everyone will have a better time.

In the final fifteen minutes of his drug lecture, our instructor introduced the subject of marijuana. He was quick to advise that this was the most widely abused drug in the country, and I was just as quick to question when it had replaced alcohol as Number One. Although somewhat startled by this question, he immediately acknowledged that I was correct, but added that he was referring only to the abuse of illegal drugs. To familiarize us with marijuana, our instructor let us smell its distinctive odor. He broke off a small amount from a large brick on the front table, placed it in a rusty coffee can, and carefully ignited it with a propane torch. He then carried the can around the room, allowing us to smell the burning contents.

When smoke clouds began to form, we were given another break and immediately descended on the front desks for further inspection of the samples. It was almost impossible to keep from laughing as I watched my classmates systematically appropriate ever-increasing portions of the official Bureau stash. The lecturer returned after disposing of the burning marijuana, gathered up the remains of his display, and graciously thanked us for our interest. If he noticed his losses, he made no comments about them.

Our private cocktail party that evening turned into the most memorable social event of the week. We hurriedly left the classroom building and followed a variety of circuitous routes to the dormitory before arriving at the Buddha's room. Bottles were out, glasses were iced, and towels were neatly folded in preparation for use under the doors.

The regular freak contingent was in attendance as we gathered around the study desk to "demo" the official Bureau stash along with the usual Columbian back-up. Since it was show-and-tell time, I pulled out a small piece of hash for inspection by the group.

"Who's got a knife that will cut this official Bureau-approved, Red Lebanese?" I asked. "Gonna make you weak in the knees."

"Right here, C," answered Panda. "Wow, what a beautiful chunk. The L.A. Connection scores again!"

"What are we gonna do for a pipe?" queried Pigeon.

"Shit, man, I just happen to have a genuine, Bureau-approved, smoking device right here," said Walrus, "also known in the freak world as a hash pipe. Probably approved by ol' J. Edgar himself."

The Walrus nonchalantly passed the hash pipe that had belonged to our instructor. We all stared in amazement. Even Leroy arose from his prone position on the bed to move over for a better look.

"You gonna make that poor dude go back to the head shop one more time, man," said Leroy, obviously unconcerned.

"It'll be good for him to get some undercover experience," chimed in Jay. "I wonder what he puts on his expense voucher, hash pipe or educational materials."

"No, man, he just covers it under pay telephones and parking meters," replied Pigeon. "That's the way it's done in the Big Apple."

After a large piece of light blond hash appeared on the desk, it was obvious we had an abundance of smoking material for the remainder of the week. But our small pipe could complete only one tantalizing pass around the room before going out.

"Reload, reload," hollered Buddha, watching the small red glow disappear into ashes shortly before being passed to him. "Man, this must be what they mean in the army when the sergeant says, 'Okay men, if you got 'em, smoke 'em.'"

Jay slowly looked up after taking the final killer hit on the hash pipe. His eyes rolled back as he stood up to pass it over to the desk for another refill. "Yeah," he said, "and most of the troopers are smokin' this same brand, Buddha, brand X."

We collectively awarded the official Bureau hashish a B plus, but the marijuana, which was at least five years old and incapable of producing a high, was a total failure. As we joked about smoking the FBI hash, in an FBI pipe, in the FBI Academy, we speculated that perhaps this was the "new" Bureau we had heard so much about. In any event, I was beginning to develop a high regard for our new leader, L. Patrick Gray III.

For an undercover agent preparing to enter the drug culture it was far better to get stoned for the first time with fellow agents who were known and trusted than to attempt to fake it in front of total strangers in an undercover situation. The increased awareness produced by marijuana could often be accompanied by feelings of paranoia and insecurity among inexperienced users, leading to disastrous results in a hostile environment.

The supervisors of the Revolutionary Activities Section had become reconciled, at least among themselves, to the fact that deep cover agents would be smoking marijuana. But unfortunately, they failed to comprehend that this activity required a much higher degree of training than merely smoking a cigarette. If an agent was passed a lid of grass, would he be able to separate the stems and seeds, roll a presentable joint, and take a hit as if he knew what he was doing?

8

Weatherman In-Service: How To Go Underground

As the week progressed, we began to receive more of an insight into the new undercover program officially adopted by the Bureau for penetration into the Weather Underground. Perhaps the general scope of the program is best described in a section of the FBI document entitled "Working Guide For Utilization of Undercover Special Agents."

There are presently over 50 men and women fugitives who are believed involved in the underground apparatus, over 25 of whom are Weatherman affiliated, based on violations of Antiriot Law, Federal Bombing and Gun Control statutes, Sabotage and for various local violations where UFAP process has been issued. In addition to these fugitives being in an underground status, there are also a considerable number of missing Weathermen who are supporting fugitives from their underground status as well as over 200 individuals considered part of surface/support or legal Weatherman apparatus.

There are a number of collectives and communes wherein Weatherman support individuals reside. There are also other collectives and communes the true nature of which has not been fully determined, but whose members appear to be aligned with Weatherman and following basic Weatherman philosophy. These collectives, communes and related individuals must be investigated to determine if they are acting in support of Weatherman and are willing and capable of participation in violent terroristic revolutionary activity against the existing Government structure of the Nation. The above defined groups and individuals are suited for targeting by undercover Agents looking toward attaining the following objectives:

1. Location and apprehension of Weatherman fugitives.

2. Penetration of Weatherman underground and revolutionary collectives or communes which appear to relate to or support Weatherman underground apparatus.

3. Neutralization of Weatherman underground apparatus which will lead to stoppage of their terrorist bombings and other violent revolutionary activity.

According to the head of the Revolutionary Activities Section, Domestic Intelligence Division, there would be three distinct levels of agent participation within the new program: the handling agent who would provide support and paperwork functions; the undercover agent, involved primarily in surveillance and short-term projects, and the deep cover agent, the most covert level assigned to long-range infiltration.

The overall success or failure of the program depended on the agent in deep cover status. He was to be relatively young and unmarried, preferably with experience in security matters and able to live with revolutionary activists for an extended period of time. He would be expected to adopt a similar appearance, life-style, and political philosophy to that of the Weathermen and to travel throughout the country if necessary. His true identity, location, and assignment would be maintained on a strict need-to-know basis within the Bureau.

After volunteering for participation in the program, agents would be required to undergo a thorough interview with the Special Agent In Charge (SAC) of their respective field division. If the SAC believed the agent qualified, a coded teletype was forwarded to the Domestic Intelligence Division, FBIHQ, containing his personal recommendation that the candidate was physically and psychologically qualified for such an assignment. This communication would not refer to the agent by name, but rather by his credential card number. It would also include his assumed identity, his cover story, and a code name to be used in telephone contacts with the handling agent. The target for penetration was also described, along with a justification for this selection and the benefits to be received. If the appropriate supervisor in the Revolutionary Activities Section concurred with the recommendation, the initial communication was then reduced to memorandum form and forwarded to the Assistant Director, Domestic Intelligence Division, for final approval.

Agents accepted for deep cover status were to be provided with extensive false identification to aid in the development of a logical cover story. Fictitious background records covering education, employment, and draft status would be planted by the handling agent so that the cover story would withstand scrutiny by suspicious Weathermen or outside law-enforcement agencies. After assuming this new identity, the deep cover agent would be provided with cash from the confidential fund, traditionally used for informant payments, to purchase a suitable vehicle. The car would be registered and insured under his assumed name. Cash funds would be made available for the rental of a house or apartment near targeted individuals. We were cautioned, however, that all expenditures for vehicles and housing required prior approval from Division Five.

It was apparent from our early discussions that several policy decisions concerning the basic structure of the program had undergone heated debate among the FBI leadership. These officials knew that the only capability possessed by the Bureau for immediate implementation of the deep cover assignment was the nucleus of less than a dozen agents who had been operating unofficially for years. This nucleus was further reduced by the policy that married agents would not be accepted for deep cover status. Experienced married agents like Rodent were to be allowed to remain in the program as undercover level agents assigned to projects which did not require extended travel. They would retain their fictitious identification and hippy appearance but would not be given a detailed cover story.

The officials from the Revolutionary Activities Section candidly admitted that this policy decision had been reached to avoid embarrassment to the Bureau, which would surely result if an agent's wife became upset over his prolonged absence or the prospect of his sexual encounters with liberated members of the radical community. The most frequently used justification for this policy was the possibility that a married agent assigned to a deep cover project might catch a venereal disease and then give it to his wife. It was obvious that from the very inception of the new program, sex was considered an integral part of the deep cover assignment and a way in which information as well as credibility could easily be obtained.

Agents who had previously been assigned to Weatherman and extremist cases in traditional investigative roles would now be designated handling agents. They would continue to function within the field division offices where they would be responsible for reporting and disseminating the information gathered by the deep cover agent. They would also serve as liaison between the deep cover operative, squad supervisor, and the Revolutionary Activities Section.

In addition to assisting in the development of a credible cover story, the handling agent was responsible for maintaining the personal affairs of the deep cover agent. He was expected to deposit pay checks, pay apartment rent, utility bills, and forward mail if necessary. He was also required to submit vouchers for confidential funds, convert these funds into cash, and arrange for delivery to the deep cover agent. In effect, the handling agent functioned as the paper man, money man, and personal representative of the deep cover agent; but most importantly, he was the last link with the straight world.

Since the role of handling agent would require a substantial amount of time and paperwork, he was to be assigned only one case. This case would appear to be a security informant matter but would be captioned with a new and slightly different numerical designation, an internal code designed to disguise the fact that the informant was a regular FBI agent, functioning in a deep cover capacity. Although the FBI had historically refused to divulge any information regarding its security informants, Division Five devised this coded method of identification to maintain the secrecy of the program within the FBI itself. I would suspect, however, that it was also anticipated that sensitive counterintelligence information maintained in this form would be exempt from future dissemination under the Freedom of Information and Privacy Acts.

To complicate matters further, this was perhaps the only instance where the actual agent who conducted the interview or investigation did not personally record the results. The raw intelligence information gathered by the deep cover agent would be passed along by telephone or at periodic debriefings held at secure locations. The handling agent was then responsible for putting this verbal information in writing as though he had received it from an informant. Unfortunately, the very nature of the deep cover assignment made it impossible to review the final product for accuracy.

The changes in Bureau procedures were not confined solely to the new undercover program. With the approval of Acting Director Pat Gray, a companion program was formulated by the Domestic Intelligence Division under the code name of SPECTAR. The Special Target

Informant Development Program (SPECTAR) was designed to improve the efficiency of the deep cover agent and to provide more immediate avenues of penetrating Weatherman support groups. Repeated efforts by the Bureau to develop reliable informants among close friends and associates of the Weatherman fugitives had proved fruitless. It was reasoned that this failure was due in large part to the traditional method of payment for Bureau informants.

Until the advent of SPECTAR, all informants, both criminal and security, were paid on a COD basis for information received. The agent who received the information would attempt to verify it through other sources before calculating its value in dollars. If his supervisor and SAC concurred, the informant was then paid cash in the authorized amount.

Under SPECTAR, agents were instructed to evaluate as potential targets the former friends, associates, classmates, and relatives of the missing Weatherman fugitives. It was hoped that a cooperating target could be located whose past relationship and position of trust would allow him to recontact the fugitives. If there was a reasonable basis for believing that the target would have an opportunity to make such contact, he or she would be offered a monthly cash payment in advance for "best efforts." These payments ran as high as one thousand dollars per month.

Deep cover agents were instructed to take note of any particular circumstances or personal weaknesses which might lead to future cooperation from a presently hostile source. These included financial or employment difficulties, extramarital sex or secret affairs, homosexual or lesbian relationships, parental problems, pending or potential criminal charges, draft board classifications, jealousies, and dissatisfaction with revolutionary philosophy or tactics.

If it appeared that information developed by a deep cover agent could compromise potential targets to a sufficient degree to gain cooperation, the targets would then be contacted by regular FBI agents at a time when they were away from their associates. In the typical communal situation, the deep cover agent would be in the position to determine if the target reported this approach by the FBI to the rest of the group. If no mention was made of this meeting, the target might be recontacted at a later date, even though the initial request for assistance might have been declined. In the event the target began working for the Bureau, the deep cover agent would be in a position to determine whether the informant was reliable or was merely furnishing meaningless information in return for a monthly income.

Based on my later experience in the deep cover role, I would suspect that much of the compromising information was ultimately used for harassment and retaliation, born out of the continued frustration over being unable to recruit SPECTAR informants. I recall isolated instances where pretext phone calls, anonymous letters, or "official" inquiries resulted in loss of employment, embarrassment, and strained relationships. At the very least, these questionable tactics produced mistrust, suspicion, and paranoia.

Initial response to the undercover program was divided among members of our in-service class. Agents who had recently expressed an interest in volunteering appeared enthusiastic over the basic concept and design of the program. They seemed to believe, and justifiably so, that the implementation of the undercover and SPECTAR programs signaled a major change in fundamental Bureau policy, indicating a move toward more aggressive and sophisticated intelligence-gathering techniques. On the other hand, those of us who had previously engaged in similar undercover operations, though admittedly on a more limited and unofficial basis, felt strongly that these agents did not comprehend the full impact of what the Bureau was asking of them. It was evident that many of the prospective volunteers, not to mention Division Five officials, had no conception of the unique life-style into which they were being asked to submerge themselves. It was impossible to convince them that successful penetration of the Weather Underground was not simply a matter of growing a beard and wearing old clothes. The most intricately documented cover story was totally useless unless the deep cover agent felt at ease in his new identity and possessed an understanding of his targets.

To make the situation even more difficult, the frequent antiwar demonstrations of the late sixties and early seventies had almost ground to a halt. No longer were the various student and political groups actively soliciting support for massive street actions or for membership in their respective organizations. Thus these new Bureau recruits would not be allowed the luxury of making their first mistakes among thousands of marchers. They would be compelled to make their initial approach to targets without the benefit of previous exposure to the formative years of the antiwar movement.

In response to questions from class members, we were advised that there would be little financial incentive for participation in the program. Division Five officials, who were always aware of possible internal criticism, had decided that there would no no increase in pay, even though the deep cover assignment would require a twenty-four hour

143

commitment for as long as necessary. Since some assistant agents believed that hippy agents would be jumping from bed to bed with an assortment of beautiful young women, they should be overjoyed at being selected for the assignment.

What these officials and many of the potential recruits failed to realize was that while the regular agent might work exceptionally long hours from time to time, once he left the office, he could go home to his wife and family, pour himself a drink, and enjoy his favorite television program in comfortable surroundings. Deep cover agents, on the other hand, would seldom be allowed any time off, and the very nature of their assignment, not to mention their appearance, would preclude any meaningful social contact with anyone other than the targets with whom they associated. It was to be an existence of continuous tension, of living the big lie during every waking moment.

Although there was widespread dissatisfaction over financial arrangements and the exclusion of married agents, the most hotly debated issue of the new program was "office of assignment." We were advised that every agent assigned to deep cover operations would be subject to official transfer from his present office to any other Bureau office where a better opportunity existed to infiltrate known Weatherman associates. In my situation, this would mean that if the Revolutionary Activities Section determined that little opportunity existed for successful infiltration in Los Angeles, while Detroit had located targets with maximum potential but possessed no qualified deep cover agents, then I would be transferred to Detroit.

Like nearly all of my bachelor colleagues in Los Angeles, I had adjusted readily to the relaxed southern California life-style and had absolutely no desire to end up in Detroit. And what was to happen after I completed my assignment or grew tired of the program? We were told that upon leaving the undercover program, either through completion of assignment or voluntary termination, we would receive our "office of preference" or be transferred "as close to that office as possible."

Perhaps the personal goal of every agent in the Bureau was to obtain enough seniority to rise to the top of the "office of preference" list. During the Hoover era, new agents had been assigned to offices geographically remote from their previous residences, friends, and relatives to avoid any potential conflict in the performance of their official duties. They also remained subject to transfer at any time for the needs of the Bureau. Every agent assigned to what he considered an undesirable office, seemed to dream continuously of eventually returning home on an official transfer. It was not uncommon for agents to wait patiently for transfer after twenty years on some lists. In return for our voluntary participation as deep cover agents, we were now being offered the unparalleled opportunity to be transferred to our office of preference in the foreseeable future.

There was, however, the usual bureaucratic *Catch-22*. Domestic Intelligence Division officials claimed that they were unable to provide us with written agreements stating we would receive an official transfer to our office of preference. They said we would simply have to trust them, and they could foresee no problem in obtaining an office of preference for a deep cover agent who had made great personal sacrifices in the performance of his duties. No problems, but no written guarantees. In effect, this meant that an agent assigned to Los Angeles might volunteer for the program and be transferred to Cleveland where he would work in a deep cover capacity for perhaps a year, then ask to leave the program, only to discover that he must remain in Cleveland. We were all troubled by the constant references to "office of preference" or "as close to the office as possible." Since Pat Gray had not been formally confirmed as Director, and the program was adopted with his approval over the objections of several senior officials, it was not inconceivable that at some future date, Cleveland might be considered "as close as possible" to my office of preference in Dallas.

Many of the Division Five officials were outraged by our skepticism of their personal assurances regarding office of preference. What they failed to understand was that the majority of single agents assigned to offices they enjoyed had no desire to give up a year or two of their lives, as well as all of their social contacts, for a nebulous verbal assurance of a future transfer.

After discussing the various structural details of the new program, we plunged into the controversial area of investigative techniques. This was a matter of paramount interest since investigative techniques in security cases had typically included the use of surreptitious entries, listening devices, and mail covers. It was an extremely sensitive area previously avoided by Domestic Intelligence Division officials, even though several class members had requested clarification of current Bureau policy. There was increasing speculation among agents in the field that substantial changes in fundamental policy and investigative emphasis were evolving under the leadership of Pat Gray. In the relatively short period since the death of Mr. Hoover, we had witnessed changes in areas ranging from personal grooming to the acceptance of women agents.

We were all aware that surreptitious entries, or "black bag jobs,"

145

had been standard operating procedure in the Domestic Intelligence Division for as long as one could remember. I recall lecturers at the time of my New Agents Training who boasted about illegal entries of foreign embassies and consulates in Washington and New York City. Many of these entries were reportedly made on a regular basis, often through the cooperation of inside sources, to plant or replace listening devices and to photograph documents. Although these were considered legitimate techniques in foreign counterintelligence matters, it was assumed that they were widely used in domestic security cases involving suspected Communist Party members of the fifties. These actions were apparently justified by rationalization that "those who seek to subvert the government should not be allowed the protection of its Bill of Rights."

I often noted with amusement various newspaper reports that Director Hoover specifically discontinued the use of surreptitious entries in 1966. I can recall no mention ever being made of this directive while I was undergoing New Agents Training in late 1968. I would suspect that Mr. Hoover actually believed that he did ban illegal entries, just as he apparently believed that the FBI had no long-haired hippies working undercover, but in reality the handful of senior officials who actually ran the Bureau during that period realized only too well that when the Director demanded results, they had to produce them, never mind how. And if these practices were actually discontinued, then why did the Bureau continue to provide intensive training in them? My personal experience leads me to conclude that if a directive was issued in 1966 prohibiting these questionable tactics, then by 1970 it was universally disregarded by agents involved in security matters.

Prior to the Supreme Court ruling in the landmark case involving the White Panther Party, warrantless wiretaps could be authorized by the attorney general in domestic security cases under the guise of protecting the national security. But after the White Panther decision, the attorney general could no longer authorize the FBI to conduct wiretaps against United States citizens in purely domestic matters. These cases would now require the showing of probable cause before a federal magistrate or judge prior to the issuance of a warrant authorizing a wiretap. The court left unresolved the troublesome question of foreign involvement.

The Bureau reportedly removed several wiretaps on domestic organizations after this decision, primarily among the Weathermen and Black Panther Party. While Bureau officials were quick to point out publicly that the attorney general could no longer authorize wiretaps in purely domestic security cases, they left unanswered the question of whether surreptitious entries for intelligence-gathering purposes were still allowed.

Prior to the Supreme Court decision, if a field office had a domestic security case where they felt it necessary to seek Bureau permission to install a listening device, they would submit a written request to conduct a "survey." If the Bureau concurred with the request, they would then forward a communication to the field office authorizing them to conduct a survey to determine the feasibility of a future installation, prior to requesting official authorization from the attorney general. This authorization for a survey was, in effect, Bureau sanction for a surreptitious entry to photograph documents and search for intelligence information.

When specifically questioned as to whether the Revolutionary Activities Section would approve requests to conduct surveys on Weatherman associates, we were advised that "all pertinent requests regarding any 'investigative techniques' should be forwarded to the Bureau for consideration." These officials would not publicly state that surveys, or surreptitious entries, would be authorized, nor would they privately state that they would not be authorized. With an understanding wink, they would only reply that "surveys should still be considered by the field as one of many 'investigative tools' available."

In retrospect, I'm sure these vague public replies stemmed from the fact that the top officials in the Domestic Intelligence Division, as well as many of us who had been involved in Weatherman investigations, were aware that surreptitious entries, illegal wiretaps, and mail openings had been periodically conducted by agents in New York City since the original Weathermen entered the underground. Some of the earlier entries were apparently approved as surveys, while many were reportedly conducted by individual agents without specific Bureau approval. As a general rule, veteran agents would never request Bureau permission to conduct an important survey if they felt it would be denied. They would simply recruit a sufficient number of trusted agents to provide back-up assistance and handle the job themselves. I was personally involved in such a situation on the West Coast in which virtually all of the participants, including myself, believed that the entry had been authorized, only to discover some three months later that a request had never even been made.

It should also be pointed out that the nature of the typical New York City apartment house actually contributed to these activities. Nearly every building had a maintenance superintendent who was generally underpaid, uneducated, and usually a member of a minority group. By flashing a phony badge and credentials, an FBI agent would identify himself as a NYPD detective, narcotics agent, or member of some other law-enforcement agency. With an appeal to patriotism, civic responsibility, or law and order, accompanied by a crisp twenty dollar bill, the cooperation of most supers was quickly obtained. Since they generally resided in, or had access to, the basement area where the building's telephone junction box was located, they could easily provide total security for an inspection of the phone system.

Once access was gained to this area, the super was told to take a walk. An agent with only minimal experience could locate the pairs in the junction box which belonged to a particular apartment, and he was then able to monitor conversations through a headset. It was a crude but effective method of wiretapping. There were no telephone poles to climb, no apartments to enter, and best of all, the super had no idea of the agent's true identity.

After surveillance teams had discovered that many of the Weatherman associates were using a designated series of pay telephone booths for communication at prearranged times and dates, it became even easier to monitor their conversations. Agents installed a small FM transmitter in each of the phone booths, and then listened to the conversation broadcast on a receiver in their car, parked several blocks away. After the calls were completed, they simply removed the transmitters.

Building superintendents also provided master keys which could be duplicated for future use. Many of these keys were obtained on a legitimate basis so that surveys could be conducted for warrantless wiretaps. But after the Supreme Court ban, the master keys were not returned even though their legitimate use had ended. Agents could wait until all of the occupants of a particular apartment left and were tracked by a surveillance team outside. The apartment could then be entered and thoroughly searched. The agents would remain in radio contact with the surveillance team who were aware of the occupants' whereabouts at all times. I was told that many such entries were made on a weekly basis, although little information of value was ever located.

Building mailbox keys could also be obtained in a similar fashion, and envelopes resembling personal correspondence were reportedly steamed open on more than one occasion. While I never witnessed an FBI agent opening mail, we did rely heavily on "mail covers" obtained through the cooperation of the U.S. Postal Service. The Post Office would supply the Bureau with all information contained on the outside of each piece of mail delivered to a specific address, but would not open the envelope. The mail cover would then provide us with the names of all individuals receiving mail at a particular address, the return address on the correspondence, as well as the postmark indicating the city from which it was mailed.

Although the tactics of unauthorized entries, wiretaps, and mail openings employed against American citizens are patently illegal and can never be condoned, it should be remembered that the agents who engaged in these practices were under tremendous pressure to produce results. The Nixon administration had little patience with "radicals" who publicly criticized foreign and domestic policies. Each time there was a bombing or violent student demonstration, intense pressure from the White House would reportedly be brought to bear upon Director Hoover to restore law and order. As the disruptions continued to escalate, Mr. Hoover became increasingly infuriated over the inability of the FBI to locate the missing Weathermen.

Under J. Edgar Hoover, the Bureau functioned as an autocratic, paramilitary bureaucracy whose employees were ruled by a climate of fear. Those unfortunate enough to provoke the wrath of Director Hoover would find themselves transferred to some remote outpost at considerable expense and family hardship, or suspended without pay for a period of weeks. Agents whose transgressions were considered more serious were generally provided the option of submitting a letter of resignation or being fired. Most vulnerable were the upper level supervisors and Assistant Directors. In the Domestic Intelligence Division, for instance, most of the top officials had been assigned to Bureau headquarters in Washington for ten to twenty years, enjoying increased status and higher salaries than regular agents in the field. They realized only too well, however, that "inadequate supervision," "sustained mediocrity," or "insubordination" could produce a transfer just as easily as a "personal indiscretion," if investigative results expected by the Director were not forthcoming.

When the missing Weathermen first became federal fugitives, attempts to apprehend them were conducted by the Special Investigative Division as if they were ordinary criminal fugitives. But even after placing many of the Weatherman leaders on the "Top Ten Program" for the country's Ten Most Wanted criminals, no tangible results were achieved, and the situation was becoming an embarrassment to the Bureau, not to mention its Director. It was then suggested that since the Weathermen were actually a radical political organization whose activities were a threat to internal security, the investigation should come under the supervision of the Domestic Intelligence Division. It was further reasoned that the abundance of security informants involved in radical political organizations, who were already under the control of Division Five, would be in a far better position to help locate the fugitives than traditional criminal informants.

This unprecedented reassignment between divisions produced a unique situation, since agents assigned to security type cases were generally involved only with intelligence-gathering projects, not with gathering admissible evidence for a criminal prosecution. The majority of agents would ever even consider making a surreptitious entry for the purpose of obtaining evidence which would subsequently be used in a court of law in a criminal case. If questioned about such evidence an agent might feel himself forced to commit perjury. On the other hand, agents assigned to security matters seldom had any dealings with the criminal justice system. Now, for the first time, security agents were actively attempting to locate and apprehend criminal fugitives.

Most of the Weatherman fugitives were initially sought on a variety of local and state charges before federal warrants for "Unlawful Flight to Avoid Prosecution" were obtained. The primary goal of the security agent assigned to these cases was to make an arrest so that the individuals could be returned to the appropriate state or local jurisdiction to stand trial. Since they were not concerned with gathering evidence against the fugitives or faced with the possibility of having to testify in court, it becomes somewhat easier to understand why they were willing to participate in surreptitious entries. The discovery of a letter from the underground, a telephone number, or an address book left lying around could provide the one lead needed to locate the missing Weathermen. And once they were arrested, agent participation in the matter was ended, for the FBI was never required to reveal exactly how they located fugitives.

It should also be pointed out that most of the agents assigned to Weatherman investigations were young and inexperienced. Veteran security agents were too knowledgeable to become involved in cases receiving such prominent media coverage and the personal attention of the Director. They could also successfully argue that younger agents were better suited for use on surveillance teams, unofficial undercover projects, and for developing informants among younger age groups.

The typical agent involved in Weatherman cases was, like me, in his late twenties with less than three years of experience in the Bureau.

We were all cast from the same conservative law-and-order mold, and our knowledge of counterintelligence matters was confined solely to briefings in training school and James Bond novels. Since information concerning security investigations was disseminated on a strict need-to-know basis, we were reluctant to ask detailed questions for fear of revealing our obvious inexperience. In addition, we began to adopt the prevailing attitude that by its very nature, the intelligence function prevents any clear distinction between activities which are legal or illegal, moral or immoral, right or wrong. We all shared the sincere belief that our country was undergoing a severe internal crisis that demanded positive and immediate action.

Mr. Hoover's displeasure over the ineffectiveness of the Weatherman investigations was directed at the Assistant Director of the Domestic Intelligence Division, and more particularly at the Revolutionary Activities Section which had primary responsibility for the cases. These officials in turn put tremendous pressure on agents in the field to produce results. I would suggest that most of the illegal activities which occurred in New York City were a direct result of this pressure, aided by the climate of fear which existed in the Bureau at that time, and the personal frustrations of the agents involved. Weatherman associates had flatly refused to speak with agents or provide them with any cooperation. Their usual reply to the display of FBI credentials was a brief and direct, "Fuck off!" It may seem naive to some people, but the hierarchy in Washington was unable to comprehend this lack of respect for the FBI, often criticizing the agents for not "dominating the situation" and conducting a "thorough and forceful interview."

Based on my experience in undercover Weatherman investigations, I would think it virtually inconceivable that the leadership of the Domestic Intelligence Division, and especially the Revolutionary Activities Section, had no knowledge of the investigative techniques being employed in New York City. Had we been able to develop reliable informants among known Weatherman associates, we would have had no need for the deep cover and SPECTAR programs. And if official Bureau policy was opposed to surreptitious entries, why were our leaders unwilling to say so instead of using gobbledygook to create exactly the opposite impression? The message we received from these officials continued to be "Do what you have to do to get the job done, just spare us the details."

On the last morning of the Weatherman In-Service week, we were to be addressed by L. Patrick Gray III, Acting Director of the FBI. It

151

was apparent that the Academy maintenance crew had been apprised of the visit, since virtually every floor in every building was waxed and buffed to an immaculate shine. The faculty and staff wore their most conservative clothes. Several of the older members of our in-service class were similarly dressed, although we turned up in our usual undercover attire.

We eagerly awaited Gray's arrival, since few of us had been given an opportunity to meet him or hear him speak. He had previously visited many of the FBI field offices throughout the country, including Los Angeles, but we had not been allowed to meet him because of our appearance and the uncertainty over how he would accept the fact of our existence.

Gray entered the room in a flurry of excitement, accompanied by an entourage of dignitaries that included Assistant Director Jenkins, Assistant Director Edward S. Miller of Domestic Intelligence; his Number One man W. Raymond Wannell; Robert L. Shackelford, Section Chief for Revolutionary Activities; and Unit Chief William N. Preusse. Even Sy The Spy was in attendance, no doubt reluctantly, but he seemed oblivious to our improper dress and never ventured a look in our direction. It was almost as if the President of the United States had entered the room, shielded by a phalanx of Secret Service agents and surrounded by the entire White House staff.

Gray seemed in good physical condition and carried himself like a man accustomed to command. He was dressed in a conservative gray suit, blue oxford-cloth shirt, and burgundy and navy striped tie. His appearance was that of a successful, confident business executive. He spoke in a direct and forceful manner that generated respect. He certainly made a favorable impression, and I thought at the time that he would encounter no difficulties in projecting the proper Bureau image.

After a rousing introduction by Assistant Director Miller, Gray began his brief address by emphasizing the importance he placed on the deep cover program and expressing his personal confidence in its ultimate success. He outlined the grave dangers he perceived to our democratic institutions if the substantial threat to our country's internal security were not neutralized. He complimented us on our performance during the Miami conventions, and for the personal sacrifices we had made for our country. Had there been an American flag within reach, I would not have been the least bit surprised if he had suddenly grabbed it and waved it. He closed by reiterating that the undercover program was to receive top priority within all divisions of the Bureau and would continue to have his close personal attention.

It was a brief, stirring appearance in which he thoroughly succeeded in conveying the point that our assignments were vitally important to the well-being of the country and the survival of the democratic system. We were all impressed by the fact that the Acting Director had spent over two hours traveling from Washington to deliver a short address to a single in-service class of less than forty-five agents. For many of us who were still doubtful about future participation in the program, his appearance played a major role in our final decision.

As our plane departed from Dulles International later that evening, I reflected on the significance of the week's events. After spending most of the week with senior officials of the Domestic Intelligence Division, I was deeply disturbed by several of our discussions.

It seemed that the climate of fear which characterized the forty-eight-year rule of J. Edgar Hoover had been replaced by a climate of indecision. Since the death of Mr. Hoover, the day-to-day operations of the FBI had continued, though many important decisions were postponed because of uncertainty about Gray's position. Although Pat Gray was the Acting Director, it was obvious that the small group of Assistant Directors who actually ran the Bureau were unwilling to implement many of the sweeping changes he envisioned, at least until he was formally confirmed.

We had been asked to volunteer for a new and unprecedented undercover program, but none of the Division Five officials in charge of the program had been willing to state publicly what investigative techniques could be used. We were being asked to join in a game without benefit of any rules. We were repeatedly told that several top officials at headquarters were against the program. Assuming that it did get off the ground, how long would it last? We were given verbal assurances that we would receive our office of preference, or as close to that as possible, in return for our participation in the program. But if this new program was so important, why wouldn't the Bureau provide written guarantees regarding transfers in order to encourage more volunteers? On the one hand, we were told of the substantial changes being instituted to implement the program; on the other, we were told that the details of salary, overtime, and transfers, which were all the province of the omnipotent Administrative Division, must be handled within the framework of existing Bureau policy.

I was pleased to discover, however, that after years of unquestioning acceptance of the edicts of J. Edgar Hoover, Division Five officials had discarded the ridiculous notion that the entire antiwar movement was somehow organized, orchestrated, and financed by the Communist Party. Nevertheless, I was forced to conclude that our leadership possessed little, if any, understanding of the life-style, values, or beliefs of those involved in the movement, much less of the Weathermen.

The effectiveness of Domestic Intelligence Division leaders continued to be limited by their faulty assessment of the present realities. To begin with, they were unable to comprehend how deeply committed the Weathermen were to their political beliefs. They refused to accept the fact that these revolutionary groups had no respect for the authority of the FBI and would not be intimidated by harassment or threats of prosecution. But most importantly, they failed to perceive that public opinion had begun to swing toward the belief that the antiwar movement was, in fact, a just cause, one which more and more Americans, including many FBI agents, had come to support.

9

LA 7852-S (Extremist)
or Born Again

Early in October 1972, we were thrust back into the realities of Los Angeles. Scarcely a day would pass without our receiving some priority directive either modifying, deleting, revising, or establishing our guidelines. There seemed to be a new sense of urgency about deploying deep cover operatives against their targets without delay. The Bureau wanted results, and they wanted them fast.

On the local level, our long-established undercover contingent, though now blessed with official sanction, was forced to undergo substantial change. Leroy, the newest member of our group who had performed so admirably on the Miami caravan, decided to leave the program and seek administrative advancement. He was a family man, and he saw little future in the drudgery of surveillance work or short-term projects on the undercover level.

Both Rodent and Joe were also disappointed by their exclusion from the deep cover assignment because they were married, especially after gaining years of experience in related work. The Domestic Intelligence Division had decided that deep cover operatives should completely dissociate themselves from the November Committee to protect the deep cover agents in the event that the front organization was exposed. Rodent and Joe would have to work alone now, being the only remaining "members" of the November Committee; nevertheless, they reluctantly agreed to stay on as undercover-level participants, at least for the present.

For the Panda, the decision over volunteering came easily: "Fuck it!" He had experienced all the degradation, humiliation, and abuse he would take. Although single, he could no longer date women he was genuinely interested in because of his unkempt appearance. How could he possibly explain that the outrageous freak was really an attorney employed by the FBI? According to him, his social life was practically nonexistent, his parents were upset by his hippy image during a recent visit home, and he wanted no part of this ridiculous new transfer policy. Thanks, but no thanks. A shave, haircut, white shirt, and tie would suit him just fine. To the Panda, deep cover was deep shit.

With the "retirement" of Panda, the Bureau lost one of its most competent undercover operatives. Only Jay and I now remained as potential deep cover operatives in the Los Angeles Division. Since Jay had joined our group a few months before the Miami conventions, he possessed only limited experience in undercover investigations. And since he was over thirty, his entry into this unknown world of militant freaks would undoubtedly be more difficult.

Among the many single agents assigned to Los Angeles, there were few who enjoyed the relaxed southern California life-style more than Jay did. His warm personality and good looks made a big hit with the ladies. And like most of us, he used every opportunity for weekend ski trips, volleyball games, sailing, or scuba diving. As an avid sports fan, he frequently attended games of the Dodgers, Lakers, and Kings. With a nice home, good income, and the unlimited social opportunities available in Los Angeles, Jay had absolutely no desire to risk being transferred.

I felt much the same way, though I was intrigued by the possibility of an "office of preference" transfer to Dallas. Living on the beach in Los Angeles had been a fantastic experience, but I realized that it wouldn't last forever. Land prices were skyrocketing, and it was inevitable that my aging rental unit would soon be demolished in favor of ocean-front condominiums. But my goals and aspirations would be changing too. After years of the hedonistic life, I was still attracted by the traditional American dream of owning a home and starting a family; however, I was certain that I needed a position of greater flexibility before that dream could be realized. Once an agent had mortgage payments, kids in school, and medical bills, he was economically vulnerable and exactly where the Administrative Division wanted him.

I had seen enough agents suffer through disciplinary transfers or assignments to work they despised because they couldn't afford to quit or give up their retirement benefits. They simply couldn't accumulate enough money to leave the Bureau and search for another job. If I became unhappy with the job, I wanted to be in a position to resign without having to worry about selling a house and disrupting my family. Since my parents lived near Dallas, and I was already admitted to the Texas Bar, it was the logical place to begin a law practice on short notice. Living in Los Angeles had been an interesting, rewarding experience, but somehow, it just didn't seem to be the right place for my future.

After much discussion, Jay and I decided to adopt a wait-and-see attitude. While we were enthusiastic about the program, we had strong reservations about the possibility of an unwanted transfer. The '72 presidential election was almost at hand, and the situation could change drastically if McGovern was elected, although there appeared little chance of that. Too many uncertainties stood in the way of our making a decision; we had no idea who we would be targeted against, where the operation would take place, or even when it would begin. And in reality, we didn't have the slightest conception of what the deep cover assignment would involve.

Fast Freddie, our squad supervisor, kept pointing out that we shouldn't be overly concerned with the problem of transfer. He knew many of the officials at Division Five on a personal basis and felt certain that potential transfer problems could be resolved to our mutual satisfaction. He was openly enthusiastic over the prospects of the deep cover program and viewed it as the opportunity we had all been waiting for. We would finally be allowed to conduct a highly sophisticated, covert operation unhindered by the ridiculous administrative games we had been forced to play in the past. Fred was ready for us to go head to head with the underground apparatus and prove once and for all who was superior. With the full support and all the resources of the FBI behind us, he felt it was only a matter of time until the Weathermen were located. And since I had been the first Los Angeles agent to go under cover unofficially, he naturally assumed I would jump at the assignment.

I must admit that I did little to discourage this assumption, for I was personally challenged by several aspects of the work. While I felt certain that I had the knowledge, experience, and self-confidence to pull off the deep cover role successfully, I realized that unless I actually tried, I would always wonder. My competitive instincts had been aroused, and I wanted to prove to my colleagues as well as myself that I could beat the Weathermen at their own game. If they could endure the hardships of the underground, so could I. And since they were obviously committed to their goals, I would become even more committed to mine.

While the prospect of working alone and on little more than intuition seemed exciting. I was also intrigued by the intellectual challenge. After all, many of the Weatherman fugitives were about my age and were as well educated as I. What prompted their actions? How could we have grown up at the same time, in the same country, and yet have viewpoints that were diametrically opposed? I hoped I would eventually be able to answer these questions.

Looking back, I would suspect that at this particular time I was also motivated more by a sense of protectionism than patriotism. After spending years in the antiwar movement, I had come to believe that my judgment was more balanced than that of many of my colleagues. Those experiences had taught me to be more tolerant of other life-styles and to consider unpopular viewpoints with an open mind. In the past, I had trusted our nation's political leaders implicitly, never questioning their motives or sincerity. But the seeds of doubt had been sown, and my confidence was wavering. Many of the early claims made by antiwar leaders about the conduct of the war, though outlandish at the time, had turned out to be correct. And I had long since discarded the prevailing government notion that marijuana use led directly to heroin addiction. Whether justified or not, I ultimately rationalized my participation in the program by concluding that it was far better to have someone with an open mind in the deep cover role, especially when it came to drug usage, than a staunchly conservative agent who would report *every* violation, no matter how insignificant.

Kenny, a seasoned Bureau veteran with vast experience in security investigations, was selected as my handling agent. Kenny was a likable Bostonian of Irish descent who had a dry sense of humor that made him impervious to pressure from the Bureau. No matter how grim the situation, Kenny could always find the lighter side. His detailed knowledge of the inner workings of the Domestic Intelligence Division allowed him to anticipate their questions or objections in the initial communication. He was a master at the game of paper flow and could often keep investigations current without ever leaving the office. And recognizing the Bureau's dependence on routing slips, he could successfully apply that time-honored adage, "When in doubt, route!"

Now that an informant case had been formally opened and assigned to Kenny, I would be known exclusively as LA 7852-S (Extremist) in all future communications. Unless the reader was aware of deep cover, he would not have the slightest idea that the informant represented by the code name was actually an FBI agent. Since Kenny was now responsible for establishing my legend, or fictitious background, we began meeting at remote locations in the San Fernando Valley to formulate our plans.

During our recent In-Service at Quantico, it was suggested that new deep cover operatives use the same methods as the Weathermen and assume the identity of a dead infant. This was accomplished by visiting local cemetries or searching through county records for an infant born in approximately the same year as the agent, but who was no longer living. Since birth and death records were not commonly cross-referenced, an application for a duplicate birth certificate was requested in the name of the dead child. After receiving this document, other forms of identification such as library cards, fishing license, voter registration, and Social Security cards could be obtained under the new identity. It then became a relatively simple matter to obtain a driver's license, the most important document of all.

Although the dead infant procedure would provide verification in the event birth records were checked under the new identity, there were several possible pitfalls. The FBI, as well as other law-enforcement agencies, was aware that Weatherman fugitives had used this method in the past; consequently, the Bureau began cross-referencing applications for duplicate birth certificates of individuals born during a time period similar to that of the fugitives. If the cross-referencing disclosed the fact that the birth certificate requested was that of a dead infant, then an investigation would be launched to determine the identity of the applicant. In one such case, agents discovered that a white male fugitive who subsequently obtained a California driver's license, had unknowingly assumed the identity of a deceased black. But if the infant had died in another county, or preferably another state, it was virtually impossible to discover the fictitious identity.

As a practical matter, however, the dead infant method of building a fictitious identity produced an even greater problem: you had to assume the infant's full name, which usually sounded nothing like your own. I had always felt it was far wiser to retain your first name, unless it was too uncommon, and select a surname that was as close as possible to your own. While this might seem insignificant at first glance, it is important to remember that this new name must appear to have been yours from birth. That meant using it in a normal manner, answering to it without hestiation, and signing the proper signature as though it were an everyday occurrence. All this is by no means as easy as it sounds. And in my opinion, the difficulty is increased by assuming a name completely unrelated to your own.

Since I had obtained my fictitious identification several years earlier and was already known under the name of Bill Lane, Kenny and I saw no reason to assume the identity of a dead infant. And unless I applied for a passport, there seemed little likelihood that anyone would attempt to verify my birth, especially since none of the identification documents I carried noted *where* I was born.

In addition, I had secured my California driver's license without relying directly on Bureau contacts for assistance. These contacts were trusted individuals who were often asked to help on sensitive matters relating to their employment at educational institutions, businesses, public utilities, or governmental agencies. In this way another agent who had a contact at a local draft board was able to obtain blank Selective Service cards, one of which I subsequently completed and used as identification for my driver's license. Since the Department of Motor Vehicles required a residence address, I had previously located a vacant lot in Venice where a dilapidated tenement had recently been demolished. For my mailing address, I had listed a post office box which was rented by using the draft card for identification. As best we could determine, there was no possibility my identity could be compromised by a Bureau contact, and inquiries from other government agencies would only prove inconclusive.

While it was both easier and faster to rely on Bureau contacts, especially in obtaining a driver's license, it was not without risk. Instead of slowly building an identity on a piecemeal basis, studying for the written driver's examination, and taking the driving test in a car with untraceable license plates, some agents preferred to arrange an appointment through contacts at the Motor Vehicle office.

On one such occasion, a small group of undercover agents traveled from San Francisco to Sacramento to have photographs taken and obtain drivers' licenses under their chosen names. Unfortunately, they failed to consider that their hippy appearance would attract the attention of the hippies working at state licensing headquarters. And after seeing long-haired freaks receiving preferential treatment from senior officials, the employee freaks, being of somewhat radical persuasion themselves, immediately decided that these were state narcs getting phony I.D. cards. Not only did the employee freaks attempt to take pictures of the FBI freaks; they also tried to rip off copies of their license applications so they could publically reveal their false identities. Needless to say, it was not one of your more productive trips to Sacramento.

And why, one might ask, didn't the FBI Laboratory with all its technical and scientific expertise simply forge a driver's license in the agent's chosen name? Wouldn't this eliminate the entire problem of being compromised by contacts?

Once again, a clear example of lack of cooperation at Bureau head-quarters. The Laboratory Division was a semi-autonomous fiefdom whose Assistant Director determined the extent of assistance to other Divisions. In the case of fictitious identity for deep cover operatives, the matter was quite simple: there would be no assistance. In spite of the public relations hype, the prevailing sentiment of agents in the field was best summed up by a former colleague from Seattle: "Them boys in the lab couldn't find their ass with a goddammed search warrant!"

After resolving the new identity problem, Kenny began the process of documenting our legend. This involved placing phony records, with the help of Bureau contacts, to verify education, employment, and draft status under my new name. Every year of my past was to be accounted for by planting supporting documents throughout the country. For the sake of simplicity, we decided to make the legend conform as closely as possible to my actual background. But if another field office decided it was too risky to plant a transcript at a particular college or high school, then the legend would simply be changed to reflect attendance at an institution with a more "understanding" administration.

Division Five was concerned with documentation of deep cover legends since they had received information that certain underground organizations had posed as business organizations to check out suspected infiltrators. Through the use of letterhead stationery, they had made inquiries as potential employers attempting to verify résumé information. Since most educational institutions handled these requests in a routine manner, it was a simple and virtually risk-free method of corroboration.

While various offices around the country were planting records to substantiate the background of Bill Lane, Kenny and I were completing plans for my cover story. This was the most important aspect of the deep cover operation, since it was usually the first information the target received. It had to be convincing, logical, and practical; moreover, it had to be a story that the agent felt comfortable with. If both substance and presentation were convincing, there was little chance that the agent's background would be checked any further.

The development of a workable cover story involved several inherent problems. Since I would own a van and have money to permit travel, what was the source of my income? It certainly couldn't be derived from a regular job, since I had to have the flexibility to travel on a moment's notice for as long as necessary. And not only did the explanation have to be politically acceptable to my targets, it had to be in character for a freak. The solution to the dilemma was obvious: I would become a drug dealer.

By posing as a drug dealer, I could easily explain large amounts of cash as well as brief absences from time to time for business. And since there was a certain aura of mystery and intrigue surrounding drug dealers, many of whom were viewed as modern day folk heroes, I wouldn't be expected to divulge extensive information about myself. And if my gun was discovered, I had a logical explanation: occupational hazards.

While most targets would naturally be paranoid over a possible bust by undercover narcs, nearly all of them used drugs of some type. Since there were few freaks who couldn't use another connection, especially for free samples, I would be in the position of satisfying a basic counterculture need. Although there would undoubtedly be suspicion, there was also a general awareness of the laws of entrapment. I was selling, not buying—an important distinction. The very fact that I supplied, rolled, and smoked marijuana in front of my targets would further enhance my credibility as a dealer.

To make the cover story even more attractive to those in the underground, Kenny arranged to plant phony arrest records with the Los Angeles Police Department (LAPD) and the FBI. Accompanied by a contact from LAPD Intelligence, Kenny drove me to the Venice precinct where I was escorted inside wearing handcuffs. I was processed as though I had just been arrested on drug charges, and several mug shots were taken. Unnoticed by the other police officers and prisoners, Kenny changed the date on the booking board to reflect an arrest in 1970, some two years earlier. After being handcuffed again, I was led outside for the ride downtown.

If records of the LAPD were checked under my new identity, they would disclose that I had been arrested locally several times for both possession and sale of marijuana. A routine inquiry to the FBI Identification Division would turn up a similar record, although the inquiry would receive far from routine treatment. During the course of various Weatherman investigations, the Bureau had learned that a young deputy sheriff in a Western state had been requesting FBI "rap sheets." This information was then passed along to certain underground organizations who purportedly used it to check out suspected infiltrators.

In view of this startling information, the FBI Identification Division established a special procedure. In the event a request was received for a "rap sheet" on a deep cover agent, a discreet investigation would immediately be launched to determine *who* actually made the request and *why*. Similarly, the National Crime Information Center (NCIC) computer was programmed to respond that there were no outstanding warrants on the agent. But within seconds after the response was transmitted, the Domestic Intelligence Division would be notified of the inquiry. They would then telephone the FBI field office closest to the inquiring agency and order an immediate investigation.

There was another innovative procedure developed by the Identification Division, though I suspect it was more for the protection of the Bureau than the safety of the deep cover agent. The agent's actual fingerprints were placed in the "wanted" criminal files. If he was later arrested and his fingerprints submitted, the classifier would believe a wanted fugitive had been arrested under an assumed name. Officials in Domestic Intelligence would then be notified of the incident. This procedure was promoted as another safety factor for the deep cover agent, but since fingerprints were not generally received and classified until weeks after an arrest, it seemed to be a method whereby the Bureau could keep tabs on *our* behavior.

Although Kenny had made steady progress in the development of my legend and cover story, our efforts to buy a suitable vehicle had been stymied from the beginning. Even Kenny, the unflappable master of Bureau bullshit, was frustrated by the situation. Just as I had suspected, the deep cover program was receiving little assistance from officials in other divisions. Those who had been against the program from the start seemed determined to impede its implementation.

Kenny had initially requested authorization to spend up to $2,800 for a van, justifying this amount by the fact that I would be traveling to Oregon, Washington, and Canada and required a mechanically sound vehicle with camping facilities. The Bureau replied that no expenditure would be authorized until we provided the exact year, make, model, serial number, and registration of the vehicle to be purchased. There was one other small point: $2,800 was too much money.

The following days were spent reading the classified section of local newspapers, desperately searching for the right type of vehicle at the right price. It seemed as though I traveled to every corner of Los Angeles County answering ads, talking to used car dealers, and trying to make a deal. Unfortunately, the boys back at Disneyland East, or FBIHQ, couldn't seem to understand that used vans were a rather hot item in southern California. If you didn't come with cash or prearranged financing, forget it. The van would have been sold by the time you received authorization and returned to make the purchase. And to make matters worse, the Bureau refused to authorize funds for a cash deposit pending their approval.

Kenny was sympathetic to the problem, but after weeks of teletypes and telephone calls, he was still unable to convey the big picture to the Bureau.

Then President Nixon was reelected by one of the largest landslides in history, and Pat Gray's stock shot up accordingly. Within the Bureau, this was interpreted as a resounding mandate by the American people for a no-nonsense approach to law and order. Three days later, Kenny fired off a lengthy teletype proposing that I travel to northern California, Washington, and British Columbia, stopping at selected communes along the way to identify the inhabitants. He solicited comments, recommendations, and potential targets from field offices in those areas while skillfully tying the entire proposal to a request to spend $2,000 for a van.

I had already located a '69 Dodge van owned by a freak in Monrovia. It was in fairly good mechanical condition and equipped for camping. The Bureau was enthusiastic over the commune proposal, and some six days later, we received authorization to spend up to $2,000, including tax, title, and license for the van. But by the time we received the authorization, it was meaningless. When the van's registration had been checked through the Department of Motor Vehicles, Kenny found that it was actually a '68 model with a rather dubious title history. Back to the classifieds.

As the days turned into weeks, Division Five was becoming more impatient over our inability to locate a van. After lengthy deliberations, the Bureau ultimately selected the proposal of the Seattle Division. By teletype dated December 1, 1972, and bearing the unusual heading, "FROM: FOR THE ACTING DIRECTOR, FBI, W. MARK FELT, ACTING ASSOCIATE DIRECTOR," LA 7852-S (Extremist) was authorized to travel to Seattle for deep cover penetration. The last paragraph of this communication was apparently the result of a top-level power struggle over program expenditures.

INFORMANT IS NOT TO BE PLACED ON PER DIEM WHILE ON THIS ASSIGNMENT AND ONLY ACTUAL EXPENSES INCURRED ARE TO BE CLAIMED THROUGH CONFIDENTIAL FUND. IT IS

EXPECTED THAT SOURCE WILL UTILIZE THE VAN AS HIS
SLEEPING QUARTERS, HOWEVER, IT IS RECOGNIZED SOURCE
MAY PERIODICALLY NEED NORMAL ACCOMMODATIONS FOR
WHICH HE SHOULD BE REIMBURSED IN ACCORDANCE WITH
EXISTING INSTRUCTIONS IN THESE MATTERS.

Now that my destination had been determined, all I needed was a
van. Since this would be my only means of transportation as well as my
home, it was not a decision to be made hastily. Just about everything I
looked at in the authorized price range wouldn't make it back to Venice, much less to Seattle.

With the search for a van at a temporary standstill, Fast Freddie
came up with an ingenious solution. Since the Bureau had previously
approved an amount of $2,000, we could purchase a suitable vehicle
for under this figure, and regardless of its mechanical condition, authorization would be forthcoming. Once the van was bought, Fred
would prevail on the mechanics who serviced the fleet of regular Bureau cars to provide needed repairs. And since authorization was not
required for "incidental repairs," repairs could involve anything from
a minor tune-up to a complete overhaul. In other words, as soon as the
van became Bureau property, it could be totally rebuilt.

In view of the fact that I was now considered an informant rather
than a Special Agent, Fred decided that the rules for informant expenditures should apply. This meant that amounts up to $500 could be ob-
tained from the office's confidential fund for necessary expenses. What
could be more necessary, we reasoned, than expenses for converting a
regular van into a camper? Such expenses were justifiable especially
since I was expected to live in the van and would not receive the usual
per diem allowance. As long as individual purchases were under $500,
specific Bureau authorization was not required.

Early one Saturday morning, I rushed out to Granada Hills to look at
a '70 Ford Supervan that was advertised for the first time. Having become an expert on van models, I realized that this particular body
style was perfect for my needs. It had a slightly longer wheelbase than
the regular models, providing more room in the rear living area. And
according to the ad, the van had a V-8 engine with an automatic transmission. After years of driving an underpowered VW van and having
to shift gears constantly during rush hour traffic, I considered automatic transmission a major attraction.

The van belonged to an affluent-looking, middle-aged man who used it in his carpet business. After a brief conversation on his front porch, he reluctantly gave me the keys for a test drive. It was obvious that he was apprehensive about my appearance, but then he also wanted to sell the van, and I was the first customer of the day.

The vehicle had faded to a pale blue and was undoubtedly the most basic model ever produced by Ford. With the exception of the broken cigarette lighter, there were no extra cost options. It was just your plain-vanilla, economy-model work truck with only two seats and plenty of room for hauling bulky rolls of carpeting. This austerity was to my advantage, since the absence of windows in the side or rear doors would allow me to park in urban areas and sleep in back in complete privacy. A makeshift set of curtains could be strung behind the front seat for total seclusion.

Although the engine started properly, the fact that the vehicle pulled sharply to the left required an unusual compensation in steering to prevent its crashing into oncoming traffic. Perhaps this was due in part to the tires, I thought, since an earlier inspection had revealed no visible sign of any remaining tread. But with new tires and a thorough once over by Bureau mechanics, it ought to run well enough.

We agreed on a price of $1,875 and I gave the gentleman $200 of my own money as a deposit. After verifying the registration information and obtaining verbal authorization from Washington, I returned with a pocketful of crisp hundred-dollar bills. The seller was both elated and suspicious at the sight of the money; nevertheless, he quickly counted it, signed over the title, and I was on my way.

While the mechanics at the Bureau were working on the van, I was busy locating the materials necessary for converting the rear area into living quarters. After having examined so many customized vans during my lengthy search, I knew what I wanted to build, although I had little idea exactly *how* I would build it.

I soon discovered that without having the van for measurement purposes, I didn't know in what amounts to buy construction materials. This minor delay gave me the opportunity to take care of the registration problems. With the voluminous rules and regulations governing every facet of Bureau affairs, I was amazed to learn that I would be allowed to register the van under my fictitious identity. Since most of our rules seemed to be founded on the principle that agents couldn't be trusted, it was ironic that the Bureau would spend $2,000 for a vehicle, then allow it to be registered under the name of someone who did not exist.

One problem overlooked by Division Five officials, however, was that of auto insurance. After questioning the Justice Department, they received an opinion advising that vehicles purchased and driven by deep cover agents, even though registered under fictitious identities, would be considered government-owned vehicles in case of accident; therefore, insurance by a private company was unnecessary. But if I was involved in an accident, how in the world would I ever explain that this hippy van was a government vehicle? And what if my targets were riding with me? Even the victim of a minor fender dent would ask for the name of my insurance company.

Recognizing the validity of this argument, Division Five agreed to authorize expenditures for automobile insurance under our fictitious identities. A simple solution? Hardly. The Bureau overlooked the fact that insurance companies don't just write policies for anyone who walks through the door—particularly for a freak in his late twenties with a new driver's license, no driving record, and no current employment. If anyone ever had a good reason to be suspicious of our background, it was the insurance companies. After all, how many male applicants learn to drive, obtain a license, and buy their first car at age twenty-nine?

Our previous experiences with leased vehicles ruled out any possibility of explaining the true nature of the situation. After a number of rejections, we learned that you just couldn't level with the insurance companies—not if you expected to receive a policy. The slightest mention of undercover agents in undercover vehicles seemed to conjure up thoughts of shoot-outs, collisions, property damage, and massive lawsuits involving endless litigation.

The problem was finally solved by imposing on the insurance agent who handled my own auto coverage. I provided only the barest of details, but he could tell from my appearance, not to mention my false identification and registration, that *something* was up. Since he was aware of my employment, he was discreet enough to refrain from asking any specific questions. To this day, I'm not certain how he pulled it off, but I later received a policy from the country's largest insurance company in the name of Bill Lane, self-employed photographer.

After nine days in the Bureau garage, the mechanical work was completed. Except for the color, I could hardly believe it was the same van. New tires, battery, generator, starter, shocks, and tune-up. Since the garage maintained an inventory of Ford parts for the regular Bureau cars, it was obvious that no expense had been spared.

Inspired by the work of the mechanics, I plunged into the task of equipping the van for living and smuggling. Since the rear cargo area was exposed sheet metal, I decided to panel the sides and top with a thin, pliable balsa wood. This was accomplished by drilling hundreds of small holes in the structural support braces, then using sheet metal screws to attach the wood in panels. Before mounting the panels, fiberglass insulation was glued to the top and sides for warmth. I used heavy lumber to construct long rectangular boxes over both wheelwells so that the hinged tops could be padlocked for storage while also doubling as benches.

After stapling foam padding to the wooden floor and bench tops, the real challenge began. I had bought a large roll of shag carpeting with the idea of covering all the surfaces in the rear area in one continuous piece. The carpeting would start up one side, run across the ceiling, and down the other side. Carpeting for the floor, bench tops, and rear doors would then be cut to match. I planned to attach the carpet to the wood panels by using a staple gun. By placing the staples at the base of the shag, they would not be visible.

The idea seemed simple enough, but the installation was another matter. Balancing a heavy roll of carpeting on my head while stapling under my feet in near darkness proved a bit awkward. It took only about five days of labor, forty thousand staples, and a swollen right hand to get the damn thing installed. But it did look great. The overall effect was of a subterranean cavern lined in dark gold shag.

I had decided to use the bottom portion of the side and rear doors as hiding places for my drug supply. Instead of cutting a single piece of wood the exact size of the doors, I installed two panels, each with its own set of screws. A single piece of carpeting was then stapled to each door panel. To gain access, I would simply rip out the staples holding the bottom portion of carpeting, unscrew the lower wood panel, and reach inside the metal door. After replacing the panel, I would use the staple gun hidden in the storage bench to attach the carpeting. It would take a good amount of time and a discreet location to get to my stash, but you would literally have to tear the van part to find it.

I bought a large chest of drawers in raw wood which fit perfectly against the rear doors. After a coat of brown paint and the installation of latches to keep the drawers from sliding open, it was anchored to the hinges of the rear doors, which locked from the inside. If anyone wanted to check those panels for contraband, they would have to move the massive chest wedged into the back between the storage benches. But to accomplish this, the mattress that was pushed against the chest had to be removed first. It would be a formidable, time-consuming task which I hoped would deter even the most inquisitive police officers.

A small refrigerator was bolted to the floor behind the driver's seat. Fred had arranged to have the office radio technicians wire the unit, which was powered by an auxiliary battery located in the adjacent storage compartment. By placing diodes in the wiring system, the engine could charge the auxiliary battery, but the refrigerator would be prevented from draining the main battery.

I managed to convince Lucky, my intermittent girl friend from down the beach, to sew curtains for the van. She was one of the few women fully aware of the nature of my undercover employment, and while never fully convinced that my actions were appropriate, or even necessary, she was always patient and understanding. She was also one of the most intelligent women I have ever known. Although a Phi Beta Kappa with two degrees, she chose to commute hours each day in order to teach school near Watts. Perhaps it was this association with tough, street-wise kids from the inner city that allowed her to lay things right on the line.

"I must be crazy to make these curtains," Lucky remarked as we measured the opening. "I'm just making it easier for you to hustle all that young puss! Now you've got a van with a bed in back . . . Payne's puss palace! I must be losing it." Lucky was smiling as she feigned indignation, but we both knew she was correct.

By the time she finished the curtains, which were made of an exotic Indian batik, the van was nearly completed. I bought a catalytic heater, propane tank, and sleeping bag from a local discount store. And after thinking about the many miles of driving, I decided to buy an eight-track tape deck complete with FM radio, at my own expense. With two speakers mounted up front and two in the living area, it provided a dynamite sound.

With Christmas, New Year's Eve, and the Super Bowl out of the way, I was eager to get going. My credentials, badge, revolver, and all of my personal identification were placed in a safety-deposit box. I was Bill Lane now—a wild-eyed freak who lived on the road in a van full of drugs. But assembling my stash had been no simple matter.

Shortly before Christmas, the local office had contacted the U.S. Customs Service and requested they furnish the FBI "two kilos of marijuana and a quarter-pound of hashish" for a special assignment. A letter of confirmation was then prepared to verify the telephone conversation, but the official request was abruptly withdrawn. Since there was increased speculation during this period that Nixon was about to merge Customs and possibly the Drug Enforcement Agency into the FBI, someone decided that Customs could not be trusted with such a sensitive request.

According to the explanation I received, the Bureau was afraid that customs officials might subsequently use the request to blackmail the FBI. I haven't the slightest idea how this would take place, but I was instructed to buy what I needed from my sources on the street. Since there would be absolutely no cooperation between agencies, I was forced to rely on my own contacts for supplies.

After spending the weekend packing, storing provisions, and securing my stash in the door compartment, I was ready to depart on the long-awaited journey. Monday, January 22, 1973 turned out to be a picture-perfect day for a drive up the California coastline.

Joe picked me up around ten, and we drove over to the Marina to meet Jay, Rodent, and Panda for breakfast. After so many delays, I was eager to get moving, but I realized more than ever that the days ahead would be lonely without my friends. We had worked, traveled, and practically lived with each other for months, in some cases, for years, and I'm sure we had become more mutually dependent than we cared to admit.

We returned to the apartment after a lengthy breakfast, and I checked over my gear for the last time. I experienced a strange feeling as we shook hands and said good-bye, for we had no idea when we would see each other again. It was the type of warm, sincere parting that only close friends who have shared adversity together can understand. Everything out front. So long, good luck, take care of yourself, keep in touch, and by all means, cover your ass!

I jumped into the van as my friends headed for their cars in the beachfront parking lot. Well, this is it, I thought. Here I come, Seattle, ready or not. I turned the ignition key in the Ford. Nothing. Not even a click. I turned it again. Same song, second verse. Incredible, I thought, absolutely incredible. The van had just been checked out by the Bureau mechanics on Friday, and I had been assured it was mechaically perfect. Apparently they forgot to check the ignition.

I yelled at Joe as he was turning the corner and was fortunate to catch his attention. He backed up, and I quickly explained the problem. Joe was laughing so hard he could barely talk as he pulled out the radio mike from under the front seat.

"Joe to Rodent."

"Go ahead, Joe," Rodent responded.

"It seems as though C has a minor problem with his ten thousand dollar van. It won't start!"

I could hear Rodent and Jay howling wildly. "You gotta be kiddin'," Rodent said. "We'll be right there."

"Ten-four," replied Joe. He replaced the mike and parked his van. "You may have just made the shortest deep cover trip in history, C," he said. Somehow I was not amused.

After a cursory inspection of the engine compartment, Joe diagnosed the problem: dead battery. He gave me a jump start and the van fired right up. It was obvious that the electrical wizards in the radio shop had not wired the refrigerator correctly. Either that or the diodes were defective, because the refrigerator had completely drained the auxiliary and engine batteries.

By the time the Bureau garage charged the dead battery and checked out the electrical system, it was nearly four o'clock. The radio technicians could find nothing wrong with the diodes, refrigerator, or wiring, which made me a bit nervous, but I was assured that I would have no further problems. What the hell, I thought, might as well leave right now. I didn't want to go through all the good-byes again, and the battery needed a better charge anyway.

With Jerry Jeff Walker appropriately singing about those "L.A. Freeways," I joined the thousands of rush hour commuters who were inching their way toward the San Fernando Valley. I passed Ventura just as the sun was setting, and the drive along the coast was incredible. The Channel Islands loomed crystal clear on the horizon, and the ocean was peacefully calm. How many times I had driven this road over the past years! Only this time, I wouldn't be stopping in Isla Vista.

The rugged coastline north of Isla Vista was illuminated by a full moon. The waves had grown larger and seemed to sparkle in the moonlight as they crashed against the shore. There was little traffic on the highway, and it was a perfect night for driving. An hour or so later, I stopped in San Louis Obispo for dinner. Since Cal Poly was located in the city, it also seemed like a good place to spend the night. Vans would attract little attention around the university area, and I certainly didn't want to get hassled on the first night in my new home.

Shortly before midnight, I located a fairly dark street near the campus and parked among several cars and trucks. I crawled into the back, pulled the curtains, and unrolled my sleeping bag. This was to be the first of many, many nights in the van; unfortunately, it was not one of the better ones.

A major problem was immediately apparent; I had parked the van on a slight incline. Within seconds, the blood began rushing toward my head. After several minutes of misery, I reversed my position, allowing the blood to rush to my toes. Unable to sleep either way, I decided that the only solution was to get dressed and move to level ground. This time I paid more attention to the terrain.

I awoke early the next morning feeling stiff, tired, and frozen. My discount store sleeping bag had been a miserable failure the first night out. I had no idea it would get so cold in the van, especially after installing fiberglass insulation. And if it was this cold in California, how would I ever survive in Canada? But there was no time to dwell on the temperature. I had to find a bathroom.

I stopped at a coffee shop near the Interstate for breakfast and a welcome rest stop. It was a routine that would be repeated over and over again on my travels across country. Sit down, order breakfast, head for the men's room, take care of business, then cautiously remove my toothbrush, toothpaste, and hair brush from my fatigue jacket. These matters of personal hygiene had to be conducted rather hastily to avoid detection by the management or other customers. And as one might expect, freaks who brushed their teeth in the men's room were not exactly looked upon with favor.

I made an unofficial stop in San Francisco to visit with Walrus and Buddha. How great it was to see those two crazies again! They looked even more outrageous than I remembered. I was somewhat disturbed, however, to learn that both of them had decided against taking a deep cover assignment. Like the Panda, they felt it would demand too many personal sacrifices and expose them to the likelihood of an unwanted transfer away from San Francisco. Both had agreed to remain in undercover status until the office could locate suitable replacements, which they hoped would be soon.

The Walrus was working as a dishwasher in a delicatessen, trying to get next to a cook who was a close friend of several Weatherman fugitives. For a guy who used to be able to eat deli food six meals a day and still be hungry, the Walrus was a changed man. After weeks of pearl-diving, he claimed he could no longer stand the thought, much less the smell, of chopped liver, pastrami, corned beef, and other kosher goodies. When I saw him decline an offer of cheesecake that evening, I knew it had indeed been a trying experience.

Buddha was working undercover as a part-time stock clerk in a small Haight-Ashbury grocery store. Several Weatherman supporters lived in the immediate area and frequently dropped by the store to use the pay phone. As one might expect, Buddha diligently worked the stock next to the telephone when these targets made calls.

Both Walrus and Buddha were understandably miffed about a recent directive regarding their undercover employment. I suppose some eight-to-five, desk-bound genius at the Bureau had nothing better to do than make life more difficult for agents in the field. Whatever the case, the communication serves as a good example of what we were forced to contend with.

IN CONNECTION WITH UNDERCOVER OPERATIONS OF AGENT PERSONNEL, FROM TIME TO TIME IT MAY BE NECESSARY FOR SECURITY PURPOSES, FOR THESE AGENTS UNDER THEIR ASSUMED NAMES (COVER IDENTITIES) TO GAIN EMPLOYMENT. TO INSURE THAT FEDERAL AND LOCAL TAX LAWS ARE ADHERED TO, THE FOLLOWING PROCEDURES ARE TO BE TAKEN TO THESE MATTERS. WITHHOLDING TAX IS TO BE TAKEN OUT OF WAGES CONSISTENT WITH FEDERAL AND LOCAL REGULATIONS. A FEDERAL AND STATE TAX RETURN WHEN DUE, IS TO BE FILED UNDER AGENT'S ASSUMED IDENTITY.

WAGES EARNED BY AGENT IN THESE ASSIGNMENTS SHOULD BE PLACED IN CASH (NO CHECKS OR COVER IDENTITY REFERENCE) IN HIS OWN PERSONAL CHECKING ACCOUNT AND HE SHOULD PREPARE A CHECK IN THIS AMOUNT UNDER HIS TRUE IDENTITY PAYABLE TO TREASURER OF THE UNITED STATES. A COVER COMMUNICATION IS TO BE SUBMITTED WITH CHECK UNDER TRUE NAME CAPTION OF AGENT. THIS COMMUNICATION WILL STATE THAT IN CONNECTION WITH HIS OFFICIAL DUTIES CAPTIONED AGENT RECEIVED $ . . . . ON . . . DATE . . . ATTACHED IS A CHECK FOR THIS AMOUNT FROM CAPTIONED AGENT TO TREASURER OF THE UNITED STATES. THE SAME PROCEDURE WOULD BE USED UPON REFUND OF ANY TAXES PAID UNDER COVER IDENTITY. COPIES OF ALL TAX FORMS SUBMITTED IN THESE OPERATIONS ARE TO BE MAINTAINED IN THE APPROPRIATE FIELD ONE THIRTY FOUR FILE ON THE SOURCE INVOLVED ALONG WITH MATERIAL PERTAINING TO ANY REFUNDS.

I jokingly told my colleagues that it was merely a case of poor job selection on their part. After all, drug dealers don't normally pay state
and federal taxes! But as far as Walrus and Buddha were concerned,
both the I.R.S. and the state of California would receive their fair
share.

After a night of revelry, we embarked on a counterculture tour of
San Francisco the following day. Packed into a '59 VW bus that could
barely negotiate some of the city's steeper hills, we cruised by many of
the former locations of the Weathermen. My friends also pointed out
several nearby apartments that were maintained by the Bureau for
surveillance purposes. I was amazed at how the character of the area
had changed over the past few years. Freaks were still visible on the
streets, but the atmosphere was a far cry from the psychedelic days of
the flower generation. The colorful costumes of those espousing peace
and brotherly love had been replaced by the drab rags of junkies concerned only with urban survival.

I was curious to see what changes had taken place in Berkeley, but
Buddha refused to go anywhere near the Bay Bridge. He had once
maintained an apartment in Berkeley where he occasionally lived under a fictitious identity. Several employees of a leading underground
newspaper lived in the same apartment house, and Buddha hoped to
get to know them. Because of other investigations, he was frequently
absent for days at a time. Like most of us, he found it extremely difficult to spend night after night in a dingy apartment in Berkeley when
he could jump in his van, cross the bridge and sleep in his own apartment in the city.

He returned to the Berkeley apartment one morning to be confronted by an enraged group of residents and several of their equally enraged friends. According to Buddha, it was immediately apparent that
the group had two goals in mind: to take his photograph for publication in the underground paper and to stomp his ass. When they burst
into his apartment yelling and cursing, he realized he was in trouble.
But when he noticed them waving his telephone bill, he knew it was
time to beat a hasty retreat before they discovered his true identity.
He made a speedy exit down the stairs, ran out of the building, jumped
in his van, and left Berkeley—never to return as a freak.

It seems that Buddha had become careless. Like other unofficial hippies of the period that preceeded deep cover, he was still bound by the
archaic rules of the Bureau. Unless an agent was in radio contact, he
was required to call the office every two hours to check for messages
or priority investigations.

Instead of leaving the apartment several times a day to search for a pay phone, Buddha had used the telephone in his room. When his neighbors became suspicious, they began to steal his mail from the apartment mailbox. As luck would have it, they ripped off his telephone bill and began calling all of the message unit numbers in the metropolitan area. And guess which long distance number on the bill had been called time and time again? That's right, folks, the San Francisco office of the FBI.

10

Seattle and Sex

Bright and early the next morning it was back to the van. The Seattle Division had indicated that there was no need to stop at any communes along the way since their Weatherman investigations had been progressing rapidly. Division Five therefore ordered me to report directly to Seattle. But there was one minor problem. After sitting for two days on the streets of San Francisco, the van wouldn't start. Both batteries were completely, totally, and unequivocally dead. As the electronic wizards in L.A. had said, "There's nothing to worry about. Everything's in perfect mechanical condition."

After a jump start from Walrus and a six-hour wait in a recreational vehicle service center, I was back on the road. For $29.95 I got a battery charge and another expert opinion that "Everything looks fine." Since no one could locate the problem with the refrigerator, I decided the safest procedure was to turn it off.

I was especially careful that evening about where I was going to park the van. I pulled off Interstate 5 at Redding, California and cruised the city for some time before finding a shopping center with a service station on one corner. I parked directly behind the station, since I felt there was a strong possibility the battery would require another charge come morning. If the damn thing wouldn't start, I didn't want to be parked on some quiet residential street and have to explain what I was doing there.

Around midnight, I was awakened by the slam of a car door followed by the unmistakable sound of a police radio crackling through the night air. When I raised my head slightly, I saw the reflection of a red light bouncing rhythmically off the passenger window. A glaring ray of light illuminated the curtains as the officer held his flashlight against the windshield, trying to peer inside. The van swayed slightly as he checked both doors. Apparently satisfied that the van had been parked for the night, he returned to his squad car and drove away. Since there were a few other vehicles parked nearby, he probably thought the van had been left for mechanical repairs. But between the interruptions and the weather, I was having a difficult time sleeping. My outlook was greatly improved the following morning, when the van started.

Back on the Interstate. Welcome to Oregon. If this is Sunday night, it must be Eugene. Another delightful evening spent freezing in the van at a dormitory parking lot on the University of Oregon campus. If the past few days were any indication, I was certain that living in a van in a city would be a tremendous bore. I couldn't turn on the interior lights to read, nor could I listen to music without attracting attention, and there was no one to talk to. About all I could do was think warm and hope for better times.

Late the following evening, I rolled over the last hill of darkness and saw the breathtaking panorama of the lights of Seattle. With the Rolling Stones tape going at full blast, it seemed the perfect time to fire up a joint for my triumphant return to the city. The combination of Mick Jagger, marijuana, and the sparkling lights of Seattle almost made me think I was coming in for an instrument landing on an Interstate runway. The memories of my previous year in Seattle flashed through my brain: my first field office, the agents I had worked with, the taverns in Madison Park, the people I had met, and a girl named Wade. It was a great feeling to be returning to the city which had provided so many wonderful experiences.

As I neared the downtown area, I couldn't resist a swing through the city. I turned on Madison Street and drove down the steep hill to Elliott Bay. The waterfront was just as I remembered and the taverns along Pioneer Square were doing a thriving business. I stopped at an isolated parking lot under the Alaskan Way viaduct to relieve myself and noticed that there were still plenty of winos stumbling down the grass embankment from the bars along First Street. Time had changed nothing in this section of the city.

Even though it was after midnight, I wandered around the downtown area for nearly an hour before deciding to drive out toward the University.

After a full day and night of driving, I was beat. I turned north off of Forty-fifth Street into an area of older houses rented primarily by university students. There were several vans and trucks on the well-lighted street, and this seemed as inconspicuous a location as any. The only available parking space was just off a corner intersection, right under a glaring streetlight. It shone through the thin curtains, but I was so tired, it didn't seem to matter. I quickly undressed, unrolled the sleeping bag, wriggled inside, and zipped it all the way up to ward off the January cold.

Sleep came swiftly. It was a peaceful, relaxing slumber, my first really sound sleep in days. I was soon dreaming that I was lying atop a rubber air mattress on Lake Washington, just outside my old apartment near Leschi Park. As a boat would pass by, its wake would gently rock the mattress from side to side as the water rolled toward the shore. But the rocking was becoming more pronounced, more violent. Must be a helluva boat to cause a wake like this, I thought.

"Ummph," came a muffled groan from outside the van, almost as though someone were straining.

Shit, this is no dream! Some idiots outside are leaning on the van, rocking the damn thing back and forth. And in the middle of the goddammed night, no less. I was still drowsy and wishing I could continue my dream. Oh well, I figured, they'll soon go away, and I can get back to sleep.

Snap! The piercing sound of breaking metal reverberated through the van. The front vent windows! My fuzzy brain finally developed the big picture: some bastard's trying to break in!

I fumbled with the zipper on the sleeping bag, trying to pull it down far enough to squirm out. Where did I leave the flashlight? It's got to be on the floor nearby, somewhere in all this junk. And where in the shit's my gun? Adrenaline and fear ran through my body. Don't panic, dammit, think. Bottom drawer of the chest, under some clothes. But I would have to hold the mattress up to allow room for the drawer to slide open. I scrambled around silently on my knees, yanked the mattress up on one end and held it with my body while I searched frantically through the drawer.

Suddenly, I heard the unmistakable sound of the door-lock button being pulled up, followed by the unlatching of the front door mechanism.

Son of a bitch, I thought. While I was floating around in dreamland, someone had broken into the van. I quickly located my Walther automatic and turned to face the front of the van. My left knee landed on the missing flashlight. I crouched down slightly, gun in my right hand, flashlight in my left, and not one stitch of clothes on. As the passenger door swung open, I cocked the hammer of the automatic.

I was wide awake now, and my heart was about to pound out of my chest as I tried to decide what to do. There was only a split second to think, but for some strange reason, I knew that I didn't want to blow some half-assed car burglar away unless I had to. And if there was any shooting, both my identity and the deep cover program would be revealed.

Then another thought bolted through my mind: what if *he* has a gun!

I could see the head and shoulders of the burglar silhouetted against the streetlight as he cautiously slipped into the passenger seat. He paused momentarily, then turned to crawl between the seats into the rear of the van.

This is it, I thought. I hope to hell I don't kill him.

My left arm was extended straight out in front with my thumb positioned on the flashlight switch. My right hand felt clammy as it held the gun close to my body, aiming at the narrow passageway between the seats. As he crawled through the curtains, I flicked on the flashlight, blinding him with light from less than a foot away.

It was over in an instant. The burglar nearly tore his head off trying to get out of the van and trampled his partner outside in the process. The next thing I saw was two black dudes setting a new world's record in the fifty-yard dash. They flashed by the van's windshield like tracer bullets as they ran through the intersection and into the darkness of an alley. In their haste, they dropped a large crowbar that had been used to pry open the window frame. I hurriedly dressed and drove several miles from the area, not wanting to risk the possibility that they might return.

Sleep did not come so easily the second time. It was hard to say who had been more frightened, them or me. I had never even considered the possibility of having the van burglarized, especially on a well-lighted residential street, and with me *inside*; likewise, they had never considered that someone would be sleeping in the van during the middle of winter.

My first night of deep cover in Seattle had indeed been an eventful one. Needless to say, I never spent another night in the van without a gun and flashlight right by my side.

The following morning, I telephoned the local FBI office and talked with Stu, who was to act as my handling agent. I had known Stu during my earlier assignment in Seattle, although he had arrived only a few months before my transfer to Los Angeles. While we were never close friends, I had been impressed by his energy, enthusiasm, and dedication. He was a few years my senior, married, and had three children.

His smile and his Southern accent were always present. I remembered him as a conscientious agent who didn't mind working long hours to get the job done. I hoped the intervening years hadn't changed his outlook.

We scheduled a meeting for noon in a public parking area across the street from Elliott Bay. Stu would be accompanied by Harry, the security squad supervisor who was in charge of Weatherman investigations. They would walk down to the waterfront from the office on Second Street and we would talk in the van.

When I drove past the Federal Reserve Building where the FBI was located, I noticed a couple of veteran agents from the fugitive squad standing on the street corner. Two authentic Bureau heavies, I thought, recalling the many arrests we had made together. They walked right in front of the van as I stopped for the traffic light and made no attempt to disguise their hostility at yet another California hippy invading the city. If looks could kill, I would have been in serious trouble. How strange it seemed to see my old agent friends after all these years and be unable to talk with them. And how strangely they regarded me now that I didn't look like one of them. I was beginning to realize that I would be treated quite differently on this visit to Seattle.

I spotted Stu and Harry as they strolled through the parking lot during the noon rush hour. With the Seattle Ferry Terminal and a number of waterfront restaurants across the street, the area was usually crowded. Although they had license plate numbers and a description of the van, they seemed reluctant to approach me until I flashed a broad smile of recognition and unlocked the passenger door. I crawled into the rear area as they opened the door.

"Jesus Christ!" Stu exclaimed as he climbed in. "I don't believe it. I just don't believe it. You look great, Cril." Stu shook my hand warmly. "I wouldn't have recognized you in a million years."

Harry struggled through the narrow opening between the seats, snagging his coat in the process. Being a squad supervisor, he didn't usually have to crawl around on his hands and knees. "Good to see you again, Cril," he said, reaching out to shake my hand. I could tell that Harry was shocked. He just stared at me with a perplexed look on his face. "My god," he finally said, "how long has your hair been growing? You look more like a hippy than the real hippies. I'd never guess it was the same agent who was here a few years ago. Would you, Stu?"

Stu was unable to answer because we were both cracking up at Harry's genuine amazement. Since he seldom worked the streets, I'm sure he had had only limited exposure to freaks. But whatever the case, it was apparent that Harry wasn't expecting me to look so outrageously realistic.

They were most impressed with the van conversion and sleeping facilities until I related the events of the previous evening. All of a sudden, living in a van wasn't such a simple matter. Like me, they had never considered the possibility of a van burglary with the owner asleep inside. But the mangled vent window provided graphic evidence of the unexpected. The entire frame would have to be replaced before the van could be locked securely. Since I would be needing money from the confidential fund, I mentioned another priority item: a new sleeping bag. If these were to be my sleeping quarters, I didn't care to freeze my ass off each night.

Harry suggested that I spend a few days in an outlying motel so that agents assigned to Weatherman cases could brief me on their investigations. After several sleepless nights in the van, I accepted his suggestion readily. They had located a small motel just off Interstate 90 near Issaquah, Washington. Since it was a substantial distance from Seattle, there was little possibility of running into potential targets.

While I had been excited about the prospects of working undercover in Seattle, and possibly in Canada, I was a bit apprehensive about how the Special Agent In Charge (SAC) would view the assignment. Having worked for him before, I knew he was a stern disciplinarian in the finest Hoover tradition. He ruled the office with an iron hand through the time-honored devices of fear and intimidation. While we had never been involved in a major confrontation, the SAC made no secret of his attitude toward single agents. He seemed to view them as walking time bombs whose free spending, carousing, and after-hours activities could easily embarrass the Bureau—and him.

Like most SAC's, he realized that statistical accomplishments were the name of the game. Steady increases in categories such as fines, savings, recoveries, arrests, and convictions were what kept a SAC a SAC. Under J. Edgar Hoover, if the stats went down, the SAC was likely to go down with them, occasionally not stopping until he reached the bricks. Since security investigations produced few, if any, statistics, many SAC's refused to assign sufficient manpower to those squads. Pat Gray had supposedly changed that practice by making the Weatherman fugitives a top priority and directing that more agents be assigned to those investigations. It remained to be seen if the SAC's would comply with these directives.

When I questioned Harry about this matter, he said that the SAC was one hundred percent behind the deep cover program. He went on to say that the SAC had been most cooperative and was vitally interested in the deep cover program, so interested that he wanted to meet with me that very afternoon. I wasn't sure whether this was good news or bad. Stu would smuggle me into the basement of the Federal Reserve Building for a three o'clock meeting.

It was eerie sneaking back into the building where I once had worked. Stu pulled the green panel truck into the alley just off Spring Street at the rear entrance of the fortress-like building. I crouched motionless in the back. A uniformed guard behind a bulletproof glass enclosure immediately recognized the truck, since it was usually parked in the basement, waved at Stu, and pressed a button allowing the massive steel doors to roll up. Stu drove through the opening and toward a concrete ramp as the doors banged shut behind us.

Inside the basement there were several armored cars backed to a loading dock. Armed guards moved large bags of money around as if they were sacks of potatoes. Other guards looked on nonchalantly as they held sawed-off shotguns in the ready position.

On another level, there was a limited number of underground parking spaces for high-ranking Federal Reserve officials and for three FBI emergency vehicles. Stu parked the truck in its assigned space and went to check out the labyrinthine hallways. Finding everything in order, he returned to the truck, opened the door, and I scrambled out. We hurried down the dimly lit passageway that housed the building's mechanical section. As we rounded the corner of a steel boiler, we ran smack into the Bureau radio technician whose workshop was just down the hall. I had known the guy fairly well during my earlier assignment, but it was obvious he didn't recognize me now. He probably wanted to question Stu about his bizarre companion, but we never slowed down or looked back until we reached a small corner room that was used as the office photo lab. Stu locked the door and immediately telephoned Harry and the SAC to notify them of our arrival.

A short time later, Stu responded to a sharp rap on the door and J. Earl Milnes, Special Agent In Charge of the Seattle Division, strode purposefully into the small room. Milnes was a large, barrel-chested man with big hands and a powerful grip. For a man in his fifties, he was in surprisingly good physical condition. He wore glasses, had a slightly receding hairline, and a wry, disarming smile which had earned him the nickname of the Smiling Surgeon among office veterans. According to the old-timers, he could cut an agent to ribbons while grinning from ear to ear. The many stories of how he punished recalcitrant agents through transfers, squad reassignments, and delayed pay raises were legendary. But while he was feared for his misuse of authority, he was also respected for his leadership ability.

Milnes seemed to go out of his way to be cordial. He professed a strong interest in the deep cover program and was most appreciative of my assistance. He pledged his full cooperation while also voicing concern for my safety and well-being. Taken at face value, the man's attitude couldn't have been more supportive. I wanted to believe his assurances were sincere; nevertheless, I remained somewhat skeptical.

Although our meeting with the SAC was amicable, he made certain that everyone present knew exactly who was in charge of the deep cover operation. In that regard, he enumerated several guidelines pertaining to my activities in the Seattle Division. I was not to contact any of the agents I had previously worked with, and my presence in Seattle was to be kept on a strict need-to-know basis. Milnes knew I had many good friends in the office, and he specifically cautioned me against contacting them. The same prohibition held true for friends outside the Bureau, especially former girl friends. Under no circumstances was I to contact anyone who had known me as Cril Payne. In fact, he suggested that Stu and Harry refrain from using that name and refer to me exclusively as Bill Layne.

As the meeting was about to conclude, Milnes added another requirement. He wanted to see me on a regular basis, perhaps once a month, in order to review our progress and assess my physical and psychological condition. I felt like saying that it was obvious I was crazy or I wouldn't be here in the first place; however, I managed to keep my thoughts to myself. I realized that it was only another part of the game we were all playing. After lengthy tenure as a SAC, Milnes was well aware that the most important aspect of Bureau survival was to cover your ass.

The following days were filled with briefings by Stu, Harry, and the handful of agents assigned to Weatherman investigations. They presented profiles on local activists which typically included information on their residence, employment, associates, and extent of political involvement. The majority of this information had been obtained through background investigation, surveillance, and informant coverage. Most profiles contained the subject's photograph, often cross-referenced to photographs of known associates. License numbers and vehicle descriptions were filed the same way.

We discussed the various communes, collectives, and political organizations in the area, both aboveground and underground. Particular emphasis was given to the Students for a Democratic Society (SDS) as well as the Seattle Seven, a group of University District war resisters who stood trial in 1971 for an alleged assault on the federal court house in Seattle. Based on investigation and surveillance, agents offered their own theories about which individuals or groups might be in contact with the Weathermen.

We initially held these sessions in my motel room at Issaquah, but after the manager became suspicious of the frequent visitors, Stu rented a conference room at the Holiday Inn near Bellevue. He advised the management that he was conducting training seminars for new employees of a market research firm. These employees would allegedly be going from door to door with questionnaires on the marketability of a new detergent. This cover story was used to explain the disparity in the appearance of those attending the meetings.

Toward the end of the week, we began to focus our attention on potential targets for deep cover penetration. During a morning coffee break, Stu mentioned that Harry wanted to speak to me privately when the meeting adjourned. I had noticed that Harry seemed more nervous than usual, although he was always inclined to worry.

After the other agents left for lunch, Stu closed the hall door, and the three of us moved our chairs to the far corner of the room. Something was definitely bothering Harry, but he appeared uncertain as to how to approach the matter. I was sure that it involved me.

"Say, Bill," Harry began in a soft, confidential voice, "did you know a girl named Tracey Everett when you were here before?"

"Yeah, I sure did."

A perplexed look came over Harry's face. "Did you know her well?" he asked.

Hell, yeah, I thought. Real well, Like *intimately* well. "Fairly well, Harry," I said matter-of-factly. "I used to go out with her some when I was assigned here."

Harry's eyes grew wide as saucers. His face was flushed and contorted. "Oh, no," he whispered painfully.

"Jesus, Harry, she was straight as hell when I dated her. In fact, another agent here introduced me to her. She was a naive little Southern belle from Georgia. Very proper, and a little slow. I used to call her 'Spacey Tracey'."

"Son of a bitch," Harry muttered. "Of all the luck. I knew we shouldn't have opened that broad up." Both Harry's anger and the volume of his voice were building steadily. "That goddammed Johnson.

Him and his female informants. I knew she was gonna be trouble."

"You mean she's an informant?" I asked incredulously. Harry nodded his head silently in the affirmative. "A security informant?" I continued. "What the hell could she tell you?"

"She joined a revolutionary group," Stu interjected.

"One of Johnson's harebrained ideas," Harry added. "I knew it was wrong from the start."

"Wait a minute, Harry," I interrupted. "Let me get this straight. You mean to tell me Tracey's a 134 informant and she's infiltrated a revolutionary group?"

"That's right," he said gloomily. "But that's not all. She worked it for over a year. Then Johnson was transferred and Abbott took over the case. Then it was reassigned to Miller. She got totally out of control and started making all sorts of demands. Said she would tell everything—about how she spied for the FBI and was paid to infiltrate political groups. I told 'em to cut her loose, not to go near her." Harry looked ill. "She's gone over to the other side, Bill. She's joined nearly every radical group around, and we don't even pay her. She's a convert—no doubt about it."

I was dumbfounded. The whole thing sounded impossible. Spacey Tracey a security informant? Forget it. She was straight, conservative, and completely nonpolitical. The idea was simply preposterous. It was as if J. Edgar Hoover had just told me that my mother was president of the Communist Party. "You mean she's *really* into the radical trip?"

"You better believe she's into it," Stu answered quickly. "And there's a damn good chance you might run into her. Could she identify you?"

Only without my clothes on, I thought. "No way," I said emphatically. "She wouldn't recognize me in a million years. Hell, my parents don't even recognize me anymore." I hadn't come all this way for nothing, and I was concerned that Harry might feel obligated to tell the Bureau. He was a real stickler for following each and every rule to the letter. "I'll just have to keep on my toes and be on the lookout for her. If she heard my voice, I could have problems. She might pick up on my accent. I'll just split if I run into her."

"I don't know, Bill," Harry said cautiously. "It's taking too big a chance. If you were identified and we hadn't told the Bureau, the entire program could be compromised. Maybe I should take it up with Earl."

"I don't think we need to bother the boss with it, Harry." Stu could see trouble on the horizon and was coming to my rescue. "Chances are Bill won't even run into her. I don't think she'd recognize him anyway. It's been over three years. Let's just see what happens, and if things get tight, we can pull him out."

Harry reluctantly agreed to take no further action, at least for the present time. He was certainly not one to make unnecessary waves, especially with Division Five. I'm sure he realized that the result would only be more delays and the distinct possibility that Seattle might never receive a deep cover operative. Nevertheless, it was mutually understood that we had a potential problem on our hands. And I would definitely be on the lookout for my old friend Spacey Tracey in the days to come.

"Mornin', Stu."

"Well good morning, Bill," Stu replied cheerfully. "Boy, am I glad you called in. We need to get together right away. I've got some promising news on the location of our friends up north."

"Terrific! It's about time we got a break. I can be downtown in thirty minutes. Wanna meet in the same place?"

"No, we'd better change," he said. "How about the Sears parking lot, down the street. You remember where it is?"

"Not really, Stu, but I'm sure I can find it."

"Just head south on First Avenue. It's on the right-hand side, about a half mile before you hit Spokane Street."

"Oh yeah, I remember. How does eleven o'clock sound?"

"That's fine," he answered. "I'll be driving the green panel truck. We can talk in back."

"Okay, great. I'll be lookin' for you."

After driving around downtown Seattle to clean myself, I quickly located the Sears store, arriving some twenty minutes early. A casual swing through the massive parking lot revealed nothing out of the ordinary, and I parked among several other cars near the store's main entrance.

The panel truck appeared shortly before eleven. Stu cruised the parking lot, observing both the cars and the people. He cast a vacant, unrecognizing glance in my direction, parked several rows away, then strolled into the store. After watching the entrance for a few minutes, I followed.

Stu was standing near the front, rummaging through the men's shirts while discreetly observing everyone entering the store. I walked on past him and over to the sporting-goods department to look at camping equipment. A short time later, Stu was examining the saltwater fishing reels.

We often used large retail stores like Sears for clandestine informant meetings since they were frequented by a wide variety of customers and were usually crowded. Long hair attracted little attention, and by leapfrogging through the store as shoppers, we could readily observe each other as well as anyone who might be following. It was also not uncommon to position a third agent in the parking lot to watch our cars.

Stu wandered aimlessly throughout the store, often stopping abruptly, turning, then retracing his steps before moving on to another department. Satisfied that he had successfully cleaned himself, he walked casually toward the front door. I waited for a few more minutes to give him time to reach the panel truck and make radio contact with the agent positioned outside. If the outside man had spotted a problem, or if Stu just didn't like the look of things, he would simply drive off, and the meeting would be cancelled.

As I walked out into the parking lot, Stu returned a knowing glance, then moved into the rear compartment of his truck. I opened the door on the driver's side as if it were my own vehicle, briefly checked out the parking lot, then crawled back to join Stu. The floor of the truck was carpeted to prevent noise, and two folding lawn chairs were set up. Since the van was used for photographic surveillances, black drop cloths could be pulled over every opening, making it impossible to see what was inside. Stu was pouring steaming coffee from a thermos into Styrofoam cups.

"I'll have two over easy, please, with a side order of sausage and whole wheat toast."

Stu smiled broadly and passed me a cup. "The grill's not open yet. How about black coffee and a day-old donut?" He produced a crumpled bag of donuts left from a previous surveillance, and we munched away.

"What's up?" I inquired between gulps.

"Well Bill, I think we may finally have the break we've been looking for." It was obvious from Stu's expression that he was excited by the news. "I went up to Whidbey Island yesterday to debrief a new informant," he continued. "A friend of mine in Naval Intelligence put me on to her. The girl's in the navy, a WAVE, and she's stationed at the Whidbey Island base. She'll be discharged in less than a year, and she

187

In 1968, as a member of the New Agents Class at the FBI Academy, I was recently out of a Texas law school with all my patriotic ideals and provincial ideas intact. Conservatively garbed and barbered, clear-eyed and confident, I am the very model of a modern FBI man. Less than four years later, I had transformed myself into the bonny, brawny lad with the golden tresses. Our undercover group, known as The Beards, caused considerable consternation when we turned up at the Miami office for special briefings in connection with our coverage of the 1972 nominating conventions. It was in this "hippy freak" disguise that I was severely beaten and subsequently arrested by the Miami police.

I first sure
damn' looked like Angel!
↓ matching mustaches

When one of our undercover colleagues
left the FBI to take up the practice of
law, The Beards gave him this memento.
The photo was taken after hours in the
LA office, where we posed for
posterity—and for possible future
documentation of our existence—under
the baleful glances of Attorney General
Mitchell, President Nixon, and J. Edgar
Hoover himself. I seem to be especially
pleased by my sandals.

190

This mug shot, backdated to 1970 as part of a complicated scenario involving my supposed association with the Weathermen, was being shown by FBI agents in Seattle with the notation that I was "wanted" for political crimes as well as for assaulting a police officer at the Republican National Convention in Miami. I now had a "legitimate" explanation for being a "fugitive" in Canada.

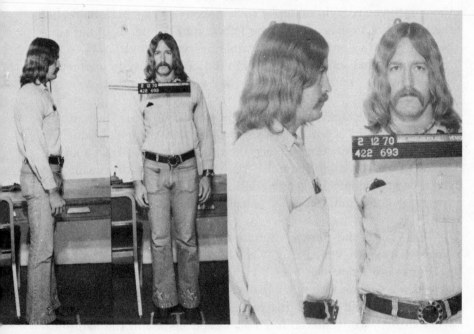

approached my friend about working for the government. Seems she has a stepbrother who's a Selective Service fugitive and former activist. He's living in a hippy commune in Canada, just north of Vancouver. Well, she started writing to the guy, and last weekend traveled to the commune to see him. As best I can tell from talking to the Royal Canadian Mounted Police (RCMP), it's a place we've both been interested in for some time. Special L says Weatherman support people from Toronto have visited the commune, but they don't know who's actually living there. But get this, Bill. They think there's a damn good chance Cameron David Bishop may be hiding there."

"Did your girl identify anybody up there?" I asked.

"No positive I.D.'s," Stu replied, "but several possible look-alikes. I showed her the whole Weatherman album, plus several other photos of missing support people believed to be living in Canada. She did manage to get some license plate numbers, and we're checking them out now. But get this. *Visitors* are supposed to be coming to the commune this weekend. Her stepbrother invited her back because Monday is Washington's Birthday, and she has a three-day weekend. She says these visitors are some of his old political friends from the States who now live in Canada. And another interesting point. She says there's a log cabin about a hundred yards behind the main house that's built right in the middle of the forest. You can't even see the damn thing until you're right on top of it. Somebody's living back there, but she never got to eyeball 'em. She knows they're friends of her stepbrother, but they never came out while she was around."

"Shit, Stu, that sounds like a great shot!" It was easy to understand why he was so excited. "I'd love to have a look inside that cabin myself."

"Well, that's exactly what we had in mind," he said. "I've already talked to the girl about it. Her stepbrother said she could bring her boyfriend along next time. In fact, she thinks it would attract a lot less attention and be more natural if she did go back with a man. And you'd be in a helluva lot better position to eyeball the residents. Once you get to know 'em, you could go back on your own if it looks productive."

"Yeah, but is the Bureau gonna let me go into Canada?" I asked. "And what are we gonna tell the chick?"

"Harry and I talked it over last night," Stu began, "We think the best idea is for me to tell her that you're another Bureau informant, just like she is. I'll tell her that since you can identify several of the Weathermen, we want you to go along and help with the identifications. You can drive up in your van and give 'em the story about being a drug dealer and political fugitive. It'll also be a great opportunity to see if she's telling the truth and really wants to work for us."

"That's okay with me, Stu, but will the Bureau buy it?"

"Well, the only problem I see is that she's still on active duty with the navy, and they'll raise hell about our making her an informant. Plus she's a woman, and that'll scare the living shit out of 'em. But I'll find a way to cover that with my buddy in Naval Intelligence. Maybe call it a joint operation or something. Give 'em the impression that she's really *their* informant. Write it up as a naval request for Bureau cooperation. I think they'll let you go into Canada if they believe we can locate a 'Top Ten,' and Bishop's been on there a helluva long time."

"You're the paper man, Stu. Whatever you think best. I'll let you and Harry handle the creative writing. What's our next move?"

"I'll go back to the office and get a teletype out to the Bu. She'll have to leave for Canada Friday afternoon after work. That gives the Bureau less than two days to make a decision. We'll go up to Whidbey tomorrow and talk with her, then if all goes well, you two will leave the following afternoon. You remember where Mount Vernon is, on the way to Bellingham?"

"Sure I remember."

"Okay. Go through Mount Vernon and pull over about a mile north of town. I'll meet you there at noon tomorrow and you can follow me on over to Whidbey. I'll talk with the girl tonight."

"Okay Stu, but does this chick know anything about radical politics?"

"Not a thing," he replied. "But she's giving her stepbrother the impression that she hates the navy, which is probably true, and that she's against the war and the establishment."

"How about drugs?" I inquired.

"I don't know, Bill. She mentioned they smoked pot in the commune, and it didn't seem to bother her to talk about it. But I have no way of knowing if she uses anything else. You can find out about that when you meet her." Stu began groping for his black vinyl briefcase to replace his notes. "Well, I better get back and work on that teletype."

"One more thing, Stu," I said. "What's this chick look like?"

Stu broke into his deep-South, moon-pie, shit-eatin' grin. "Well, Bill," he drawled, "she's nothing like you used to date when you were a regular agent 'round here, but she's not ugly either. I mean, she's attractive, a little heavy maybe, but seems to be a real bright girl. I think you two'll get along just fine."

"Yeah, right. Just fine. Okay," I said with resignation, "see you in Mount Vernon."

I decided to spend the remainder of the day scouting around for a good location in which to park the van each night. Aside from the break-in my first night in town, the biggest problem I had encountered with my mobile living accommodations was the recurring "call of nature." I had experienced little difficulty finding rest-room facilities while traveling cross-country since I usually needed gas anyway. But once in the city, it was a completely different story. One did not stop and piss at will on a residential street—not unless one wanted to go to jail.

It was funny to note how infuriated most gas station attendants became at the thought of some dirty, long-haired hippy trying to cop a free pee at *their* station. No sir, no way. If you don't buy gas, and it better be a fill-up, you don't get to piss. And of course no toiletry articles are allowed inside the restroom. "Whaddaya think this is, a goddammed hotel?" After level terrain, close proximity to a bathroom became the second most important consideration when looking for a place to park the van at night.

Since I would be heading north the following morning, I drove up Interstate 5 past the university area toward the outskirts of Seattle. I eventually spotted a large motel complex just off the west side of the freeway. There was a twenty-four-hour restaurant to the right of the motel and a Texaco service station off to the left. Since most of the parking spaces for motel guests were located behind the three-story structure, they couldn't be seen from the street. The rear of the parking lot was bordered by a high concrete retaining wall that made it virtually impossible to look through the windshield into the van. There were even two telephone booths located in front of the station.

The motel provided another unaccustomed luxury: ice. Since self-service ice machines were located on each floor, the evening cocktail hour could be conducted in fine style. And when nature called, I could discreetly amble over for a quick piss without even being seen by the service station attendants. It seemed the perfect place for the urban van dweller: discreet location, level terrain, rest room, telephone, and ice-maker.

As I passed through Mount Vernon the following morning, I noticed Stu at a service station, filling up the Bureau car. A short time later, he joined me a few miles outside of town.

"You ready to go north?" he questioned.

"You bet," I replied. "Any word from the Bu yet?"

"No, not yet. I just got the teletype off last night; it'll probably be to-morrow before we know. I talked with Jeannie last night though."

"Is that the chick?"

"Uh-huh. One thing I better warn you about. She mentioned that the other girls in the commune would most likely ask her what kind of a lay you were. And since you're supposed to be her boyfriend and all, she says you two better get to know each other real well before you go up there. Otherwise, she's afraid they might not believe her story. She said they'll want to know all the details of your sex life."

"You gotta be shittin' me, man!"

"No, really, Bill, that's what she said."

"You mean to tell me I gotta service the chick just to pose as her boyfriend? Amazing, man. Absolutely fucking amazing. This really is the new Bu."

"Well, just look at it this way," Stu said, struggling to keep from laughing, "you're doing it for your country."

"Yeah, right, man, for my country. Like put a flag over her face and hump for Old Glory, huh."

I followed Stu over the narrow, two-lane highway which headed west toward Whidbey Island. As we neared the naval facility, he flashed a prearranged signal for me to pull over and wait while he entered the base to pick up his new informant. A short time later, he sped past the van and motioned for me to follow. We traveled several miles down a winding asphalt road until he stopped at a small frame house. I drove on past, turned around, then parked where I could observe his car.

Several minutes later, he backed out of the drive and drove off toward the base again. He then turned onto a small dirt road and traveled for some twenty-five minutes through the forest. Stu finally pulled off the road and parked in a small clearing which provided a commanding view of the route we had just traveled. I had absolutely no idea where we were, but it certainly was remote.

I parked the van about ten yards behind the Bureau car and waited anxiously while Stu and Jeannie engaged in animated conversation. I still hadn't seen my new girl friend and was growing more apprehensive about the deal by the minute. Finally, the doors of the Bureau car swung open, and Stu and Jeannie came walking back toward the van.

A *little* heavy! Is that what he said? If that stupid bastard thought this chick was a *little* heavy, I'd sure as hell hate to see one that's *over-*

weight! I mean, like, she hadn't missed a meal in years. Maybe a life-time.

The lady was rather short, not more than five feet, and constructed like a Coke bottle, with most of her ample poundage located below the waist. Her brown hair was worn short in tight curls that called attention to her round, cherubic face. Attempts at counterculture involvement were indicated by her wire-rimmed granny glasses, her jeans, and a blue denim work shirt.

Stu could see the horror in my eyes as the two of them walked toward the van. He was grinning from ear to ear, trying hard to maintain his composure. I climbed out of the van to face the music.

"Bill, this is Jeannie," Stu muttered quickly. "Jeannie, meet Bill."

"Hi, Jeannie," I responded while looking away from Stu. "It's nice to meet you. I've heard a lot about you."

"And I've heard a lot about you," she replied, flashing a warm, knowing smile.

Son of a bitch, I thought. Stu's probably pumped this gal so full of shit about me, I'll never live it down. And knowing him, he's described me as a three-speed sex machine.

"Well, I'd better get on back to Seattle," Stu interjected. "You two can spend some time together and get to know each other. Jeannie can fill you in on the commune and what to expect up there. Better get your stories straight as to how you met, how long you've dated, and so on. And Jeannie, be sure to give Bill a rundown on your stepbrother and what he's been involved in."

"We'll get it all worked out before we leave, Stu," I said with a note of confidence. "No sweat."

"Okay, but remember, Bill, be sure to call me in Seattle before you leave tomorrow afternoon. I've explained to Jeannie that because of your legal problems, you can't go into Canada without approval from Washington. I think we'll get it, but it'll be my ass if you go without authorization."

Jeannie and I followed Stu back to the highway, then turned in the opposite direction. We stopped at a store near the base and bought a couple of six-packs, then drove around the island. It was obvious that while Jeannie had only recently been exposed to the so-called hippy life-style, she was intrigued with what she saw. From what she told me, she had traveled down the straight and narrow path. But her experience in the navy had not been a happy one, and she was more than ready to move on to something new and exciting. She was fascinated by the idea of living in a van with all one's worldly possessions right at hand, ready to roll on down the highway at a moment's notice. My adopted life-style appeared to represent all of the freedom the daily regimentation of naval life had denied her.

Jeannie was totally oblivious to revolutionary ideologies or the issues of women's liberation, and I knew right away she could never assume the role of a revolutionary woman. But she was bright, friendly, and open-minded, and her innocence would produce credibility. She sincerely wanted to become a part of this new counterculture or at least find out for herself what it involved. Although she was the type who could walk down a crowded city street without receiving a second glance, the inner person was warm, gentle, and remarkably forthright.

We drove around the island for hours, drinking beer and rapping about her background, family, and stepbrother. I soon learned that Stu had failed to inform me of another small matter. Jeannie was married to a guy in the navy. According to her, the infatuation was short-lived, and the relationship had deteriorated quickly. Her husband was away on sea duty, and she saw no compelling reason to seek a divorce, at least not until he returned; nevertheless, the marriage was over as far as she was concerned.

Perhaps it was my instinct for self-preservation, but I was somewhat concerned about why Jeannie wanted to become a government informant, especially against a relative she admired. Judging from our conversations, she really didn't know the answer herself. But she did want out of the navy, and the sooner the better. She seemed to feel that working for the FBI would provide a good income and the possibility of an early discharge. She wanted to believe that patriotism was also a factor, but I think that for the first time in her life, she felt the kind of excitement that gives a special meaning to living. Here was something new and different, and it sure as hell beat the boring routine of navy life.

But while Jeannie may have been uncertain about her motives, she was inquisitive about mine.

"How long have you been working for Stu?" she inquired.

"Oh, on and off for a couple of years, I guess."

"He seems like a pretty nice fellow, but then he's the only FBI agent I've ever met."

"Yeah, Stu's a good dude," I said. "He'll shoot you straight. No bullshit, you know. But that don't mean they're all like that. Some of those dudes can get you blown away if you're not goddamn careful. Always remember that. You and me, we're on different sides from those dudes, and don't ever forget it. Always cover *your* ass first, then worry about gettin' the shit *they* want."

"Is the pay good?"

"It beats workin' for a livin'," I answered, "but you ain't gonna get rich doin' it. Sometimes it's a piece of cake, other times it's a real ball-buster."

"Well, why do *you* do it then?" she shot back.

"Partly for the bread, but mostly 'cause ol' Stu got my nuts in a big vise and can squeeze 'em any time he wants."

"Oh, you mean the drug thing? He told me you'd been busted for dealing."

"Right. But what he didn't tell you was I got popped again by the federal narcs a year ago. The whole goddammed buy was a fuckin' set-up, man, like they were waitin' for us. Anyway, next thing I know, Stu's rappin' on my brain 'bout workin' for the FBI. The fuckin' feds are all freaked out over the antiwar movement and all the Weather-man bombings, not to mention communes and underground newspa-pers. So he lays it out for me. I help him, he helps me. If I do a good job, the narcs'll just forget the whole thing. If I don't, or if Stu gets pissed at me, they'll file the federal charges and my state probation from the first bust'll be revoked. So when you get right down to it, I ain't got a helluva lotta choice."

"That's terrible," Jeannie remarked. "How long do you have to work for them?"

"Until Stu decides I've paid my dues, I guess. Shit, I don't know. But I'll tell you one thing: it sure as hell beats jail. I'd rather live in a van any day. Besides that, a man still finds time to do a little dealin' every once in a while."

Jeannie threw her head back and laughed heartily. "I've got some pot back at the house. Want to go get it?"

"That is not the least big necessary, my dear, for I just happen to have an ample supply right here. Just step back into the master bed-room and get the little tin box out of the top right-hand drawer."

I fired up a joint as Jeannie opened the last beer. After driving around the island for hours, I had absolutely no idea where we were. Jeannie directed me to a narrow dirt road that looked as though it had been used for logging operations. We traveled several miles through the dense forest until we suddenly came upon a small clearing, reveal-ing a beautiful blue lake. The area was peaceful and deserted; so we drove around the lake and parked where the road dead-ended, just a few yards away from the water.

I retrieved a half-gallon bottle of red wine from my supply box, and we both took a hefty belt. Rock music blared out of the stereo speakers as we sat there in the wilderness talking, smoking dope, and drinking wine. It sure beat driving and seemed as good a place as any to determine how my new girl friend would react to grass. Better to find out now than the next day, I thought, when we'd be sitting around in a remote commune in Canada.

The sun was setting above the shimmering water as I returned to the van from my second visit to the nearby woods. How uncomplicated life was in the wilderness. Just step out of the van, breathe the crisp, clean air, and piss away. Not a disgruntled service station attendant for miles!

As I opened the front door, my eyes instantly focused on Jeannie's wire-rimmed glasses which were carefully positioned on top of the engine cover. No sign of Jeannie, but the wine bottle was missing, the curtains were partially pulled, and Eric Clapton's guitar was belting out "Layla" at around 105 decibles.

I closed the door and glanced anxiously through the batik curtains into the shadows of the rear of the van. Jeannie was lying on top of the mattress, completely nude. The clothes she had been wearing lay neatly arranged on the floor. In the darkness, her folds of milky-white skin seemed to be covered with fluorescent paint. My first impression was of a young whale that had been beached and was now lying quietly, trying to preserve its energy. I mean, the lady had looked *big* with her clothes on, but with nothing on, she was *enormous!*

Now I had always been an admirer of fine, foxy young ladies. But never, never had I seen a woman this large without clothes on. It certainly wasn't her fault, but it sure as hell shocked me.

I fired up another joint, thinking I could smoke her pretty, and hurriedly pondered the situation. After all, we were going to pose as lovers. And what the hell, we both worked for the same government, not to mention the fact that we were stoned out of our gourds on grass purchased with government money!

Another pertinent fact suddenly emerged. It had been an unusually long, dry spell for me. I locked both doors and moved into the back, unbuttoning clothes along the way.

"I thought you'd never get here," Jeannie whispered softly.

I took a generous swig from the wine bottle and passed her the joint.

"Well, if I'd only known what was waitin', I'd been here a lot sooner."

Jeannie raised up partially from the mattress, her small round breasts looking strangely out of proportion with the rest of her body. "I know the girls in Canada will ask me about this beautiful cock," she said, deftly stroking the object of her affection. "They'd know for sure if I tried to lie. Besides, we'll know and trust each other a lot better."

"For sure," I replied with a smile. "If you can't trust your dealer, who can you trust!"

For the next hour or so we kissed, caressed, fondled, stroked, copulated, rotated, ejaculated. In short, we balled our brains out. The lady truly seemed to enjoy herself, and I must admit, so did I. She could reach intense levels of excitement without ever breaking stride.

Later that evening, we slowly made our way back to town and picked up a pizza. After all the physical activity, I was famished. We drove back to Jeannie's house, ate, drank a few more beers, and smoked some of her hash. Before I could even reload the pipe, the lady had unzipped my fly and was struggling with the belt buckle. In seconds, we were both naked, bodies entwined on the ancient couch, and right back where we started. This time, Jeannie was even more passionate, screaming with delight.

Shortly after midnight, I crawled outside to the van parked in Jeannie's driveway. She had insisted that I sleep with her, but I was concerned that someone might come in, like her husband, and be most unhappy about my presence. And for all I knew, the guy could be living on Whidbey Island instead of on a ship. In addition, I figured that the chances of my getting any sleep were two: slim and none. If the last ten hours were any indication, Jeannie would not only need, but demand more attention. I was totally exhausted and realized that the next day would require many hours of driving.

It was near freezing in the van as I placed my weary body in the new mummy bag and fell fast asleep. It seemed as though I had scarcely rolled over when I heard a sharp rap on the front door and turned to see the first rays of sunlight filtering through the windshield. I struggled out of the sleeping bag and peered cautiously through the curtains It was Jeannie, dressed in her white navy uniform and ready for work.

"Hi, Bill," she said warmly while climbing into the van. "How you feeling this morning?"

"Tired, man, like *real* tired." I hurriedly crawled back to the mattress and the warmth of the down-filled bag. "What time is it anyway?"

"Almost six-thirty," she answered.

"Jesus Christ, I don't know how you're gonna make it to work. I'm fuckin' beat. You really gave me a workout last night. I probably got a negative sperm count!"

"That's ridiculous," she said, reaching into the sleeping bag. "This cock was hard as a rock last night."

"Yeah, but that was last night," I answered, "and many, many climaxes ago." Thank god the lady has to go to work, I thought. "See, ol' Jake's still asleep."

Jeannie smiled coyly and removed her glasses. She threw back the top of the sleeping bag and slithered down for a closer inspection. "Well, I'll bet he'll be wide awake after I finish sucking him," she whispered.

As it turned out, the lady was right. Absolutely right. Some service in the Whidbey Island hotel, I thought. But could my body possibly survive four more days with this lady?

"Ummh, such a nice breakfast," she remarked with a big smile, "and you said there were no sperms! Here's the key to the house. Go in and make yourself at home. Gotta run. I'll be back after two."

"Okay. Have a good day," I yelled halfheartedly as she slammed the van door. Thank god for the navy, I thought, and quickly returned to a peaceful slumber.

By three o'clock, the van was packed and we were ready to leave. I stopped at a telephone booth near the naval base, and Jeannie waited in the van while I called Stu in Seattle.

"Will you accept a collect call from a Mr. Bill Lane?" the operator inquired.

"Yes I will, operator," Stu replied.

"Hey, asshole," I said without giving Stu a chance to interrupt. "I damn near had to crawl into the phone booth, I'm so fuckin' tired. This chick's turned me every way but loose. Up, down, and around. The navy must be keepin' her locked up in a cell somewhere, isolated from all the sailors. Son of a bitch! Anyway, we're ready to head out. What's the word?"

"The Bu won't let you go," Stu said timidly. There was a deafening silence on the line.

"You got to be shittin' me, man. I mean, why? What's the problem?"

"They're afraid she might compromise you. Since she hasn't worked for us before, they're afraid she might tell her stepbrother you're an informant. Then the whole project would be blown. I'm really sorry, Bill, but there's nothing I can do. They still want her to make the trip though. Better let me talk to her and explain things. You try to get her on the road, then come back to Seattle."

"Okay, Stu," I said dejectedly. I knew there was no use arguing with him over a decision made at Bureau headquarters. I pushed open the folding glass doors and hollered for Jeannie to come to the phone. She had an apprehensive look on her face as she reached for the receiver. I walked back to the van and watched from the outside mirror as Jeannie and Stu talked. It was obvious from her expression that she was unhappy, and she gave the door a resounding slam upon her return.

"Shit, Bill, it's stupid! Damn stupid! I don't see why you can't go with me. Besides, I'm too tired to drive all that way by myself."

"Yeah, I know, I don't understand it either. Stu says they're afraid the Mounties will check me through the computer when we cross the border, and I'll get arrested again. Hell, I don't know. He may be right, but I sure did wanta go."

"Well, fuck it then!" she shouted. "I'm not going without you. Let's just stay here and spend the weekend together. There's a lot we can do around here."

"Believe me, honey, I'd love to. But when Stu finds out that you didn't go to Canada 'cause we stayed together, he'll have my ass in a sling. I just can't risk pissin' him off right now. Anyway, he says they need me back in Seattle for a job this weekend."

We headed back toward Jeannie's house, passing through the naval base and down the winding asphalt highway. She said little during our brief journey, but she did become reconciled to the fact that she would have to leave for Canada, though not until early the following morning. After unloading her bags from the van, we sat on the ragged couch, sharing the last beer left in the refrigerator.

"Couldn't you just stay here tonight?" Jeannie pleaded. "Stu won't know when I leave for Canada anyway. I've been thinking about you all day, and I was really looking forward to our trip." Her right hand slid adroitly to my crotch and began moving in a rhythmic, stroking motion.

"You know I'd like to, Jeannie, but I just can't chance it. Stu wants to see me tonight, and if he gets pissed, it's back to jail."

"Well, when will I see you again?" she asked softly, never once missing a stroke.

"Soon, I hope, real soon. You talk to Stu, and I'll do the same. Try to get him to let us work together. We'll make it to Canada yet."

It was well into evening when I finally arrived at my newfound home in the motel parking lot. I mustered up enough energy to walk over to the ice machine, filled a small cooler, then returned quietly to the van. After pouring myself a hefty scotch, I unrolled the sleeping bag and prepared to crash.

As I sat alone in the chilly darkness, I couldn't help thinking about what had happened during the last two days. I didn't feel at all guilty about deceiving Jeannie or about having sex with her. At that time, I simply wasn't enlightened enough to realize that I had exploited a lonely woman who hoped that I could provide the freedom she so desperately needed. And it never entered my mind that she might suffer emotionally from that brief, intense encounter. This was my job, I rationalized, and Jeannie was merely the means to an end.

As I reviewed the events that had taken place, there was little doubt that I had learned an important lesson. Although I had been to bed with a number of beautiful women over the years, I somehow always equated physical beauty with sexual performance. Jeannie had successfully destroyed that myth. Perhaps less attractive women try harder to provide sexual satisfaction, but whatever the case, the lady had definitely changed my way of thinking.

Although I wasn't particularly bothered by *my* actions with Jeannie, I was deeply disturbed by the actions of the Bureau. With such a golden opportunity to visit an important commune accompanied by a lady who was already accepted by the inhabitants, why had they refused authorization? Wasn't this the very purpose of the deep cover program? If not, why was I living under a fictitious identity in a freezing van crammed full of drugs? And moreover, why was the scenario with Jeannie staged in the first place?

Many months later, when I finally saw the Seattle teletype requesting travel authorization, the riddle was solved: the Bureau had been told that Jeannie, who was identified only by an informant symbol number, was a *male*! Since this was a new informant of unproven reliability, Division Five could see no valid reason for allowing two *men* to visit a Canadian commune together, especially since both were ostensibly informants for the FBI. They were concerned that a new, untested informant might expose *me* as an informant while we were at the commune. The end result would be as devastating as if I'd been identified as an actual agent.

Based solely on the information provided, the Bureau made a sound decision in denying the request. But in reality, Jeannie was already convinced I was a fellow-informant when the decision was received. In effect then, the damage had already been done, for Jeannie could just as easily expose me in Seattle as in Canada.

The foregoing situation seems to underscore the bizarre communications gap which has historically existed between agents in the field and supervisors at Bureau headquarters. While field agents were under intense pressure to locate the missing Weatherman fugitives, they were ever-mindful that many of the antiquated rules, regulations, and prejudices of the Hoover era were still the order of the day. Even though Pat Gray had become Acting Director, all were aware that the Bureau was still run by the handful of Assistant Directors who, after spending their entire careers under J. Edgar Hoover, were committed to preserving the status quo. Many senior officials seemed to consider it an act of disloyalty even to suggest that certain long-standing policies were no longer appropriate.

This is not to imply that the Seattle agents were remiss in not providing the Bureau with all the facts. They simply realized that if they disclosed the full story, there wasn't a chance in hell that the Bureau would approve their plan. The Bureau was demanding positive results, but only on its own terms. In other words, no operation would be approved if there was the slightest possibility that it might tarnish the FBI's image of infallibility.

Since there was a stringent requirement that informants work exclusively for the FBI and have no contact with other state or federal agencies, how could Seattle possibly reveal that Jeannie was on active duty in the navy? To do so would have required formal notification to Naval Intelligence of the scope and purpose of the operation; consequently, the Bureau would be in the unaccustomed position of giving information rather than receiving it.

To complicate matters further, the Bureau would discover that Jeannie was a woman as soon as her service records were obtained. There seemed to have been an innate prejudice against using women as informants since they were generally considered emotionally unsuited for such work. During the Hoover regime, female employees were tolerated only to perform the boring clerical functions required to keep Bureau paper flowing. The prevailing attitude seemed to be that it was perfectly all right to bullshit 'em and ball 'em; just don't tell 'em any secrets.

Later that week I checked in with Stu and learned that I had an urgent message to contact Fast Freddie in Los Angeles. Stu mentioned that it sounded important; so I placed the call from the same phone booth. I felt a twinge of nostalgia upon hearing the familiar voice of Linda, our secretary, answer "Squad Nineteen." After a brief though informative chat, she put Fred on the line.

"Well, hello, C," Fred said cheerfully. "How you doing up there?"

"Fine, Boss, just fine," I said. "How you?"

"Great. Couldn't be better. Fighting the usual paper battle, but that's nothing new. Everything going okay?"

"Yeah, pretty good. I guess Stu told you we had a little problem with the Bu over goin' north. I can't figure those guys out back there, boss. They're livin' in an ivory tower."

"I heard about it," Fred said dejectedly. "Sounds like they're all afraid to take responsibility for a decision. Maybe it'll get better. It's got to."

"How things in the Marina?" I asked. "Any women beatin' on the doors tryin' to get in and ravish your body?"

Fred laughed. "No, they must know you're out of town, C. But I'll do my best to entertain any that drop by. By the way, that's one reason I called. You know a girl named Tracey?"

Oh shit, I thought. This was beginning to sound like a bad dream. And more and more people seemed to be joining in. "Yeah, I know her. Spacey Tracey."

"Said her name was Tracey Everett. She called your apartment the other night and I answered. Is she an old girl friend or something?"

"Not exactly, boss. I used to see her occasionally when I worked in Seattle, but I haven't seen or heard from her since I moved to L.A."

"Well, she sure seems to know a lot about you," Fred said emphatically. "She asked if you were still in the FBI. I was evasive as hell about where you were, but she was damn persistent. In face, she's a real wise-ass. Wouldn't take no for an answer. I had a hard time getting rid of her. She left a number for you to call, but I told her I had no idea when I'd see you. When I noticed the area code was in Seattle, I got a little nervous."

"I haven't seen that chick in years, boss. How the fuck did she get my unlisted phone number?"

"She must have got it from your mother, because she mentioned she'd talked with her. I think that's why she didn't believe me. She kept saying that your mother said you were in L.A."

"I can't believe my mother would give her my unlisted number. Especially over the phone. I've cautioned her about that. She won't even give it to friends from college without checking with me first. But Tra-

cey did know I was from Denton. She probably called information and
got my parents' telephone number."

"What do you want me to tell her if she calls back?"

"Don't tell her a goddammed thing, boss. Just bullshit her again. Did
you mention this story to Harry or Stu?"

"No, why?"

"Because that straight little Southern belle I used to go out with has
become a kick-ass revolutionary. Some agent opened her as an informant a couple years back and got her to join some radical groups. The
word from the guys on the squad is that the case agent was screwing
her on a regular basis. He got transferred, she got pissed, and the shit
hit the fan. She's gone over to the other side and making all sorts of
threats about exposing the Bureau."

"You sure know how to pick 'em, C."

"Well, when I picked this one, she was as all-American as apple pie.
They fucked her up, not me."

"Do you think she's spotted you around town?"

"Not really, Boss. I haven't been out that much yet. We spent over a
week on briefings; then I went up to Whidbey Island on Stu's fiasco. I
know she couldn't recognize me, but she'd probably pick up on my accent. For the life of me I don't know why she'd be calling after three
years."

"It beats me, but you better watch yourself. She might be on to
you."

"Okay, look. Let's keep this between us. Harry'll go wild if he finds
out she called my unlisted number in L.A. I'll call my mother right
now and get the full story. And I'll make certain she doesn't give out
any more information. You put another line on Tracey if she calls back.
Then contact me."

"All right, C, but you watch yourself, understand? Don't take any
chances. And stay in touch."

I immediately called home and talked with my mother. Just as suspected, that sweet little Georgia peach had done the "yes ma'am," "no
ma'am" routine and thrown in enough facts about my employment in
her down-home Southern drawl to charm my mother into giving her
the phone number.

Tracey had given my mother the impression that I had provided her
with their Texas phone number so that she would always have a way of
reaching me. I wasn't altogether surprised, for Tracey was a crafty
and very determined young lady. It suddenly dawned on me that she

had tried to check up on me by calling the office, my apartment, and several of my favorite watering holes several years earlier. But the basic question remained: why was she calling me now? After more than three years of silence! And why was she so determined to find out where I was and what I was doing? Was it mere coincidence that her interests were suddenly revived two weeks after I returned to Seattle? But even if she had seen me, how could she possibly have recognized me? Surely I would have recognized her. Or would I? Perhaps her appearance had changed as dramatically as mine.

11

Deep Cover:
(I Make the Right Connections)

To the casual observer, there was nothing particularly distinctive about the exterior of the Red Sun Tavern. Located near the University District, the Red Sun had large tinted windows that looked out on a major traffic artery. Since the four-lane thoroughfare was always congested, parking was not permitted in front of the establishment. Space could usually be located on one of the nearby residential streets, necessitating a chilly walk in the winter drizzle.

There was one unique aspect about the entrance to the Red Sun, which went unnoticed by those who frequented it. On many nights, this entrance served as a backdrop for the surveillance photographs that were snapped by FBI agents across the street. Inside the surveillance truck parked well away from the tavern, agents used a Bessler Topcon camera with a five-hundred-millimeter telephoto lens to photograph customers entering and leaving. High-speed recording film was used to obtain portrait-like pictures in a dimly lighted area. Both the motor-driven attachment and camera body were soundproofed to avoid detection. One agent wore an earplug device in order to monitor Channel Four, the Bureau surveillance frequency.

Except for the poor light, it was a perfect setting for photographic surveillance. No parked cars blocked the view of the entrance, and because customers had to walk a substantial distance to reach it, ample time was provided for photography. Passing automobiles presented the only problem, although traffic diminished considerably by closing time, when patrons tended to congregate on the sidewalk out front.

The interior of the tavern contained a jukebox, a few battered tables and chairs, and several booths along the walls. The small bar had only five stools and was used primarily as a stand-up conversation area. It was a rather austere environment, in keeping with the times and the radical clientele. Posters advertising rock concerts and antiwar demonstrations were about the only adornments on otherwise blank walls.

No one seemed to notice however, for it was usually so dark you couldn't see more than a few feet.

The customers were a fiercely loyal group whose lives seemed to revolve around activities at the tavern. For the regulars, The Sun was like a family headquarters. Everyone knew everything about everyone else. The crowd could be characterized as freaky, drug-oriented, sexually liberated, and politically radical. And if you obviously didn't belong, the regulars would oftentimes bring that fact to your immediate attention. It was a small, closed society that had absolutely no desire to expand its membership. Unless, that is, you offered a commodity that interested them.

Hardly a night would go by without someone openly smoking a joint. The closet-like rest rooms were so dense with marijuana clouds that a visit would get you almost as high as a joint. Other popular activities included coke snorting and pill popping. And oddly enough, whiskey drinking.

Since taverns could sell beer and wine only, no hard liquor was available—legally, that is. Most of the freaks soaring high on coke, speed, or psychedelics liked to smuggle in a half-pint and sit in back where they could gulp down shots of their favorite spirits.

How did a public facility licensed by the state get away with allowing such outrageous behavior? Primarily because the manager, bartenders, and waitresses who were the cohesive force behind the Red Sun family were exactly like the regular customers. They liked to smoke dope, snort coke, and drink whiskey too. Why should a little thing like a job prevent you from doing something you enjoy, they reasoned. But above all, they were street-wise. They knew when to clean up their act and when to tell their customers to do the same. If there were strangers in the tavern who didn't look like freaks, the level of illicit activity dropped off substantially. And when employees discreetly warned the regulars, it ceased completely.

It was in these surroundings that I began my deep cover efforts. According to the briefings I had received, the Red Sun was the meeting-place for everyone who was anyone in radical politics. Judging from the number of photographs of Seattle Seven members I reviewed, it was obviously a favorite spot with them. Since most local agents believed that certain of these individuals were in touch with the Weathermen, they were a frequent target of surveillance cameras.

After several nights of drinking in the tavern, I began to recognize many of the activists whose profiles I had studied. Within a week or so,

I could associate names and organizations with individual faces. In time, I would know who they talked with, what they drank, and where they preferred to sit. With a judicious choice of location and any luck at all, I could almost make them come to me. If I was already seated when they arrived, I could overhear most of their conversations without attracting undue suspicion.

Observing the actions and reactions of unsuspecting individuals provided valuable insight that gave me a distinct advantage in selecting potential targets and determining when and how I might approach them. If a guy consistently acted as though he was a loner and overly paranoid, why even bother to approach him? Why not just wait patiently and watch. Each time he saw me with someone he knew and trusted, my credibility would grow through association.

My prior undercover experience had taught me that before I approached anyone at all, I should try to determine who the radical heavyweights were. Who among this group seemed the likeliest contacts with the Weathermen? Who possessed the lengthy movement background, the capability for militant activism, and the requisite political ideology? Who were the leaders? When the leadership was bitterly divided in controversy, who could command the most loyal following? It was not necessarily the person you might read about in the newspapers as a spokesman for this or that particular movement, but rather someone whose rhetoric, intellect, and charisma could generate decisive action on the part of others.

Although the leaders were the logical targets for deep cover penetration, they were also the most difficult. Most movement leaders were justifiably paranoid and virtually impossible to approach. They generally spent their time with a few longtime friends who shared a similar political philosophy. One didn't just sit down uninvited and strike up a conversation on revolutionary politics. Not unless you immediately wanted to draw suspicion to yourself. After several years of this type of work, I had made it a personal rule never to approach the radical heavyweights without a good reason; nevertheless, these were the people I eventually wanted to know—and well.

During the days that followed, my primary goal was to spend enough time in the tavern to make myself known as a familiar face— someone who was usually around laughin', gettin' high, and buyin' a few beers; someone who enjoyed friendly conversation, but at the same time was uninquisitive and a bit mysterious. Night after night, I watched the small group of individuals who always encircled the heavyweights. I was looking for someone on the periphery of that circle of old and trusted friends whose acquaintance would provide me with credibility; someone who could be manipulated to deliver my cover story to the heavyweight so that it would be heard for the first time from a friend. It was a technique that had usually worked well.

With prior experience firmly in mind, I soon developed more than a passing interest in Karen, a waitress and occasional bartender at the Red Sun. I had noticed that she often engaged in whispered conversations of considerable length with the heavyweights who treated her as though she were a close friend. But then Karen was friendly with everyone. She had an outgoing, effervescent personality, and no matter what line you threw at her, she always had a witty comeback, usually delivered with the rapidity of a submachine gun. But she could be a genuine wise-ass when hassled, and if a customer gave Karen a hard time, everyone in the tavern would be aware of the incident before it was over.

Karen had long, dark hair which she usually pulled back to accentuate her radiant smile. She was pretty rather than beautiful, and her manner of dress was stylishly bizarre, combining an assortment of unrelated, hand-me-down garments. She could somehow assemble these relics in various combinations so that she ended up looking together, a bit freaky perhaps, but together. Karen was frequently overweight, sometimes by as much as twenty-five pounds. This excess poundage never detracted from her overall appearance; in fact, because it seemed to settle in her enormous breasts, her physical attraction increased with her weight.

While there was a distinct air of self-confidence about Karen, something seemed to be lacking. As our conversations became more frequent, I began to suspect that her cocky attitude was nothing more than a defensive front. But at that particular point it was of little concern, for we were both physically attracted to each other. When Karen asked for a ride home one cold, rainy evening, I was more than happy to oblige.

After a brisk walk to the van, which I had wanted Karen to see, we drove to an old, run-down house near the Wallingford district. The house was the absolute epitome of a hippy crash pad. A mangled wooden frame that once held a screen door hung precariously from a single hinge. The front door would barely close, let alone lock. Faded blankets were nailed to the inside window frames to prevent prying eyes from seeing what went on inside. A ragged, stained couch of

1930s vintage was in the center of the living room; an overstuffed chair with no legs and a protruding spring was positioned nearby. A red light bulb glowed eerily from inside the fringed shade of an antique floor lamp. Magazines, comic books, and paperbacks littered the floor, and the overwhelming smell of cat shit filled the air.

According to Karen, there were thirteen cats in residence. There was Willie, Easy, Annie, Clara Bell, Fritz, and Gray Cat, to name a few, all purring, jumping, clawing, and staring as we sat on the couch smoking Karen's hash. I felt very apprehensive about these dark, shabby surroundings. In fact, the place felt downright *weird*, like something in the occult or supernatural world.

But the macabre atmosphere didn't inhibit our physical progress. Sparks of passion were flying between us like cosmic lightning bolts. It was the unique sensation that a man and woman experience when body chemistry, emotions, and mutual vibrations are exactly right— and they both know it. Perhaps the mind is too intent on the excitement of the moment and the prospects of sensual pleasures, but whatever the case, my thoughts didn't include the FBI or deep cover.

Karen led me into a small, cluttered room with an unmade bed. After hurriedly dispensing with clothing, our naked bodies were passionately entwined in the chilly darkness. Her firm pink nipples stood out like an eraser on a new pencil. As I began to explore the shape of her warm body, she suddenly tensed up. I knew that I hadn't forced the issue and certainly had no intentions of doing so. But I sensed that Karen was afraid to go on. Maybe she was afraid of me, I thought. Or maybe she just wasn't into men. For some reason, that explanation immediately flashed through my mind as I recalled her intimate embraces with several women at the tavern. I caressed her body slowly, making a deliberate effort to be as gentle as possible. Karen seemed to be afraid of something, and I was determined to find out what. It wasn't as though she was playing games; that was a genuine fear, a fear that only time, patience and tenderness could overcome.

After a lengthy period of silence and exploration, the emotional intensity began to build again. Suddenly, almost without warning, Karen returned to the height of passion. And I must add, I was not far behind. It was as though I had just undressed her and the intervening hour had never taken place. The lady definitely had me turned on, and at this particular point, my assignment was the farthest thing from my mind. Lust was the only consideration. My thoughts were apparently infectious, for Karen got cranked up pretty tight herself. To say that our sexual appetites were well satisfied would be a classic understatement.

All in all, it was a goddammed heavy beginning. There was mutual, unspoken agreement that this was something more than a one-night stand. But the environment had certainly not contributed to our sexual performance. Between the freezing cold of an old, unheated house and the marauding pack of cats that constantly attacked my gyrating posterior, it was a wonder things ever got off the ground.

When I was awakened by the first rays of daylight, I got a good look at the rest of the house. In a frantic search for the bathroom, I stumbled upon the kitchen that was piled high with dirty pots, pans, dishes, and glassware. Nothing had been washed here in weeks, maybe months. A slimy green mold floated in the pots and pans that were soaking in the crowded sink. Ants and roaches swarmed over the crusted, decaying food left on dishes and counter tops. At least a half dozen cats were in the kitchen, perched atop mounds of dishes, the breakfast table, and stove. It was a sickening sight for such an early hour. The odor of decaying food was so repugnant it even overpowered the piles of cat shit on the floor.

I made a quick right turn and ended up in a room containing a rectangular dining table surrounded by six chairs. In the middle of the table sat a large candy dish of the type my grandmother had in west Texas. It was a dime story variety of cut glass that faintly resembled crystal but had a distinctive greenish tint. But instead of containing the usual peppermints or chocolate kisses, this candy dish was overflowing with "white-crosses"—tablets of bootleg amphetamine that stimulated the central nervous system, causing the heart and other body systems to race full speed ahead. Unless one was a dedicated speed freak one needed chemical assistance in order to come down. The assistance was there too.

An ashtray full of the remains of marijuana cigarettes sat on the table alongside a small, hand-carved wooden box full of hash that brought back memories of the previous evening. Very pleasant memories, I might add. A bottle of niacin, a paper cup containing chewable vitamin C, and an assortment of roach clips and flavored rolling papers completed the dining room decor.

I wandered down a long, dark hallway and peered into the first open door. The frames of two dormitory-style bunk beds housed six separate levels of metal shelving. Over each level, two fluorescent tubes shone brightly on the countless marijuana plants positioned below. Much larger plants in gallon metal cans stood in the lighted closet at the far end of the room. The mattresses from the bunk beds were pushed together on the floor, and two grimy sleeping bags lay on top. A candle,

213

incense sticks, and a large plastic bag of marijuana were placed on a wooden crate that served as a bedside table. A small mongrel dog looked up with lack of interest from his position atop the sleeping bags.

Farther down the hall, I located the only bathroom in the house. It was comforting to reach my destination, although the tiny cubicle was just as trashed out as the other rooms. There was an old-fashioned, undersized bathtub on pedestals. It looked as though it hadn't been cleaned in years. An exposed light bulb dangled dangerously overhead from a single, frayed strand of electrical wiring. What a convenient way to be electrocuted, I thought. A small discolored sink, a mirrored medicine chest, and a cracked porcelain toilet completed the room's fixtures. Soiled clothing, towels, and underwear covered the cracked linoleum floor. A cat litter box was placed under the sink—unused.

I noticed a tattered, water-spotted postcard wedged in the lower corner of the medicine chest mirror. It reminded me of the old *Believe It Or Not* series and depicted the grotesque caricature of a human who was part man and part elephant. "Ralph The Elephant Man," the card proclaimed, "Skin as tough as an elephant's hide!" Sure enough, ole Ralph had sagging folds of rough, wrinkled skin that made him look exactly like a member of the pachyderm family. I was uncertain as to the significance of Ralph The Elephant Man, but it was apparent that his likeness had been displayed in the same location for a long time.

After using the facilities, I made my way back to the relative warmth of Karen's bedroom. My curiosity no longer compelled me to wander from room to room. I had seen about all the filth and squalor I could take at such an early hour. Anything else would have to wait.

The succeeding nights with Karen were reenactments of our first night together. I would drop by the Red Sun, drink and bullshit until closing, then the two of us would head for her place. After learning that the house was freezing because gas service had been discontinued for nonpayment, I brought in my catalytic heater and propane tank. We were now provided with sufficient heat in the small bedroom, but once you opened the door, it was back to the deep freeze.

Perhaps it was because it was warmer, or possibly because the cats were shut out of the room; whatever the reason, our nightly sexual encounters continued to escalate in intensity. If I failed to drop by the tavern for a night, our next meeting would be outrageously intense. Karen acted as though she would never see me again if I took a night off. But when I returned, she made a diligent effort to make up for lost time.

214

Midway through our second week, Karen moved to the offensive as we lay comfortably in bed one morning.

"I mean, it's fucking ridiculous, Bill. You're here every night, but you leave every morning. It's such a hassle to lug all your shit in at night and back out the next day. And it's too cold for you to be sleeping in that van. You'll freeze your balls off out there! Why don't you just move in with me? There's plenty of room here."

"Well, I—"

"And besides," she continued, "You're going to get hassled by the pigs out there sooner or later. Why take the chance?" Karen snuggled closer and smiled. "And why sleep alone?" she asked softly.

"You got a point all right," I replied jokingly. Having already revealed the main items of my cover story, I convinced Karen that I couldn't run the risk of getting busted. She was right about the van, however, for attempts at sleeping had become a miserable and chilling experience. But then I wasn't completely certain that a freezing commune containing thirteen cats and two dogs was much better. "What about your roommates?" I questioned. "Do you think they'd mind?"

"Fuck, no. They're not here half the time anyway, especially when the rent's due. I have to cover somebody's share nearly every month. Last month I had to pay the whole fucking thing! But if you start dealing, maybe you could help out a little bit."

"Well, sure, man, I'll split it with you. No problem. I wouldn't expect to stay here for nothin'. I'm gettin' some things lined up right now, as a matter of fact. I'll kick in for the food too." I suddenly recalled the sordid condition of the kitchen. "I mean like, ah, if we decide to start eatin' here." As far as I was concerned, there was damn little chance of that.

Stu was predictably elated when I informed him of Karen's invitation. We were both aware that Karen was a good friend of several prominent activist leaders, but Stu had also discovered that she was formerly involved with the Seattle Liberation Front. After reviewing photographs taken at antiwar demonstrations several years earlier, he was of the opinion that she had lived in a Weatherman-style commune but had never been identified. At any rate, he was certain that she had once been associated with people we were vitally interested in. Perhaps she still was.

The rent money would be no problem according to Stu, and he suggested that I move in right away. Communications would become more difficult, however, and I tried to prepare Stu for the inevitable late night telephone calls at home. I was reluctant to disturb his family, but in all likelihood, there would be no alternative. If he was bothered by this prospective intrusion, he gave no indication. Stu was as emotionally caught up in the search for the Weathermen as the rest of us.

After years of bachelorhood, I was finally moving in with a woman. I had been tempted on previous occasions, but to have done so and been caught would have meant the risk of dismissal from the FBI. It often seemed that a married agent who was discovered being unfaithful to his wife had a much better chance for administrative survival than a single agent found living with a single woman. Clerical employees caught living in sin had no chance at all. Now the FBI not only sanctioned my illicit liaison—they would even pay the rent.

It also seemed strange that the lady who had so convincingly persuaded me to accept her invitation didn't have any idea of who I really was or what I was doing. At that particular point, I wasn't bothered by my deceit. As I had done in the episode with Jeannie, I rationalized it as part of the job. But I was beginning to wonder if perhaps I hadn't overloaded my ass. While I had bullshitted quite a few folks over the years, crashed in communes, marched in demonstrations, and smoked a little dope, I had never attempted to live with real freaks on a daily basis—and for an indefinite period. As the days passed, would my conservative upbringing betray the fact that I was appalled at living amidst cat shit and filth? Or could I act out my cover story to the limit and pull off this charade?

After living in the commune for nearly two weeks, I finally met all of the residents, or at least those who were supposed to contribute regularly toward the rent. Since many of the group were frequently on the road, you never knew when they might suddenly reappear; however, it was a safe bet that it wouldn't be around rent time. But it seemed as though somebody was always around. My first night with Karen had been unique in more ways than one; it was one of the few times that the house was deserted. I would quickly discover that the communal life-style did not allow one to become overly concerned with personal privacy.

Sherman, Patty Cakes, and a German shepherd called "Raja" lived, and frequently fought, in the bunkroom. This was the bedroom used as the greenhouse for the communal marijuana crop. Sherman, who was hovering around the age of forty, had been a conservative Jewish businessman with a wife, children, and a comfortable home in suburban

*Sherman 4/0
coke-head lawyer? on 66th st.*

Bellevue. Then he discovered various mind-altering chemicals, not the least of which was LSD, and things were never quite the same again.

Sherman, who I referred to as "Sherm the Sperm," had a three-years' growth of grizzly beard that was the prominent feature of his round, puffy face. The Sperm had only two predictable characteristics: he always wore the same pair of leather pants, and he was always loaded on something. Unlike the vast majority of freaks, Sherm had money. He had not bolted from suburbia unprepared for his new life-style. According to both Karen and Patty, the Sperm had a sizeable savings account. I would hasten to add that he was the tightest freak I've ever known. To get rent money out of him took guile, perseverance, and superhuman effort.

Patty was Sherm's ol' lady. She was a good fifteen years younger than he was, relatively quiet, unattractive, unwashed, and usually spaced out. I was never quite sure whether she viewed Sherm as a security blanket or a father figure, but it seldom seemed to be in the role of a lover. Those needs were frequently taken care of when the Sperm was not around.

Patty was about the most unmotivated, laid-back woman you could ever meet. She adamantly refused to help with housework or cleaning because to do so gave her bad vibes. With no discernible ambition, she was content to hang out, vegetate, and depend on the Sperm for survival. The only energy expended by Patty was the requisite trip to collect unemployment checks and buy food stamps.

Sky King and an assortment of young, wide-eyed girls with one-night tenures resided upstairs in the attic, commonly known as the Ice Palace. Sky had been a reluctant draftee into the United States Army who had served in Vietnam. He was now a part-time university student in order to receive veteran's benefits, and a full-time drug dealer. Since he was required to make token appearances at the university, he also serviced the demand for speed that flourished toward the end of each semester. Come exam time, Sky King was busy as a beaver.

Perhaps it was because he constantly sampled his merchandise, ostensibly for the purpose of quality control, that he suffered from the malady that has plagued many a drug dealer—paranoia. Because he was constantly worried that the big bust was imminent, he and many of his friends felt compelled to sleep at different residences. "If they can't fucking find me, man, how they gonna bust me?" he reasoned.

Two or three times a week, Roberta would appear at the commune in the company of various women. In private conversations among the male residents, she was known as Roberta the Rooter, code name "Roto." Although she reportedly lived with a guy, Roberta also had a strong interest in women. While Roberta's appearance was decidedly masculine, I was constantly amazed at the quality of women she attracted. She and Karen had been friends since high school, and neither made the slightest pretense of disguising what was going on.

I soon learned that this type of activity was not at all uncommon among women involved in similar life-styles. I wasn't shocked, but my male ego had to adjust to the fact that an attractive young lady would rather go to bed with a member of her own sex than with me. The irony lies in the fact that if I had been out-hustled by a man, I probably would never give the incident second thought.

In addition to the thirteen cats, two dogs, and six intermittent residents, there was always at least one prostrate body crashed out on the floor each night. These were transient freaks passing through town on their way to nowhere. They would appear without warning at any hour of the day or night, indicate that a friend of a friend gave them the address, and ask if they could bed down. They usually moved on the following day, although a few would have to be reminded that it was time to leave.

A typical day in the commune began around nine o'clock when the first strains of "Black Sabbath" came blasting out of the stereo speakers. After staggered visits to the bathroom, everyone routinely gathered around the massive dining table and without further discussion, Karen, Sky King, and Patty reached into the candy dish and nonchalantly gulped down a hit of speed. By the time that ritual was completed, Sherm the Sperm had already loaded up the hash pipe, taken three to four real nice hits, and started it around the table. If things were running according to schedule, the coffee would be ready after a couple of passes.

The aforementioned activity usually took place on five out of seven mornings. On the other two mornings, residents were still too fucked up from the night before to get out of bed. But if Karen was working lunches at another tavern or Sky was going to class, each one began with at least one hit of speed, a generous helping of quality hash, and plenty of caffeine.

After watching my roommates conduct this ritual for several weeks, I was completely astounded. I managed to confine my participation to coffee and hash, since I had neither the reason nor desire to stagger out of bed and swallow a white cross. I just couldn't believe that they could consistently get up, start speeding, smoke hash, drink coffee, and then gobble another hit of instant energy on the way out the door. But that's exactly what they did.

The experience did give me an invaluable insight into heads who were stoned during every moment of the day and night. Until I moved in with Karen, I viewed marijuana primarily as a social alternative to alcohol. It was a relaxing, tension-relieving diversion after a hard day at the office. I didn't wake up in the morning wanting a scotch and water *or* a joint. Naturally, I assumed that a lot of heads turned on during the day, but I never even considered that some of them jumped out of bed and toked on a hash pipe as routinely as they brushed their teeth.

After a few weeks of hashish breakfasts, I had a thorough understanding of the problem: the hash never got out of your system. I was smokin' when I got up and smokin' when I went to bed. By the time noon rolled around, I can honestly say that I really didn't give a shit one way or the other. I was laid back, relaxed, floating along with my thoughts, and nothing else seemed important. Or for that matter even relevant. It was a helluva way to start the day.

When Karen was working lunches, I usually drove her downtown around eleven o'clock. She'd ordinarily work until two or three, then hitchhike over to the Red Sun if she couldn't catch a ride with another waitress. Being a rather ballsy, outgoing woman, she had hitched rides from early morning to late at night until a recent incident completely unnerved her.

According to Karen, she had hitched a ride with an elderly man one afternoon near the University District. As they crossed over the Interstate on Forty-fifth Street, the old codger pulled out his log and began to whip it—quite frantically by all reports. When the old gentleman stopped at the next traffic light, Karen bolted out of the car.

"Can you imagine the nerve of that ol' fart!" she said disgustedly. "He was trying to jack off a limp dick, drive, and watch me at the same time. That chauvinist pig! The nerve of that fucker! The streets just aren't safe anymore when a working woman can't hitch a goddamn ride."

On mornings when I chauffered her to work, I often had a long, leisurely breakfast at a nearby coffee shop. During these hours away from the commune, I read the Seattle papers from first page to last. Karen had previously noted my regular habit of reading newspapers and news magazines.

"Why do you waste your money on this shit?" she questioned one morning after stumbling over a pile of old papers. "Newspapers are so depressing. There's never anything good in them."

"I just skim over 'em and read the sports," I answered. "Least I know how bad we're gettin' fucked by the government. And if they come lookin' for me, maybe I'll read about it first." Karen seemed to accept my explanation, although it was obvious that she wasn't in complete agreement. Perhaps it was out of character for a freak to be so interested in current events. I made a mental note to do my future reading away from the house.

At this time, I devoured every bit of available information. Not only was the Bureau's handling of the Watergate scandal coming under scrutiny, but the debacle of Wounded Knee made daily headlines. With many close agent friends assigned to the Wounded Knee "special," I was eager to learn what was going on. It seemed inconceivable that the FBI would send untrained agents into a military situation. Like most agents who hadn't been in the military, I had never even held an M-16 rifle, much less tried to load one. The fiasco of Wounded Knee would be the classic example of on-the-job training.

If Watergate or Wounded Knee didn't make the headlines, then reports of Pat Gray's confirmation hearings before the Senate Judiciary Committee did. The hearings, which had begun on February 28, the week I moved in with Karen, had gone steadily downhill. Then one morning I'm greeted with the news that Pat Gray has been providing John Dean with the actual FBI interviews of various Watergate subjects! A few days later, Gray offered to give committee members a similar opportunity to review *raw files*. It was an unbelievable admission and an unprecedented offer.

After completing breakfast and the newspapers, I would drive to a distant telephone booth and call Stu. I had located approximately a dozen pay phones which I rotated among each day. Our conversations almost always began with a discussion of what was going on at the Bureau. Unfortunately, Stu didn't know much more than I did.

Since there was a distinct possibility Pat Gray would not become the Director, where did that leave us? Would our next leader continue the deep cover program, or would the whole thing be scrapped? If a senior official from the Hoover era was selected, I felt certain it would be the latter. Most of the positive changes instituted by Gray, an outsider, would suffer a similar fate. It was definitely a time of uncertainty.

If Stu didn't request a meeting or have any leads for me to check out, I would sometimes spend the late afternoon at the downtown YMCA. After a hard, strenuous workout I always felt more relaxed and mentally alert. But there was another compelling reason to visit the "Y": a shower.

Ever try to wash a couple of years' growth of long, thick hair in a miniscule bathtub with no hot water? Believe me, it's not easy. I could barely fit in the communal bathtub in the first place, much less get on my knees and try to bend my head under the water faucet. If I was to wash that unruly mop of mid-shoulder-length hair, it had to be in a shower.

It seemed strange to see familiar faces around the "Y" from my earlier days in Seattle. Acquaintances from the past never even gave me a second glance now that I was a freak. I ran into an assistant United States attorney with whom I had worked fairly closely in 1969. We nearly collided in the steam room one afternoon, but it was obvious that he didn't have the slightest idea who I was.

If the house was deserted during the early evening hours, I would try to catch the network news on the small television. It was also a good opportunity to digest *Time* and *Newsweek* without attracting suspicion. If there were others around, I would try to find a relatively quiet corner of the house and read a book. Karen had a large supply of old paperbacks, and I recall reading a number of Kurt Vonnegut's books. His writing provided the only humor in an otherwise bleak and lonely situation. Another diversion was music. I listened to Dave Mason's *World in Changes* album so many times that I had the words memorized.

As the days passed, I began arriving at the Red Sun later and later each evening. I felt an obligation to pick Karen up when she got off work, but I was really getting burned out on the place. And since I had become known as Karen's ol' man, I could visit with several of the radical heavyweights at *their* houses. The primary reason for my delayed appearances had become the after-hours activities.

Several nights a week, the employees and a few regulars gathered in the back room after closing for all-night drug sessions. Since these get-togethers didn't begin until after two A.M. closing, there was little reason to arrive early.

Neal, the manager, and Hondo, a bartender, were both heavy cocaine users. We were no more than social acquaintances by virtue of my affair with Karen, but after observing them for some time, I figured that their frequent absences during business hours were for a quick toot of nose candy. They would return to work wired, wild-eyed, and sniffing.

The first time I attended an after-hours gathering, the coke was flying through the air like a Rocky Mountain snowstorm. Tiny glass vials with coke spoons attached to the caps were passed around time after time. There were no tightly rolled one-hundred-dollar bills or fashionable sterling silver straws in evidence here. These people were interested only in *what* they snorted, not the ritualistic manner in which it might be accomplished. Their main concern was to get that finely chopped white powder up the nose, into the bloodstream, and "all 'round the brain." Assembling in the back of the tavern where they couldn't be seen from the street, the group would shoot pool, snort coke, and drink whiskey until the early hours. There was also a generous supply of hash and psychedelics for those who were so inclined.

The way Neal and Hondo were passing out cocaine, I knew they had to be dealing. Even at 1973 prices, they couldn't afford that kind of generosity unless they were snorting free. But they were damn cagey about it. They made plenty of contacts through their jobs at the tavern but sold only to a very limited clientele. Although they knew I was a dealer, they would conduct business only through Karen until they finally decided they could trust me.

It would be several weeks later before I learned how badly I had underestimated Neal and Hondo. I figured they might buy an ounce or two of coke, step on it a few times, then pedal grams so they could snort free. Once I got to know them, I discovered they were moving almost a pound a month!

But big volume was accompanied by big problems: they had snorted so much coke that they couldn't get high without going through several grams a day. Even dealers couldn't afford that kind of habit; consequently, they abandoned the nose in favor of the arm. Once they started shooting coke for a better high, they went downhill both physically and professionally. As one might expect, they became both greedy and careless; so it wasn't long before Neal was busted by DEA agents. Shortly thereafter, I discovered that Neal and Hondo were male lovers who had lived together for nearly three years.

There were many late night gatherings when Neal and Karen would get loaded and shoot pool until daybreak. They seemed to spend hours intently studying the table and lining up shots, usually to no avail. Karen kept the jukebox going, and the evening wasn't complete unless she played Lou Reed's "Walk On The Wild Side" at least a half-dozen

times. It was her favorite song and she loved to sing along as she glided around the pool table. Perhaps it was because the subjects of drugs, transvestites, and kinky sex were so near and dear to her.

Although I had been around many people involved in the antiwar movement who exhibited liberal attitudes towards sex, I was totally unprepared for the number of activists who were openly bisexual. After working as an agent in cities like Seattle and Los Angeles, I was aware of that segment of gay society, both male and female, that tends to be highly visible. But I was astonished by the number of men who looked like your typical, macho, all-American freak yet swung both ways.

Fortunately, I had never suffered from the prevailing law-enforcement notion that I could spot a fag in any crowd. It just seemed as though these people looked decidedly unfag. A dude might be hittin' on a chick one minute, then turn around and hit on you the next. What perplexed me was the fact that the dude really didn't seem to give a damn which one he landed—you or the chick.

I had certainly logged my share of time in singles bars, but I'd never run across such a large number of people who were so openly *adaptable*. The situation progressed to the point where I felt apprehensive about even approaching women. Maybe straight women suffered a similar problem, since they didn't know about me either; nevertheless, it was an experience that I was unprepared for.

It seemed there was peer group pressure among women of political commitment to prove they were "liberated." One could never become a truly independent, revolutionary woman, they reasoned, unless one could put men aside. This was not to say that men were not acceptable, or even necessary, from time to time. But for most of these women, it seemed imperative that they demonstrate the *capability* of making a choice.

Perhaps it was this same type of pressure that made women more dedicated and potentially more dangerous than men as urban terrorists. Women who were passionately committed to their political beliefs took unbelievable risks to gain acceptance. For the most part, these risks involved brazenly illegal acts that their male counterparts would never even consider undertaking. I was never sure whether the difference resulted from women's seeking to justify their relatively new status as equals, but I am certain of one thing: female activists were the moving force behind the fundamental changes that occurred during those years of protest.

The primary location for the counterculture merry-go-round of sex was the tavern-disco where Karen served lunches on weekdays and drinks on the weekends. It was a cavernous structure with a long bar and seatings on two different levels. Nightly live entertainment was of the acid rock variety. Colored lights pulsated over the enormous dance floor which was surrounded by deafening speakers, and a mind-blowing strobe provided the requisite synch for the psychedelic journey.

Many of the regulars from the Red Sun frequented the disco on weekends to drink, dance, and get rowdy. It also was *the* place to buy or sell psychedelics. LSD, mescalin, MDA, psilocybin, and STP were always available. If you were in the market for something a little more sedate such as grass, hash, or coke, the Red Sun was your best bet—if they knew you. For those on downers or smack, there was a small bar near the University District which was frequented by a predominantly black clientele.

Perhaps it was the influence of the disco or maybe just a matter of availability, but the longer Karen worked at the place, the more deeply involved she became with psychedelics. She was no stranger to the world of hallucinogens; on the contrary, she had journeyed down that magical road many times. Only now she seemed more like a prisoner. She often dropped a hit of acid on the way to work, gobble another hit during the evening, and trip along merrily through the entire night.

"Everybody in the place is tripping anyway," she'd argue. "Who the fuck's gonna notice?"

I noticed. There were many nights when Karen came home so spaced, she couldn't hit her ass. The disco had a younger clientele that was boisterous, bisexual, and messed up. The piercing rock music made attempts at conversation an exercise in futility. And since I was adamantly opposed to the use of acid, the whole scene got old pretty quick.

When I didn't show up at the disco, Karen would have to find a ride home, and she'd generally arrive totally spaced out, energized, and ready to go. Unless it was to be an evening of hysterical crying—by far the toughest type to deal with—she began by playing a Rolling Stones, uptempo, boogie number. She would turn the volume up and dance, and dance, and dance until she could dance no more. In a typical evening, she might dance through twenty albums before she crashed to the floor in complete exhaustion. The first time I saw her pull this stunt, she ended up with blisters on her feet and was unable to wear shoes or work the following day.

It seemed that Karen went into this routine because I wouldn't stay at the disco until closing, or because I refused to do acid with her, or both. During one week, on the third sleepless night in a row, when her blistered feet prevented her from dancing, she talked to herself and wrote in a notebook until dawn. I heard her banging around the living room, hurling books and records, babbling, and then frantically ripping pages out of her notebook.

It was too weird for me. Karen was a witty, intelligent woman until she got loaded. But now she was *always* loaded. The typical day would see her consume grass, hash, speed, acid, coke, alcohol, and occasionally a downer to "sleep on." She was continuously out of touch with reality because she was always soaring on some type of chemical. If she had ever really come down, maybe she could have coped. But her fantasies were apparently too good to give up.

I sincerely wanted to help Karen, and I tried, but I didn't have a comprehensive view of the drug or the person. Acid scared the shit out of me, and watching Karen freak out night after night certainly didn't help. But it seemed imperative to appear completely unbothered by her erratic behavior. Maybe people freak out like this all the time, I rationalized. Perhaps if I had actually been what I seemed—a real dealer rather than an actor—my experience would have allowed me to take more positive action. Instead, I acted as though this were an everyday occurrence among regular acid freaks.

I returned to the commune early one evening and was surprised to find it peacefully deserted. Karen was working at the disco, and after spending the afternoon checking out rural communes for Stu, I was beat. The opportunity for undisturbed sleep was too inviting to resist. I closed the bedroom door and turned in around ten.

Several hours later, I heard footsteps in the living room and figured it was probably Karen coming in from work. Since the doors were never locked and people were constantly coming and going at all hours, there was little cause for concern. I quickly returned to a deep sleep in the hope of missing the nightly dance marathon.

Some time later that evening, I was awakened once again, this time by the sound of voices. Karen and Sherm the Sperm must be rapping, I thought. But the voices were growing louder and angrier. There was more commotion followed by shouting and what sounded like a muffled scream. Something was wrong! I threw on my jeans and went to investigate.

As I tiptoed silently through the dining room, Karen's familiar voice boomed out, "Fuck you! Now get your ass outta here or I'll call the cops."

An inaudible response came from the depths of the long hallway. A young boy was standing partially outside the bathroom, his profile framed by the light. He was so intently focused on what was happening inside the bathroom that he never heard me approach. What the hell is some underweight, pimple-faced, teenager doing in here, I thought, and in the middle of the goddammed night.

A few feet away from the doorway, I heard Karen scream out again. "Now look, you little fuckers! Scram! Get outta here or I'll whip your ass! Right now, dammit! Leave . . . Go! Look, asshole, I said clear your butt outta here! Keep hasslin' me, man, and I'm gonna call the cops."

What the hell's going on here? I wondered. I was eyeing the kid closely while trying to maneuver into position to look over his shoulder and into the bathroom. Suddenly, I heard the sickening, unmistakable sound of a revolver being cocked.

I peered into the bathroom and saw Karen sitting naked on the commode facing a second young boy who was standing in front and slightly to the right of her. His extended right arm shook noticeably as he balanced a steel-blue .357 magnum on her lower row of teeth. From the look of things, Karen had almost half of the four-inch barrel in her mouth. Her eyes were wide as saucers, yet she had a composed, almost defiant look about her.

"Shut the fuck up, bitch!" the boy snapped. "Or I'll blow your shit away." Then, as if he were surprised at what he'd said, the young kid's tone became more conciliatory. "Hey lady, dig it. We don't want no hassles, no shit . . . understand? But we know ya got the bread, man! Like, we saw ya cash the check." The boy's mouth must have been dry as sandpaper as he struggled valiantly to swallow. "Now we're hurtin', lady, ya understand? Me an' my pal gotta make a score, and we need the fucking bread—like now!"

The scrawny teenager's whole body seemed to be swaying as he precariously held the cocked pistol inside Karen's mouth. His face glistened with sweat as he nervously fingered the trigger. I knew that he had sensed my presence before his head darted around to look at me.

"Don't fuck with me, man!" he screamed excitedly.

"I'm not about to fuck with you, brother," I said as calmly as possible. "Specially when you got a gun in my lady's mouth."

The kid was obviously strung out on something. He was nervous as a cat and so hyper that even the wrong look could spook him. I was furious with myself for leaving my automatic in the van, although I realized it didn't make one bit of difference at the present time. A strung-out teenage smack freak was holding all of the cards. If Karen or I even *thought* of a sudden move, that nervous, jerking reaction would provide sufficient trigger pressure to send the rear contents of Karen's skull splattering against the wall.

"Whatever it is you need, brother," I said in my most deliberate Texas drawl, "just take it and go. We don't want no trouble. You want drugs, take what we got. You want the bread, we'll give it to you. Hell, take the whole damn house if you want it. Just lighten up with the gun, man. There's no need for that."

"Okay!" he snapped. The boy pulled the cocked revolver out of Karen's mouth but moved it only a few inches away from her face. "Now look, man," the kid began, "I don't want no more grief outta the chick, understand? We're tired of fucking around. We know she's got the bread. We're hurting bad, man, like real bad. We gotta score some scag."

"Hey, brother, okay, okay," I said. "We can deal with it. But remember, we don't have a lot either. Just take what you need and split."

Our youthful intruders proceeded to rip off eighty bucks from Karen, which was most of the pay check she had cashed at the disco, a fistful of speed from the dining room table, and a large plastic bag of home-grown marijuana. When they ran out of the front door, Karen wanted to chase them down and rip out their hearts; then she accepted the futility of the whole affair. It was frustrating enough to get ripped off in your own home, but that the perpetrators were two teenage smack freaks added insult to injury.

Fortunately the young desperados were smart enough not to return for a second try. As for me, I never spent another night in the commune without my gun hidden by the bed.

My weeks in Seattle had been a profound personal experience as well as a professionally rewarding one. Through Karen, I had become acquainted with several activist leaders. After numerous conversations with her and her friends, and background information developed by Stu, many of the pieces began to fall into place. Her friendship with members of the Seattle Seven went back to the time when she attended the University of Washington and was involved with the Seattle Liberation Front. In fact, Karen had formerly lived with some of these people in revolutionary-style communes around the city. She subsequently told me about their assault on the federal court house and the plan for a violent confrontation with police. The details of their preparation for the street action reminded me of Miami and were facts which would only have been known by a participant. After reviewing the many surveillance photos taken during the disturbance, Stu tentatively identified Karen as one of the demonstrators.

I had also become good friends with a lady who possessed every qualification for the designation of radical heavyweight. Agents from the local office were unanimous in their opinion that she was in contact with the Weatherman fugitives. In the interest of anonymity, I shall refer to her as the "Queen of the Underground," a title borrowed from the Rolling Stones' song "Dead Flowers." The Queen was a complicated, fascinating personality who was totally committed to her political beliefs. She was one of the few activists who always led by example rather than by rhetoric. In Bureau terminology, the Queen had "brass balls." Moreover, the Queen was smart as a whip. In the area of political theory, she was easily the most formidable target I had ever encountered. Cunning, cynical, and totally disarming, the Queen seemed to trust no one completely. I was amazed at her ability to dissect, analyze, and recall even the most minute details of a conversation. One learned early in the game that the Queen was not susceptible to bullshit. If you made a mistake, she'd be the first person to pick up on it. I couldn't help wondering whether the Queen and Weatherman leader Bernardine Dohrn had similar personalities. While the Queen never provided me with Bernie's address, she did inadvertently pass along some interesting information.

In one conversation, she spoke at length about a couple called Timmy and Shirley, referring to them as Weathermen who had been driven underground. She mentioned that Timmy had dyed his hair and that he had passed stolen travelers' checks around the Seattle area for almost a year without detection. The main thrust of the Queen's discussion was that we were too preoccupied with our own paranoia. In fact, she pointed out, Seattle had a flourishing underground and little in the way of police harassment. The only reason Timmy and Shirley moved to San Francisco, she added, was that they had grown tired of the political inactivity and wanted to see their old friends.

The Queen didn't realize that *I* was aware of the true identities of the Weathermen who used the aliases Timmy and Shirley. And while I knew *who* they were, I had no idea *where* they were. After one simple conversation, I learned they had lived in Seattle for over a year, passed

228

travelers' checks, and had moved on to San Francisco. I now knew I was on the right track. These people discussed the Weathermen and made no secret of openly supporting their political philosophy.

A short time after Karen had delivered my cover story, apparently in a convincing manner, the Queen put me on to "Betty Blotter." Betty, who was also known as Betty Box, and sometimes as Sweaty Betty Box, was a longtime friend of Karen's. I later learned that Betty had grown up on the East Coast with Timmy and Shirley, and that all three had traveled West together after a brief stop in Chicago during the Weatherman-sponsored "Days of Rage."

At the insistence of the Queen, Betty Blotter let me know that she might possibly be of help in establishing my new identity. In less than a week, she provided me with a blank Selective Service card obtained from a friend employed by the local Selective Service Board. It seemed that Betty Blotter had connections exactly like the highly prized contacts of the Bureau.

Early one Saturday afternoon Betty Blotter called the commune to tell Karen that she had to talk with her right away and in person. She arrived a short time later and related every detail of a call she'd received from Shirley in San Francisco. According to Betty, Timmy had been busted by the feds after they followed a chick to his residence. Timmy had apparently been recognized by accident, she said, and was presently in jail on charges of assaulting a Chicago police officer. Although he felt he could beat the Chicago rap, he was worried that the FBI might find out about his check-passing activities in Seattle as well as extensive welfare frauds committed in several Western states. Betty said she had pleaded with Shirley to return to Seattle before she was arrested too.

During our lengthy conversation, Betty always referred to Timmy as an "underground Weatherman," and once mentioned that he should have gone "up North" with "Jeff" rather than return to San Francisco. Could this be my old buddy, Jeff Jones, I wondered, doing an underground number in Canada? After all, agents had been within twenty feet of him at the Western Union office in San Francisco, but all they came away with was a great surveillance photo. Maybe he and Timmy had lived together at the Pine Street commune.

Karen seemed to know just as much about the Canadian situation as Betty did. It was obvious from the conversation that she was deeply concerned about the welfare of Shirley. She also shared Betty's opinion that it would have been wiser for them to have gone to Canada. Both women now seemed to be victims of the paranoia that infects people after a political ally has been busted.

"Let's get out of here for a while, Bill," Karen suggested. "I've got plenty of friends in Vancouver we can stay with, and you'll be safe there. I need to get away from Seattle, and this is a damn good time. The pigs are gonna be coming around as soon as they find out Timmy lived here for a year."

As one might expect, I was most receptive to Karen's suggestion. She constantly referred to her fugitive friends in Canada, although she never mentioned specific names. She did reveal that one of her friends had traveled to Cuba with the Venceremos Brigade, which immediately got my attention. But I couldn't discount the fact that Karen just wanted to get away and try to clear out her head.

An old friend of Karen's had questioned me earlier about her drug use and mental state. She was concerned that Karen's frequent bouts with drug-induced depression might send her on a return trip to Edge City. Only then did I learn that Karen had attempted suicide on more than one occasion. I was well aware that Karen displayed schizophrenic tendencies, but I certainly hadn't seen anything to indicate she was contemplating suicide; nevertheless, I would be watching closely.

Stu had been encouraged by my progress and believed that we were moving in the right direction. He was fascinated by the quality and volume of intelligence information I provided. After years of working security cases, Stu, as well as other agents on the security squad, found it difficult to understand that information revealing where a subject lived, worked, or spent free time was easily obtained through casual conversation. While they might have to spend weeks reviewing utility, telephone, or other records, I could accomplish the same task in a matter of minutes.

Since Stu functioned as my only communication link with the Bureau aside from an occasional conversation with Fast Freddie, I depended on his evaluation of local activists for guidance. He had closely followed the development of Seattle's radical world and possessed detailed knowledge of the leadership. His familiarity with the history of radical organizations and individuals allowed him to piece together many connections I was not aware of. Having investigated several of these people *before* the mass migration underground, Stu remembered exactly who was associated with the element of SDS that subsequently evolved into the Weatherman faction.

Based on the information developed through our deep cover efforts,

Stu felt it was imperative that Karen and I travel to Canada. I had learned that Betty Blotter, the Queen, and Karen were all aware of Timmy's true identity while he and Shirley lived underground in Seattle. But what was more important was our own information that Timmy had been close friends with Weatherman fugitives Bernardine Dohrn, Jeff Jones, Cathie Boudin, and Bill Ayers before they dropped out of sight. The Queen of the Underground shared many of these same friendships. Investigations in other parts of the country had produced strong indications that several of the Weatherman fugitives were in Canada. The opportunity to travel into Canada and meet Karen's fugitive friends seemed almost too good to be true.

Within hours after I relayed the information regarding Timmy's arrest, Stu was requesting Bureau authorization for my trip to Canada, but he advised me to delay our departure as long as possible. Since I had previously met two members of the Special L Squad, Royal Canadian Mounted Police (RCMP or Mounties) when they toured the November Committee headquarters in Venice, we felt this would be a distinct advantage in gaining approval. In addition, Stu discussed the project with Special L members on the phone and received their support and cooperation; however, we soon discovered that things were not going well at Bureau headquarters.

Only a few days earlier, on March 22, 1973, Pat Gray's testimony before the Senate Judiciary Committee indicated that John Dean had lied to FBI agents when he was asked whether Howard Hunt had an office in the White House. Newspaper headlines across the country screamed "Gray Says Dean Lied to FBI." After three weeks of stormy confirmation hearings, this would be Gray's last appearance before the committee. And while Pat Gray was left to "twist slowly, slowly in the wind" at the advice of John Ehrlichman, the organization known as the Federal Bureau of Investigation was now doing the same thing.

It seemed that a moratorium had been placed on decision-making at Bureau headquarters. I would suspect that many Bureau officials, especially in the Domestic Intelligence Division, were more than a little concerned over Gray's dismal showing before the Judiciary Committee. Those who had publicly supported his innovative programs no doubt realized that the ship was sinking and they might go down with it, since by supporting an outsider, they had made enemies among the lifelong Hoover loyalists who still controlled positions of power. If an insider was to be appointed Director, he would not be likely to look favorably on those who demonstrated their disloyalty to Mr. Hoover by supporting change within *his* organization. The supporters of the deep cover program, which had been instituted by the Domestic Intelligence Division over the objections of many senior officials, would have ranked high on the "enemies list."

Although Stu sent out teletype after teletype and made daily telephone calls, no one at Division Five wanted to take responsibility for a decision. It was cover-your-ass time at FBIHQ. I could appreciate the fact that this was a delicate decision requiring thorough consideration by the leadership of the FBI, but at the same time, what the hell was I supposed to tell Karen? That the bureaucrats who were paid to make such decisions were floundering in a sea of uncertainty?

After numerous delays, Stu finally received permission for me to leave. I don't know how high up the chain of Bureau command the proposal traveled, but it was made abundantly clear that I would be conducting a clandestine operation in a foreign country and under no circumstances was I to reveal my true identity or employment. While the FBI had sent informants into Canada on assignments, they had never sent agents. The day before my departure, Stu smuggled me back into the basement of the Federal Reserve Building so that the SAC would be certain I understood the ground rules. If something went wrong in Canada, I would be on my own.

At this time, the implications of working undercover in a foreign country were not at all apparent to me. Perhaps I was too caught up in the excitement of the assignment. I would be the first deep cover agent to enter Canada, and with any luck at all, I'd find the Weathermen. It seemed inconsequential that I looked like a long-haired freak, drove a van loaded with assorted drugs and weapons, and would have a passenger who was spaced out and suicidal.

12

Canada, Here I Come!

It was with a great sense of personal relief that Karen and I pulled out of Seattle on a Wednesday morning in late March. For the first time in several days, Karen was in good spirits. Just getting out on the open highway seemed to give both of us an immediate lift.

The drive from Seattle to Vancouver can usually be accomplished in about three hours. It was not an unfamiliar route, but since the border crossing at Blaine is one of the busiest in the country, it seemed advantageous to cross during the day. Considering our appearance and mode of transportation, I could suddenly foresee several potential problems.

In order to amplify my cover story, explain my income, and especially to justify the repeated delays, I had told Karen that we couldn't leave Seattle until I had lined up some action through a drug connection in Bellingham. She was led to believe that I had previously smuggled hashish across the border for a major supplier who then delivered it to a distributor in Vancouver. I explained that although it was a high-risk business, the financial rewards were equally high.

"It's no sweat if you just stay calm," I said. "Wear a straight-lookin' dress, lots of makeup, and act normal. Like a couple of tourists on vacation. If somethin' did go wrong and I was to get popped, I'd tell 'em you were hitchhiking."

"Oh, I'm not worried," she said convincingly. "Besides, we could sure use the bucks."

If Karen had been at all upset by the prospects of smuggling drugs across the border, it was certainly not apparent in Seattle. But the closer we got to Bellingham, the more paranoid she became. With great reluctance, she ultimately accepted my argument to refrain from smoking dope until we had crossed the border. She agreed only on the condition that I stop for some beer to help settle her nerves.

In order to impress Karen with the validity of the smuggling operation, Stu had arranged to stage a sinister-looking production with the help of an agent assigned to the Bellingham Resident Agency. After arriving in Bellingham, we were led through an intricate series of contact points using various public telephone booths before finally receiving a neatly wrapped parcel for delivery in Vancouver. Although she never actually saw my connection, she did get a good look at the parcel, which was exactly the right size and weight. The scenario was staged to perfection, but it appeared we had overdone it. Karen had become so nervous she could scarcely function.

I drove to a remote rural area to hide the small box in the rear-door panels. Karen remained in the front seat drinking beer while I dismantled the door. Just as we returned to Interstate 5, she announced that she *had* to smoke a joint before we crossed the border. After a somewhat animated conversation, I learned that while I was busily storing the hash, Karen was using our last beer to wash down a hit of acid. Now she was so hyper that she couldn't even sit still.

Hell, if anybody oughta be smokin' dope, it's me, I thought. I'm within twenty miles of the busiest border crossing in the country, look like a freak, Karen's tripping on acid, and my drug-laden van smells like the world's largest joint. I recall thinking how embarrassing it would be to get busted before I even made it into Canada.

I stopped at a roadside park just before we reached the border and hurriedly went over the van. While searching for roaches, beer cans, and anything else that looked illegal, I tried to air out the van. For at least the fifteenth time, I asked Karen to check the contents of her purse for drugs. She nervously went through the motions without even glancing inside.

As we approached the large canopied structure at the border, Karen's face looked paralyzed with fear, but it was apparent that her brain was speeding out of control. Her fingers shook uncontrollably while fidgeting with her handbag. The silence inside the van heightened our tension. When a female customs officer casually waved us through one of the stalls, we were both astonished. We passed by the Peace Arch with sighs of relief and traveled silently toward the Canadian side.

Stu had advised me that the Canadian government was cracking down on activist-freaks who were entering the country as tourists and then applying for landed immigrant status. Having previously briefed Karen on what to tell Immigration, I saw little reason in trying to go back over our story. She definitely knew what to say, but at this particular point, it was far from certain whether she would be able to say anything at all.

The Canadian officer was disarmingly polite as he asked the usual questions. Things seemed to be going surprisingly well until he suddenly ordered us to park the van and step inside for a chat with the "immigration man." Karen looked as though she had just suffered cardiac arrest but managed to note, in a rather graphic fashion, that she was about to wet her pants. I quickly assured her that she wasn't alone.

Once inside the building, we immediately located the rest rooms, then sat down for the agonizing wait before we were summoned into the immigration officer's glass-enclosed cubicle. It was not particularly comforting to note that virtually everyone else waiting had long hair. The immigration officer was businesslike and asked where we were going in Canada, for what purpose, and for what length of time. I replied that we were tourists on a brief vacation to Vancouver. He requested our identification, observed that we were not married and from different states, and then asked how much money we had.

After about a ten-minute conversation in which Karen remained admirably attentive, the officer advised we would be allowed to enter Canada. But there was one small hitch. He filled out a form with my name, address, and license number, and handed me the carbon copy. It was similar to a tourist visa, he said, and would be valid for two weeks. We would both be required to leave the country by that time and were instructed to return the form to Canadian Immigration prior to our departure. Karen and I fit into the profile of undesirables who were fleeing to Canada in search of landed immigrant status.

We were elated to return to the van, but just as we started to drive off, we encountered more customs officials. In our nervous condition, we had both forgotten that the van was never inspected. Karen was visibly agitated as I scrambled around the rear area opening drawers, storage lockers, and the refrigerator. After what seemed like an eternity of anxiety, the officer sent us on our way. At long last we had arrived in Canada.

I left Highway 99 at Cloverdale and stopped at the first available store for a couple of six-packs. We were both emotionally drained after the ordeal at the border, and Karen was beginning to jabber uncontrollably. After opening the beer, I crawled into the back of the van to retrieve some grass. Smokin', jokin', and drinkin' beer seemed the only way to complete our journey.

Shortly after nightfall, we arrived at the outskirts of Vancouver.

235

Having visited the city on two earlier occasions, I turned off of Granville onto Broadway and headed toward the University of British Columbia before Karen directed me to an older section of residences, apartments, and duplexes located off to the right. Even in darkness the area bore that characteristic look of the counterculture. It stretched all the way down to English Bay, crossing Fourth Avenue, Cornwall, and Kitsilano Beach. I would subsequently discover that it was a vibrant area, alive with a diversified and talented population.

With considerable confusion and little assistance from Karen, we finally stumbled on the residence of her friend Joy. It was a run-down, three-story tenement in which Joy occupied a small top-floor apartment. After attending college in Seattle, she had moved to Vancouver where she landed a well-paying job. She was now a Canadian citizen, and she remained highly critical of U.S. foreign policy. With the exception of brief trips to visit relatives, she had no desire to return to a country she considered imperialistic.

After lugging sleeping bags, packs, and cardboard boxes stuffed with Karen's clothing up the stairs, the three of us sat around the kitchen table rapping. Joy produced a bottle of cheap red wine that tasted a lot like vintage battery acid, and she and Karen talked about their mutual acquaintances in Seattle. Joy seemed shy, almost timid, and much to my surprise, she wasn't the least bit interested in drugs other than alcohol.

Karen and I slept on the living room floor that evening, and while it was much warmer than the van, we woke up with aching backs and stiff necks. Joy had left for work hours before. Karen made a futile attempt at cooking breakfast, and we drank cup after cup of instant coffee. It was mid-afternoon before we finally left to deliver the smuggled hashish.

Passing over the Burrard Bridge, we viewed the jungle of sprouting high-rise apartments framed against the distant mountains. We drove through downtown Vancouver, past the public library, and on to West Hastings where we turned toward the Gastown section. I cruised the area for some time before finding exactly what I needed: a self-service multilevel parking garage, conveniently located on Water Street. Similar facilities had proved to be the most discreet city locations for dismantling door panels and retrieving the stash. There was generally little foot traffic, and you could hear vehicles approaching from the floor below.

For Karen's benefit, I suggested a walk around Gastown to be certain that we hadn't been followed. If everything looked normal, we

236

would return to the van and remove the hash. After browsing through several nearby shops, we headed back to the garage. Karen, my lookout man, sat in the front seat smoking dope while I removed the small parcel that was meticulously wrapped in brown shipping paper. The package had been carefully sized and weighted to represent five pounds of hashish. I locked the parcel in one of the rear storage compartments, and we drove out of the parking garage.

Since I was about to make a big score, it seemed only natural that we should celebrate. We parked on Cordova Street and walked to a fancy restaurant where we stuffed ourselves with steak and scotch.

This was one of many charades designed not only to convince Karen I was a major drug dealer, but also to elicit her response to particular locations. For example, the Bureau had previously received information that Weatherman fugitives John Fuerst and Roberta Smith had lived in a Gastown flophouse later used as an underground contact point. Consequently, Karen and I had walked by the place several times, ostensibly for the purpose of casing the layout before my nine o'clock meeting with the distributor. If the hotel had any significance at all, it was hoped she would make some comment. None was forthcoming.

Upon returning to the van, I crawled into the rear area while Karen sat up front reloading the hash pipe. She watched silently as I located the package and ceremoniously shoved the Walther automatic into my left boot. I tried to engage her in lighthearted conversation, but she was noticeably uneasy. What she didn't know at the time was that I was a bit edgy myself.

Having been told only that I would be met by an undercover Mountie from the Special L Squad, I could foresee plenty of room for error. I had been bothered all day by the nagging thought that I had no idea what "undercover" meant to the RCMP. Stu mentioned that the guy had a beard, but did that mean he'd be a freak or a straight-looking, scholarly type? And after drinking numerous cocktails, a liter of red wine, and smoking hash, I was not exactly in the best condition for stopping total strangers on the street.

Karen had a distressed, apprehensive look on her face as I slammed the van door and scurried off into the darkness. It was only about a ten-minute walk to the run-down establishment that advertised hotel rooms by the day, week, or month. The sidewalk was dimly lit, and there was a public telephone just outside the main entrance. It seemed the ideal location for a mugging.

My pace slowed as I crossed the street and moved toward the hotel.

There was a barrel-chested seaman standing near the pay phone as though he were waiting for a call. The man was about my age, of short, stocky build, and wore a seaman's pea jacket and watch cap. He also sported a flaming red beard.

Since my contact man had been provided with a description of the Western-style cowboy hat I was wearing, the best course of action seemed to be a slow pass by the hotel in the hopes that someone would approach me. I stared intently at the seaman without getting any reaction.

"Howdy," I said. "You fixin' to use the phone?"

"No, mate, just waiting for a call," he answered cheerfully. "Go right ahead." I fumbled through my pockets searching for change. "Say," he said edging closer, "aren't you Bill, a friend of Stu's?"

"Yeah, right. And you must work with Jack?"

"Sure do. I'm Walt," he replied, thrusting out his hand in greeting. "Welcome to Vancouver."

"It's great to be here, Walt. I'm Bill." We shook hands warmly. "Here's a little present from Stu." I passed him the neatly wrapped package which was quickly enveloped by his bulky pea jacket.

"And this is from Stu to you," Walt said as he slipped me an envelope crammed full of crisp hundred-dollar bills.

I shoved the money into the pocket of my field jacket and glanced toward the hotel. "Sure appreciate the help, Walt."

"Anytime, Bill, anytime." Just as I was about to walk off Walt whispered, "Call us when you can."

I nodded, and we both turned and walked in opposite directions. The evening was damp and chilly, and I wasted little time in returning to the van.

Karen was jubilant when I displayed the envelope full of money. As best I could tell, she was totally convinced of my involvement in drug trafficking. We left the Gastown area and traveled over the Granville Street Bridge back to Broadway, to a popular pub near General Hospital. Joy had recommended it as a good place to celebrate our arrival in Canada.

After recalling the hard, uncomfortable floor in Joy's living room, I persuaded Karen to sleep in the van that night. In our exhausted and drunken condition, the thought of sleeping on a mattress seemed much more appealing than waking Joy up at such a late hour to sleep on the floor. I parked on a level street three blocks away from Joy's apartment, and we settled in as best we could.

In addition to the prospect of a good night's sleep, there was a more important reason for not returning to Joy's apartment: I was neither physically nor mentally ready for another crisis. And if things had gone as planned in Seattle, there was certain to be a "red alert" upon our arrival. As far as I was concerned, it would have to wait until morning.

Through the foresight and Bureau contacts of Kenny, FBI agents in Seattle had used my mug shot from the Los Angeles Police Department to orchestrate yet another intricate scenario. Within hours after Karen and I left Seattle, Bureau agents began interviewing virtually all of the local activists who had known and associated with Timmy and Shirley. Each activist was asked to review a group of mug shots of various Weatherman fugitives. My arrest photo had been included among the group, and along with my description, it bore the notation that I was wanted for assaulting a police officer at the Republican National Convention in Miami. While none of those who were interviewed admitted knowing me, Stu later mentioned that my photograph produced a number of perplexed reactions.

Perhaps a certain amount of confusion was attributable to the fact that most of these people knew me only as "Chief." For some unknown reason, Karen began referring to me as "the Chief" shortly after I moved in with her. She in turn became known as "Ralph" or "Ralphie," in honor of Ralph the Elephant Man. While virtually everyone interviewed would have recognized my arrest photo, I doubt that any one would have been familiar with the name William Allen Layne. In any case, it seems highly unlikely that they would have acknowledged the fact to the FBI.

We arrived at the apartment the next morning to find the door unlocked and an urgent message inside for Karen to call Joy at work. From all indications, everything was going as planned. Just listening to Karen's side of the telephone conversation and observing her frightened reactions told me the scheme had worked.

"Chief!" she screamed. "The FBI's showing your picture all over Seattle! They wanta arrest you for political crimes!"

"You're kiddin'," I replied with feigned amazement. "Who says so?"

"Betty called Joy last night. She waited up all night for us, but we never came in. The pigs have been hassling everybody that knew Timmy and Shirley. They musta traced 'em to Seattle after Timmy got busted in California. But Chief," she stammered, "they had *your* picture. Betty said they wanted you for political crimes, and they think you've been in Seattle! What are we gonna do?"

"Shit, man, I don't know. I just can't believe they would've traced me to Seattle."

"Well, they damn sure did!" she exclaimed. "Betty talked to the others, and they agreed you can't possibly go back. Rob says if they know you were in Seattle, they're watching the border. Oh Chief!" she cried. "What are we gonna do?"

"I don't know, Ralph," I replied dejectedly. "But it looks like we're gonna have to run. For all we know, they might have traced the call to Joy."

During the remainder of the day, Karen vacillated between states of silent depression and near-hysteria. Long-distance calls to Betty Blotter and the Queen of the Underground certainly didn't help matters. Each one described a confrontation with FBI agents, and it was soon evident that paranoia was rampant in Seattle. Luckily, Joy's arrival brought some stability to a rapidly deteriorating situation.

I provided her with a rundown of my cover story that evening, including my previous political activities and my present drug dealing. While she took everything in, she gave out little information in return. I remained uncertain as to how much, if anything, she knew about the Weatherman underground. When she offered to arrange a meeting with a fugitive friend the following day, it was all I could do to disguise my astonishment. Joy mentioned that the guy, who was also an acquaintance of Karen's, had lived underground after fleeing to Canada and would be in a position to offer some helpful information.

Since Joy and Karen slept late the following morning, I had a good opportunity to contact the Special L Squad before my Saturday afternoon appointment. Jack answered the office telephone with an innocuous "Hello" and advised that Walt was not in. Apparently recognizing my Texas accent, he identified himself and asked if he could be of any help. Since Jack and I had previously met in Los Angeles, we would be able to recognize each other. He was one of the senior members of Special L, and made no attempt to change his appearance. His official position within the RCMP seemed similar to that of Fast Freddie at home.

Jack mentioned that Walt had been most impressed by my hippy look and asked whether everything had gone all right. He noted that a discreet, spot-check surveillance of Joy's apartment was being maintained, and advised that one of the primary suspects associated with the Weatherman underground lived in a commune only two blocks away. According to Jack, I had landed in the right area.

I gave Jack the background on the person I was going to meet, and he replied that the guy's name sounded familiar, although he wasn't quite sure why. He said they would check the name through their files, and I agreed to recontact him at the first available opportunity.

Joy had supplied me with the telephone number and address of her friend Marvin, who lived in a tiny, subterranean flat several blocks west of Nelson Park. After several attempts, I located the aging structure amidst towering new apartment buildings.

Marvin, who was privately known as "Marvelous Marv," greeted me at the doorway of his one-room basement apartment. He was a slight, studious-looking guy who had a receding hairline and wore thick, wire-rimmed glasses. While Marvelous was relatively cordial, it was also apparent that he was cautious.

I noted large posters of Ché Guevera and Chairman Mao as we struggled through the customary small talk. I was certain that Marvelous was trying to size me up without revealing himself. But in doing so, he conveyed an overbearing, elitist attitude, acting almost as though he were conducting an interrogation.

I supplied Marvelous with the basic elements of my cover story, although certain segments were intentionally presented in a cryptic manner. While he could readily confirm my story through his acquaintances in Seattle, he seemed much more interested in the details of the Miami arrest. According to Marv, he had an activist attorney friend in Miami who could verify that the incident took place.

Much of Marv's reluctance to talk about living underground resulted from the fact that he had only recently become a Canadian citizen and was afraid to do anything that might jeopardize his new status. He talked at length, but abstractly, about using the deceased infant method of establishing a fictitious identity; this was a method successfully employed by *others*, rather than by himself. And although he implied a sympathy for the Weatherman philosophy, he was careful to deny any knowledge of their activities or whereabouts. In view of the fact that I had never even mentioned the word "Weatherman," I found his disclaimer quite interesting.

About the only tangible advice Marvelous Marv could offer regarding my present situation was to leave Vancouver and "lay low" until he could talk with his associates in the States. He was firmly of the opinion that the number of police officers in the city made the risk of being stopped and deported much higher. I mentioned several rural areas where Weatherman fugitives were thought to have been hiding, but

Marv showed no signs of recognition, nor did he offer any further suggestions. I agreed to recontact him when I had a better idea of my future plans, and we parted amicably.

Before returning to the apartment, I located a telephone booth and placed a call to Stu. As I expected, he instantly recognized Marvin's real name. According to Stu, Marvelous Marv was indeed a radical heavyweight. After losing a lengthy appeal in federal court, Marv had decided several years ago to leave the United States rather than submit to induction into the armed forces. In short, Marvin was officially considered a draft dodger.

Stu told me that before fleeing to Canada, Marvin had been active in the Seattle Liberation Front and SDS. But after his long absence from the U.S., no one was quite certain about what he was up to. In order to be on the safe side, Stu planned to ask the Miami Division for assistance in determining the identity of Marvin's attorney friend. If at all possible, he would also have the Miami office plant a fictitious fugitive warrant indicating that I was wanted for assaulting a Miami police officer.

After reviewing the events of the past few days, Stu felt it was an ideal time for me to leave Vancouver and travel with Karen to a remote mountain area called the Slocan Valley. The Bureau had received numerous reports that Weatherman fugitives were living in the area with the support and assistance of Canadian activists. In fact, the suspect mentioned earlier by Jack, who was appropriately named "Fred the Head," was known to make regular trips from the commune near Joy's apartment to the Slocan Valley. Both RCMP and FBI informants had reported the existence of a secret commune called "Weatherman Haven North," which was thought to be directed by Fred the Head. But since Slocan Valley was inhabited almost entirely by American freaks, many of whom were wanted in the United States, the RCMP had been unable to gain any assistance in locating the commune.

Stu was also of the opinion that a trip to Slocan Valley might produce further information from Karen about her fugitive friends, especially since I was on the run myself. He would call Jack right away, brief him on my conversation with Marvelous Marv, and advise him of our travel plans. I reminded Stu that it would be extremely difficult for me to maintain contact with anyone while Karen was traveling in the van. I wanted to be certain that both he and Jack were aware of the communications problem so that neither side would become overly concerned at not hearing from me. Stu assured me that he would thoroughly explain the situation.

By late Sunday morning, we were ready to leave the city. Joy would serve as the communications link with Seattle during our absence, and we planned to contact her periodically for messages. At my insistence, she also agreed to telephone Marvelous Marv and request any additional help he might be able to offer. I felt certain that Joy's call would not only increase my credibility but also give Marv the impression that I was following his advice.

In view of our belated departure, we didn't arrive in Hope, British Columbia, until mid-afternoon. From Hope, we traveled east on Highway 3 through a scenic stretch of snow-covered forests and mountains. After crossing Allison Pass, I stopped at a campground in the Manning Provincial Park just before nightfall.

Although the campground was covered with snow and completely deserted, several of the campsites still had stacks of firewood. The outdoor toilets were unlocked, and from all indications, the area was officially open for winter camping. After discovering that all of the wood was too wet to burn, I could understand why we were alone. There would be no hot meal cooked over an open fire on that particular evening.

The temperature inside the van plunged to well below freezing that night, and we tossed and turned constantly as we vainly struggled to find a warm, comfortable position. The single-size mattress wasn't big enough for two people, and it was impossible to spread both sleeping bags out in the usual manner. After hours of frustration, we decided to unzip both bags. We then placed one on the mattress and the other on top of us. It was a workable solution but far from ideal.

Early the next morning, we continued our journey, stopping for breakfast in the town of Princeton. The hot food seemed to relax us both after the misery and discomfort that had interfered with the night's sleep. But in addition to suffering from fatigue, Karen was also worried about my fugitive status and the possibility of being arrested. The combination of all these factors made her nervous and irritable. When she crawled into the rear of the van for a beer, a joint, and a hit of speed, I knew it would be a long day.

I stopped in Castlegar for gas that afternoon, and when I returned from the rest room I noticed Karen rummaging frantically through her cardboard boxes. Just as I pulled out of the service station, she nonchalantly swallowed a hit of acid.

"Wanna do some acid, Chief?" she said tauntingly. "It'll make you feel lots better."

Karen was well aware of my feelings about psychedelics. "Sure, Ralphie, sure!" I answered in mock excitement. "But will it make my drivin' any better?"

It was almost dark when we turned onto Highway 6 at the tiny village of South Slocan. Even though Karen was soaring like an eagle and babbling incoherently, I was elated to reach Slocan Valley. After hearing so much about the area, I was eager to see what it was actually like.

Karen had been smoking intermittently throughout the afternoon, and had placed a hefty chunk of hash, a pipe, and my pocketknife on top of the engine cover. I had agreed to join her in the last pipeful, and she was skillfully slicing more hash off the large chunk as we were passing through Slocan Park. Suddenly I noticed an RCMP squad car parked off to the left in front of a small store. Within minutes after I relayed this observation to Karen, we heard the wail of a siren and noticed the reflection of flashing red lights in the outside mirror.

We both went into a state of panic. Since I wasn't speeding, I knew this couldn't be a routine traffic stop. The van was littered with empty beer bottles, roaches, and tiny slivers of artfully carved hashish. Karen was hysterically spaced, I was half-loaded, and the interior was permeated with the odor of illegal smoking material. If this wasn't "probable cause," the Canadian legal system was in big trouble. And at the moment, so were we.

The chase had begun so suddenly that we had no time to hide things. Since the guy had apparently followed us without his lights on, I didn't even know he was behind us until we heard the siren. Karen was frantically kicking beer bottles under the seat and grabbing for her drugs as I pulled off the narrow two-lane road. The van had scarcely rolled to a stop before I jumped out and walked back to the patrol car. The police officer was just stopping when I arrived at his door.

If there was ever a time in my life when I was friendly, courteous, respectful, and downright humble, that was it. We chatted amiably for at least five minutes before he even ventured a glance toward the van. It was all "yes, sir" and "no, sir" as I made a conscious effort to answer each of his questions. While many of his questions seemed innocuous, it was obvious that his primary interest was our identity, destination, and where we would be staying.

After requesting a radio check of my driver's license through the FBI's National Crime Information Center (NCIC), he ambled over to the van and glanced in at Karen. She flashed a big smile and greeted him warmly. It never ceased to amaze me how the lady could be floating in outer space one minute, then suddenly return to earth as though she had never left it. Even so, it was a good thing the officer couldn't see her eyes. Before he had a chance to start a conversation, the radio in his squad car squawked abruptly, and he returned to answer the call. The NCIC inquiry was negative, as I knew it would be, and he seemed satisfied. We parted cordially, and by the time I returned to the van, Karen had already started reloading the hash pipe.

Although it was another fifty miles farther, I had seen a listing on the map for a campground north of Rosebery. At the moment, it looked like our only choice. What I didn't know was that those fifty miles would involve some unbelievably tricky driving, especially at night. The twisting road, much of which was unpaved, had a myriad of tight mountain switchbacks. Some stretches were hewn out of the mountainside, and several of the spooky tunnels were wide enough for only one vehicle at a time. The darkness obscured the sheer dropoffs into Slocan Lake several hundred feet below. It was definitely not the type of road to explore in the dead of the night while stoned on hash.

It seemed as though we'd been traveling for weeks when we finally saw the sign for Rosebery Park. I noticed only two other cars as I drove through the campground and pulled into the first available campsite. A quick trip to the outhouse located just across the way, and we were huddled under the sleeping bags.

By daylight, we saw that Slocan Valley was an isolated, undeveloped area of incomparable natural beauty. The area I was interested in stretched approximately seventy miles along Highway 6 from around Winlaw on the south to our campground north of Rosebery. The town of New Denver, about six miles south of the campsite, was our headquarters for gasoline and groceries. The tiny community stretched only a few blocks west to the shore of Slocan Lake which occupied virtually all of the valley between two mountain ranges. Above the far shore of the ice-blue lake, five windswept miles from New Denver, loomed the majestic, snow-covered mountains.

Five miles past New Denver was the village of Silverton, and another twenty-five or so farther along was the town of Slocan. Only a few communities were scattered through the thirty-mile area of unspoiled wilderness.

At the town of Slocan, the lake narrowed into the Slocan River. To the south toward Winlaw were rolling valleys criss-crossed by dirt roads running east and west from Highway 6. This was the heartland of the valley's agriculture. The family farms, which generally had only a few acres in cultivation and a few head of livestock, seemed just large enough to provide the necessities of life for the owners.

Most of the farms were owned by descendants of the Doukhobors, a religious sect of Russian peasants who emigrated to Canada in 1898 to escape persecution. From what I was told, the Doukhobors were a hardworking, self-sufficient group who lived by their old beliefs and traditions. These views occasionally clashed with those of the Canadian government, especially in the area of public education. During the past few decades, this conflict had erupted in a rash of bombings and arson for which a number of Doukhobors were now reportedly serving prison sentences.

These old fashioned Slocan Valley farmers were perturbed by the influx of long-haired, American hippies, and their occasional hostility was not without justification.

What seemed to infuriate them most was the fact that the freaks had no respect for their property. During the summer, tents, teepees, and shelters would spring up everywhere. The problem was almost impossible to control. If a cabin, barn, or outbuilding was vacant, freaks would move in and stay until the farmers ran them out. Some of these dilapidated log structures were owned by Doukhobors who were in prison. It was frequently mentioned that when the rightful owners were freed, the long-haired occupants would be dealt with severely.

The atmosphere of antagonism didn't seem to faze the great majority of freaks. While many simply lived off the land as squatters, a surprising number of Americans had bought acreage with the intention of settling permanently. For the most part, these people had fled the United States to avoid military service and had since obtained landed immigrant status in Canada. Land in Slocan Valley was cheap, isolated, and incredibly beautiful. With an abundance of timber, water, and fertile soil, self-sufficiency was possible. The increasing population of dissident Americans provided a constant supply of drugs, and the absence of any meaningful law enforcement made dealing hassle-free. It wasn't difficult to understand the reason for the area's popularity.

In the days that followed, Karen and I explored nearly every one of the meandering dirt roads between Winlaw and Slocan. The number of dwellings was overwhelming, and I could understand why the RCMP had difficulty policing the area. Everywhere there were battered cars, vans, and trucks bearing American license plates, oftentimes parked in the middle of nowhere. Many of the cabins could only be reached on foot after a lengthy walk through the dense forest. Without specific directions from the inhabitants, they were virtually impossible to find. The amazing thing about the whole region was that if you confined your travels to Highway 6, you would never know about all those people, houses, and vehicles in the backwoods.

After a long winter of snow, many of the resident freaks were starting to get out and visit one another. I picked up every hitchhiker and had many fascinating conversations. We were invited to visit one commune where we sampled homemade wine and smoked the most recent crop of homegrown grass. Since it was early spring, the main activities in the valley were gardening and socializing. But just about everyone we met spoke of the annual spring festival to be held in late May as the social event of the year for valley residents.

Driving north from Rosebery Park one morning, we rounded a sharp curve and were startled to see a wild-looking freak trudging out of the forest. He was a gaunt figure with a scraggly black beard and a mass of hair that jutted out from his head in corkscrew ringlets. When he casually stuck out his thumb for a lift, I couldn't resist.

This was my introduction to "The Chicken Man," or "Man," as he would later be known, "Mr. Chicken." The very moment he climbed into the van, I was certain he was a genuine space case. From the far-away look in his eyes, I figured he had done one microgram too many, and was now in a permanent short circuit.

The Chicken Man lived a few miles up the road near the tiny hamlet of Hills. When he cheerfully invited us in for a visit, I turned off the highway and followed his directions through a fenced pasture toward a surprisingly well-built residence. As we neared the house, the Chicken Man guided me past the structure to a rickety, two-room shack some thirty yards away. A piece of rusted tin roofing served as the door, and the entire place was no bigger than a walk-in closet. Furnishings consisted of a broken chair, small table, and a pallet. There was no plumbing, electricity, or water. The two window frames were covered with sheets of cracked, yellowing plastic.

We accepted the offer of some tea to be brewed with mint just gathered by our host from a nearby meadow. After he chopped kindling for the wood-burning stove, and while the tea steeped in a dented pot, we sat on the floor and attempted conversation. The Chicken Man was originally from Oakland, but like many of those in the valley, he had fled the United States to avoid military service. He was now a Canadi-

247

an citizen and supported himself by working only one month each year. In two weeks of picking apples and two weeks of planting trees, he earned about three hundred dollars, which was all the money he needed to live comfortably.

As I sipped the steaming mint tea from a tin cup, there was something about the layout of the house that reminded me of my grandparents' farm in central Texas. When I peered through a section of broken flooring and saw a foundation of gray-white dung, it all came back: this was a chicken coop!

In response to my inquiry, the Chicken Man readily acknowledged that the structure had once been a chicken house.

"But doesn't all that chicken shit smell?" I asked incredulously.

"It ain't too bad in the winter," he replied. "Gets a little rank in the summer though. When it's frozen, you can't smell it. But like I don't pay no rent, man, and when it's warm, I sleep outside."

The Chicken Man then proceeded with a lengthy discourse on mind control and cosmic consciousness. But since the chicken house was no more than a windbreak at best, I was curious about how he survived the bitter winters.

"You've got to program your conscious being to think warm," he answered earnestly. "In the higher states of consciousness, your mental awareness can block out any physical reactions to the cold. If your mind thinks you're warm, then your body'll be warm."

I was going to ask whether this consciousness allowed him to program his nose to disregard the pungent odor of chicken shit in warm weather, but decided against it.

Karen offered to share some hash with our host, but he refused. Though once a serious abuser, he claimed he had given up all drugs because they interfered with his consciousness level. We thanked him for his hospitality and headed back to the van.

"Come back anytime," he yelled. "I don't get to talk to many people up here."

It wasn't difficult to understand why.

Looking back, it seems inconceivable that after having lived intimately with Karen, I wouldn't have anticipated our difficulties in camping and living out of a van. I think the lack of foresight resulted from the fact that although we had lived in the same house, we frequently went our separate ways. We had seldom been alone together for long periods of time; now we were together twenty-four hours a day, seven days a week. There was no getting away.

It was frightening how confining the van became when two people tried to live inside in subfreezing temperatures. In the commune, I could shut the bedroom door and try to sleep through the early morning drug marathons. And if the situation became unbearable, I'd take a night off and crash in the van. Even a drive to a local store would provide a few moments of peaceful solitude. But now there was no store nearby and besides, what would I do with Karen? The van was her only home.

Perhaps it should have also occurred to me that Karen just wasn't cut out for roughing it. After camping nearly all of my life, I must have assumed Karen had done the same. It was quickly evident that this was an erroneous assumption.

The increasing tension that was steadily building between us was not entirely Karen's fault. My brain was getting as scrambled as hers because of the continuous mental stress of living the big lie and constantly weighing every word before speaking. I had also failed to realize the importance of my frequent conversations with Stu, Fred, and other agents. They served as my only link with the past and gave me the opportunity to speak openly with people who knew my true identity and occupation. Now I was more like a prisoner of my mind; my inner thoughts were my only escape.

A typical evening of camping in Rosebery Park found me gathering wood before nightfall. The van would be pulled into a secluded, U-shaped clearing alongside the picnic table. Its side doors were opened to allow the stereophonic sounds of Stephen Stills to float into the wilderness. Once I got the campfire going, we would sit outside in the crisp, clean air smoking dope and drinking whiskey, wine, or both.

Having been elected "Outdoorsman of the Year," by default, I was given the responsibility of preparing all meals. It wasn't that I didn't do a good job, but the unavailability of supplies didn't allow for much variation in menu planning.

Immediately after our outdoor meal, we'd head for the van. Early April was still a bit nippy in the Canadian forest. Once inside the cramped quarters, there was little to do in the way of diversion. If we had been driving that day and the battery was sufficiently charged, we might use the interior lights for reading. We generally kept the stereo tape deck going, but always with an eye on the alternator gauge. A dead battery out here would be disastrous.

Most evenings, our entertainment centered around sex and drugs. After being together all day, there usually wasn't much left to talk about, and by nightfall we were generally so loaded that a passionate round of hard-core sex seemed the most viable alternative. But as the nights passed and the pressures between us continued to build, Karen began to use more and more drugs. Between the camping, the cold, and the confining environment of the van, she was simply over-whelmed. And without the conveniences of urban living, she became increasingly irritable.

Aside from just grating on my nerves, Karen had also become a problem from a professional standpoint. While traveling the back roads around Winlaw, I had noticed a large number of vehicles whose registration information could be of special significance. For several years the Bureau had indexed lists of license numbers, vehicle descriptions, and aliases used by Weatherman fugitives and their suspected supporters. But with Karen in the van, it was impossible to write down license numbers without her becoming suspicious.

Late one morning, we stopped at the Winlaw general store which also served as the post office and gas station, just in time to see three freaks jump into a beat up old Chevy and roar off toward Slocan. From no more than a quick glance at a distance of twenty yards, one of the guys looked exactly like our most recent photograph of Weatherman fugitive Mark Rudd. With Karen right by my side, however, I was un-able to get a license number or follow them. I watched helplessly as the vehicle disappeared in the distance.

A similar situation occurred when we visited communes. I couldn't vary my cover story from the one Karen knew even though it might have been advantageous to do so.

It had also become obvious that Karen had no "fugitive friends" in the valley. In fact, she didn't know any more about the region than I did. Before leaving Seattle, we had discussed traveling to the Banff area, and although I was now of the opinion it would be no more pro-ductive than our present location, we had to do something before we drove each other crazy. At least while we were traveling, we could stop for a decent meal. A night in a motel with a hot shower and a comfortable bed didn't sound that bad either.

Early the next morning, we broke camp and drove north to the town of Nakusp, on the shores of Arrow Lake. From Nakusp we took an incredible wilderness journey up Highway 23 to Galena, where we rode the ferry across Upper Arrow Lake to Shelter Bay. Although it didn't look far at all on the map, the drive was tedious and time con-suming. When we arrived in the city of Revelstoke, it was almost dark.

We checked into a cheap motel and immediately indulged ourselves with a hot shower. The opportunity to have clean hair again and the expectation of sleeping in a bed with crisp white sheets elevated our spirits. Refreshed and clean, we went out to a nearby restaurant and gorged ourselves. It was easily the most enjoyable night we'd had since leaving Seattle.

We slept until almost checkout time the following morning, ate a hearty breakfast, and after gassing up the van in Revelstoke, we traveled through Glacier National Park to Golden. Though it was late in the day, we pushed on toward the province of Alberta and Banff National Park.

Shortly after we entered Yoho National Park, I noticed a prominent road sign, located right in the middle of the wilderness, which somehow belatedly called attention to the fact that there were no gas stations for the next seventy miles. A check of the gas gauge indicated we could be in for serious trouble. But it was getting late, and by the time we doubled back to Golden, it would be dark. I decided to go for it.

Even the unpleasant thought of being stranded without gas couldn't diminish the incomparable beauty of the Canadian Rockies. Although the highway was clear, everything else was covered in a blanket of glittering snow. Since there were few visitors at this time of the year, bighorn sheep had moved down from the high country in search of food. They walked right up to the van when we stopped and stared at us as though wondering what we were doing there in winter.

Driving slowly through the mountain valley, I glanced off to the right and noticed a large elk trudging through the field just as the sun was going down. He sported a massive rack of antlers and was pushing through unbroken snow that almost reached his shoulders. It was an unforgettable sight and a reminder that this pristine wilderness belonged to the wildlife; man was simply a seasonal visitor.

After a stop to view the awe-inspiring beauty of Lake Louise, I noted that the gas gauge was edging ominously close to "E." As we pushed through the darkness toward the town of Banff, what concerned me the most was that in the entire trip through Yoho and Banff National Parks, we had seen a grand total of three cars. Not exactly one of your better roads to be stranded on. But we had to be getting close to Banff. Judging from the mileage indicator, I figured we had to be within ten miles of our destination.

We were approaching the crest of a small hill when I first felt the engine hesitate, then begin that sickening sputter that can only mean one thing: you're out of gas, dummy! After trying to coax a few more yards out of the engine, it coughed one last time and died as we coasted to a stop by the side of the road.

Karen didn't seem that upset over our predicament until I started to dig through the drawers in search of insulated underwear and heavy clothing. Only then did she realize that if I hiked for gas, she would be left alone in the van. I didn't like the idea any more than she did, but there was no other choice. We might be there all night before another car came by, and if I didn't get to Banff within the next few hours, the gas stations might well be closed.

I was concerned about leaving Karen behind in the van, but she couldn't possibly make the walk in subfreezing temperatures without proper clothing. It would be cold enough *inside* the van. I cautioned her against playing the tape deck for fear of running down the battery, and I instructed her to keep the doors locked and remain inside. I slipped the automatic in my boot, primarily to keep it away from Karen, and climbed out of the van.

The stars were shining brightly and provided plenty of illumination. But at the same time, the absence of any cloud cover, combined with a light wind, made it bitterly cold. For the first few minutes, the cold air seemed to paralyze my lungs, and it took several minutes of brisk walking to adapt. Fortunately, since I had on plenty of warm clothing, it wasn't unbearable as long as I was moving.

Having become resigned to the fact that a walk into Banff was inevitable, I was beginning to question whether I'd seriously misjudged the distance. I heard the sound of an approaching car but there was no sign of headlights. Then suddenly, lights appeared from behind me. Standing near the center of the road, I waved frantically to be certain the driver saw me. Not only did he see me, he damn near ran over me as he sped into the darkness. There was nothing for me to do but keep walking.

Some ten minutes later, I was surprised to hear another car approaching from the direction of the van. This time I stood by the side of the road and casually held out my thumb. I might not get a ride, but at least I wouldn't get run down. The car slowed as it neared me and pulled to a stop only a few yards beyond where I was standing.

The driver was a middle-aged traveling salesman from Calgary. Having passed the van several miles back, he had correctly surmised the problem. Since he traveled the road regularly, and frequently at night, he carried a large can of gasoline in his trunk. After convincing him that I had the money to pay for the gas, he agreed to drive me back to the van and then follow us into Banff where I could reimburse him. He noted that we were only a couple of miles away from town, and after driving back to the van, he advised me that I had just completed a six-and-one-quarter mile trek. At the time, it didn't seem that far.

I hastily emptied the contents of the can into the tank and replaced it in his trunk. I briefly greeted Karen, and noting that she was nervous and frightened, I thought it wise to get moving as soon as possible. When we got to Banff, I filled up the van and gas can.

After accepting our thanks and the gas refill, the good samaritan from Calgary resumed his journey, and we stopped at a small coffee shop on the main street. Once inside the brightly lighted establishment, it was obvious that Karen was messed up. Although she wouldn't admit to it, I was certain that during my absence she had taken speed or acid, or quite possibly both. When our dinner arrived and she obstinately refused to eat, I knew it would be a long night.

Had I been able to locate a motel that evening, perhaps things would have been different. But this was the beginning of spring skiing, and Banff was packed. Our only choice was to head back out the road we had just traveled and stop in one of the numerous National Park campgrounds. According to my road map, they were all open for winter camping.

When I pulled into a snowcovered campground near the ski area road, I was surprised to see a number of large mobile homes and recreational vehicles. They apparently belonged to weekend skiers from Calgary and were all equipped with generating systems that provided light and heat. While the generators were noisy, I would soon discover they were also essential.

That first evening, parked in the snow of Alberta, turned out to be the longest, coldest, most miserable and frustrating night I ever endured in the van. Having become depressed and withdrawn, Karen ceased to communicate. She must have undergone some frightening experience when I struck out for gas and she was left alone. I had an idea that she had taken LSD and freaked out in the chilly darkness of the van.

Now she was speeding like a runaway freight train, and the only solution was to ride it out.

It was unmercifully cold inside the van, and I tried to warm it up by using the catalytic heater. I was always reluctant to run the heater when two people were inside the cramped quarters because it might tip over. If the shag carpeting caught on fire, the whole interior would go up in seconds. And while the heater didn't produce carbon monoxide, it did consume oxygen. For this reason a window had to be opened a little to provide air. The warm air was therefore quickly dissipated.

253

Karen was justifiably furious about the cold, and I wasn't all that happy about it myself. But what could I do? There were no rooms available at any price. I finally persuaded her to get under the sleeping bags for warmth. Sleep appeared out of the question. Our breath seemed to freeze as we lay there shivering. Karen began to toss, turn, and cry.

The only possible solution was to put the catalytic heater between the front seats and crack the windows open a bit. It would be one helluva fire hazard, but it was better than freezing. Karen was placated by my attempts, though I doubted they would produce much in the way of tangible benefits.

Later that night, I felt that I was drowning. My head was pounding wildly. I gasped for air, and struggled with all my might to reach the surface. In sheer terror, I bolted up from the sleeping bag, gulping desperately. The temperature was almost tropical. I jumped over the front seat and flung open the door to discover that a light snow was falling. Just as I expected, Karen had closed the windows, and the propane-powered heater had consumed most of the oxygen.

The temperature inside the van plunged rapidly as the frigid air rushed through the open door. Apparently unaffected by the lack of oxygen, Karen screamed wildly that I was trying to freeze her out. She was on the verge of hysteria and clearly beyond reason. The fact that we might have suffocated was of no importance. What mattered now was that she was hysterical, irrational, and freezing, and it was all my fault. Not only had I *deserted* her earlier during my walk to Banff, now I was *intentionally* trying to freeze her. Her pent-up frustration, stress, and anxiety were now directed squarely at me.

She threw off the sleeping bag and began putting on layers of clothing. It was too cold to sleep, she screamed. She would stay up all night. She alluded to a conspiracy that would result in her freezing to death while sleeping. I refused to comment on her theory; instead, I started the engine to allow the van's heater to warm up the interior. As I silently crawled back under the sleeping bag, Karen violently jammed a tape into the deck and cranked up the volume.

"A little music won't bother you will it, Chief?" she screamed over the furor. I didn't offer a reply.

"Hey Chiefie! Chief!" she yelled. "If I gotta stay up all night freezing my ass off, I might as well be tripping, huh? Wanna do some acid, Chiefie? Come on, Chiefie, whadaya say? How about just one hit of windowpane?"

I heard her rummaging through her purse but made no reply. What good would it do, I thought. This was going to be another midnight-to-dawn marathon.

Neither of us slept a wink that night. Karen remained in the front seat while I stayed in back on the mattress. She played tape after tape, often singing along at the top of her lungs. But once that speeding roller coaster was replaced by a spaceship, she became quiet and introspective.

At one point, she crawled back and retrieved a spiral-bound notebook. I could hear her frenzied scribbing as she filled page after page. While talking to herself, she flipped through the pages as though reading in the dark. Then she would violently rip out each sheet and fling it across the seat. A pencil snapped noisily and suffered a similar fate as it bounded off the window.

Lying there in the frigid darkness and witnessing her pitiful behavior, I was overwhelmed by a feeling of hopeless frustration. I was fed up with this recurring psychedelic scenario, but at that particular point, I just felt sorry for Karen and wanted to help her. But how? What could I do short of revealing who I was and what I was doing? And most agonizing of all, what if *I* had caused this problem?

My god, I thought, this wasn't just some deep cover target I was living with, this was a human being. Behind that outrageous, drug-crazed facade, Karen was really longing for something to believe in—anything, anybody. But it seemed as though everything she had committed herself to ultimately fell apart: education, politics, employment, religion, relationships. Try as she might, it just never came together.

I could never decide exactly what prevented Karen from facing reality, but somehow she couldn't—or wouldn't—allow herself to find happiness. It was almost as though she wanted to destroy a relationship because she feared it wouldn't last. It was a self-destructive cycle, and I had compounded the anguish.

The only logical course of action was to get Karen back to Seattle and fade graciously out of her life. Maybe I couldn't help her, but at least I wouldn't make matters worse. In addition to concern for her well-being, I was also motivated by my own selfish considerations, not the least of which was my sanity. On several occasions, I had felt myself edging dangerously close to violence.

Upon examining the relationship, I think I basically resented the constant intrusions on my peace of mind. While I was content to smoke dope and go with the flow, Karen was always chemically energized, constantly bombarding me with questions, comments, and opinions. In a very real sense, she had served as my guide into an unknown world that was totally, completely, and unequivocally drug-related. Now I realized that I was in over my head.

When the first rays of sunlight peaked over the mountains, I rolled out of the sleeping bag and moved up to the driver's seat. The front compartment resembled a disaster area. Hundreds of torn, crumpled pages littered the floorboard along with two full boxes of used Kleenex. Tapes, beer cans, and pieces of clothing were scattered over the seats and dashboard. Karen sat leaning against the door, wrapped in blankets, ski jacket, and sleeping bag. She stared blindly into space and said nothing.

After getting the van started and the heater going, I began to clean up the mess. Only then did Karen show signs of life. It was evident that she didn't want me to see her drug-induced scribbling. A fleeting glance revealed the reason why: most of the writing looked like that of a six-year-old. Fragmented words and letters were crudely scrawled four to five lines high. An entire sheet of paper might be consumed by a phrase or partial sentence. Then the writing became miniscule and almost impossible to decipher.

I was more certain than ever that we were returning to Vancouver. Once the ice and snow were scraped off the windshield, we left the campground and drove to the coffee shop in Banff. Karen sat impassively as I went inside. The place was packed with happy, carefree skiers who were enjoying breakfast before driving out to the ski area. I desperately wanted to go with them.

Armed with the thermos of black coffee, I sped out of Banff with an overriding purpose: to reach Vancouver and put an end to this madness. It was almost an hour before Karen spoke to me.

"Where we going, Chief?" she said softly.

"Vancouver."

"How come? I thought we were gonna drive up to Jasper."

"It's too cold to camp, Ralph, and besides, we need to get back."

"Well Chief, you can't possibly drive all the way to Vancouver."

"You're exactly right, Ralph," I snapped. "That's why I wanna borrow a couple of those Christmas Trees."

Karen's mouth fell open in shocked disbelief. Through all of our times together, I had never taken a hit of speed. But I had a reason now, and it seemed like a damn good one. I was exhausted after the freezing, sleepless, chaotic night, and I was determined that it wouldn't happen again. The fact that Vancouver was six hundred tedious miles away was inconsequential. I popped the green and white

Dexamyl Spansule into my mouth and washed it down with the coffee. Karen moved back to the mattress as I psyched myself for some high-speed, cross-country driving.

Karen slept soundly throughout the day while I pushed the van and my body to the limit. She awoke late that afternoon as though nothing unusual had happened and seemed in good spirits. In our subsequent conversations, she apologized profusely for her behavior. Even though I assured her that the incident was forgotten, I'm certain that she sensed I was fed up and in no mood for a repeat performance.

At Karen's suggestion, we camped that evening at Nicolum River Park, just east of Hope. Considering my mental and physical exhaustion, it took little persuasion to get me to stop for the night. Trying hard to make amends, Karen even cooked dinner.

We arrived in Vancouver the following day and learned that nothing of significance had occurred during our absence. Joy offered the use of her bathroom to allow us to clean up. Since Karen had to return to her job in Seattle or lose it, the realization that we would no longer be together was beginning to sink in. She became depressed, irrational, and demanding. She slept in Joy's apartment that night while I stayed outside in the van.

Late the next morning, I loaded her possessions into the van and drove her to the bus station in downtown Vancouver. Once again she offered copious apologies, and once again, I accepted. In reality, I think she was overjoyed by the fact that I had even bothered to bring her back. I bought her bus ticket and gave her a couple of months' rent in advance. Since she was always short of money, I didn't want her to go hungry until she received her first paycheck.

While waiting for her bus, we devised a telephone communications system, and I instructed her to send any correspondence to the post office at New Denver. Based on advice given Joy by Marvelous Marv, Karen would take our tourist visa to Seattle, where she would mail it to Canadian Immigrations with a note explaining that we had forgotten to stop off and return the form. According to Marv, the Seattle postmark would convince Canadian authorities we had left the country.

After a tearful, emotional parting, Karen reluctantly boarded the bus for Seattle. I was both relieved and saddened.

Within twenty-four hours after Karen's departure, I had crossed the Canadian border and was sitting comfortably in the living room of my "drug connection" at Bellingham, Washington. I had been summoned to a debriefing on the deep cover operation with representatives of the RCMP and FBI. My drug connection, an FBI agent assigned to the Bellingham Resident Agency, was present, along with Stu from the Seattle office, and Jack from the Special L Squad in Vancouver.

According to the sketchy information I received when I first arrived in Seattle, the Royal Canadian Mounted Police (RCMP) were charged with the responsibility for both law enforcement and intelligence activities. In other words, various divisions within the RCMP performed the functions divided between the FBI and CIA in the United States. From what I was told, the Security Services (SS) Branch of the RCMP was composed exclusively of college graduates who worked in a plainclothes, semicovert capacity in areas of intelligence-gathering, counterintelligence, and national security. The Criminal Branch was composed primarily of the traditional, uniformed Mounties who handled everything from traffic enforcement to criminal investigations.

While the Security Services Branch possessed sophisticated surveillance and informant capabilities, they had steadfastly refused to assist the FBI in locating the Weatherman fugitives. Officially, they reasoned that since the Weathermen were legally considered criminal fugitives, any assistance provided by the RCMP should come from the Criminal Branch. Unofficially, I was told, they were concerned about the sweeping implications of the Watergate scandal and the current leadership crisis in the FBI.

There were also strong indications of rivalry between the two branches. The security branch was said to consist of intellectual elitists, while the criminal branch was supposedly composed of cop-on-the-beat types. On the surface at least, it was a rivalry not unlike that of the CIA and FBI.

In view of the refusal by the Special Services Branch, the RCMP had designated the Special L Squad of the Criminal Branch to assist the FBI in its search for the Weathermen. The Criminal Branch had apparently once been given the responsibility for internal security as it applied to foreign, religious, or ethnic groups residing in Canada. There were a number of plainclothes squads, each designated by alphabetical letters referring to the particular group under investigation. The L Squad was now assigned exclusively to provide ongoing liaison for the FBI's Weatherman investigations.

I had already met Jack in the spring of 1972 when he toured the November Committee Headquarters in Venice. He was an outgoing type who seemed genuinely interested in assisting the Bureau. Since Jack and the Special L Squad had served as contacts for FBI informants sent on assignments into Canada, he was well-acquainted with those involved in the Weather Underground. But while he made a concerted effort to provide the necessary assistance, he frequently reminded us that the investigative resources of the Special L Squad were extremely limited compared to those of Special Services Branch.

Although he was certainly aware of my deep cover objectives in Canada, I don't think he had the slightest idea of how we were trying to accomplish them. On the occasion of the Bellingham debriefing, he was openly irritated by my failure to maintain regular contact while traveling with Karen. This was exactly the problem I had sought to avoid by having Stu explain the inherent difficulties in communications. But I could readily understand Jack's displeasure, for he had been placed in an embarrassing bureaucratic squeeze by two separate governments.

When Karen and I had been stopped by the RCMP officer in Slocan Park, he had checked my identification through the NCIC computer. Though the officer received a routine reply that I was not "wanted," all hell broke loose at FBI headquarters. The Revolutionary Activities Section of the Domestic Intelligence Division was immediately notified that the RCMP had inquired about the fictitious identity of a deep cover operative in Canada. Red Alert! What's gone wrong? Was he arrested? Is he in jail? Did he have an accident?

Frantic calls from the Bureau to Seattle. Seattle ordered to contact Special L immediately and find out what was going on. Jack doesn't have the slightest idea, because I haven't called in. Then Jack's superiors jump his ass because the RCMP is supposed to be assisting an undercover FBI agent, and they don't even know where the guy is! It was a bureaucratic nightmare. Evidently, no one ever stopped to think that Karen wasn't my colleague in the deep cover operation.

Jack finally solved the problem by contacting the Mountie who stopped us, and one night after that, I had called him from a pay phone in New Denver. While discussing the incident during our debriefing, Jack mentioned that the RCMP officer in the Slocan Valley had been instructed to stop and identify the occupants of every vehicle bearing U.S. license plates.

Jack couldn't resist throwing a subtle barb about my hippy image. "The officer mentioned there was something very suspicious about you, Bill."

"Yeah, what's that, Jack?" I asked.

"He said he'd never seen a hippy who was so damn polite. Said there was something strange when a long-haired Yank didn't act like a smart-ass."

"Guess it's just my respect for authority, Jack," I said jokingly. I felt like saying, you're goddammed right I kissed his ass, Jack! With Karen flying on speed, acid, hash, grass, and alcohol, the van looking like a mobile pharmacy, and me half-loaded, what would you do, tell him to get fucked? As I recall, I'd tried that approach in Miami and ended up with a rebuilt asshole!

With the exception of the communications problem, the general tenor of our debriefing session was decidedly optimistic. Jack and Stu were both of the opinion that we were proceeding in the right direction with opportunities for a major breakthrough in Seattle, Vancouver, and Slocan Valley. And when I related my experiences with Chicken Man, Jack was instantly elated.

According to Jack, Chicken Man was believed to have been a former resident of the mysterious "Weatherman Haven North." And what was important, he was thought to have witnessed a murder that had occurred near the commune. Among the many nonfugitives who supported the Weathermen was a young physician from San Francisco—I'll call him "Doctor Demento." It seems that the good doctor and his ol' lady regularly smuggled drugs across the border for delivery at the commune. But Doctor Demento became enamored of another communal resident, and in a drug-induced fit of passion, murdered his ol' lady. Her body was then buried in the wilderness, and Jack said that the Chicken Man was now the only living person who knew the location of the grave. A few months after the murder, Doctor Demento and his new ol' lady stopped at a shabby motel room near the Canadian border. The doctor and his companion had swallowed balloons full of heroin in order to smuggle it across the border. As fate would have it, their stomach acid dissolved the balloons, and they died instantly from massive overdose.

Based on this startling development, the RCMP requested that I return to Slocan Valley and recontact the Chicken Man in the hope that he would eventually give me a lead to the location of the secret commune as well as to the grave. I was less than ecstatic over the prospect of living in a decrepit chicken house with the strange, mind-controlling Chicken Man.

By the next afternoon, my van had been hidden in Stu's garage outside Seattle, and we were on our way to Sea-Tac International Airport. After twelve weeks on the road, I would be allowed to return to Los Angeles for debriefing and three glorious nights of peaceful relaxation in the privacy of my own apartment. I couldn't get there fast enough.

13

Deep Cover: Commune Life in the Canadian Wilderness

It didn't seem at all unusual to be riding around the streets of Spokane in search of a discreet parking location; in fact, it had become a nightly ritual since traveling and living in the van. I was in Spokane because the Bureau had found out that Weatherman fugitives were using the smaller, less frequented border crossings in eastern Washington, and I had been instructed to return to Slocan Valley by a similar route.

The whirlwind trip to Los Angeles had been more of a culture shock than a quiet, relaxing visit. After twelve weeks of the van, Seattle, Karen and Canada, to be sitting in my own living room seemed unreal. Joe, Rodent, Panda, Jay, and Fast Freddie were all on hand to greet me, and it was great to see them after such a prolonged absence. But I found it extremely difficult to sum up my experiences for them. Many of my more vivid memories had to be worked out in my own mind before I could communicate them to others.

As far as Bureau activities were concerned, nothing seemed to have changed in Los Angeles during my absence. Although the investigation of the Weathermen appeared to be progressing at a snail's pace, few agents seemed overly concerned. The popular Bureau saying, "Every day pays the same and they all count toward twenty," was a realistic way of explaining it didn't make any difference whether the Weathermen were caught next week or next year; career agents would still receive the same amount of money and need the same twenty years for retirement.

On my final day in Los Angeles, I met with the SAC of the Security Division so that he could personally certify me as physically and psychologically fit to continue in deep cover. After I arrived in Seattle early the next morning, Stu again smuggled me into the office basement so that the Seattle SAC could certify the same thing.

When I got to Spokane, I purchased a propane-powered cook-stove and a five-gallon gas can. At least I could have a hot meal when there was no dry wood around, and I would avoid future hikes for gasoline. I crossed into Canada near the town of Nelway and could readily see why it would be a popular spot. There was only one tiny guardhouse at the border. It was situated in the middle of the forest, and it was reminiscent of many European border crossings. The officer never even looked in the van or questioned me about my intentions. The entire procedure took less than three minutes, and I was on my way.

On my way back to Slocan Valley, I stopped in Nelson, B.C. to telephone a member of the RCMP Intelligence Unit. In order to prevent any future communications problems while in the valley, Jack had arranged for a local intelligence officer to serve as my contact man. After advising him of my future plans, I returned to my old home in Rosebery Park and set up camp.

The following morning I drove up to Hills in search of the Chicken Man. There was no sign of the elusive mind-control expert, and the chicken house was closed as tight as the rusted sheet of tin roofing would allow. Since I couldn't locate him, I decided to drive the back roads around Winlaw in search of American license numbers. Now that I was alone, I could begin to identify individuals who were residing in the valley.

I drove into Silverton that evening and placed a call to Karen from the town's only pay phone. I had previously spoken to her from my apartment in Los Angeles, although she was under the impression the call was coming from Canada. On that occasion, she had sounded depressed and distraught over our separation.

Before her departure, we had worked out a communications system involving long distance calls. It was similar to one of the methods employed by the Weathermen and consisted of my placing long-distance calls from Slocan Valley at specific times to prearranged pay phone numbers in Seattle. While living in Seattle, I had compiled a long list for Karen of pay phone numbers and their locations. Karen would wait at a predetermined phone in Seattle for my long-distance *collect* call, answer with a casual "Hello," and advise the operator she would accept the charges. It worked every time.

When Karen answered the pay phone as planned, she did seem to be in better spirits. She filled me in on all the latest happenings around the commune and Red Sun. Our conversation rambled on for several minutes before Karen dropped a bombshell: she was pregnant!

I was stunned. This was a situation I had never even considered in the context of the deep cover program. The problem of venereal disease had been discussed during our in-service at Quantico, but pregnancy was not even mentioned.

"What about the birth control pills?" I finally stammered after a prolonged silence.

"I quit taking those things weeks ago," Karen replied. "They fucked up my system and made me gain weight. Look, Chief, don't worry about it. I'm going to the Free Clinic tomorrow and see about an abortion." She sounded as though it were no bigger problem than a minor cold.

"Okay, Ralph," I said dejectedly, "but look, if you need more money, just let me know, and I'll send it right away."

We made plans for another collect call in two days. I had intended to call Stu at his residence, but after the conversation with Karen, I just wasn't up to it. Instead, I returned to the campground and attempted to make some sense out of what was happening.

I went back to the chicken house the next day, but once again there was no sign of the Chicken Man. While I made attempts at investigating communes around Winlaw, my heart and mind just weren't in it. The situation in Seattle occupied all my thoughts.

When I finally spoke with Karen again, I got right to the point.

"What did the doctor say?"

"I didn't go to the doctor, Chief," she answered. There was a long silence.

"Well, how come, Ralph?" I asked plaintively.

"I've been thinking about it, Chief. I really want a child, and it would be a great opportunity to raise it as a true revolutionary. Our child could grow up in a liberated atmosphere free from all the petty establishment bullshit. I could teach him myself. And—"

"Hey, Ralph," I interrupted. "What's the kid gonna do for a father? Have you forgotten that I've got a small problem with the government? And what are we gonna do for bread? Jesus, Ralph, I don't wanna have a kid I can't even see."

"Well, I'll move to Canada then," she announced defiantly.

"Ralph, let's get our act together before we start thinkin' 'bout havin' a family."

Our conversation continued for some time without even approaching a resolution to the problem. About the only concession I could wangle out of Karen was a reluctant agreement to see a doctor. We made plans to talk again the following evening, and I slowly drove back to camp.

I sat dejectedly in front of the campfire wondering how my personal life had gone so hopelessly out of control. Perhaps this was my reward for exploiting and manipulating people in the name of national security. Were the Weathermen actually capable of starting a revolution in the United States? Or was it essentially just a matter of wounded pride among the pompous bureaucrats and the egotistical politicians? How easy it must be to sit in a plush Washington office with a fat paycheck and nonchalantly talk about penetrating the innermost thoughts of deep cover targets. Hell, these targets weren't paper cutouts! They were *people* with hopes, aspirations, and human frailties exactly like mine. And now one of them wanted to have my child.

Out of all the confusion, only one thing was certain: if Karen had my child, I would be haunted for the rest of my life. How could I ever hope to see the child, or even provide support, without revealing my true identity and employment? That course of action would almost certainly result in my immediate dismissal from the Bureau. On the other hand, if things just rocked along and Karen somehow discovered my true identity, she would probably initiate a paternity suit.

The only practical solution was to argue strongly for an abortion. But since Karen was well aware of my views on the subject, that would be no simple matter. I had long ago formed the opinion that a woman should have the fundamental right to determine what happens to her body.

Now I found myself in an impossible situation made even more frustrating by the fact that I had to argue for a position diametrically opposed to my beliefs. But while I felt strongly that the ultimate decision about pregnancy should be made by the woman, what about the prospective father? Shouldn't he have some say in the matter? He would, after all, bear much of the financial responsibility for the child. And in a very real sense, isn't the child as much a part of him as of the mother? Perhaps the freedom of choice I had long espoused for women could, in certain situations, effectively abridge the rights of the potential father.

I slept fitfully that night and had a hard time getting up the next morning to face the day. As I was cleaning up, who should walk into the campsite but the Chicken Man. He had been strolling by the park and decided to see if I was around. In response to my inquiries about his absence, he mentioned that he had been visiting friends in a commune south of Nelson. Naturally, that got my immediate attention.

Apparently the Chicken Man had sought me out because he needed transportation to the town of Kaslo, some thirty miles away on the shores of Kootenay Lake. I was more than happy to oblige, and in a short time we were traveling down a winding dirt road through the Selkirk Mountains.

Since the Chicken Man was such a space case, it was almost impossible to sustain conversation. He seemed to wander off into prolonged periods of silence. Then, after a fifteen-minute lapse, he would suddenly resume the conversation exactly where it had ended.

Mr. Chicken gave me a guided tour of the town of Kaslo before we stopped at a health food store to buy his supplies. After a trip to a hardware store and a used bookstore, we were back on our way. Passing through New Denver, I noticed a girl standing near the outskirts of town waiting for a ride. She looked strangely out of place since she was relatively clean, without possessions, and wearing a dress. She seemed like an affluent coed spending her spring break as a hippy.

"Hey, that's Debbie!" Mr. Chicken yelled. "She's going up to my place. Let's give her a ride."

I pulled over, and Debbie jumped into the van. She was a friendly, outgoing lady, and I wondered how she and Mr. Chicken knew each other. From what I could tell, they had little in common. Imagine my surprise at learning that some two years earlier, they had spent the entire winter together in the chicken house. In fact, Debbie had just traveled to the commune, which she called Wild Horse Mountain, with Mr. Chicken.

Upon arriving at the chicken house, Debbie prepared some fresh mint tea and, we chatted amiably for a while. There was something very strange about her relationship with Mr. Chicken, but then Mr. Chicken was far from normal. Since I didn't want to miss my call to Karen, I thanked my friends for their hospitality and sped back to New Denver.

Karen answered on the second ring. She was bubbling with excitement because she had been given the name of a contact in Vancouver who could provide false identification and an entree into the underground. In all honesty, I was excited too.

Through the efforts of the Queen, Betty Blotter, and several others, a longtime Seattle activist had been persuaded to provide the name, address, and telephone number of a trusted underground contact in Vancouver. The activist had been involved in radical politics for such a long time that I knew his name, although we had never met. He was no youngster by any means, but exactly the type of person the Weathermen would trust.

Karen provided me with the name of the underground contact—I'll call him "The Professor"—along with his post office box and telephone number in Vancouver. In addition, she told me to mention the name of Wes Black as a mutual friend from the Seattle area. In the event I was unable to contact the Professor at the number provided, I was instructed to ask for Peter, who was a close associate of the Professor's.

Although excited by the news, I was more concerned about Karen's visit to the doctor.

"Did you go to the doctor, Ralph?" I inquired.

"Yes I did, Chief," she replied without elaboration.

"Well, what'd he say?"

"He said I'm too far along for an abortion. But look, Chief, don't worry about it. I've heard about a doctor who'll do 'em anytime. Betty told me about him. I'm gonna go see him next week."

"Okay, Ralph," I said, "but I wouldn't waste any time."

We made plans to contact each other again toward the end of the week. Karen said she was becoming rather paranoid about our telephone system. She was afraid that the police would drive up and bust her in the phone booth after she had accepted charges on a collect call. I agreed to cut down the frequency of our calls and also told her to write to me in New Denver.

On the way back to the campground, I was struck by the thought that things weren't making sense. One day Karen wants to have the child and raise it as a true revolutionary. The next day she agrees to have an abortion. Then she visits a physician, only to find out that she's too far along for an abortion, but at the same time she doesn't seem all that concerned. Though by no means an expert, I had read that therapeutic abortions were generally uncomplicated during the first ninety days of pregnancy. After examining a calendar, I realized that I hadn't even known Karen that long, and during the time we lived together, she claimed to be taking the pill. Very strange indeed.

I drove into Nelson the next morning to telephone Stu. He was beside himself when I told him of the underground contact in Vancouver. Stu knew the Seattle activist and had long suspected him of being in touch with the Weather Underground. Though unfamiliar with the Professor's true name, he said he would check it through Bureau files in Washington and also have Jack review RCMP files in Ottawa. When I gave Stu a list of license numbers I had obtained in the Valley, he said he would try to have the registration results by the time we met for our next debriefing session.

Although I was eager to make contact with the Professor, I felt it would be advantageous to know as much about him as possible in advance. I decided to await the result of Stu's background investigation before proceeding further.

On the following day, I was driving down to Winlaw when I noticed Debbie hitchhiking just outside of Silverton. I pulled over and she jumped in the front seat. She was traveling back to the commune at Wild Horse Mountain where her friends had promised to help cut poles for a teepee she was building. She had bought a teepee kit in Spokane and smuggled it into Canada to avoid paying taxes, and planned to live in it during the coming summer.

Perhaps because I represented free, nonstop transportation, Debbie eagerly invited me to visit the commune and meet her friends. If this was, in fact, Weatherman Haven North, it would be interesting to meet the inhabitants. After the trip to Kaslo, I was certain that it would be more pleasant to ride with Debbie than with Mr. Chicken, though I was compelled to inquire about him.

"He's out in the woods someplace," she replied with some disgust. "You never know what he's gonna do anymore. For that matter, neither does he."

"Didn't you mention that you two spent a winter up there?" I inquired.

"Yeah, but that was before he weirded out. Won't even communicate most of the time. When he was my ol' man, we used to make it all the time. Now he won't even fuck me! Says if he comes, it'll interfere with his mental concentration and keep him from reaching higher levels."

"If ya don't mind my asking, what's sperm got to do with brains?"

"Fuck if I know! To hear him talk, you'd think one climax would make him go crazy."

"Sounds to me like he's crazy already," I commented. "But didn't it get cold in that chicken house during the winter?"

"Cold!" she shouted. "There were times when I thought we'd freeze in our sleep. Snow would blow right through the walls and cover us during the night."

I couldn't help laughing. "You mean you couldn't reach that elevated state of cosmic consciousness where your mind told your body it was warm?"

"Shit, no!" she snapped. "I damn near froze my ass off."

After about an hour of driving, Debbie told me to turn off the highway onto what she called a dirt road, but it was more like a cow path.

It wound up into the Selkirk Mountains where the deep ruts and tight switchbacks were a real challenge for the van. We passed only one house as we traveled some twelve miles before reaching our destination.

The Wild Horse Mountain commune was situated on a gently sloping meadow surrounded by timber-covered mountains. The buildings consisted of two log cabins located some twenty yards apart, and an unfinished shed enclosed on one side by a small corral. A clear stream meandered behind all of the structures and flowed down the sloping terrain before joining a larger river at the base of the mountain.

Debbie introduced me to Kevin, Kath, and JoJo, who were the only permanent residents of Wild Horse Mountain. They were a friendly group who immediately impressed me with their openness and sincerity. Kath and JoJo were originally from New York; Kevin was a native Canadian. I would subsequently learn that JoJo and a friend of his named Aaron had fled the United States in the late sixties to avoid military service. They were accompanied by Kath, who was Aaron's girl friend, and Sher, JoJo's college sweetheart. They eventually made their way to Wild Horse Mountain where they hoped to start a new life free of Vietnam, the draft, and Richard Nixon. Fortunately, JoJo's parents, who were affluent and supportive, gave him enough money to buy forty acres of remote wilderness called "Crown land" from the Canadian government.

With nothing more than a dream, determination, and copies of *The Whole Earth Catalog* and *Foxfire*, these young Americans lived in tents during the summer and early fall as they worked daily on a log cabin to house the four of them. But when the snows came, the house was far from finished. JoJo told me how he and Aaron took turns hiking into the nearest town on snowshoes, some twelve miles away. It was generally a two- to three-day trip, and they could bring back only what supplies they could carry on their backs.

Finally, after months of labor, the two-story structure was completed. They moved in shortly before the holidays, and on Christmas Eve, they staged a celebration. A celebration naturally consisted of drugs, and according to JoJo, all four dropped acid. At some point during the early morning hours of Christmas Day, the log cabin caught on fire, and before they could get their collective act together, it had burned to the ground. They managed to save a few personal items, but for the most part it was a total loss. They found themselves in the midst of winter, with several feet of snow on the ground, and no place to live but a tent.

Both Aaron and Sher eventually left, unwilling to face the ordeal of rebuilding. But JoJo and Kath stayed, later to be joined by Kevin, who developed an attraction for Kath, and by the Chicken Man, who wandered by one day and stayed on.

They built a large cabin the following year in another location. JoJo bought a horse for the monthly trips into town. After the spring thaw, JoJo built his cabin down the hill, and the Chicken Man took up residence in the loft.

I was never exactly clear when Debbie arrived on the scene, but for a brief time, she, JoJo, and Mr. Chicken enjoyed a relatively successful ménage à trois at Wild Horse Mountain. But the situation changed, and Debbie followed Mr. Chicken to the chicken coop. Apparently, one winter was enough. Debbie had spent this past winter living with JoJo at Wild Horse.

I was fascinated by Kath, Kevin, and JoJo and their unique life-style. Considering what they had accomplished and the primitive way they had gone about it, the entire commune was an amazing display of human perserverance.

Light was provided by candles or kerosene lamps, For plumbing, you stepped out on the porch, took a deep breath of unpolluted air, and pissed away. Running water was always available, since one end of a rubber garden hose was positioned in the sink, with a faucet-like clamp attached, while the other end ran through the log wall and was placed well upstream. It was an ingenious, practical way of creating constant water pressure that would never freeze if the flow was constant. When I think of ingenuity, I'm always reminded of the evening's entertainment. And by that I mean *each* and *every* evening. After dining on a healthy but unfilling array of vegetables—all of the residents were strict vegetarians—we'd walk down the hill to JoJo's cabin for the nightly festivities.

On a previous summer, two visiting friends of a friend who were antiques freaks went crazy over a rusting, potbellied stove that had been sitting out back since the disastrous fire. The city chicks figured they could get it for nothing from a bunch of backwoods yokels, but as negotiations progressed, JoJo got exactly what he wanted from the scheming visitors: the eight-track stereo system out of their car.

We'd sit around the one-room cabin, usually smoking my finest hash, while JoJo attached the wires from the tape deck to the twelve-volt battery from his truck. Since the vehicle seldom ran, the battery was almost always located in the cabin. Once the system, complete with two minuscule speakers, was ready to go, JoJo would ceremoniously plug in the tape. It should be noted that this was the one and only tape. Others had been included in the original deal, but they had long since broken.

Even now, virtually every word of every song on that tape remains indelibly etched across my mind. It was Joni Mitchell's *Blue* album and we would sit there night after night listening to it over and over. I can still see us sprawled around the floor, rapping, smoking dope, and watching the sunsets through the plastic sheets that served as windows. After nightfall, our only illumination came from the flickering fire in the stove. As we sat there in the shadows, the log walls seemed to come alive with an endless variety of shapes and textures.

In order to support themselves and keep from going crazy during the long winters, the residents worked on various projects. JoJo made leather shirts, tops, and dresses that were magnificently crafted from the finest skins and constructed with hand-sewn leather strips. Many of the women's tops were highlighted with drawings, beadwork, and feathers. A Vancouver boutique sold much of his work which had the look of authentic Indian craftsmanship.

"But how does a Jewish kid from New York, living in the Canadian wilderness, manage to come up with such realistic designs?" I asked. JoJo laughed as he pointed out each one, as well as the shirt patterns, in the pages of *The Whole Earth Catalog*.

Late each spring, he hitchhiked into Vancouver to sell his winter's production to a number of specialty shops. With a portion of the proceeds, he purchased more skins from a tannery in the city. The remainder of the money was used for communal expenses.

After spending a week at Wild Horse Mountain, I got to know the inhabitants pretty well. I helped JoJo and Kevin finish work on the small barn—a learning experience in itself. Since the group had recently acquired a milk cow and another horse, the barn was badly needed. We went into the dense forest with the chainsaw, selected and cut the trees, dragged the logs out to a clearing, and pulled them back with the truck. We employed the technique of the early pioneers to stack the logs in place: leverage, muscle, and sweat. We also cut poles for the teepee, and the women began the task of removing the bark to allow them to dry. It was to be Debbie's new home and would be erected some forty yards away from the cabins near the river.

The most difficult thing for me to understand was how the group could spend years busting their butts to develop the land, then give serious consideration to moving further north, leaving everything behind to start all over again. But as incredible as it sounds, that's exactly what they were about to do. The Canadian government had decided to allow the cutting of virgin timber several miles beyond the commune on Crown land. Large, diesel-powered logging trucks had already begun traveling past Wild Horse Mountain each day, kicking up suffocating clouds of dust and scaring the animals. Their drivers must have been well paid, for on those roads and with a full load, driving was hazardous at best. For Kevin, Debbie, and JoJo, this was an unacceptable intrusion into a wilderness that had been their sanctuary. They planned to sell their property during the coming year and move to an isolated area in the Coast Mountains just south of Prince Rupert.

While both JoJo and Kath had been well educated in the States, they had forsaken the opportunity for affluence in favor of basic, uncomplicated existence in the wilderness. While their resettlement had initially been motivated by political considerations, they had reached the point where they were decidedly nonpolitical. In fact, they had no information about what had happened in Vietnam or in the United States, and clearly, they didn't care.

When Kath noticed some back issues of American news magazines in the van one afternoon, she asked if she might look at them. I didn't yet know that she hadn't seen such publications in years. The following evenings were spent answering countless questions about Vietnam, Nixon, Watergate, and the antiwar movement. While Kath and JoJo were astounded at what had taken place during their absence, I was equally amazed at their ignorance.

I experienced mixed emotions upon leaving Wild Horse Mountain, although I had no choice in the matter, since a debriefing was scheduled at Trail, B.C. I gave all my magazines to Kath and tried to leave them some stereo tapes, but they wouldn't hear of it. We made plans to see each other at the upcoming spring festival, and after saying good-bye, I headed down the mountain.

As I drove back to Slocan Valley, I reviewed the profound experience of my week at the commune. The people I met had been genuine, sincere individuals dedicated to establishing a new life in the wilderness. I think they realized that *more* is not always *better*, and that the quality of life takes precedence over materialistic quantity. Everything they had was shared freely. In essence, all they really wanted was to be left alone to live their lives in the way they saw fit.

After their warm hospitality and interesting conversations, I was forced to ask myself what right an FBI agent had to violate the privacy of hardworking Canadian citizens in an attempt to learn their political views? The answer was alarmingly simple: none!

I arrived in Nelson around mid-afternoon and decided to cruise the main street before locating a pay phone to call Stu. The area was crowded, and since the town's largest pub looked packed, I parked several blocks away and walked back toward the place. As I passed a downtown newsstand, my eyes instantly focused on the banner headlines. Holy Shit! Haldeman, Ehrlichman, Dean, and Kleindienst had resigned over Watergate! I damn near collapsed. Grabbing a paper, I quickly unfolded it to see a story proclaiming "Ruckelshaus Named Head of FBI." How ironic that I should have kidded JoJo and Kath about being out of touch with current events. I bought *Time, Newsweek,* and a half-dozen papers, and rushed back to the van. I needed uninterrupted quiet so that I could concentrate and try to find out what the hell was going on.

For me, the news was a major disappointment. The resignations of the White House staff members weren't completely unexpected. As for the departure of FBI chief Pat Gray under a cloud of criminal disgrace, it was beyond my comprehension that the Acting Director of the FBI, and a lawyer to boot, would intentionally destroy vital evidence in the Watergate investigation for the sake of political loyalty.

I had admired Pat Gray. He had bucked the entrenched FBI bureaucracy, instituted meaningful, long overdue change, and diligently tried to move the organization into the twentieth century. But this was simply too much. How could he knowingly break the law in the name of political expedience?

Given the benefit of hindsight and years of reflection, I now realize that I was breaking the law just as Pat Gray was, though at the time I rationalized my activities in the name of government, duty, and national security. But on that earlier occasion, my judgment was certainly influenced by the emotional letdown of discovering that someone I respected and trusted had sold out the organization.

My greatest concern after reading the news reports centered around our new leader, William D. Ruckelshaus. Since the President had already politicized the Bureau by involving Pat Gray in the Watergate scandal, I wasn't overly impressed by the fact that another member of the Nixon team had been appointed to run the FBI. The only information so far available indicated he was a Republican who had served as head of the Environmental Protection Agency. It didn't seem like much of a law-enforcement background for the nation's top cop, especially considering the demoralized organization he would govern.

It also appeared evident that Nixon had decided to discard a few key players regardless of the political fallout. If he was a contributing force behind the deep cover program, which I strongly suspected he was, then we might be expendable too. I might just accidentally get myself busted in Canada with a van full of drugs and find out that the Bureau never heard of me. It wasn't a "set-up" that I feared, but rather the fact that the Bureau had no legal authority to conduct undercover investigations in a foreign country.

When I reached Stu at the office in Seattle, he said that he knew nothing more than what had appeared in the papers. It seemed that everyone in the organization was so deeply shocked by the recent developments that they were afraid to speculate on what would happen next.

The only bright spot in an otherwise dismal conversation was the information Stu and Jack had uncovered on the Professor. My underground contact in Vancouver was indeed a heavyweight, Stu noted, and apparently of the highest importance. Although a Canadian citizen, the Professor had taught briefly at a state university in Colorado during 1968 where he was associated with SDS, the White Panther Party, the Industrial Workers of the World (IWW), and the antiwar movement. He was acquainted with Cameron Bishop and Stephen Knowles, who had made the Ten Most Wanted list for sabotage in connection with the bombing of power transmission lines. Both the RCMP and FBI believed the Professor was responsible for spiriting Bishop and Knowles into Canada during 1969 and setting them up in the underground network. Stu was quick to point out that although the RCMP had been aware of the Professor's activities for years, they had been unable to penetrate his organization or close circle of friends.

I told Stu that I would telephone the Professor in the next day or so and make a pitch for assistance. Since Stu and Jack had arranged for a debriefing early the next week at a motel outside the town of Trail, we would discuss developments at that time. I also asked Stu to find out what was going on at Bureau Headquarters in the meantime. Though I didn't mention it to Stu, I had an uneasy feeling about working undercover in a foreign country without approval from the head of the FBI.

In view of the late hour, there wasn't sufficient time to return to the valley and place the scheduled call to Karen. I decided to splurge and check into a seedy downtown hotel for the night. After almost two weeks without a bath, I could hardly stand my own smell in the unventilated van at night.

After a lengthy soak in an antique bathtub, I walked to a pay phone and called Seattle. There was no answer. Karen had not shown up to take the call.

Upon returning to Slocan Valley the following day, I placed a call to the Professor. It was a brief, friendly conversation in which he seemed aware of my fugitive situation but was completely noncommittal about providing assistance. He gave me his address in Vancouver, and we agreed to meet the following week.

On the chance that Karen might have confused the dates, I called the designated phone booth again with the same result. In desperation, I telephoned the commune, but there was no answer. The remainder of the evening was spent at the campground contemplating the many possible reasons for the communication breakdown. They were all bad.

On the way down to Trail for the debriefing session, I stopped at the post office in New Denver to check for mail. Sure enough, there was a letter waiting from Karen which had been sent care of general delivery. It was a rambling four-page discourse which began with an apology for missing the phone call and ended with one brief sentence saying that she had had an abortion.

Except for Vancouver, Trail seemed to be the largest place I had yet visited on my journey. Our meeting-place was one of the self-contained cabins that were part of a motel on the outskirts of town. There was no danger of being overheard through common walls.

Lee, the Intelligence Unit officer from Nelson, attended the meeting, along with Stu, Jack, and Willie, a deep cover agent from San Francisco who had only recently arrived in Canada. Although Willie and I had never actually worked together, we had met on several occasions. Like myself, Willie was an attorney but a few years my senior. With his long salt-and-pepper beard and flowing silver hair, he looked like the swami who had been the Beatles' spiritual adviser.

Willie had just completed a week's trip to Slocan Valley. He had been as surprised as I had been at the number of Americans living there; moreover, virtually everyone had mentioned the spring festival as the social event of the year. We both agreed that if the Weathermen were living in or near the area, it was likely they would make an appearance at the festival. When Jack mentioned he had found out from his sources that Fred the Head and his freaky musical entourage would show up at the festival, we felt certain we were on the right track.

I now sensed that our friends from the RCMP seemed more cautious and less candid. In view of the political turmoil in the United States and the scandal within the FBI, their wariness was understandable. While I was dying to question Stu about what was going on in Washington, I didn't want to air our dirty linen in front of the Canadians.

Everyone present felt that I should travel to Vancouver at once and pursue my contact with the Professor. Stu felt it represented the most vital breakthrough to date in the investigation of the Weathermen. And according to Jack, the RCMP considered the Professor a major figure in the underground apparatus.

After hearing about my talks with Mr. Chicken and Debbie, and my visit to Wild Horse Mountain, Jack sheepishly acknowledged that a further review of RCMP files indicated that Mr. Chicken could not be identical with the individual who witnessed the murder and burial. While both had the same names and looked somewhat alike, Mr. Chicken was originally from the U.S. while the witness was a native-born Canadian.

It was decided that Willie would remain in the valley while I went to Vancouver to meet the Professor. If at all possible, I would return in time to attend the festival with Willie in order to determine if any of the Weatherman fugitives were present. It was also hoped that we would connect with Fred the Head.

When the meeting adjourned, I buttonholed Stu so that Willi and I could speak with him privately. After Jack and Lee left, we learned little of value. According to Stu, the whole situation at Bureau Headquarters was very hush-hush. Ruckelshaus was an unknown quantity, untrusted, inexperienced, and viewed primarily as another political appointee. Most of the top Bureau officials seemed to regard this interim appointment as another affront to the integrity of the organization.

Stu noted that during the past week, on his very first day in office, Ruckelshaus had been greeted with a copy of a telegram sent by Bureau brass to President Nixon, requesting that the next Director be appointed from within the Bureau hierarchy. That same day Ruckelshaus met with all the Assistant Directors and assured them his appointment was only temporary and that his primary goal was to locate a suitable successor. It appeared that Ruckelshaus was trying to quell the palace revolt before the first shots were fired.

"Well, how does he feel about deep cover?" I asked.

"Who knows," Stu replied dejectedly. "Your guess is as good as mine. Chances are he doesn't know."

Since the motel room was paid for, I saw no reason to pass up my second opportunity in a week for a hot bath and a night in a bed. I went out that evening intending to have a big meal and a night on the town; instead, I had a big meal and returned to the motel to reread the Watergate reports in magazines and newspapers I'd purchased.

I reached Vancouver around ten the next evening and headed the van to Kitsilano Park for the night. It was an ideal location because the Professor's apartment was located only a few blocks away, and so were the residences of Joy and Fred the Head. I awoke the following morning to a beautiful spring day. After a visit to the park's rest-room facilities, I took a leisurely stroll along Kits Beach.

Noticing a wild-looking young lady who seemed vaguely familiar, I sauntered over to her. It turned out that I had seen her before, working in a health food store up on Fourth Avenue. She was rough-looking, but you couldn't ask for a more pleasant individual. She laughed continuously, revealing a glittering silver front tooth with an inlaid, while enamel star. A three-colored, rainbow-shaped tattoo graced her upper right arm.

We lay on the beach in the spring sunshine for almost two hours before Molly—"Black Molly" to her good friends—had to leave for work.

"Say, Bill," she said before leaving. "If you're like ah, into rock music, somma my friends are doing a live gig tomorrow night at a party. Oughtta be a real fine time."

"No kiddin'!" I said. "I ain't heard any live music in months."

"Well, come on over then. It's at the Alpen Auditorium on Victoria and Thirty-third. You can buy drinks there too."

"I'll be there," I replied eagerly. "What time?"

"Eight, I think. My girl friend dates one of the guys in the band. I'm sure we'll be there by then."

The next day I drove over to a newsstand on Broadway that sold American newspapers and magazines. I was eager to find out about the latest revelations in the Watergate investigation, but I wanted to read about them from an American perspective. Once again, I was shocked beyond belief. The Pentagon Papers trial had ended and after nearly two years of courtroom drama in Los Angeles, all charges against Daniel Ellsberg and Anthony Russo had been dismissed by U.S.

District Court Judge Matt Byrne because of *government misconduct!* Even more startling was the revelation that Judge Byrne had met with Nixon and Ehrlichman while the trial was in progress to discuss the possibility of his appointment to another federal position—that of FBI Director!

After reading the news accounts for the third time, my anger and indignation began to subside. After all, there was nothing I could do, I reasoned. I changed into clean clothes and went off in search of food and the Alpen Auditorium. It was located in a low-rise building that was the headquarters for a fraternal organization similar to the Elks or Eagles. The upstairs area seemed to be used by members for meetings, dining, and drinking, while the downstairs auditorium, which was more like a basement, was rented out to other organizations when not in use. Inside the Victoria Street entrance, there was a long, steep flight of stairs leading to the basement. The downstairs area was relatively small and supported by a number of structural columns. I noticed a makeshift stage at the far end of the rectangular room and a couple freaks who were just beginning to set up their equipment. A few people were scattered throughout the dimly lighted area. There was no sign of Black Molly.

What appeared to be a storage closet with the half-door opened on top was being used as the bar. When I went over and ordered a drink, the bartender inside, who seemed to be a genuine bad-ass, gave me a contemptuous look and gruffly announced that I had to buy drink tickets. Since they seemed a real bargain, I bought ten bucks' worth, grabbed my drink, and sat down alone at a long wooden table surrounded by metal folding chairs. A guy seated one table over stared at me in disgust.

I couldn't understand the problem. It was a Saturday night dance with an open bar and live rock music. I'd worn my finest freak attire: boots, leather-patched jeans, embroidered workshirt, beads, rings, a well-worn suede coat, and my black cowboy hat with the silver Navajo band. With long hair flowing to the middle of my back and a face full of whiskers, I figured I'd look as freaky as the next guy.

During the next hour, I cashed in a few more drink tickets as the place began to fill up. There was something very strange about these people, but in the near-dark, it was impossible to see clearly. In my immediate area, however, I noticed that every long table was occupied by only one guy, a couple, or a small group. There was no intermingling among tables. And unlike most freak gatherings where the women were friendly, talkative, and uninhibited, these women seemed more like slaves.

There was a big, mean-looking dude seated one table over on my right who was giving his ol' lady grief. An unintelligible grunt, or a scowling look from his pockmarked face, and she bounced up, rushed to the bar, and returned quickly with a fresh drink. And there was hardly any conversation in the room. The guys just sat there quaffing down shots of whiskey while their women stared silently and waited for them to finish each drink.

With the crowd steadily building, the wait for drinks became a lengthy affair. After standing in line for several minutes, I returned with my drink to find that every table in the room was occupied by at least one couple. I sat down at the opposite end of the long table of the bad-looking dude and the slave woman. There were at least a dozen other vacant chairs shoved up under the same table.

"You want something, cowboy?" the dude shouted tauntingly.

"Howdy," I greeted him. "Mind if I sit down?" By that time I was already seated.

"Somebody ask you to sit with Frenchy?" he sneered.

"Didn't know they had to," I drawled in my best Texas accent. "But it's tough to drink standin' up. You savin' these seats for friends?" I figured it was time to be a bit humble. From the looks of things, I had offended the guy by invading his turf, and he would like nothing better than to rearrange my face. He looked at me with a murderous stare, but before the situation could progress any further, the band began to play. Since he couldn't shout over that kind of volume, the near-confrontation passed without incident. Just to be certain that it had, I ambled over to the drink line to cash in another ticket.

Once the music started, a steady stream of humanity rushed down the stairway. As I stood in line facing the bar, it seemed as though every dude that walked past gave me a noticeable shove, push, or bump. Growing a little impatient of all the bullshit, I turned around to view the jostling, unruly crowd that had grown to some two hundred strong. Since the stage lights had been turned on for the band, it was possible to see beyond a few feet: the room was filled with bikers! Not hippy bikers, mind you, but dirty, arrogant, kick-ass outlaw bikers decked out in their grimy, oil-crusted biker regalia and sporting the colors of the Satan's Angels.

"Christ almighty!" I thought, "what the hell am *I* doing here?"

A short time later, I noticed Molly walking toward the drink line.

After exchanging greetings, I ushered her over to the side where we couldn't be overheard.

"What's with all the bikers?" I asked as casually as possible.

"Whadda ya mean?" she answered in her rat-a-tat-tat style.

"I'm 'bout the only guy here not wearin' colors except the band."

"Oh don't worry about that," she said laughingly. "It's *their* party. Satan's Angels rented the place and hired the band. But they're nice guys, ya know. I went on a weekend run with 'em once. There's supposed to be bikers from as far away as Oakland here."

"Well where I come from, lady, the bikers don't take too kindly to freaks crashing their parties."

"Oh, don't worry about that, Bill. The party's open to the public. Besides, I know these guys. Look for me when the band takes a break, and we'll go out back and smoke some hash."

Molly scurried off into the crowd. The break couldn't come soon enough for me.

I went out on several breaks that evening, managing to return each time feeling carefree. Had I not been so light-headed, I would have had sense enough to get the hell out of there. But I was fascinated by the whole biker subculture—the way they treated their women, bluffed each other with threats of violence, then went about the business of getting drunk.

It was interesting to sit near the bottom of the stairway and watch the elderly couples dressed in their Saturday night finery leave the building from the party upstairs. Intrigued by the rock music blaring out of the basement, they tiptoed halfway down the staircase to look in on the party below. Once they saw what was waiting down there, they refused to venture one step further. And if a biker unexpectedly started up the stairs, they scattered like quail.

Shortly after midnight, two classic-looking bikers came roaring down the stairs on chopped Harleys, and once they arrived on level terrain, they drove those chromium monsters through tables, chairs, and people! It was one of the most unbelievable events I've ever witnessed. They raced out to the dance floor, gunning the engines while spinning around in donuts, fishtailing across the linoleum floor, then abruptly chasing anyone in sight. The sound from the bikes was so deafening that it completely overwhelmed the rock band, and in minutes, the basement was filled with a thick blue cloud of sickening exhaust fumes.

And what was the reaction of those in attendance after their biker-buddy crazies had trashed the room, filled it with carbon monoxide, and busted half the furnishings? They loved it! Everybody went nuts. The band finally gave up and began to concentrate on saving their equipment from destruction.

Scattered fighting was breaking out, and as the scene progressed to an out-and-out brawl, I realized that I was about the only one without a chain, club, or blade. It seemed the perfect time to leave.

While cautiously threading my way toward the stairs, a flying beer bottle bounded off my shoulder and shattered on the floor. I glanced back quickly to see my bad-ass buddy Frenchy charging at me from across the room like a rampaging bull. I caught him in the shins with a folding chair and knocked him screaming to the floor. For the first time, I noticed that Frenchy was wearing the traditional Levi's jacket with the sleeves hacked off, but there were no colors sewn on the back. No club, no nothing. Oh shit, I thought, maybe he's trying out for the team!

Still certain that retreat was the only answer, I started toward the stairs, but the big ox was back on his feet. I hit him with everything I had, caught him squarely on the jaw, and sent him reeling to the floor. That was a *big* mistake. The bones in my throbbing hand felt like mush, and my powerhouse right didn't even faze the bastard. He was getting up again!

I didn't have to study Frenchy's facial expression to tell he was pissed, especially at having been tagged by a hippy in front of his biker buddies. I was hastily backing toward the stairway when another dude lunged at me from the right. I turned quickly to see what he had in mind and at the same time backed into a table. Luckily, I staggered against the table at the exact instant that Frenchy smacked me with a glancing blow that felt like a sledgehammer. If the shot had landed squarely on my jaw rather than ricocheting off the back of my skull as I fell, I think my head would have come off. As it was, he sent me flying over the table, bouncing off two chairs, and crashing onto the floor.

Primarily out of fear and a sense of self-preservation, I raised up only slightly to see what was coming next. Frenchy was rolling around on the floor with a Satan's Angel while another dude was undergoing a ferocious beating at the hands of three brutish-looking outlaws. Had any of the combatants paused to notice, they would have thought Superman had just vaulted up the stairs. I damn near made it in a single bound.

Back on the street, I moved hurriedly up the hill toward the van. Rounding a corner, I saw six bikers pummeling a young freak who had been at the dance. He had managed to set off a nearby fire alarm and was now paying heavily for having summoned the authorities. Sprawled on the sidewalk, he was being kicked like a rag doll by heavy motorcycle boots. His battered, bleeding body looked lifeless.

The bikers suddenly noticed my presence and turned to give me a similar greeting. I darted into the nearest alley and ran for several blocks before they gave up the chase.

In front of the Alpen Auditorium, a constable from the Vancouver police was surrounded by a group of Satan's Angels who were kicking him unmercifully as he lay helpless on the pavement. As the officer writhed in anguish, they brutally attacked his head, ribs, and groin. His police dog was encircled by other bikers who were attacking the animal with clubs and chains.

A passing motorist stopped to offer assistance but was immediately knocked to the ground and stomped by the unruly mob. When several police cars converged on the scene, the crowd instantly scattered into the darkness.

It was well into Sunday afternoon by the time I ventured out again. The only souvenirs of the dance were a mild hangover and an aching right hand. After a couple of unsuccessful attempts at telephoning the Professor, I stopped by Joy's apartment. She mentioned that Marvelous Marv had called to inquire about my whereabouts, but since Karen had written that I was in touch with the Professor, she had told Marv that his assistance was no longer needed. I wasn't overly concerned at the turn of events. If things didn't work out with the Professor, I could always recontact Marv.

Monday's edition of the *Vancouver Sun* contained yet another startling front-page headline: "Ellsberg's Wiretap File Found in White House Safe." The most troubling part of the report indicated that Hoover's former assistant William Sullivan, who had been forced out of the Bureau by his boss in late 1971, had removed the files before leaving and given them to then-Assistant Attorney General Robert Mardian because he feared Director Hoover might use the files to blackmail the Nixon administration. Now, two years later, the missing files were discovered in John Ehrlichman's safe.

Aside from the fact that the secret wiretaps appeared to be a blatant abuse of power by the both the President and the FBI, I was at a loss to explain why someone in the Bureau hierarchy hadn't let Ruckelshaus in on the more than two-year-old secret. After all, he was serving as the head of the FBI.

14

LSD and Me

I finally reached the Professor later that afternoon, and we made plans to meet that evening at his apartment. He sounded cordial and eager to offer assistance as he provided the directions to his apartment building. I had already looked the place over. It was an older, three-story walk-up much like the building Joy lived in, and I subsequently learned that many of the apartments were occupied by political associates of the Professor.

The Professor turned out to be totally unlike my expectations, although I'm really not certain about what I did expect. He was about my age, of medium height and thin build. His thick, dark hair was cut short and parted on the side and he wore thick-lensed rimless glasses. He was dressed in blue jeans and a simple denim workshirt. I was immediately impressed by his friendly manner. From the moment I stepped into his tiny, three-room flat, he seemed to go out of his way to be hospitable. I was introduced to Margo, the Professor's girl friend, and to his friends Peter and Janis. I was surprised to see so many people and was afraid the Professor might be reluctant to talk candidly. It was quickly apparent that my fears were unfounded.

Not only had he been thoroughly briefed on my fugitive status; he had also been contacted by Karen, who had called to find out if I had arrived in Vancouver. We discussed my particular situation at length, and the Professor offered a number of tips on how to avoid detection in Vancouver. Having been associated with the Canadian Aid To American War Objectors organization and the American Deserters Committee, he possessed a vast amount of practical knowledge on the subject.

In response to my request for fictitious identity, the Professor said he could obtain a high-quality Canadian birth certificate in about six weeks. He even offered the use of his apartment as a mailing address while I was in Vancouver. That act of generosity took me completely by surprise.

"Look man, I really appreciate what you're doing," I said. "But aren't you afraid the pigs 'll check your mail?"

"Oh no, Bill," the Professor answered in a tone of finality. "This is Canada, not the United States. They don't do all that shit here."

I remained skeptical although he sounded thoroughly convincing. I was also troubled by his failure to question me on political ideology. I had assumed that he would be dogmatic in his views and would want to ascertain mine before offering assistance. But his only comment along those lines was that he was in the Wobblies, the organization officially known as the Industrial Workers of the World (IWW). If he was curious about my politics, he certainly didn't show it.

In hopes of eliciting some meaningful response, I told him of my plans to return to Slocan Valley in order to lessen the chance of detection. I wondered whether he knew Fred the Head, and mentioned that I hoped to see some movement friends at the spring festival. He concurred in my plans and supplied me with a crude map detailing the mountain location of Christina, a political associate who lived near the town of Balfour, B.C. If I should need assistance while in the valley, I was to follow the directions on the map and use his name as a reference.

We made plans to meet again, and after a cordial goodbye, I left the apartment. I was more than satisfied with the meeting. Unlike Marvelous Marv, the Professor was a trusting, straightforward type who could seemingly get along with anyone. But I couldn't rule out the possibility that I might not have an insight into the personality and behavior of a native Canadian.

Later that week, I reached Fast Freddie at my L.A. apartment. I wanted to fill him in on the Professor, and I wanted to know what was going on at the Bureau. It was great talking to him after such a long period, and he seemed genuinely excited over my meeting with the Professor. I was happy to have the opportunity to talk to him when he was away from the office. I trusted Fred completely and knew he was one of the few officials I could speak to freely. It was evident that he was deeply troubled, and like everyone else in the organization, he had no idea what would happen next.

"But Boss," I said. "What does Ruckelshaus think about the program and our deep cover operation up here? Is he gonna back us up if something goes wrong?"

"I honestly don't know, C," Fred replied. "The word I get from Division Five is that since he's only temporary, he won't even be told about it."

"Well, who's running the goddammed Bureau then?"

"That's a good question," he said. "Did you hear about Felt throwing it in?"

"Mark Felt?" I was incredulous. Felt was the Number Two man in the Bureau who had run the day-to-day operations during Pat Gray's tenure. It was also common knowledge that he aspired to the position of Director.

"Yep, he's retiring at the end of June."

"Well how come?" I stammered.

"Don't know, C. Guess he's had enough of the bullshit."

You couldn't help but feel sorry for dedicated agents like Fred who had devoted their lives to the FBI and were now seeing everything they'd worked for come tumbling down. J. Edgar Hoover had been such a masterful public relations man that agents had historically enjoyed respect, trust, and prestige from practically all Americans. But now, most agents felt that through no fault of their own, the organization was without credibility, leadership, or esprit.

From a personal standpoint, the conversation with Fred was far from reassuring. If the Acting Director of the FBI was unaware of deep cover and our covert operation in Canada, where did that leave me?

Back in Slocan Valley, the roads were clogged with hitchhikers traveling to the area for a summer of inexpensive outdoor living. Everyone I picked up mentioned the spring festival. But while everyone knew *of* the festival, no one knew exactly *where* it would be held—a typical counterculture situation.

It was to be a three-day event, beginning on a Friday afternoon and ending on Sunday night. Camping facilities would be available and homemade food would be sold; live entertainment would be provided—and drugs would be supplied. There was no admission charge since the festival was viewed as a gathering for area residents rather than as a moneymaking enterprise. The time, talent, and energy required to stage the event were provided by volunteers.

I left Rosebery Park early Friday morning after finding out that the festival was being held in a provincial park north of Castelgar. I arrived to find a beautiful setting of rolling hills and large shade trees. A natural, amphitheater-like clearing about the size of a baseball field served as the main spectator area. An old-fashioned bandstand at one end would be used for the entertainment. The campsites around the clearing had been claimed early by various communes seeking to sell homemade goodies. The road leading down the hill had been closed to vehicles.

Since I planned to sleep in the van, I parked on the hill overlooking the area and hiked in. I took a walk through the festival grounds where people were busily setting up booths, outdoor cooking pits, drink concessions, and equipment. I ran across Fred the Head's contingent which had driven over in a school bus outfitted for camping. I was interested to note that they were situated in the most isolated, inaccessible spot in the park. They would certainly bear watching during the next few days.

By late afternoon, the turnout was much smaller than anticipated. But within the next few hours, the park became more crowded, and the chief topic of conversation was the reason for the delayed arrivals. The RCMP had set up a roadblock just outside the only park entrance where they stopped and searched every car for drugs. The fact that they had already made several arrests put a considerable damper on both enthusiasm and attendance. After hearing that unexpected news, I was more than happy to have arrived early.

The spring festival was an unstructured, laid-back affair in which everyone did their own thing. For the most part this consisted of eating, drinking, smoking dope, and just generally having a good time. It was all friendly and low-keyed. There was virtually no violence, and most of those present were older freaks who could handle their drugs.

The general level of amateur entertainment during the festival ranged from marginal to terrible. Music usually began in the early afternoon, although that was also a popular time for nude swimming in the nearby lake. It continued until midnight when the electricity was shut off. Anyone who wanted to perform was given the opportunity, but most of the groups were scheduled for the evening when the crowds were larger. By that time, nearly everyone was well-oiled, and if a group could play at all, most of the crowd would be on their feet dancing wildly around a roaring bonfire.

On Saturday afternoon, I ran into my friends from Wild Horse Mountain. Kevin and Kath were selling hot vegetables and homemade oatmeal cookies from a makeshift concession stand. JoJo and Debbie sat nearby smoking a joint and listening to a lengthy discourse by the Chicken Man. I bought a plate lunch and joined my friends.

Shortly before dusk, our little circle was passing around a hash pipe carved from a deer antler when I spotted Willie. How ironic, I thought. A few hundred people are holding a spring festival in rural British Columbia, and now there are *two* undercover FBI agents here in search of the Weathermen.

I greeted Willie and introduced him to the group as a friend of mine from Berkeley. Since he was with a lady from Vancouver and a group of her friends from Nelson, we didn't have an opportunity to talk candidly until later that evening. Neither of us had yet been able to meet any of Fred the Head's entourage. We had tried to observe the group and noticed a number of freaks visiting the school bus throughout the day. Unfortunately, the problem here was the same as in the United States: you could be sitting next to one of the Weatherman fugitives and nine times out of ten not recognize him.

It wasn't until Sunday that I noticed a bizarre-looking lady chatting with one of the women from the school bus. I watched her throughout the afternoon, and when the opportunity presented itself, I sat down beside her to say hello. The lady's name was Samantha, and she wore an ankle-length buckskin skirt, a fringed leather shirt, and beaded moccasins. Strands of multicolored beads hung round her neck interspersed with tiny jingling bells. Her long dark hair was braided and tied by leather thongs adorned with dangling feathers. On the back of the lady's right hand was an intriguing Aztec tattoo, while her derriere, I subsequently discovered, featured a tattooed butterfly.

Samantha impressed me right away as an intelligent, articulate woman strangely out of place as an Indian-style mountain mamma. After growing up in suburban Phoenix, she had become a Canadian citizen. She was a strict vegetarian who disdained the use of alcohol but abused just about every other drug. She spent the winters in Vancouver and hitchhiked during the spring and summer months with nothing more than her dog and backpack.

For some unknown reason, I was highly skeptical of her story. Somehow she seemed too intelligent to be a carefree child of the highway. Moreover, I wondered why a bright, good-looking woman from Phoenix would emigrate to another country and become a professional hitchhiker.

Toward the end of the evening, we walked over to Samantha's campsite opposite the school bus. A backpack, dog, and two grimy sleeping bags lay near the coals from a recent campfire. Being less than enthusiastic over her offer to sleep in the bag, especially if it rained again, I suggested that she join me in the van. But having made plans to hitch into Nelson with a girl named Maria, who was apparently missing in action, Samantha was afraid they would be unable to locate each other the following morning.

As we were discussing our sleeping arrangements, a group of six to eight crazies stumbled over from the direction of the bus, generously offering to share their dope and wine. Although the festival had officially ended, they were just beginning to get cranked up. "It's party time!" one dude shouted. Samantha wanted to join them, and thinking that they might be friends of Fred the Head, I agreed. After gathering more wood, we sat around the blazing fire passing joints and a half-gallon jug of red wine.

Within an hour, I began to feel rather strange, almost as though chilled by the crisp night air. But we were laughing so uncontrollably hard that I tended to discount the unusual feelings. Every spoken word or action was hysterically funny. I wondered if I would ever stop laughing. I looked across the campfire and noticed that the people seated only a few feet away were at the far end of a narrow, wavy tunnel. The coals in the fire looked like molten lava. Although I could snap out of the distortion, I suddenly realized that my depth perception had gone haywire. I hastily thanked the group for their hospitality, told Samantha I would see her the next morning, and staggered off into the darkness in search of the van.

By the time I located it, my entire body knew it was in for some type of frantic rush. There was no one specific symptom but rather a series of exhilarating, sporadic rushes resembling an amphetamine trip. I was certain that I'd never felt exactly that way before.

While sitting in the driver's seat, I stared into the windshield and suddenly possessed high-speed, microscopic vision. My eyes zoomed in on the glass, then went from the surface of the glass to the inner composition and molecular structure. The magnified pores of the windshield shone as brightly as the stars in a darkened universe. Then without warning, those millions of tiny pores began to breathe! They expanded and contracted like a miniature lung. I finally realized that those were *my* lungs, and that I could control the movement of the pores in the windshield! Once I got past the point of being scared shitless, I was totally engrossed by the show. I also reached the conclusion that I had unknowingly taken some LSD.

There appears to be continuous motion or flow in psychedelic situations. No matter how interesting a particular segment might be, changing external factors require a commensurate change in mental focus. What might be a wonderful, pleasant thought for one minute—or one hour—might be followed by an intense experience that would prove terrifying as hell! It's like sailing on the ocean in a small boat, and as the waves grow higher and rougher, the inexperienced sailor might become seasick, throw up until his stomach is empty, and then relax while the storm abates and the sea calms. But all of a sudden, here comes the goddammed waves again, this time bigger than ever! Those who understand what happens when they've ingested LSD try to relax, and like the big folks say, "go with the flow." Sometimes it works, sometimes it doesn't.

At some point during the evening's entertainment, the windshield exploded with a blinding flash of bright red light. My entire being seemed consumed by the power of the brilliant fireball. I was so startled by the explosion that my body was shaking uncontrollably. Then I realized that the exploding meterorite resulted because the freak parked in front of me had stepped on his brakes, causing the rear brake lights to blaze in the dark.

After determining the origin of the U.F.O., I felt a surge of self-confidence for a brief period. Then that shit came rushing back, full speed ahead. I fumbled through the tape box, shoved *Led Zeppelin II* in the deck, crawled to the back, and fell on the mattress. The ceiling in the van looked as if it were easily twenty feet high. Time and space were a mystery of flowing distortion. The carpeting seemed to be alive, as if each gold strand were a living organism undulating to its own rhythm. Then the Led Zep tape came blasting out of the stereo speakers and damn near scared me to death. In that state of timeless suspension, I had forgotten all about the music, but now it was bombarding my senses as the sound waves traveled through my prostrate body.

The exposure to rock music under those circumstances was an unprecedented experience. It was as though I could actually *see* the music and *hear* the colors as their vibrations changed in intensity. It was the phenomenon of synesthesia, a state of consciousness in which one particular sensation is converted to another.

Some time later, I decided to pull off my boots. My legs looked ten feet long and well out of reach. Upon discovering that I could grasp the boots, my arms appeared equally long. My depth perception was so altered that my extremities seemed to stretch to infinity. Upon examining my hand, I could inexplicably see the bones, muscles, and blood vessels as though I had X-ray vision.

It has often been said that a successful journey into the phantasmagorical world of psychedelia is dependent on "set" and "setting." Set refers to the particular frame of mind, the emotional and psychological makeup of the individual; setting is the actual environment where the drug is experienced. Fortunately, because I was aware that—for good or ill—I was embarking on an LSD trip, I was able to reach the familiar confines of the van before the drug took effect. At times it was a harrowing experience, but at least I was alone in a secure environment, and I had some vague idea as to what would take place.

While tripping for the novice is haphazard at best, it can be one helluva profound experience. For me, while it was initially terrifying, it produced a mood of detached introspection in which I began to see myself as only an infinite part in the overall structure of the universe. Viewed from that perspective, and considering the billions of years during which the universe has evolved, our physical life on planet earth seemed infinitesimal. Were those revelations merely the result of drug-induced reasoning? Perhaps. But whatever their source, they dramatically altered my basic outlook on human existence.

It was daylight by the time I finally fell asleep. Shortly after noon, I heard a knock on the van door and crawled up to see Samantha, her dog Simon, and friend Maria. According to Samantha, during the previous evening's festivities, I had graciously offered to drive the three of them back to Vancouver.

"Oh wow," I muttered while trying to clear the cobwebs from my brain. "Some party, huh?"

"Well, I hope you survived better than the others," Samantha remarked. "They were screaming all night. We had to move to get any sleep."

"Yeah, I can imagine."

"Can you still give us a ride to Vancouver?" she asked.

"Ah, yeah, sure. But look, I've got to see some people in the valley first, then I have to make a stop over near Balfour. It'll be a week or so before I can leave. That too late?" After seeing the size of Samantha's dog Simon and the age of her friend Maria, who looked about fifteen, I was hoping it would be much too late. I did have other leads to cover in the valley, and I wanted to meet the Professor's friend Christina.

"No, that's fine," Samantha replied. "Maria's got friends in Nelson we can visit till you're ready to leave. Are you heading in that direction?"

One of your more persistent ladies, I thought. "Sure, I can take you as far as South Slocan. But I've gotta find a friend of mine first. He was camped down from you."

"Everybody pulled out this morning, Bill," she said. "I don't think there's anyone down there."

How wonderful, I thought. After leaving Samantha and Maria at the van, I walked down to the festival site. Sure enough, the school bus was gone. Fred the Head and his freak entourage were nowhere in sight. After three days and an unscheduled acid trip I hadn't met a single one of them. All of a sudden I felt worse than ever.

15

How Important Is the Professor?

Late that afternoon, I dropped my three passengers off at South Slocan and turned north on Highway 6 for the valley. Because I was in no condition for the grueling mountain drive to Rosebery, I left the highway for a secluded dirt road where I could spend the night.

I pulled off the road and parked where the van couldn't be seen from the highway above. Within seconds, I was zipped into the sleeping bag and trying to catch up on lost sleep. Perhaps it was due to the previous evening's encounter with LSD, but my mind was like a movie screen with an unending lineup of events flashing by.

Later that night, my mind focused on an approaching train moving at high speed. I could hear the clicking of the rails growing louder and faster as the train moved closer. The sound level continued to build from the direction in back of the van until it was overpowering—then deafening! Just as I bolted up from the mattress in terror, the locomotive of a speeding freight train passed within five yards of the van. The air turbulence from the train buffeted the van back and forth as the engineer sounded a shrill blast from the horn. It damn near scared me to death. Once I realized it wasn't a dream, I thought for sure the train was about to run me down. By the time I got out of the sleeping bag and scrambled frantically to the front window, the long freight train had flashed past. Only then did I realize that I had parked parallel to a railroad track. In all the weeks that I spent in the Slocan Valley, it was the only time I saw a train use those tracks.

Upon returning to the highway the next day, I noticed "Weird Wally Winkle" hitchhiking south with a guitar strung over his shoulder. Weird Wally was from Houston and we had met at the festival. He was a lanky guy who was fond of drugs and claimed to be a professional sailor. Recognizing me behind the wheel, he waved broadly and I drove over to see what he was up to. Weird Wally was on his way to a jam session at a nearby farmhouse, and since he was in need of transportation, I was invited along.

When we arrived at our destination, I was surprised to discover that I had already met the lady of the house, a black chick from San Francisco named Maureen who was formerly associated with the Black Panther Party. She had been accompanied by her husband during our earlier meeting, but he was now down South looking for work harvesting fruit. Maureen had an electronic pickup to amplify an acoustical guitar, and she and Weird Wally jammed for hours. Other friends dropped by, and Maureen provided some homegrown marijuana to enhance our listening pleasure. She sat on the floor leaning against the wall, humming softly while breast-feeding the baby held tightly in her arms.

When we left Maureen's place, Weird Wally invited me to visit another one of his lady friends. He directed me down a nearby road and had me turn into a narrow pasture adjacent to the mountain. Having driven that way on several occasions, I was certain there wasn't a house visible from the road. We parked the van and walked through the meadow for nearly half a mile before coming upon a treehouse built into an enormous shade tree and wedged against the mountainside.

We climbed up a wooden ladder fastened to the massive tree-trunk before arriving on an open deck with an entrance door. Weird Wally rapped on the door and we were greeted by "Mountain Woman" and her infant daughter "Chan." The interior of the treehouse consisted of one large room and a sleeping loft. Toward the back of the room was a smaller addition on a higher level which was used for sewing and crafts. Furnishings consisted primarily of pillows and a log table with benches. A few toys were scattered about.

Mountain Woman and her ol' man, an American selective service fugitive, had built the treehouse three summers earlier. He had long since departed. It had been a marriage of convenience, she noted, which allowed her husband to obtain Canadian citizenship. Chan had been an unplanned by-product of the brief relationship. But if Mountain Woman was at all bothered by the experience, it wasn't discernible. She and the baby lived on Vancouver Island during the winter months, and each spring traveled to the Slocan Valley treehouse. She was a tall, buxom woman who seemed totally self-sufficient and attuned to the outdoors.

Later that same week, I passed Weird Wally on my way into Nelson. I stopped to say hello, and he asked if he could accompany me. Not that he had planned on going to Nelson, but the opportunity just seemed too good to pass up. As I would soon learn, Weird Wally had been known to drink a beer now and then while shooting a friendly game of pool. And if his game was up to par, he'd also pocket a considerable amount of spending money.

I dropped him off in front of the Main Street pub while I searched for a discreet pay phone. When I joined him an hour or so later, he was guzzling beer and gliding around the pool table with the grace of Minnesota Fats. He seemed to know everybody in the place, or at least everybody who thought they could shoot pool. He was good, or lucky, or a combination of both, and he won a lot more than he lost. When he ran out of challenges, we joined several of his friends at a dimly lighted booth near the back wall of the spacious building.

It was apparent that a substantial amount of dealing was taking place in the pub. And since the establishment was packed on a midweek afternoon, something had to be going on. I noticed an older, straight-looking guy walking through the room and thought how out of place he looked. Then it dawned on me that the guy was a good ol' boy from the local police department who was about to make an arrest. He was moving in our direction, but since I was sitting between Weird Wally and another dude, there was nowhere to go.

As he neared our booth, I gave Wally's leg a resounding kick and began unloading my jacket pockets. I was holding only a small chunk of hash, but that was plenty. In one skillful swoop, the cop grabbed the wrist of the dude sitting next to me and slapped on the iron with a resounding click. The dude's left hand had been cuffed while he still clutched his beer! And just to make sure there was no problem with the other hand, two uniformed RCMP officers came bursting through the back door from the alley, not ten feet from where we were seated, and began moving us out of the booth and against the wall.

Had it not been such a tense situation, it might have been comical. The floor underneath our table was so littered with hash, bags of grass, pills, pipes, roach clips and pocket knives, it was damn near impossible to walk. Everybody in the place was frantically emptying pockets and moving toward an exit. As soon as the dude was handcuffed and walked to a waiting squad car in the alley, the whole thing was over. When the officers went out the back door, Weird Wally and I ran toward the front and out onto Main Street. In no time at all, I was looking at the town of Nelson through my rear view mirror.

Among the many long distance calls I had made from Nelson was one to Walt at the Special L office in Vancouver. He had previously visited the Slocan Valley in an attempt to verify informant information about the location of Weatherman Haven North. Although Jack had tried to describe the location to me in Vancouver, his description was sketchy at best. After spending a full day hiking through brush, forest, and along the river bank without success, I had decided to call Walt for a better description. Much to my chagrin I was nowhere near the area.

One bright sunny morning, I loaded my day pack with supplies and started out on my second attempt. The hiking was more difficult this time, since the terrain was all dense forest. But there was a peaceful serenity in walking alone through an unspoiled forest on a beautiful day.

Several hours later I reached the crest of a small tree-covered hill and started my descent down the other side. After walking another few hundred yards, I unexpectedly came thrashing out of the underbrush into a large meadow that was completely surrounded by timber.

Turning to my right, I was startled to see two women staring at me from the far end of the meadow. Behind them were an ancient log cabin with a crumbling roof and a large teepee. The women were skinning the bark from thin trees, apparently for more teepee poles. The taller of the two women wore an Indian-style breechcloth and held a hatchet in a menacing fashion. The other woman wore nothing but a leather belt with a knife scabbard. She clutched the large hunting knife she was using for bark shinning. A long-barreled rifle was propped against a tree a few feet from where they worked.

As I walked cautiously toward the women, I'm sure my unconcerned facial expression belied my astonishment at stumbling upon two naked women in the middle of the wilderness. Since their skin was uniformly bronzed, without the slightest trace of white, the size of their well-formed breasts was not evident until I got closer. Without suntan lines, it was difficult to recognize nudity from a distance. Up close, it was sensuous as hell.

I noticed the tall woman edging closer to the rifle. "Howdy," I said.

"Hello," she replied warily.

"My name's Bill."

"That's cool," she said cautiously. "So what are you doing out here, Bill?"

"Just hiking around."

"Well, take a hike someplace else, man!" she snapped. "This is private property."

"I see. Just curious, but is it your private property or someone else's?" From the looks of things, they were summer squatters.

"It belongs to me and my ol' man," she said while shouldering the rifle. "He'll be back any minute, so you better get your ass outa here."

I'd had a few guns pointed in my direction over the years but never by a naked lady. And the light breeze gently blowing her tiny breech-cloth only added to my distraction. "Gimme some slack, lady, I'm just out hikin' for chrissake. There's no need for the gun."

"Then don't make me use it," she said icily. "Now get outa here and don't come back."

"Okay, ladies. Sorry to bother ya."

I took the shortest route back to the safety of the woods and didn't pause until I was well out of sight—and range. I worked my way through the forest and around to the far side of the meadow. A higher point near the edge of the clearing provided an unobstructed view of the inside of the decaying log cabin. It was empty. The women had returned to work, and their breasts jiggled violently as they hacked away at the bark.

I was certain this wasn't Weatherman Haven North, for we had a good description of the main house and a photograph of an interior room. But this strange occurrence was a mystery that would never be solved.

While driving south the following day, I spotted the Mountain Woman hitchhiking near the Winlaw post office. Chan was strapped on her back and since they were on their way back to the treehouse, I was happy to offer them a lift. Mountain Woman had bought some fresh vegetables at the general store and invited me to stay for dinner.

While she washed the vegetables, I sat on the treehouse floor and entertained Chan. For about the tenth time that day, my senses were overwhelmed by the disgusting smell of my own body odor. It had been weeks since my last bath and two days of hiking in a scorching hot sun certainly hadn't helped. My clothes were so soaked and caked with sweat they could almost stand up by themselves. I was forced to wear my hair in a pony tail in order to keep the odor as far from my nose as possible. I apologized to Mountain Woman in advance.

"If I don't get cleaned up pretty soon, I won't be able to stand myself any longer."

Mountain Woman enjoyed a hearty laugh. "You'll get used to it," she said. "You don't smell any worse than the next guy.

"Well, that's true," I said. "But is there any place around here to take a bath?"

"Oh sure," she answered. "I've got my own waterfall up in the mountains. You never have to worry about running out of water, but it does get a little chilly."

I didn't care how cold the water was, or so I thought. The only important thing was to clean up. "Could you show it to me sometime?"

"Well sure, Bill. How about tomorrow? You can stay here tonight and we'll hike up in the morning."

The next day Mountain Woman directed me to a logging road which led us up into the heart of the mountains. We parked the van and walked for about a mile before arriving at an incredible waterfall. The rushing water from the winter runoff cascaded over a jagged rock ledge, crashed onto the boulders below, and flowed downstream in a boiling white froth.

Baby Chan squealed with delight as her mother and I threw off our clothes and scurried into the waterfall. The ice-cold water took my breath away and almost sent me into shock. After bolting through the waterfall and moving to the sun-drenched rocks nearby, I soaped my shivering body to a heavy lather. It was a great feeling to wash away the sweat and grime. I took a deep breath and ran back for another assault by the frigid water. If that bone-chilling ritual was the only way to get clean, it was easy to understand why most freaks in the valley stayed dirty.

Monday, May 28, 1973 was one of my more significant birthdays. But instead of greeting it with a riotous celebration among close friends, the day was spent camping alone in Rosebery Park with a dreadful cold and sore throat from the waterfall escapade. The big "THREE-O" had finally arrived, and I was sick, lonely, and wondering what I was doing living out of a van in a foreign country.

I had bought a thick steak and bottle of wine for my one-man celebration, but that evening, after eating everything in sight, there was nothing left to do except move inside the van and listen to music. I couldn't help thinking about my agent friends back in Los Angeles. It was Memorial Day and part of a long weekend. They were probably out at the beach, drinking beer, playing volleyball, and hustling the young ladies. How distant all that seemed now. After years of being a freak, I wondered if I would ever again be able to relate to conservative establishment types who had no conception of what I'd seen and experienced? And would I ever be able to converse intellectually without using drug clichés or gutter profanity? At that point, I was far from certain.

The special circumstances surrounding my thirtieth birthday caused me to question whether the benefits to be derived from what I was doing were worth the personal sacrifice. I wasn't getting any younger or any closer to meeting the right woman for a serious relationship. But most of all, I just wanted to live under my own name again, tell people my background, and what I did for a living. I wanted to be free from the necessity of constant lying.

While sitting in the van that night listening to tapes, I was struck by the refrain in the song "Bound to Fall" from the Stephen Stills *Manassas* album:

> From reality it seems I've strayed,
> Tired of all the silly games I've played.

Not only was I growing tired of the games, I was edging closer to the conclusion that they weren't even needed for the security of the United States. Moreover, I realized that from a personal standpoint, I was rapidly approaching the same level as the Weatherman fugitives. Both of us were willing to lie, manipulate, and break the law in order to accomplish our respective goals. And from my perspective, both the goals and the means to achieve them seemed questionable at best.

Had the Weathermen been setting off a bomb a week in the United States, I'm sure that apprehending them would have been critical to the national security; instead, they had long since retreated into the underground and reportedly disavowed violence as a political tactic. But in any event, would my continuing to live as an underground fugitive, disregarding laws, individual rights, and the very essence of freedom ultimately justify the end result? In view of the revelations flowing from the Watergate scandal, was this a crisis situation of sufficient national magnitude to sanction investigations by "whatever means necessary?" Is there any logical justification for the premise that the government can secretly violate the law for the purpose of arresting citizens who violated the law, in order to demonstrate that violating the law is wrong?

As I had done many times before, I speculated about where the Weatherman fugitives might be hiding, and wondered if they were living under conditions similar to mine. I longed for an opportunity to sit down with Bernardine Dohrn and have a straightforward conversation on her political beliefs.

Oh Bernie, I thought to myself, *where are ya, darlin'? If you're as miserable as I am right now, you're in a world of shit. The agents in the Austin, Texas R.A. still talk about the '69 SDS gala and the fantastic beaver shots you gave 'em from onstage! But seriously, do ya think it's really worth all the hassles? Was it worth givin' up friends, family, and the best years of your life for politics? I mean, has your personal sacrifice really made one goddamn bit of difference? In all honesty, do you genuinely believe the American people wanta change their political system?*

Ya know what, Bernie, I think we're both losing. Personally, it's been a great learnin' experience livin' with freaks, but has either one of us accomplished anything? You can't change the system while you're hidin', and I can't influence the Bureau long as I'm runnin' 'round the country lookin' for you. If we had any sense, we'd both be out practicin' law.

It occurred to me that our basic problems were paradoxically similar: neither of us was able to withdraw gracefully from a deteriorating situation. Ms. Dohrn was probably concerned that additional, more serious charges might be brought against her if she surrendered. For me to split in the middle of an unfolding scenario could arouse suspicion and lead to the discovery of my true identity. In addition, I might find myself without the security of employment, which, at the time, seemed a matter of critical importance. In essence, then, we were both compelled to hang on and play out the game.

On Wednesday I passed through Slocan Valley for what I assumed would be the last time. I was heading for a roadside park just outside of Nelson where I was supposed to meet Samantha for the trip to Vancouver. I found Samantha an intriguing woman who remained an enigma, but I was less than enthused by her young friend Maria and dog Simon. I was hoping they had found other transportation, but to my disappointment, they were waiting exactly as planned.

My three passengers eagerly piled into the van, and we sped off toward Balfour. I was determined to meet the Professor's friend Christina and wanted a look at her mountain abode. In addition, it would give the Professor an opportunity to verify that I had actually traveled to the valley. After debating the problem of Samantha and Maria, I had previously decided that their presence in the van would only add to my credibility.

Without the Professor's map, I would never have located Christina's house. It was well out from Balfour and situated at the very end of a twisting mountain road that angled off unmarked from the highway.

Several times it appeared that the van would be unable to negotiate the tight switchback, but somehow we finally made it. The women remained in the van while I walked up to the large, screened porch at the front of the house.

Christina seemed a bit apprehensive at first, since she claimed to be alone, but soon invited me inside. She was a heavyset woman who looked to be in her mid-thirties. Though she was politely cordial, I sensed that Christina was a cautious, deliberate woman who made few mistakes. I also had the impression there were others in the house who were listening, if not watching.

After introducing myself as an acquaintance of the Professor's and casually displaying the map he had drawn, I explained that the women outside were hitchhiking to Vancouver, and since I didn't actually know them, I had asked them to remain in the van. Christina accepted the explanation without comment and soon appeared more relaxed and talkative. She was curious about the political climate in the United States and the status of the antiwar movement. During our discussion, she was able to evaluate the extent of my involvement in movement politics.

I recall thinking that I should have visited Christina without my passengers so that I could have asked to stay for a few days. The inaccessible location was easily the best I had seen. But somehow, I felt certain that Christina would do nothing without first checking me out with the Professor.

When I said that I would be talking with the Professor in a few days, Christina asked me to tell him that she would be in Vancouver for the Wobbly meeting in late July. A short time later, I thanked her for the hospitality and returned to the van. All things considered, the visit had raised more troubling questions than it answered. I couldn't help wondering if Christina, and others who had not been visible, were questioning my unscheduled visit.

By the time we returned to Nelson, it was late afternoon. We stopped at a grocery store where Samantha purchased an assortment of fresh vegetables since she had volunteered to cook the evening meal, vegetarian of course. Several hours later we stopped at a roadside park where I unpacked the cooking gear while the women prepared the vegetables.

Samantha was an amazing cook. She transformed a variety of raw vegetables into a full-course gourmet dinner. The secret, she said, was ample seasoning with a variety of exotic spices. One entire compartment of her backpack was full of spices, each labeled and folded into paper packets like grams of cocaine.

"You ever get hassled on the road and have your pack searched by the cops?" I asked.

"Oh, a few times," Samantha said. "But never anything serious except this one asshole who made me open half of my spices to prove they weren't drugs." Samantha flashed a broad smile. "Didn't catch me dirty though."

"Well, isn't that a problem?" I asked, recalling Samantha's fondness for illegal drugs.

Samantha reached up and carefully removed the tortoise-shell comb that held her long, thick hair in a bun. As the hair spilled onto her shoulders, she removed three massive hunks of foil-wrapped hashish. "I always hitch with my hair up," she said laughingly.

It was dark by the time we finished dinner and resumed our journey. Maria and Simon were soon asleep on the mattress in back while Samantha sat up front. Maria was a troubled teenager who seldom spoke. I suspected that she might have run away from home, but whatever the case, she was definitely too young to be hitchhiking.

The uneasiness over my passengers, plus the lack of sleeping facilities, prompted my decision to reach Vancouver as soon as possible. After driving all night, we arrived in the city around ten in the morning. Samantha directed me to a battered frame house in an older, residential neighborhood. One look at the orange door, blanket-covered windows, and shabby exterior, and there could be no doubt this was a genuine crash pad.

I was introduced to the small group of men and women who were passing a hash pipe around, but after driving all night, I paid little attention. The only matter of immediate importance was sleep. I stumbled back out to the van, locked the doors, and crashed.

I dropped by the Professor's apartment on Friday afternoon to be greeted by a number of unexpected developments. While the Professor seemed his typically jovial self, he was quick to point out that he had received a letter and two phone calls from Karen inquiring about my whereabouts. As I offered innocuous excuses for my failure to contact Karen, he casually tossed me her letter.

It basically outlined my fugitive problems and seemed to enhance my cover story. I was smugly scanning it until I got to the third page when I damn near collapsed. Karen had unwittingly discovered a fundamental mistake I had made.

While living in the Seattle commune with her, I had used my propane heater to warm our bedroom. The heater quit working shortly before we took off for Canada. I left it at a factory repair center in Seattle and purchased another model. Karen was vaguely aware of the transaction but had never inquired about where the heater had been taken for repair. I mentioned the incident to Stu before leaving for Spokane, gave him the claim check, and asked that he pick up the heater when he had a chance. Karen had suddenly remembered both the heater and its brand name, tracked down the proper service center and called to inquire about the repair. As luck would have it, Stu had dropped by only two days earlier to pick up the heater, and the repairman possessed an excellent memory.

As Karen related her phone conversation with the repairman in the letter to the Professor, a conventionally dressed man in his forties had presented the proper claim check and left with the heater. Her letter went on to point out that as far as she was aware, I knew no one in Seattle who could be described as a middle-aged businessman.

I had clearly been caught in a serious mistake, and there was nothing to do but try and bullshit my way out of the screw-up.

"I don't understand this bit about the heater," I said, hoping to sound perplexed by it all. "Far as I know, the damn thing's still in Seattle. I'm sure the claim check's out in the van somewhere."

"Karen sounded upset about it when she called, Bill," the Professor remarked matter-of-factly. "But I told her you had already returned to the valley. Why don't you give her a call and let her know you're all right?" he suggested.

"Aren't you afraid somebody might see her number on your phone bill?"

"Hell no, go ahead," he said. "Remember, this is Canada. They don't do all that shit here."

Karen answered on the second ring. After the usual greetings, explanations, and questions on Seattle activities, I broached the subject of the heater with a bewildered denial similar to the one given the Professor. By now, Karen had decided that the FBI was somehow involved in a sinister plot. Since I purportedly had the claim check, she reached the conclusion that the repairman had been coaxed into lying, and that anyone who subsequently appeared to retrieve the heater would undoubtedly be arrested by waiting FBI agents. Her scenario had several obvious loopholes, but I was more than happy to accept it. She wanted to take a bus up the following weekend for a visit, and after enduring the great heater crisis, it seemed a small concession.

301

Davina?

how would you know?

There was another interesting piece of mail waiting at the Professor's apartment. It bore an Ottawa postmark and was addressed to a Mr. R. A. Johnson. The franked, manila envelope contained a Canadian Social Insurance card in the name of Robert Allen Johnson, my new alias. The Professor had provided the application during our earlier meeting and was still trying to obtain a birth certificate under the new name. With his continued assistance, I would soon be transformed from Bill Lane, American fugitive, to Bob Johnson, Canadian citizen.

Peter, Janis, and Margo arrived around six to prepare a spaghetti dinner and invited me to join them. Having lost almost fifteen pounds since leaving Seattle, I was delighted to accept. My contribution to the affair consisted of smoking material. Compared to most activists I had met, these people were only slightly involved with drugs. But they did enjoy smoking hash or marijuana, and we proceeded to stimulate our taste buds thoroughly in anticipation of the feast.

After stuffing ourselves with spaghetti, we sat around rapping, drinking wine, and smoking hash until well after midnight. It was an evening of interesting, revealing conversation. I learned that Peter had attended the college in Colorado where the Professor had been a faculty member. Peter intimated that the Professor had subsequently helped him enter Canada to avoid the draft. He was now a landed immigrant after having lived underground for several months following his arrival.

Later that evening, the Professor received a long-distance call from a friend named Dan Tompkins who was calling from an undisclosed location in Colorado. Once again, I was shocked that he would talk so openly when I was less than five feet away. From the discussion that followed, I learned that Dan was an activist friend of the Professor's who had been involved in the Wounded Knee uprising in South Dakota. Fearing he was about to be indicted by a federal grand jury for his participation in the incident, Dan asked the Professor to supply him with a fictitious identification upon his arrival in Canada. Dan was given the same response I had received: it was possible to obtain a birth certificate, but it took time, somewhere in the neighborhood of six weeks. Dan agreed to recontact the Professor when he decided on a name.

When the gathering broke up in the early hours of the morning, I thanked the group for dinner and made my way out to the van. It had been a long day, but I was so excited over the developments that it was difficult to fall asleep. I felt certain that the Professor and his friends were important connections in the underground railroad to Canada.

Karen's brief visit to Vancouver resulted in a nonstop, drug-crazed, sex marathon. I greeted her at the bus station with news of my temporary affluence from a recent drug deal. I wanted to take her to some nice places, as though it were a real vacation, and particularly because of her past generosity.

We checked into a modest-looking motel just past Lions Gate Bridge on Marine Drive in North Vancouver. We seldom left the room during the weekend except for visits with Joy and the Professor. We drank scotch, smoked dope, and snorted coke almost continuously for forty-eight hours, and the weekend just slipped away. We completely annihilated the three grams of coke Karen obtained through a gay dealer friend in Seattle. Back in the days before coke became so fashionable, it was relatively inexpensive.

At 1979 prices, some six years later, one ounce of cocaine was worth ten times more than an ounce of gold, and the coke had usually been cut beyond recognition. When educated, affluent people eagerly stuff their noses with a fine white powder that costs ten times more than the world's monetary standard, it makes you wonder if we ought to liquidate Fort Knox and switch from the gold standard to the cocaine standard.

Karen and I got along fairly well during the weekend, but her visit was not without moments of conflict. The mere thought of returning to Seattle seemed to make her irritable and unreasonably demanding. It never ceased to amaze me how the lady could be on top of the world one minute, then suddenly lapse into a deep depression the next. Similarly, I could be enthralled by her company, then outraged over her moods. If anything, my experiences with Karen produced an appreciation for the exceedingly fine line between love and hate. Since I never could view her with detached neutrality, she helped me discover the extremes of my own emotions.

Though I was frustrated and annoyed by our incessant bickering, when Karen boarded the bus for Seattle, I was sorry to see her go.

16

In From the Cold

After months of camping in Slocan Valley, life in Vancouver seemed unbelievably simple. Even though I still lived in a van, I could park on a public street bordering Kitsilano Park, where less than a forty-yard walk over manicured grounds brought me to a tidy rest room. And sitting on Kits Beach looking west over English Bay toward distant mountains afforded an incredible view of the summer sunsets. The park became my home. I would hang around each day, reading, jogging, or just rapping, sleep there at night, and walk along the deserted beach in the early mornings.

It was surprising how much idle time there was when I didn't have to gather wood, build a fire, cook meals, and wash dishes in order to eat. The variety of low-cost eating establishments turned me into a fast food junkie for a short while. How strange it seemed to be able to devour hamburgers, chicken, and pizza at almost any time of the day or night. And for a full meal, there were a number of good inexpensive restaurants in this vicinity.

To rediscover the conveniences of liquor stores, pubs, daily newspapers, movie theaters, and a variety of people was an exhilarating experience. Even television was captivating, like a new toy. Having watched a few hockey games at the pub in Nelson, I was now caught up in the excitement of the bid by the Montreal Canadiens for the Stanley Cup. I knew absolutely nothing about the intricacies of the game, but I loved to watch them go at it. I viewed nearly all of the playoff games from pubs in Vancouver, and oftentimes the Canadian spectators were as entertaining as the contest.

As the days passed, I spent more and more time with the Professor and his friends. Politically, the group's rhetoric and ideology seemed benign when compared to that of radical groups in the United States. Their approach was decidedly low-key, nor were there any of the brutal "criticism—self criticism" sessions favored by the Weather Underground and similar groups.

Of all the activists I'd met, the Professor was by far the most realistic. He claimed that he had long since given up the impractical, adventurist notion that fundamental social change could be brought about through a violent revolution by the masses. In his opinion, the only workable format for meaningful change was that of the Wobblies.

The Industrial Workers of the World (IWW) was founded in 1905 in Chicago. From what I was told, the original goal was to organize all workers into one giant labor union. By the mid-twenties, the Wobblies were a significant factor in the American labor movement. In their heyday, they claimed 65 thousand members—primarily miners, loggers, and construction workers who traveled across the country in boxcars to participate in a number of spectacular strikes. The group also held the distinction of being the only American labor union to oppose World War I as capitalistic. Their opposition drew a harsh rebuke from the federal government which sentenced some one hundred members to prison in a mass trial. Many Wobblies were driven underground to avoid government harassment and violence from vigilante mobs.

The primary objectives of the Professor's group were the political education, organization, and emancipation of unskilled, low-paid workers ignored by the major trade unions. They seemed to believe that if they could improve the conditions of unorganized workers in enterprises such as theaters, car washes, and fast-food franchises, they would gain new members for the IWW.

I stopped off to see the Professor one afternoon, and as we were talking, he vanished into a storage area near the front door. When he returned, he casually tossed a white envelope onto the bed where I was sitting.

"Congratulations on your official birth, Mr. Johnson," he remarked with a smile.

Inside was a birth certificate for Robert Allen Johnson, born May 28, 1943 at Hoffman, Saskatchewan. Although I'd never seen a Canadian birth certificate before, the document certainly looked official. It was a professional, high-quality forgery that undoubtedly had required sophisticated equipment.

The Professor mentioned that I shouldn't be concerned about using the document because it was impossible to verify the birth. Since the building that housed public records at Hoffman had been destroyed by fire several years earlier, there was no existing record of births prior to the disaster.

In the interest of security, it was decided that the Professor and his group would now refer to me exclusively as Bob Johnson. We discussed obtaining a Canadian driver's license and other forms of identification. The Professor offered some helpful advice on which local examining offices were the most crowded and the least demanding about identification requirements. I offered to pay for the phony birth certificate, but he wouldn't hear of it. The document was provided by a political associate, he said, who was more than happy to be of assistance. I thanked him profusely and left a massive chunk of hashish in return for his help.

When the RCMP and FBI eventually examined the birth certificate, they reported that the forgery could not be detected without laboratory examination.

I sat in the van late one night wondering why I'd so foolishly assumed that working under cover in another country would be such a glamorous assignment. Maybe Ian Fleming was responsible, or the Hollywood filmmakers who depicted international spies jetting around the world in the company of beautiful women. It hadn't worked out that way. For me it was a lonely, often guilt-ridden experience. How I longed to have an honest, straightforward conversation without the anguish of weighing each statement to be sure all the lies would add up. The loneliness seemed more poignant in the city, where I was continuously surrounded by crowds of people moving purposefully along their separate ways. When I had camped alone in the forest, there was little opportunity for human companionship and therefore the need didn't seem so critical.

After my recent name change, I often found myself undergoing a mental interrogation regarding my identity. Was I Cril Payne, Bill Lane, or Bob Johnson? Assuming the identity of Bill Lane had been relatively easy, though it did evolve over a period of years. But after convincing myself that I was Bill Lane, it was much more difficult to change suddenly into Canadian Bob Johnson. My calls to Fast Freddie, Stu, and friends in the States became more frequent because I felt an overriding need to talk to people who knew my real name. It seemed the most efficient method of avoiding a serious identity crisis.

When I applied for a library card at the Vancouver Public Library, I initially signed the application for Bob Johnson as Bill Lane and had to rip up the form and request another. And I was still unable to answer unhesitatingly to my new name. One explanation for the difficulty was my diminishing interest in deep cover. Since I was less than jubilant about my previous deceptions as Bill Lane, I had little desire to go out and lie as Bob Johnson.

I was in this state of mind when I first saw Connie. She was sunbathing on Kits Beach in a brief bikini that revealed almost all of her delectable bronzed body. With her radiant smile and freshly scrubbed appearance, she looked strangely out of place among the freaks who inhabited the beach. She rekindled memories of women from my college and law school days, and I suddenly wished I didn't look so outrageous. Although I seriously doubted she'd give me the time of day, I walked over and sat down in her general vicinity.

In no time at all, we were engaged in nonstop conversation. Connie was an outgoing woman who expressed her personal convictions. She was from a small town in Ontario but had attended nursing school in Vancouver and later worked as a registered nurse at General Hospital. She wasn't working at the time, and was intent on enjoying the summer. While collecting unemployment, she was ostensibly searching for a job until fall when she would most likely return to nursing.

Perhaps it was Connie's honesty, or maybe it was the identity crisis that consumed my thoughts; whatever the reason, I never considered using my cover story or latest identity. I was Bill Lane from Los Angeles, an attorney between jobs who was traveling through Canada in a van. Perhaps I just wanted to be someone she might like to know; but more compelling was the fact that I was tired of posing as a radical activist who was a political fugitive.

Late that afternoon, I drove Connie home from the beach and discovered that her house was on the same street as Fred the Head's, but a few blocks away. Once inside the spacious, newly remodeled duplex, I met her two roommates, Martha and Diane, who had similar conservative, small town backgrounds, and though somewhat shocked by my appearance, they were cordial and polite.

The duplex featured a shiny new shower which the residents graciously allowed me to use. They probably thought I'd drowned, because I certainly made the most of it. Connie and I left a short time later and drove over to Joe Kapp's, the type of restaurant patronized by a Cril Payne as opposed to a Bill Lane or Bob Johnson. It was a place where we could enjoy conversation over a few cocktails, and have a good wine and thick steak without my having to justify spending the money or explain where it came from.

The evening was the most relaxing and enjoyable time I'd had in months. Connie was a witty, intelligent conversationalist, but I think that we both realized that our mutual attraction was far more than intellectual. I suspect it was one of those rare instances where two people who are eagerly searching for companionship suddenly meet each other at exactly the right time.

We walked hurriedly to the van parked out back after what seemed like three hours of public foreplay. The parking lot was packed, and another customer honked impatiently as he waited to take our space. He finally grew tired of waiting, yelled some comment that was unintelligible from the rear living area, and roared off in disgust. It was a wise decision, because the van remained parked in the same spot for the next two hours.

Stu drove up from Seattle to join RCMP officials in a debriefing and strategy session on the deep cover operation. Willie and I were both living in the same area of Vancouver, and he was still hoping that the woman who had accompanied him to Slocan Valley would prove a valuable connection. Although we would run into each other on occasion, we hadn't had an opportunity to talk candidly since the spring festival. In the process of our joint debriefing, we discovered that there were a number of mutual friends among individuals belonging to the two separate groups we were infiltrating.

Stu brought us up to date on the Weatherman investigation in the States, but it appeared nothing of value had been learned. Having spoken with Stu earlier by phone, I knew he had made another pitch to the RCMP Security Service for assistance in the Canadian operation and was turned down. I got the impression that the FBI would do nothing of any significance until a new Director was selected.

Stu and Jack continued to talk enthusiastically about the possibilities of obtaining valuable information through the Professor. While I shared their enthusiasm, I was unable to understand why the RCMP considered the Professor such an influential radical. Perhaps they knew something that I didn't.

One of the RCMP officials questioned me at length about the physical layout of the Professor's apartment. I immediately sensed what he was alluding to, and when he asked me to prepare a detailed diagram of the floor plan, there was little room for doubt. The cards were finally laid on the table when he inquired if it would be possible for me to plant a bug during one of my frequent visits.

The officer kept questioning me about the Professor's chairs: how many does he have; what size and type; where are they located; are any of them broken or in need of repair; would it be possible to remove one without his knowledge.

Willie and I met for a beer after the meeting to talk things over. We were both a little disenchanted by the futility of our present situation. The Bureau hadn't provided any positive information about the Weatherman fugitives in months and didn't appear likely to. From the sound of things, the investigation had come to a screeching halt. After the resignation of Pat Gray, caution seemed to be the rule of the day among Bureau officials. From what I gathered, they entrusted Acting Director William Ruckelshaus with only whatever information was deemed absolutely essential.

Equally troubling was our deteriorating relationship with the RCMP and Special L Squad. After the Watergate scandal broke and spilled over into the FBI with the resignation of Pat Gray, they seemed to grow leery of their involvement with us. Where they had once vigorously pursued their own investigation of the Weather Underground, they now tolerated our presence, provided liaison assistance, and conducted further inquiries only when officially requested.

Willie and I had been left to plod along on our own with little guidance and less assistance. I caustically told him that the odds of two undercover agents locating missing fugitives in a foreign country of over twenty million people didn't look too good. It worked out to about eleven million suspects a piece, and without legal surveillance, or technical assistance, I figured we'd be there a long time.

We reminisced over how drastically both the times and priorities had changed over the past years. What was once deemed a matter of grave national importance by two neighboring countries had now become a problem that both would just as soon forget.

At the invitation of the Professor, I began to attend meetings of the local IWW chapter. They were nothing at all like meetings of radical organizations I had attended in the States. In fact, most of the Wobbly gatherings seemed more like low-keyed social functions. Many of the men sported beards and moderately long hair, but I was far and away the freakiest participant.

Most of the women members of the organization were clean, neatly dressed, employed, and noticeably lacking in revolutionary or feminist rhetoric. If they were radical, they certainly didn't look, act, or talk like it. Their primary concern centered around the plight of the worker, and it didn't seem to make any difference whether the worker was a man or woman. There were working married couples among the group, but I never heard any of the bitter criticisms of monogamy, sexism, and male chauvinism that dominated Weatherman discussions.

The local organization boasted a couple of members in their sixties who regularly attended meetings. The old-timers could spin fascinating tales about the early days of the Wobblies when they traveled around the United States battling the "bulls" and "finks" in violent labor confrontations. They also related chilling accounts of government harassment and mob violence during the formative years of the labor movement. Drug use among the Wobblies was slight. Most of those who smoked grass and hash would never light up in the presence of the older members.

On one occasion, about eight of us sat around the Professor's apartment late one night and proceeded to smoke ourselves into oblivion. As the evening wore on, the Professor and Peter began to recall their experiences in Colorado. They spoke at length of the Colorado fugitives, though not always in glowing terms, and the Professor acknowledged he had provided assistance in the form of false identification and temporary housing. It was quite obvious they were talking about Bishop and Knowles, although specific names were never mentioned, and I didn't inquire. From the drift of the conversation, however, I gathered the Professor had strong ideological differences with the two fugitives and was somewhat perturbed by their subsequent activities. Even so, it seemed highly likely that he was aware of their whereabouts.

As the discussion focused on false identification, I learned that the birth certificates were being manufactured locally by a small, underground printing company that published radical literature. The print shop was located in a Vancouver warehouse and relied heavily on volunteer labor from members of the IWW and other organizations. I had heard the name "Roger" mentioned frequently in previous conversations regarding the Wobblies, but now I discovered that Roger the Dodger was the individual who actually produced the documents. When I heard that Roger the Dodger was a Californian who lived underground in Vancouver, my interest heightened considerably.

Several weeks later, I was finally introduced to Roger, but by that point I was able to verify my suspicions: Roger the Dodger was a prominent, nonfugitive activist who had been missing for almost two years. While in California, he had been active in SDS, edited an underground newspaper, and helped produce a sabotage manual. He was later detected at an underground printing operation in Oregon that was known to have produced fictitious identification for the Weatherman fugitives. Shortly after, he dropped out of sight. According to information transmitted by Stu and Jack, Roger had subsequently surfaced in Vancouver to establish a printing company under his new identity. He had assumed the name of a British spy famous during World War II, although his Canadian idetification gave his birthplace as Hoffman, Saskatchewan. He was currently living with a woman who had been active in a militant Vancouver collective whose avowed purpose was to assist the Weatherman fugitives. To complicate matters further, the Professor noted during our introduction that Roger had recently been chosen executive secretary of the local IWW organization.

Between the Professor's assistance to Top Ten fugitive Cameron David Bishop and his association with Roger the Dodger, I felt certain that I was moving closer to the Weather Underground. Since Karen continued to send letters to the Professor's apartment, I had a reasonable excuse for dropping by periodically, although at that point, an excuse was no longer necessary. We had become good friends, and I was treated like a member of the family. He had invited me to join the IWW, and while I couldn't discount the fact that I was being recruited, he impressed me with his candor and sincerity.

For some time, the Professor and his lady had been planning a summer vacation. Before leaving on the trip, he arranged for me to see an attorney who was active with the Committee to Aid American War Objectors. The attorney was knowledgeable in immigration laws and procedures for obtaining landed immigrant status. The Professor felt that there must be some legal way for me to become a Canadian citizen and rid myself of the U.S. fugitive problems.

A few days later I reluctantly met with the attorney at his office in downtown Vancouver. He was about my age and mentioned that he and the Professor had been friends for some time. He seemed genuinely interested in my predicament, but after providing him with the facts of my situation—somewhat embellished—he agreed that life in the underground was the only answer. Unless substantiating documents for a landed immigrant application were falsified, which was quite risky, there was no way I could work within the Canadian law to become a citizen. I thanked him for his time and went on my way.

With the Professor on vacation, I spent virtually all of my time with Connie. Occasionally we would stay at her house, but for the most part, we slept in the van parked out front. Since her roommates would generally have departed for work by the time we got up, we had the house to ourselves during the day. After a hot shower and leisurely breakfast, we might head down to Kits Beach or visit friends in the neighborhood. While I never came right out and said it, Connie was under the impression that I was peripherally involved in drug dealing, which accounted for my absences during the afternoon and early evening. But in reality, I didn't want to be away from her any more than necessary.

A typical summer evening would find us driving to a nearby package store for beer, wine, or my latest favorite, Canadian whiskey, then walking next door to the Kentucky Fried Chicken franchise for an order to go. After a few tokes on the return trip, we'd arrive at Kits Beach, where we would sit in the van listening to music, drinking beer, devouring fried chicken, and watching the incredible sunsets.

Connie and her roommates introduced me to a number of their friends. For the most part, they were relatively straight, had good jobs, and maintained a conservative appearance, although many smoked grass. Without exception, they treated me like a trusted friend. Never once did they question my long hair, livelihood, or reason for being in Canada. I was invited to their parties, homes, and businesses.

I was tremendously impressed by the tolerance and warmth of the Canadians I met. Even though they didn't actually know me, they appeared ready and willing to help in any way possible. In their view, I was a close friend of Connie's, and that's all they needed to know. The irony of the situation didn't escape me. In the company of one group, I was Bill Lane, itinerant freak attorney, while among the other I was Bob Johnson, revolutionary fugitive. Neither group knew the real Cril Payne.

During the Professor's absence, Connie and I decided to take our own vacation. We drove up north and camped out at Alice Lake near Mt. Garibaldi, then traveled on to Nairn Falls, just south of Pemberton. It was great to camp in the mountains again, especially with someone I deeply cared for. We had become inseparable, and while I realized our relationship would one day have to end, I just didn't want to think about it. Our moments together were all that mattered. For the first time in my deep cover experience, I was as vulnerable as my earlier targets.

In early June 1973, Clarence M. Kelly was nominated Director of the FBI. The fact that he had served in the Bureau for over twenty years, rising to the rank of SAC, gave me cause for concern, although I was enthused by reports that he was currently serving as chief of police in Kansas City.

After Kelly's nomination, I made several inquiries regarding his opinion of the deep cover operation in Canada. The standard answer I received was that Kelly would not be briefed on the program until after his confirmation hearing before the Senate Judiciary Committee. The old guard at Bureau headquarters apparently didn't want to put the new Director in the unenviable position of having to perjure himself before he even took office.

Acting Director William Ruckelshaus resigned on July 5th as the confirmation hearings got under way. The hearing lasted only three days, and on July 9, 1973, Clarence Kelly was sworn in by President Richard Nixon as the first permanent FBI Director in more than fourteen months. Several days later, I posed the question about Kelly's approval once again, but this time, I was advised he had been too busy for a briefing from Domestic Intelligence.

During our next debriefing session, I suggested to Stu and Jack that we create a crisis to push the Professor off center. Either he knew where Bishop was hiding and might possibly put me in contact with him, or we were wasting our time. By now I was growing exceedingly tired of the lies and deceptions and was eager to resolve the matter. For months we had ostensibly been operating without the knowledge or approval of the head of the FBI, and in view of the revelations surrounding Watergate, I was growing increasingly apprehensive. Stu and Jack concurred in my suggestion to precipitate a crisis, and a few days later Division Five granted final approval.

In late July, FBI agents interviewed Karen at her residence in Seattle. They displayed my mug shot which had been taken earlier by the Los Angeles Police Department and advised her that I had been traced to Seattle. While she was given the impression that the FBI knew I had lived at her house, she was never confronted with the specific accusation. But instead of my being wanted for drug charges or rioting, this time the matter was far more serious. Karen was told that I was wanted for homicide.

In the early seventies, a bomb consisting of several sticks of dynamite had been placed in a trash receptacle in the men's rest room at the Los Angeles Federal Building. At the moment that a young Mexican-American reached for a paper towel from the dispenser directly above the trash receptacle, the bomb exploded, virtually disintegrat-

ing his body. The rest room was reduced to ashes which agents were forced to sift in search of evidence. About all they found were minute pieces of what was once a human body. As in most bombings of a similar type, the case was never solved. Karen was now told that I was the primary suspect.

Apparently she handled the interview fairly well by feigning co-operation and admitting to nothing. But just as expected, the agents had barely returned to their cars before she was telephoning the Professor in Vancouver with the news. The Professor then walked down to Kits Beach in search of the van to warn me of the developments. He was unable to locate me, again as planned, and just to be sure he was convinced of the story, RCMP officers were later dispatched to his building to display my mug shot to the residents. By the time I dropped by his apartment the next evening to check on my mail, there was little question that he believed the charade. However, he still didn't seem all that alarmed.

In a marathon rap session that lasted well into the early morning hours, Peter, the Professor, and I covered about all the bases in the Canadian underground. Although they never questioned me regarding specific details of the bombing, they assumed I was involved, and we progressed forward from that point. Now, instead of talking in generalities about the Colorado fugitives, they were mentioning specific names on the FBI's Ten Most Wanted list.

The Professor had helped Bishop, Knowles, and their girl friends enter the country all right, but neither he nor Peter had ever really liked the two fugitives when they knew each other in Colorado. They viewed the two as immature adventurers whose acts of violence were committed without forethought or political purpose. Nonetheless, they provided assistance. But once they arrived in Canada, the fugitives belligerently refused to take the Professor's advice. From what he said, it was one screw-up after another, until he finally washed his hands of the whole affair.

After an absence of more than two years, Bishop unexpectedly appeared at his apartment one day looking like a conventional businessman. The Professor told him that he didn't want to know any of the details of his current location, identity, or employment. During the brief visit, Bishop requested nothing in the way of assistance, though he reportedly boasted of new contacts in the underground who were helping him avoid capture.

We discussed the Weather Underground at length, and while my friends acknowledged hearing occasional rumors concerning the presence of Weatherman fugitives in Canada, they claimed to have seen no evidence to substantiate the reports. They pointed out, however, that specualtion regarding the whereabouts of the Weathermen was a frequent topic of conversation among Canadian activists; moreover, the group was often referred to by individuals seeking to enhance their image as macho revolutionaries.

Both Peter and the Professor were adamant in their opinion that I should not become involved with the Weatherman fugitives. Even if they were actually in Canada and I should somehow come in contact with them, the Professor believed it would only get me into deeper trouble. In addition, they felt that the Weatherman ideology was doomed to failure. They advised me to sell the van, cut my hair, try to get a regular job, and live quietly in a large city as Bob Johnson. They felt I could still live safely in Vancouver, but if I didn't share their opinion, they would put me in contact with trusted friends in Montreal who would gladly provide assistance.

After more than four hours of candid discussion, I was convinced that Peter and the Professor were telling the truth. They had recently admitted their involvement with Bishop, and if they were lying or trying to conceal something, I was unable to detect it. Even with the artificial crisis injected into the situation, they acted as predicted by offering to provide further assistance. If they were secretly hiding members of the Weather Underground, they were gifted actors whose involvement in the IWW could only be explained as a farce.

Early that morning, I thanked them for their help and friendship, but explained that I just couldn't risk involving them any further in my legal problems. The RCMP had already made inquiries, and if I continued to stay in Vancouver, sooner or later they would have troubles in their own country. I mentioned that I planned to travel to eastern Canada and if assistance was needed, they'd be getting a call. We shook hands warmly, wished each other well, and I left the apartment for the last time.

In my last debriefing with the Mounties, I discussed my conversation with the Professor and Peter. I noted that the deep cover scenario had been played to conclusion and that my targets had been advised that I was leaving the city. Having previously spoken with Fast Freddie about the matter, I suggested that it was time for me to return to Los Angeles. I was eager to move on to Dallas and resume a more normal existence. Deep cover had been a profound experience, but I'd had enough.

Willie had been successfully targeted against Roger the Dodger, and it was hoped that tangible information would be developed from that angle. Only a few days earlier, we had been told that promising information had been developed indicating that the Weatherman fugitives were living in Toronto. Since there were only two deep cover operatives in Canada and one was supposedly traveling east anyway, it was apparent who would be going to Toronto. The project was discussed again, but I quickly rejected the idea. It would require at least another six months, perhaps much longer, and I simply wasn't interested in starting over again with another deep cover charade.

My colleagues were understanding of the situation and concurred in my decision. We tentatively scheduled my departure for the end of the week, and Stu agreed to submit the proposal formally to Division Five for approval.

Driving out of Vancouver and leaving Connie was one of the most difficult experiences of deep cover. Once my decision to leave the program was out in the open and relayed back to Washington, I felt an overwhelming sense of relief. But at the same time, it signaled an end to my relationship with Connie. What had initially been accepted as an eventuality had now become an unavoidable reality.

I had been trying to prepare her for my departure by mentioning that a lawsuit I'd once handled in Los Angeles was coming up on appeal and would probably require my assistance. I broke the news to her as gently as possible, and during our remaining time together, we went out each evening and enjoyed ourselves more than ever. For my own part, this was due to the fact that I was much more relaxed, both mentally and physically, and intent upon savoring the final moments with a woman I felt very strongly about—so strongly, in fact, that it was a little scary.

After several consecutive nights in which our relationship soared to new heights, it was increasingly difficult to leave. To walk away without being able to say who I was or why I was there was one helluva dismal prospect. Not only was it frustrating, it was a traumatic first experience. I had never withdrawn from such a serious, enjoyable relationship without having the *possibility* of renewing it. But this was finality—pure and simple. I would never again see the warm, tender woman who had become such an important part of my life. Equally distressing was the fact that Connie would inevitably conclude she had been the victim of the ultimate Yankee rat fucking. In the not too distant future, she would discover that my Los Angeles telephone number didn't exist, and that her letters to a post office box would go unanswered. The man who said he loved her would have vanished into thin air.

Once back in Los Angeles, I found out that my transfer to Dallas was far from certain. For months, Fast Freddie had told me that in his frequent conversations with Division Five officials, they had consistently stated that my Office of Preference (OP) transfer would be no problem. But now that I had returned from Canada after more than six months of living in a van, all that had changed.

With Clarence Kelly as Director, the old guard of Hoover loyalists was once again firmly in control at Bureau headquarters. They had weathered the storm created by impetuous outsiders like Gray and Ruckelshaus until a respected member of the FBI family was appointed Director. From all indications, it was a return to business as usual. And with Kelly traveling to field offices and commuting to Kansas City each week to visit his seriously ill wife, the old guard continued to take charge of daily affairs.

Without the new Director around to arbitrate internal disputes, Bureau headquarters became the scene of a grim power struggle among the Assistant Directors and senior officials. Many of the innovative changes instituted by Pat Gray were the first to be discontinued. While this was not done officially the innovations were rendered meaningless by administrative barriers and a lack of cooperation between divisions.

Fred was as perturbed by the situation as I was and did everything possible, including risking his own job, to persuade Division Five officials to honor their commitment. But according to their version, the matter was simply out of their hands. All they could do was request the Administrative Division to transfer me from Los Angeles to another office for "security reasons." From the very beginning, however, it was made clear that I had to be transferred *somewhere*. After years of looking like a freak, I couldn't suddenly cut off my hair and start wearing a coat and tie without arousing suspicion. The possibility of my running into former movement acquaintances around Los Angeles who might recognize me as a straight FBI agent was considered an unacceptable risk.

During Pat Gray's tenure, he had awarded Office of Preference transfers to several deep cover agents, many of whom had been involved in the program for only a couple of months. And while Ruckelshaus was Acting Director, he had reportedly granted virtually every transfer request that came across his desk. These decisions apparently displeased the head of the Administrative Division, since he no doubt viewed them as a loss of personal power, and he therefore had decreed that any future OP transfers would be based on the seniority system developed under Mr. Hoover. Needless to say, I was bitterly disappointed. I had lived up to my commitment, and I could see no reason why the FBI should not do the same. My future now seemed more uncertain than ever.

The following week I received a call from Assistant Director Joe Jamieson who was in charge of the Los Angeles office. Jamieson was an easygoing, unpretentious guy who was respected for his competence and fairness. He enjoyed a reputation as a leader who was not afraid to challenge the Bureau if one of his agents was treated unjustly. I admired him because unlike the majority of his contemporaries, he wasn't obsessed with his position and the power which it afforded.

Since I had met with Jamieson several times before leaving for Seattle, he was well acquainted with my involvement in deep cover. Fast Freddie had appealed to him for assistance with the transfer problem, and he was calling to report on his efforts. According to the Administrative Division, Dallas had too many agents for their current case load, and therefore another agent was not justified. But Oklahoma City had an opening if I was interested in that. No I wasn't, I replied. Well how about San Antonio? It was farther from Dallas, but they were in need of agents. I wasn't overly excited about that either, but out of curiosity, I asked about Houston. Jamieson said he would call the Bureau and find out, then get back in touch. Knowing how case loads are juggled for inspections, I figured the whole thing was a fabrication, but Jamieson sounded sincere, and I had no reason to doubt him.

When he called back, he seemed disquieted by the whole affair. Houston, like Dallas, had too many agents. The only other Texas office requiring additional agents was El Paso.

El Paso! I was exasperated. I told Mr. Jamieson that based on the specific instructions given at the Weatherman In-Service, my OP selections reflected exactly where I wanted to go upon completion of deep cover. For months I had been assured that a transfer to Dallas would be no problem. Now that I've finished my assignment, I'm given some ridiculous excuse about case load and at the same time told that I have to be transferred somewhere. After busting my ass for months, I can't go to Dallas and I can't stay in Los Angeles! I did everything the bastards asked and now they're trying to screw me!

Jamieson knew I was right, and he was man enough to admit it. Then he laid things right on the line. "They won't transfer you to Dallas because you've got it down as your OP. Same thing with Houston."

I was dumbfounded. "You mean because I had Dallas down as my first choice for an OP I can't go there? The bastards told me to put down where I wanted to go!"

"I know," he said softly. "It's too bad you couldn't get anything in writing."

"We tried, Boss!" I snapped. "But they said we could trust 'em and it wasn't necessary."

"Is there any other office you'd like to go?" he asked. "They tell me you can go anywhere in the country except your Office of Preference."

"What about this great concern for case load and manpower requirements?" I asked.

"From what I gather, it doesn't have a damn thing to do with it. I talked with the Assistant Director, and he flatly stated there would be no more OP transfers—period. Try to understand, Cril. He's an Assistant Director and I'm an Assistant Director. I can argue with him all day, but I can't make him do a damn thing."

"Well, what if I submitted a new OP form with other offices, or listed none at all? Could I stay in L.A. a few months and then get transferred to Dallas?"

"I suggested that to him, but he wouldn't buy it."

"How come?" I asked incredulously.

"He said it would be a subterfuge."

"A subterfuge!" I shouted.

"He claims that a lot of the older agents watch the OP list religiously and they'd raise hell about its being unfair."

"Well, what the hell's fair about this, Boss? A guy can change his OP every day if he wants to. How can that be a subterfuge? I've been under cover for three years, done everything they asked, and now I'm getting screwed. It's just not right."

"I agree, Cril, but I can't make them do anything. Why don't you give some thought to those other offices, and let me know if you're interested. But remember, you're going to have to go someplace. At least we could get you to Texas."

"I'll think about it, Boss, but the whole thing sounds ridiculous. That's not the deal we made."

"Fred tells me they want you back in Washington next week for debriefing," he said. "Maybe you can argue with 'em better than I can."

I was livid with rage, for I was obviously the victim of an internal power struggle. "You can rest assured that I'll give it my best shot, Boss. But look, if they give me this same song and dance, would you mind if I took it up with the Director?"

"Not at all, Cril," he replied. "After all you've been through, I think you're entitled to that. I'm just sorry I couldn't have been more helpful."

I thanked Jamieson for his efforts and hung up. I was furious. The whole story about case loads and manpower requirements had been bullshit from the beginning. Had it not been for Jamieson's honesty, I might have accepted the explanation about Dallas and gone quietly to San Antonio. But to learn that I couldn't go to Dallas because I had followed instructions and listed it as my OP was ludicrous! Some pompous, power-hungry bureaucrat who hadn't investigated a case in over twenty years was trying to fuck with my life. Right then I decided that I was going to Dallas—either as an agent or a private citizen. If the FBI wouldn't honor its bargain, I didn't want to be a part of the organization.

In order to keep agents in line and SACs aware of what they were doing, there was a long standing policy that agents could not see the Director without prior approval from their SAC. This policy effectively insulated J. Edgar Hoover from the realities of life in the field at the same time that it protected SACs from the possibility that a disgruntled agent might take his complaints directly to the top. But with Jamieson's approval, I could request a meeting with Clarence Kelly, at least to make my position known. If Kelly disagreed, I would accept his decision with the satisfaction of knowing it had been made by the head of the FBI. I wasn't about to roll over for some desk-bound ignoramus on a power trip.

17

I Tackle the Bureaucracy

The days of waiting for the journey to Washington seemed interminable, and I was consumed by thoughts of my impending confrontation. I considered buying a new suit and getting a haircut but finally decided I'd wear the outmoded narrow lapels, button-down collar, skinny tie, and wing-tipped oxfords. I would look like the Joe College that had arrived for his first interview, only now I'd have hair down to the middle of my back and a flowing mustache. With my official Bureau briefcase in hand, I felt the contrast between freak and conservative businessman would get some attention.

When I arrived in Washington, I checked into the same "secure" hotel we had used during the Weatherman In-Service. I couldn't help laughing the following morning as I dressed to go downtown. The narrow lapels I had worried about could not even be seen because of all my hair, and the pants legs on my trousers didn't even come close to touching my shoes. I looked like a buffoon with a briefcase.

The Domestic Intelligence Division was then housed in the Federal Triangle Building, just down the street from the Justice Department. I checked in with the guard at the front desk who somewhat apprehensively notified Bill Preusse of my arrival. Preusse soon appeared and greeted me warmly. After obtaining a visitor's pass for me, he guided me to an elevator.

"We know you'll attract lots of attention up here," he whispered, "so we've told the staff we're expecting a visit from an undercover CIA agent. If anyone should inquire, you're with the Agency."

I nodded in agreement as we left the elevator. Preusse guided me through a series of executive offices where I was greeted by Bob Shackelford and Ray Wannall, and by Ed Miller, head of the Domestic Intelligence Division. We moved into a private office where we were joined by several other Division Five officials and began the debriefing. It was structured along the lines of an informal question-and-answer session. The group was primarily interested in my opinions, observations, and theories about the Weather Underground. It was a frank discussion, and it consumed most of the day.

One of the things that had always bothered me about the Domestic Intelligence officials who supervised Internal Security cases was their reluctance to accept the fact that young radical activists could become disenchanted with revolutionary politics and subsequently discontinue their involvement.

Perhaps this unrealistic attitude was partially attributable to the fact that most of the reports on the movement leaders of the mid-sixties were prepared by security agents from the red scare days of the House Un-American Activities Committee and Subversive Activities Control Board. Subversives and radicals were typically characterized with an inflammatory rhetoric that was designed to please Bureau headquarters and Director Hoover. As the years passed, many agents simply filed new reports that perpetrated the same over-zealous characterization. Unfortunately, many younger agents like myself who were on security assignments didn't understand the earlier motivation for political overkill and consequently took the reports at face value.

It was late in the afternoon before the subject of my mandatory relocation was mentioned. Since these were the same officials who had originally made personal assurances of an OP transfer, I was happy to discuss the subject. They began by giving me the same excuses I had heard from Assistant Director Jamieson regarding case load and manpower requirements. I wasted no time in presenting my objections.

Wasn't it true, I asked, that several deep cover agents had received OP transfers from East Coast offices to San Diego after spending only a few months in the program and accomplishing little of value?

Well, yes it was, came the reluctant reply, but that was before Clarence Kelly became Director. The situation had now changed, and the Administrative Division adamantly refused to consider any requests for OP transfers except those based on seniority.

"You're a young, single agent," one of the officials pointed out. "Why not transfer to the Honolulu office and have yourself some fun on the islands?"

"Mainly because it's not Dallas," I answered, "and that's where we agreed I'd go. I've lived up to my part of the bargain. Why can't the Bureau live up to theirs?"

The replies continued in a circuitous manner that conveyed the message that the head of the Administrative Division was still pissed about Pat Gray. All prior obligations are hereby cancelled!

Well, could the high-minded egomaniac possibly be persuaded to let me change my OP to Honolulu and then be transferred to Dallas?

Absolutely not, came the reply, for he had already decided the procedure would constitute a subterfuge and thus be unfair to agents with more time in the Bureau.

One of the younger Bureau Supervisors decided to explain the situation. "You've got to understand, Cril," he began. "There are lots of agents out there who watch that OP list faithfully. If an agent with only five years in the Bureau suddenly gets an OP to Dallas, they're going to be screaming bloody murder. There's no question you've made a tremendous sacrifice, but agents trying to locate deserters in Harlem feel the same way."

"Perhaps they do," I countered. "But *you've* got to remember that no matter how late they work, once they sign out they can go home and relax. But in deep cover you never get off. The day never ends, and there's no place to go except the back of your van. Your only source of companionship are the people you're infiltrating. There *is* no relaxing, you're on the job twenty-four hours a day, seven days a week. I doubt the agents working on deserters in Harlem would equate the two assignments. If they do, they're full of shit!"

I think it was clear to everyone that our discussions had reached an impasse. I was advised to think the situation over that evening, and we would resume our talks the following morning. As we were leaving the office, I was incensed by a veiled threat that it might be better to accept a transfer to San Antonio rather than to risk a selection by the Administrative Division.

Our talks resumed the following morning with no change in attitude. I had already decided that if the Bureau was going to maintain an inflexible, uncompromising position on the matter, I would do the same. If I couldn't get what had been promised, I would raise the issue with Clarence Kelly.

The first offer of the day was a suggestion that instead of being transferred, I could move to a distant part of Los Angeles and be given the highest FBI incentive award possible: Five hundred dollars less state and federal taxes!

I responded with a succinct thanks, but no thanks. If I was to remain in Los Angeles, I wanted to stay on the beach. But once again, I reminded my supervisors that our original agreement called for an OP transfer to Dallas. Money was the least of my concerns.

Then, quite unexpectedly, the ante was upped tenfold. "How would you like to come back to Division Five as a Bureau Supervisor?" Shackelford asked. "You'd get your Grade Thirteen right away and a Fourteen in another year."

"You gotta be crazy!" I exclaimed. "I wanna go to Dallas!" It was an honest, gut reaction expressed without thinking. They had offered me a chance for administrative advancement along with a hefty increase in pay, a real opportunity that many agents only dream about. But I had no desire to become a desk-bound genius dependent upon internal politics for advancement. The silence and the stern faces told me I had just insulted the entire group. "Well, what I mean is, after being out of the office for three years, I don't know the first thing about paperwork. I couldn't possibly read a report and evaluate it properly. I'm just not qualified to be a supervisor."

The group seemed to relax as though placated by my belated explanation.

"I'm sure you're a little rusty on your paperwork," Shackelford said. "But we could certainly use your knowledge and experience back here."

I thanked him again for the generous offer and finally put the issue to rest by saying that after a year or so of regular work in the field, I would reconsider the proposition. However, it suddenly dawned on me that they would go to any lengths to avoid a confrontation with the Administrative Division. It seemed the ideal time to play my trump card.

"In all honesty," I said, "I don't see why a transfer should have become a problem in the first place. Personnel may have changed, but it's still the same organization. The FBI made the commitment, and the FBI ought to keep it. Sure, we've got a new Director, but I haven't heard anyone suggest that he's refusing to honor past commitments. As I understand it, the matter's out of your hands because the Domestic Intelligence Division can't make the Administrative Division do anything. You've asked for an OP transfer and they've refused. Okay— fine. I can understand your reluctance to take on the Administrative Division. In the end you'd probably lose a lot more than you'd gain. But that's not necessarily true for me. I think the only man who can settle the controversy is the Director. If I present my side of things, that'll keep you out of it. If the Director doesn't think I deserve an OP, then fine, that's his prerogative. But at least it'll be his decision."

The Director! Power plays would come and power plays would go, but the fundamental uncertainties of life at Bureau Headquarters remained the same. Regardless of anyone's position in the pecking order, he could never be sure how the official above him on the Bureau totem pole would react to a decision on a particular issue.

As my hosts regained their composure, they began to grope for reasons why I shouldn't try to see the Director. One official mentioned that he was still in Kansas City visiting his sick wife. But I had already checked and knew that he was right down the street. Another noted how busy Mr. Kelly was, and that it would be impossible to interrupt his tight schedule; moreover, I needed prior approval from my SAC in order to request an appointment. That's true, I replied, but I'd received permission from an Assistant Director, and I was more than willing to wait patiently until the Director could see me for a few minutes. If need be, I could take annual leave and wait for days. I'm sure the idea of a long-haired freak spending his vacation sitting in the Director's waiting room was somewhat intimidating. But how could they stop me? After serving five years as an FBI agent, I was certainly entitled to see the Director.

"Did I understand the risk involved in seeking an audience with the Director?" someone asked. If he became angry or disturbed by my appearance, it might mean the end of my career. If the Director's gonna get upset about long hair on an undercover agent, he can have my career, I thought.

When I returned from lunch, Bob Shackelford called me into his office and told me that he and Assistant Director Ed Miller had decided to submit a memorandum to Director Kelly recommending that I be transferred to Dallas. I was ecstatic over their decision to plead my case officially, but Shackelford warned that it would not be an easy battle. They would need all possible ammunition for the justification memo, and he advised me to hold nothing back: drugs, sex, disease, and the Miami beating were to be discussed in detail. He instructed me to get together with Bill Preusse and assist him in drafting the memorandum.

Since I was scheduled to leave for Los Angeles that evening, we wasted no time in getting to work. We shut ourselves up in Preusse's office, and I provided him with the gruesome details. After all the information was assimilated, we prepared the first draft, which he dictated to his secretary. While Preusse was reviewing the typed copy, Ed Miller unexpectedly appeared at the door for a private, heart-to-heart talk.

Miller had been conspicuously absent from our transfer discussions, apparently preferring to rely on his top assistant, Ray Wannall, to keep him advised of our progress. It was a brief conversation, but from the very inception, it had all the characteristics of a classic stroking session. Miller made a number of flattering comments which didn't sound overly sincere.

When the five-page justification memorandum was completed, I returned to the hotel, packed my bags, and rushed out to the airport. On the flight back to Los Angeles, I reviewed the events of the past two days and was still somewhat surprised by what had happened. It had crossed my mind that perhaps the memo would never be sent up and was only a ploy to get me out of Washington and away from the Director. But surely they wouldn't take that kind of chance, I thought. The head of the Domestic Intelligence Division had assured me the issue would be raised with Kelly. If not, I could always fly back at my own expense.

Almost two weeks went by as I waited impatiently for my transfer orders. Fast Freddie made repeated inquiries of Division Five officials but continued to get the runaround. I was finally told that the memo had been held up in the office of Nicholas P. Callahan, the former head of the Administrative Division who had been elevated to the position of Associate Director by Clarence Kelly. Callahan had been assigned to Bureau Headquarters in 1945, and had come to personify the old guard of Hoover loyalists. Now that he was second in command, he was correcting many of the frivolous policies conceived by Pat Gray.

Fortunately, Assistant Director Joe Jamieson made several calls to the Bureau on my behalf. In early September, I received a letter dated August 30, 1973, which began, "Your headquarters are changed for official reasons from Los Angeles, California to Dallas, Texas."

Interestingly, the lengthy justification memo from R. L. Shackelford to E. S. Miller, dated August 17, 1973, contained the following recommendation: "That informant be transferred from Los Angeles Division to Dallas based on comments set forth above."

Directly under that sentence were the handwritten comments of Clarence M. Kelly, Director of the Federal Bureau of Investigation: "By all means *Yes*. CMK."

18

Dallas and Disillusion

When I reported for duty early on Thursday morning, September 20, at the FBI's Dallas Field Office, it was like a dream come true. I'd finally made it home to Texas, and I had every intention of staying there the rest of my life.

My old friend "Bear" introduced me around the office and took me in to see the Special Agent In Charge. This same SAC had interviewed me when I first applied for a Special Agent position five years before in 1968. He had been in charge of the Dallas office for a number of years and was widely respected throughout the Bureau.

It was frustrating to learn that I would be assigned to the security squad, for I wanted nothing more to do with investigating people's politics and thoughts. But the excitement of being back in Dallas seemed to outweigh the disappointment. Fortunately, the assignment only lasted for a day because the Domestic Intelligence Division pointed out that I might run into some of my former radical acquaintances while working security cases. I was reluctantly shuffled over to a criminal squad where I was assigned to work on civil rights cases involving police brutality.

For the first few weeks, I felt completely lost. After not having worked in an FBI Field Office for over three years, I had only a vague idea of how things were now being done. Under the leadership of Gray, Ruckelshaus, and now Clarence Kelly, the day-to-day operations, report writing, and overtime requirements had continued to change, and I had to learn rules, regulations, and procedures all over again. For an agent with five years of experience in the organization, it was annoying and embarrassing.

I was also suffering from the shock brought on by the sudden change in my appearance. Sometimes I would casually glance at my clean-cut reflection in the mirror without any sense of personal recognition. And like an amputee, I could still *feel* the long hair falling down over my shoulders, or I would instinctively stroke my chin only to discover the beard was gone.

Shopping for clothes was another shocker. I had to buy a completely new wardrobe, since everything I owned from the past was hopelessly out of date either in fit or style. After wearing only jeans and work-shirts for the past years, I was astounded by the astronomical prices of conventional suits, shirts, and ties. And if purchases were made with a personal check, I had to stop and think about how to sign my real name.

During my efforts to locate an apartment or house, I stayed in a mo-tel near downtown Dallas and pored over the classified section of the daily newspapers. On Saturday evening the television set was going while I intently mapped out my Sunday house-hunting stops.

An officious voice suddenly filled the motel room. *"We interrupt this program for a special announcement."*

I glanced at the screen and saw NBC correspondent Carl Stern standing in front of the White House. He looked distraught and seemed unable to breathe. When he did speak, his voice sounded like the voice of doom. I recall thinking that the country must be at war. At the time, the news seemed even worse. President Nixon had fired Ar-chibald Cox, the Watergate Special Prosecutor! Attorney General El-liot Richardson had resigned, and Deputy Attorney General William Ruckelshaus, former Acting Director of the FBI, had been fired. The White House had ordered the FBI to secure the offices and files of all three men.

"Incredible!" I mumbled to the television set. It was beyond com-prehension that the President of the United States would fire the pros-ecutor who was investigating presidential involvement in the Water-gate scandal. How could this happen in America? Nixon's actions during the "Saturday Night Massacre" seemed more like those of a king or dictator than of a U.S. President. Once the reality sank in, my initial reaction of shocked disbelief turned into a feeling of personal outrage.

I arrived at the FBI Academy in March 1974 for a three-week In-Service course that would certify me as an FBI Police Instructor in Le-gal Matters. Since I had attended law school in Texas and was licensed to practice in the state, the SAC had decided I was the logical choice to fill a local vacancy.

Once the course was completed, I would conduct seminars, lectures, and classes on legal subjects at police academies throughout the state. I would also be expected to assist the other legal instructors in reviewing affidavits and warrants for Bureau cases, as well as keeping agents advised on recent court decisions affecting Bureau investigations. These instructional and advisory responsibilities would be added to my normal investigative duties.

I was less than enthusiastic about attending the In-Service, but I had little choice in the matter. It did seem like a good opportunity to get back into the study of law, and after a lengthy absence, I was badly in need of an update. In addition, the thought of establishing a private practice was still in the back of my mind.

When my thirty-first birthday arrived, I recalled that only one year earlier I had been in the Slocan Valley of British Columbia. While everything had changed during the intervening months, the memories of my deep cover experiences remained vividly clear—on this birthday, I was in a Dallas hospital awaiting surgery the following morning. My recycled asshole, courtesy of the Miami police, had not healed properly after the first operation and additional surgery was now required. Once again, I would have to pay the amount that was not covered by my group insurance policy. It was a vivid reminder, both physically and financially, of my encounter with the Miami police.

I returned to the FBI Academy in July, this time for two weeks of intensive training in Special Weapons and Tactics. I had lobbied long and hard to be selected as a volunteer member of the five-man SWAT team from Dallas and was pleased that I had been chosen. Although living in Dallas proved to be everything I'd expected, my routine work was boring as hell. After years of high intensity life, I couldn't get excited about investigating hot check cases. I hoped that being on a SWAT team would make things a little more interesting.

Of all the Bureau training I received, SWAT training was by far the most thorough, professional, and physically demanding. The program was one of the few benefits resulting from the debacle of Wounded Knee. After that unfortunate episode, the need for highly trained, specially equipped, paramilitary teams capable of dealing with terrorist confrontations was fully realized.

The program was designed around the military concept of stress training and was conducted at the Quantico Marine Corps Base. After hearing so many former marine officers reminisce about the obstacle course and the Hill Trail, it was interesting to experience those grueling forms of physical torture—interesting, but far from enjoyable. The majority of our time on the firing range was spent with the M-16 automatic rifle, the M-79 grenade launcher used for tear gas projectiles, the sawed-off shotgun, and a sniper rifle. These were the basic weapons carried by each SWAT team, and since I was proficient with a rifle, I was designated team sniper.

Our last evening at the academy was a bewildering occasion that mirrored the disparity in current opinion, especially among different age groups. FBI agents from all over the country, young and old, Republican and Democrat, were crowded around every available television set, silently awaiting the resignation speech of President Richard M. Nixon.

I noticed tears in the eyes of one crusty Bureau veteran as the speech got under way. Several of the older agents were visibly moved by the event. Some appeared sympathetic to his plight, but most seemed disgusted and demoralized that he had disgraced the country.

When Nixon's speech came to an abrupt end, the majority of agents seemed dismayed. One younger agent commented in a loud voice that could be heard throughout the room, "That cocksucker didn't admit to one goddammed thing!"

"He's running for reelection already!" shouted another.

The room was soon buzzing with heated conversation. Impassioned arguments generally developed between the young and old. It was amazing to hear FBI agents arguing politics, but I suppose similar confrontations were taking place among every segment of American society. These were indeed times full of contention and excitement.

I was summoned back to the FBI Academy in September for a two-day seminar on the deep cover program and the ongoing Weatherman investigation. The meetings were held in the executive conference room above the auditorium rather than in the usual classrooms, and were attended by approximately twenty people. In addition to supervisors from Field Office Weatherman squads and Revolutionary Activities Section officials such as Bob Shackelford and Bill Preusse, three deep cover agents, including myself, were present. Our discussions centered around the inability of field offices to recruit sufficient volunteers for the deep cover assignment. This personnel problem was viewed as the primary reason for the failure to locate the Weatherman fugitives. The same administrative barriers that existed some two years earlier were still in evidence, coupled with the fact that most younger agents regarded the inactive Weather Underground as a problem that had disappeared with the draft and Vietnam War.

It was gratifying to learn that after years of trying to explain the basic facts of movement life, our analysis had finally been accepted: women were the moving force behind the radical underground. The possibility of infiltrating revolutionary communes and collectives of dedicated feminists was negligible. Because men were not allowed to attend their meetings, most undercover police officers were automatically eliminated.

Domestic Intelligence Division officials now offered a possible solution for discussion by the group: female FBI agents would be recruited as deep cover operatives. It was the most ridiculous idea I'd ever heard. The Bureau only had a handful of women agents and they were a pretty straitlaced bunch. It wasn't that women couldn't handle the assignment, for they were superbly suited for undercover work in criminal cases, but the odds they faced in trying to infiltrate those groups at that late date seemed insurmountable. Moreover, to have any success at all, a female agent would have to engage freely in sexual activities with both men and women, especially the latter.

I tried to explain the realities of the situation to Bureau officials, but as usual, it was hard to get the point across. After a lengthy discussion, my final comment to the group seemed to convey the message. "If you're really planning on targeting deep cover agents against revolutionary women's groups, you'd better find a female agent who's prepared to eat lots of puss! She's gotta understand that her sisters are gonna be divin' on her muff, and they'll expect her to do the same."

The idea was dropped.

At the request of the Revolutionary Activities Section, Domestic Intelligence Division, I traveled to Washington in December for the purpose of briefing a newly recruited deep cover operative. Since all Bureau operations were now housed in the new J. Edgar Hoover Building, I was instructed to obtain a hotel room which could later be used for the training session. I checked into the Marriott Hotel near Washington National Airport, and the next morning took a taxi downtown.

Since this was my first visit to the new FBI building, I wandered through a maze of hallways and out-of-the-way cubbyholes before locating the office of Section Chief Robert Shackelford. We chatted amiably while waiting for his new recruit to arrive. I was asked to give the agent some practical advice on how to dress and act in order to avoid detection, as well as to tell him what to expect from his new life-style.

As our conversation progressed, Shackelford squirmed noticeably in his chair and appeared flustered. He was trying to ask me a question without coming right out and asking, a not unusual habit of Bureau officials, but I wasn't about to take the ball and run with it. I knew what he was alluding to, and it seemed advisable to sit quietly and watch him squirm. Sensing my reticence, he finally broached the subject.

"Did you happen to bring any 'stuff' with you?" he inquired in a soft but deliberate voice.

"Stuff?" I asked.

"Yeah, you know, ah . . . pot. To show Herb. We could never get it around here without formal requests to DEA."

I couldn't help laughing. Probably half the clerks working in the building smoked dope, and the Bureau couldn't even score a lid for training! "Yes, I brought some," I answered. "I figured if the poor guy had to depend on the Bureau, he'd never know what grass was till he walked into a commune."

A secretary ushered Herb into the office and after Shackelford introduced us, he reiterated what he wanted me to cover. Shortly thereafter we left the building and caught a cab back to the Marriott. Herb was a friendly guy who was assigned to an East Coast office. Although we were about the same age, he had come into the Bureau only recently, following a hitch in the Air Force. With his scraggly, two-week-old beard and neatly trimmed hair, he looked nothing like a freak, but he seemed genuinely interested in learning. It was apparent that he had a long way to go.

The remainder of the day was spent in my hotel room answering Herb's questions about deep cover. I laid things out candidly and continuously stressed that he faced an extremely difficult, if not impossible, task. When he questioned me about drugs, about which he knew nothing, I did my best to prepare him for the realities of communal life. My comments were a poor substitute for experience, but they were better than nothing.

I showed Herb how to clean marijuana, roll joints, and use the more common items of drug paraphernalia. He wanted to try smoking grass, and I certainly didn't discourage the idea.

It wasn't long before he was stoned out of his gourd. I never anticipated he would get totally zonked on one joint. Paranoia set in, and

Herb was beside himself with panic each time a maid walked past my door. After a couple hours of trying to guide him through his maiden voyage, I suggested we go down to the lobby and have dinner in the coffee shop.

Herb seemed fine until we got off the elevator, when he suddenly became immobilized. We finally made our way into the coffee shop, and after convincing him that every person in the place wasn't staring because they *knew* he was stoned, Herb got the giggles. He laughed in hysterical, uncontrollable fits until he somehow regained his composure. Then he realized everyone in the room *was* watching him! Zap! Back to the panic button.

I finally got him up to my room again. It was touch and go for a while, but after warning him that arrest was a distinct possibility, he straightened up considerably. As he lay sprawled across the bed, snoring lustily, I promised myself that this would never happen again. If the FBI really needed a dope-smoking instructor, they had better start looking right away. I had just turned on my last recruit.

In the ensuing months, I discovered that the employees of the FBI's Dallas Field Office were a friendly, conscientious group. Several eminently qualified Special Agents as well as a number of younger clerical employees possessed the ability to find humor in the overbearing, regimented bureaucracy. But it seemed that every time I had coffee or lunch with some of the office veterans, the only topic of conversation was "that 'thang' we're not supposed to talk about." In actuality, the topic was discussed so extensively that by September a group of inspectors, collectively known as the goon squad, were dispatched to Dallas to harass, intimidate, and get to the bottom of the malicious rumor that had been picked up by the press.

That "thang," as the good ol' boys called it, was a handwritten note that Lee Harvey Oswald had delivered to a receptionist in the Dallas FBI office shortly before the assassination of President Kennedy. The note was intended for Special Agent James P. Hosty who had been assigned to the security case on Oswald. The exact contents of the note remain in dispute even today, but it is generally agreed that serious bodily harm to persons and/or property was threatened. The note was reportedly destroyed shortly after Oswald was murdered, though the question of who ordered the destruction remains unclear.

The fact the note remained a closely guarded secret for almost twelve years, even though many Dallas employees were aware of its existence, is an excellent example of the climate of fear that pervaded Hoover's FBI. From what I could tell after reviewing the file, Hosty had conducted what appeared to be a routine security investigation in a competent manner. Hoover rewarded Hosty with a thirty-day suspension without pay and a disciplinary transfer to Kansas City. A number of other heads rolled, but the SAC escaped from the incident unscathed.

Bureau inspectors descended on Texas and began to interview employees who had been working in the Dallas office during the assassination. In typical bureaucratic fashion, they threatened, insulted, and cajoled these employees—most of whom had eagerly told the true story—for participating in a cover-up instead of coming forward with the facts. Both the inspectors and the employees were well aware that if the incident had been officially reported while Hoover was alive, the information would probably never have left the Bureau, but the disloyal employee would have been forced to leave immediately.

What did the inspectors learn after hassling all the clerks and brick agents who actually do the work? A reasonably consistent version of the events that had occurred in 1963, a version that conflicted with statements from local officials who denied any knowledge of the incident under oath.

To accept the implication that many loyal, dedicated, low-level employees acted strictly on their own by destroying vital evidence in the political crime of the century is to disregard the tyrannical, autocratic rule that characterized the FBI as an institution. Equally absurd is the notion that those in management positions within the Dallas office would have ordered destruction of the note before consulting with Washington. It is inconceivable that they would have considered such a directive without receiving specific instructions from the highest possible Bureau authority. The prevailing office rumors were that J. Edgar Hoover had personally ordered the destruction of the note and had subsequently treated those involved with some degree of compassion in pending disciplinary actions. Only one thing is certain: the true story will never be known.

Early in 1976, rumors began to circulate throughout the field regarding an investigation headed by Assistant Attorney General J. Stanley Pottinger into allegations of surreptitious entries, wiretaps, and mail openings conducted by agents of the New York Weatherman squad against relatives and associates of the missing fugitives. The Justice Department had begun its probe by selecting twelve FBI agents, none of whom had worked on security cases, to conduct the necessary investigations. The agents chosen were characterized as being more loyal to the United States than to the FBI, earning them the dubious title of the Dirty Dozen. The group would subsequently be doubled in size although their unofficial name remained the same.

In an unprecedented move, the Dirty Dozen reportedly formed a raiding party that conducted an armed assault on the J. Edgar Hoover Building in hopes of seizing critical evidence before it could be destroyed. After seizing control of a number of offices, they searched through everything they could find. They didn't find much; according to rumor, practically nothing. Could it be that one of those loyal men from the Dirty Dozen who placed his commitment to the government above that of his own agency had in fact alerted the agency of the impending raid? This question remains a point of intense speculation.

Early Friday afternoon, on July 30, 1976, I walked out of the Dallas Field Office for the last time. After almost eight years as a Special Agent of the Federal Bureau of Investigation, I had resigned.

The decision to leave the FBI had not been easy, but it was the only possible one for me. I had a number of close agent friends in the office, the pay was adequate, and the retirement benefits were great. But I had reached the point where I could no longer lie each day in order to play the ridiculous Bureau games and still live with myself. Somewhere along the way, possibly after deep cover, I simply lost the desire to try. The situation had become so ludicrous that I no longer wanted even to *pretend* to play the games. It just wasn't me.

I also reached the conclusion that nothing of substance had actually changed in the organization. I had served under three Directors since the death of J. Edgar Hoover, and although each tried to institute meaningful reform, the Hoover loyalists at Bureau Headquarters did exactly as they pleased. They seemed to act on the premise that the American people, or for that matter Congress, could not be trusted with the truth, and that they alone knew what was best for the country. Implicit in that notion was the belief that the memory of J. Edgar Hoover should be protected and defended at all costs. If that required deceiving Congressional Oversight Committees, then so be it.

In retrospect, I would suspect that this zealous, uncompromising defense of the myth of Hoover's infallibility did more to discredit the organization than help it.

By late afternoon on Thursday, August 19, 1976, there were few agents who hadn't heard of the day's startling developments. The news spread through the Bureau like wildfire leaving no question that the Justice Department was vigorously pursuing its investigation.

According to the information I received, the Dirty Dozen had descended on Bureau headquarters and seized twenty-two file cabinets containing documents describing the investigation of the Weather Underground. I was told that Section Chief Bob Shackleford's office had been "cleaned out and hauled away."

"Did they get the deep cover files?" I asked nervously.

"From what I hear, they took everything that was there," my friend said. "But that's not all. They transferred Shackleford and a bunch of his men out of Division Five. Word is that anybody who had anything to do with supervising Weatherman cases will be filing fingerprints come morning."

My friend went on to say that the Department had also raided the New York City office, though he was unaware of the details. I seriously doubted that their documents were as sensitive as those maintained by the Chief of FBI's Internal Security section. Back when it was known as the Revolutionary Activities section, everything pertaining to deep cover was locked in Shackleford's office.

Early in September, I received a call from the SAC of the Dallas office informing me that investigators for the Department of Justice were in town and wished to interview me regarding the Weatherman In-Service held in October 1972. Members of the Dirty Dozen had finally arrived. They were interviewing another agent at the Dallas-Ft. Worth Airport, and I was requested to contact them at that number.

I placed the call reluctantly and spoke with one of the agents working for the department. It was vitally important that we talk, he said, but he and his partner were flying to San Antonio when they concluded their interview at the airport. Could I possibly come out to the airport right away? No, I certainly could not, I replied. I wasn't about to drop everything in the middle of a business day to make a forty-mile round trip to the airport. If it was a matter of such grave importance, they could come see me.

The agent then decided that this important interview could be conducted over the phone. He asked a few general questions about the Weatherman In-Service but never mentioned the deep cover program. After some four years, and without the opportunity to refresh my memory on the subject, I could honestly recall little in the way of

ALTAGALLERIA

www.AltaGalleria.com
Berkeley, California 94705

510-414-4485

Email:altagalleria@sbcglobal.net

Edith Yu

Reception Saturday, April 17, 1 - 3 PM at Alta Galleria

Exhibition April 15 - May 28, 2010

specific details. But his questions sounded so innocuous that even a precise answer would have been insignificant.

Then suddenly the line of questioning moved from generalities to specifics: Do you remember a conversation with agent "John Doe" of the New York office when he talked about illegal wiretaps against relatives of the Weathermen? A feeling of rage surged through my body. Here was an FBI agent conducting an important interview by telephone, and without the slightest mention of the Miranda warning, was asking me to implicate a fellow FBI agent by recalling the details of a conversation that allegedly took place some four years earlier. I was overwhelmed. Had the question been posed by someone from outside the organization, perhaps I would have been more understanding. But this bastard knew exactly how the Bureau was run during the period in question. Agents on the street either followed orders without questioning their authority or they were out of a job.

After caustically explaining my views, I hung up. If the Dirty Dozen wanted to shaft members of their own organization, they would do it without any assistance from me.

For the first time in the history of the FBI, a retired agent was indicted on criminal charges. In April 1977, with the approval of Attorney General Griffin Bell, the Justice Department obtained an indictment from a federal grand jury in New York charging John J. Kearney with five felony counts stemming from illegal wiretaps and mail openings allegedly committed by agents under his supervision. Kearney had been the supervisor of the Weatherman Squad in the New York City office until his retirement in June 1972, after twenty-five years of service. Kearney was indicted only weeks before the statute of limitations would have barred his prosecution. This fact did not go unnoticed among present and former agents.

Rumors concerning pending indictments had been circulating for months as the Civil Rights Division of the Justice Department continued its proble. Approximately sixty FBI agents, most of whom had worked on Weatherman cases in New York, were granted immunity from prosecution in return for their testimony before the grand jury. For many of these agents, the burden of substantial legal fees was a financial disaster. Their counsel argued that since they were granted immunity by the government in return for their testimony, and since they had never been charged with a crime, the government should pay their legal costs. Not so, claimed the Justice Department, it would be improper to pay legal fees in a criminal case that the Department itself was investigating or prosecuting. *Catch-22* revisited.

I returned home late Wednesday evening on July 27 after a business trip to San Antonio and checked the recording device on my telephone for messages.

"Mr. Payne, this is Richard Johnston. I'm an attorney with the Department of Justice in Washington, D.C. I'd like to speak with you regarding an investigation we're conducting into surreptitious entries by the FBI. Would you please call me at area code 202, 324-3761."

The chase had begun.

19

The Hunter Hunted

One week had passed since the message from Washington, but I still hadn't returned the call. During the previous months, I had spoken with agent friends from around the country who had been summoned back for similar interviews and then unexpectedly paraded before a federal grand jury in Washington. From the information I received, the inquiry was more in the nature of a fishing expedition. It was obvious that under the circumstances, a less than candid reply given under oath could result in perjury charges. Questions along the lines of "Have you ever heard an employee of the FBI discuss surreptitious entries?" posed a genuine dilemma. To begin with, most agents heard about bag jobs in New Agents Class, if not later in the field. But even if they had heard idle gossip around the office—which was the rule rather than the exception—should they unjustly accuse a fellow agent? Rumor had it that a number of those who testified committed perjury.

What concerned me most was the fact that I had no idea what was in my deep cover file. Since I prepared none of the written reports, I had no way of knowing how my years of undercover activities were depicted. To testify under oath without the benefit of reviewing those files seemed an open invitation to perjury charges. But to request the files through a departmental attorney might expose the existence of deep cover.

I spent the afternoon preparing four separate requests to the FBI for my files based on the provisions of the Freedom of Information Act (FOIA) and Privacy Act (PA). The four letters covered requests for my Bureau personnel file; deep cover file, which was disguised as an informant file; and information on the SPECTAR and deep cover programs.

I returned home to find another recorded message from Mr. Johnston in Washington. It was similar to the first message in substance although I detected a hint of impatience in his voice.

I worked late that Wednesday evening and didn't arrive home until about eight. As luck would have it, I couldn't have picked a better night to catch up on paper work.

Less than thirty minutes before my return, Deputy Henry B. White of the United States Marshall's Office attempted to serve me with a subpoena to appear before a federal grand jury in Washington. He was advised that I was out of the city.

Ironically, I had visited with Henry on several occasions as an FBI agent while depositing or interviewing prisoners. I wondered if he recognized the name and associated me with the Bureau?

What a bizarre turn of events! Because I don't return a guy's call, he has me subpoenaed. After nearly eight years of being the hunter, I had suddenly become the hunted. How foolish I'd been to assume that my Bureau life was behind me. Though disturbed by the subpoena, I wasn't all that upset. With years of experience in the underground, I knew a lot more about hiding than they did.

I was a bit depressed over the prospects of hiding until I reviewed three days of telephone messages left on my recorder. The last message provided the only good laugh of the day:

"Mista Payne, this is Debbatee Henry B. White of the U-nited States Marshall's office. Now Mista Payne, *you know*, that *I know*, that *you know* you're supposed to appear before that federal grand jury in Washington, D.C. on Monday mornin' at eight o'clock. Now Mista Payne, I expect you to be there!"

But Henry, I shouted to the machine, that's not the way the game is played. In law school they always told me you had to find me first, then physically hand me the subpoena. Sorry Henry, but a recorded message just won't get it.

In view of the continuing investigation into the Bureau's search for the Weathermen and the indictment of John Kearney, I had assumed that the deep cover program had been quietly discontinued. Consequently, I was shocked to see news reports describing the FBI's arrest of five individuals closely associated with the Weather Underground.

Several of those arrested had been active in the antiwar movement at the University of Washington in Seattle, and three of them had been wanted since 1970 on fugitive charges. In 1973, one of the individuals had left the Red Sun Tavern only fifteen minutes before FBI agents came to arrest him.

What surprised me most about the media coverage of the arrest was the apparent effort by the Bureau, through press conferences and interviews, to reveal the full story of how two undercover agents had spent years infiltrating the Weather Underground. Agents were still being interviewed about earlier abuses, and here the national press was reporting a successful deep cover operation. Was it possible that this was part of a public relations effort on the part of the FBI?

Only a few weeks earlier, the press had reported a top secret FBI report linking the Weathermen with espionage agents from Cuba and North Vietnam. Apparently this report was an attempt to justify past abuses as legitimate counterintelligence measures conducted against secret agents of a foreign power. We were aware that the Cuban intelligence service had assisted certain Weatherman fugitives to flee the United States, but by and large these contacts had been made through the Vinceremos Brigade's annual visits to Cuba. If there was ever any tangible evidence that the Weatherman fugitives were functioning as espionage agents for a foreign power, I was certainly not made aware of it. In fact, as late as August 1976, Ed Miller, the former head of the Domestic Intelligence Division, publicly rejected that contention by stating that the FBI's investigation didn't justify the suspicion of espionage.

Early in February 1978, I was contacted by a former Bureau associate who told me he had recently been interrogated by members of the new prosecution team at the Department of Justice. He had noticed my name prominently displayed on an office bulletin board with a notation that it was essential I be subpoenaed. Upon inquiring further, he was informed that I was an uncooperative troublemaker who was playing games to avoid a subpoena. A fairly accurate description, I thought. But the government shouldn't have been unhappy with my elusiveness. After all, they taught me how!

After more than seven months of waiting, writing, and dodging subpoenas, I had not received a single page of the Bureau documents I had requested. It was apparent that I was getting the runaround, but I couldn't understand why. I would soon discover that attempts to obtain sensitive infromation from the FBI under the relevant provisions of the Freedom of Information (FOIA) and Privacy Acts (PA) can become an exercise in futility. Based on my experience, any potentially embarrassing information requested is subsequently classified to prevent its release. In my opinion, this tactic is another example of the way in which the FBI disregards the will of Congress in order to protect and perpetuate its image of infallibility.

After I sent my four separate FOIA/PA requests on August 3, 1977, I received a letter asking for a notarized affidavit of signature. Since I had been employed by the Bureau for almost eight years, submitted the request on letterhead stationery, and provided the exact file number, it seemed a bit strange. Even more perplexing was the fact that my four separate requests had been assigned only three reference numbers, making it impossible for me to determine which request was missing. The letter was a masterpiece of confusion:

> Should you find it necessary to correspond with us concerning this matter prior to release of any documents, please refer to number 51,331 which has been assigned to your personal record request. Number 51,340 is to be utilized concerning the SPECTAR request and *the final request number* to be used is 51.330. (Emphasis added)

When I forwarded the notarized affidavit of signature, I pointed out this discrepancy and asked for clarification. Some two months later I received another letter stating that "a preliminary review of documents pertaining to your request" would involve processing charges of approximately three hundred dollars; accordingly, I must provide written notification of my willingness to pay fees in excess of twenty-five dollars. Since no mention was made of the reference number, I didn't know what request they were referring to.

I sent yet another letter indicating my willingness to pay processing fees and pointed out that four requests do not equal three reference numbers. Then in late December, I received a letter acknowledging my request dated August 3, 1977. There was no mention of a reference number, but I was advised that documents pertaining to Revolutionary Activities would cost approximately $855. Once again, written notification regarding fees would be required.

This time I replied with a lengthy letter to Director Clarence Kelly summarizing all correspondence, the discrepancy in reference numbers, and a detailed synopsis regarding each of my original four requests.

In early February, I was advised by telephone that my personnel file would be released in one week. It finally arrived some six weeks later, but the covering letter was characteristically cryptic about the afore-mentioned discrepancy:

> The records you requested are being processed and on re-quest, information contained in your official Bureau personnel file and assigned request Number 51,331, has been completed and 309 pages are being released.

The last paragraph of the letter only added to the confusion:

> Your *other three requests* are presently being processed and as soon as determinations are made whether the information in our files is classified or releasable, you will be so notified. (Emphasis added)

They finally acknowledged that there were four separate requests even though they steadfastly refused to assign four reference numbers. But upon examining my personnel file, I discovered that the justifica-tion memo from Section Chief Bob Shackelford to Assistant Director Ed Miller, which I had helped prepare while in Washington, was miss-ing. The memo was referred to on the actual transfer documents as the basis for my official transfer, but the justification memo itself, which was personally approved by Director Kelly, was nowhere to be found.

I fired off a lengthy letter to the Justice Department's Office of Pri-vacy and Information Appeals outlining the circumstances and formal-ly appealing the withholding of the memo. After more than eight months, I had received nothing that would indicate my past involve-ment with deep cover.

On April 6, the day's mail produced the most asinine correspon-dence to date from the Chief of the Bureau's Freedom of Information-Privacy Acts Branch:

> Reference is made to our disclosure letter to you dated March 8, 1978. Additional information concerning your Free-dom of Information-Privacy Acts request pertaining to your-self and assigned request Number 51,331, has been processed and ten pages are being released.

After a quick glance at the ten pages, the reason for the delays, dis-crepancies, and dilatory tactics became patently clear: the FBI did not wish to acknowledge the fact that investigation conducted by an actual agent had been reported as though it had come from a confidential informant. The ten heavily censored pages were from the security informant file of LA 7852-S (Extremist). They were described as "additional information concerning your . . . request pertaining to yourself," and curiously assigned the same reference number as my official personnel file.

Suddenly a government employee's personnel file, with a 67 classification, is inexplicably lumped with that of a confidential security informant, which is always designed as a 134 classification! Even stranger was the fact that all ten pages released to me were copies of teletypes taken from records of the Communications Section instead of the actual informant case file. But more preposterous was the asserted basis for withholding an *undisclosed number* of "other documents" in their entirety. I was advised these documents were exempted from disclosure because they were "currently and properly classified . . . in the interest of the national defense or foreign policy," and that the disclosure of these "investigatory records compiled for law enforcement purposes" would "reveal the identity of an individual who has furnished information to the FBI under confidential circumstances . . ."

The FBI was now telling me that they could not release *my* informant file, the contents of which were obtained, developed, and reported by me as a deep cover operative, because the disclosure might possibly reveal *my* identity! How comforting to know they were looking out for my best interests, especially since the Justice Department remained intent on having a heart-to-heart talk—under oath before a federal grand jury. The literary masterpiece which so diligently sought to protect "properly classified" information in the interest of national defense or foreign policy failed to point out that the information hadn't been classified until *after* I requested it.

I suppose I should not have been surprised, for the FBI had been lying to the American public about similar requests ever since the inception of the Freedom of Information Act. Any information obtained by a deep cover source was routinely exempted from disclosure by alleging that its release might possibly reveal the identity of a confidential source. But the Bureau was well aware that information wasn't obtained by a confidential source—it came from an FBI agent. In effect, information that was obtained by a government employee was intentionally withheld from the American public in defiance of an Act of Congress. All of a sudden, it was much easier to understand why the word *subterfuge* had become such an indispensable part of Bureau terminology.

The ridiculous charade would continue for another six months without producing any tangible results. The Bureau would ultimately advise me that everything concerning my SPECTAR request was classified, as were all but twenty pages of documents regarding the establishment of deep cover, and these pages were excised beyond recognition.

I eventually learned that administrative appeals to the Justice Department, which theoretically assures compliance among all government agencies with the Freedom of Information and Privacy Acts, were equally futile. After another four letters appealing the FBI's action and requests for review of classified documents by the Departmental Review Committee, nothing of value was obtained. In fact, about two years after my original request, the Justice Department still had not notified me of the outcome of two administrative appeals.

But the appeal process was not a total failure. The Justice Department did acknowledge that the missing memorandum from Bob Shackelford to Ed Miller, dated August 17, 1973, did not appear in my personnel file "but appears instead in a file which is the subject of one of your other requests." I guess it didn't matter which "other request" because the memorandum in question was "classified in its entirety." I was certain they were referring to my informant file. A subsequent letter from the Department denied my appeal "on your request for access to your F.B.I. Security Informant file" since the remaining 174 pages were all classified.

I was courteously advised that judicial review of the Justice Department's action on both appeals was available through the United States District Court. Sure it was, I thought, and in addition to a review I'll also get a subpoena! No thanks, fellows, I think I'll go about it in another way. I might not know exactly what the files say, but I know their substance better than anyone. I was there.

In an unprecedented announcement made in April 1978, Attorney General Griffin B. Bell revealed the indictment of three former FBI officials for conspiring to "oppress citizens of the United States who were relatives and acquaintances of Weatherman fugitives" by violating their constitutional protections against unreasonable search and seizure.

Those indicted included former Acting Director L. Patrick Gray III,
W. Mark Felt, second in command under Gray, and Edward S. Miller,
former Assistant Director in charge of the Domestic Intelligence Division.

At the same time, Bell announced that the Department was dropping all charges against John Kearney, indicted one year earlier. This
move appeared to reinforce his stated policy of prosecuting the high
officials who gave the orders rather than the street agents who carried
them out. Those indicted were once high officials all right, but in my
opinion, Bell didn't go high enough. But perhaps the Attorney General
was not unmindful of recent events which demonstrated clearly that
those at the very highest levels of government would not be held ac-
countable for criminal acts.

Bell also ordered William H. Webster, who had been appointed FBI
Director less than three months earlier, to conduct an investigation
into the concealment of the sensitive Bureau documents which
formed the basis of the indictments, and to take disciplinary action
against sixty-eight unnamed agents who carried out the illegal acts under orders from superiors. But Bell didn't allow Director Webster to
discipline Assistant Director Wallace LaPrade, head of the New York
City office; the Attorney General relieved LaPrade of his duties, ordered him back to Washington, and requested his resignation, reportedly for committing perjury before the grand jury.

While I was not altogether unsympathetic to the plight of Felt and
Miller, I couldn't help feeling that they were an integral part of the
Bureau hierarchy that had created and fostered the fundamental problems of the FBI. Nonetheless, I respected them for publicly acknowledging that they had ordered the break-ins, and then along with Pat
Gray, refusing to follow the example of other high government officials who had accepted the offer of plea bargaining in exchange for a
misdemeanor charge.

I couldn't help feeling sorry for Pat Gray. He had been sold out by
his Republican cronies. Moreover, he had been deceived, perhaps be-
trayed, by high Bureau officials whom he had mistakenly trusted. I seriously doubt that Pat Gray ever knew the full extent of what was going on in the FBI, just as his successors didn't. I respected Clarence
Kelly for publicly admitting he had been deceived and then getting
rid of the officials responsible for his deception. Up until that point,
even Kelly, an insider, was unable to achieve full control of the old
guard, which time and again caused him public embarrassment by
providing erroneous information.

346

If Pat Gray personally ordered the resumption of surreptitious entries because of orders from the White House, he was being manipulated. If he tacitly agreed to recommendations from top Bureau officials to reinstitute the practice, he was being misled. After twenty-five years of employing those investigative techniques within the Bureau, there was nothing to resume or reinstitute. Regardless of the pious denials, bag jobs were an everyday occurrence when Pat Gray took office in May of 1972. After all, Gray served as Acting Director for less than two months before John Kearney retired from the FBI.

One of the most disgusting aspects of the entire episode is the fact that many people seem unwilling to recall the panic and outrage that swept through the country as the Weathermen claimed credit for bombing the Capitol and Pentagon during the early seventies. They were setting off bombs at will, and it was obvious the government was powerless to stop them. The agents who actually performed the illegal acts were doing so, in a crisis situation, on the orders of what they considered to be legitimate authority. They were honest, dedicated, well-meaning people conditioned to following orders without giving consideration to moral judgments. They believed in the American form of government to such a great extent that they never stopped to question the character or motivations of its leaders. Without a charter clearly defining the power, authority, and conduct of the FBI, it seems ludicrous to suggest some seven years later that street agents should have realized they were breaking the law.

In my opinion, Congress must assume its fair share of responsibility for failing to control the FBI or provide a meaningful charter governing its conduct. I would suggest that the politicians who failed to question or criticize the policies of J. Edgar Hoover during his forty-eight-year reign are just as guilty as those of us who faithfully carried out his orders.

Given the benefit of hindsight, the deep cover program seems a far greater intrusion into the personal liberty of American citizens than surreptitious entries. But as federal court records would subsequently reveal, the former Chief of the Bureau's Internal Security section acknowledged ordering the destruction of forty-seven file drawers containing more than fifteen hundred folders of documents in apparent defiance of orders from Director Kelly. More than half of the FBI's files detailing the search for Weatherman fugitives were destroyed. Speculation continues regarding the fate of deep cover files.

The three former officials who were indicted may have been overzealous and misguided, but given the times and the nature of the organization, it would seem they responded to what they perceived as a crisis situation by condoning investigative techniques that had been successfully employed for years; moreover, their allegedly "illegal" conduct reflects no indication of criminal intent or personal financial gain. Can the same be said of Richard Nixon?

And what about the senior officials who ran the Justice Department during those years? The same Republican appointees who endorsed implementation of the Huston plan and actively prosecuted political activists in the name of internal security can suddenly recall nothing about the FBI's use of questionable investigative techniques. For my own part, I find their self-serving denials absurd. I would suggest that not only did they know what the FBI was doing; they also encouraged the practice and continuously pushed for more of the same.

After the long, agonizing period of national self-examination following Watergate, I think we have all learned from the lessons of the past. Of far greater importance, it seems to me, is the culpability of the present high-ranking officials at FBI headquarters who knowingly misled Congressional committees, whitewashed the internal inquiry into the U.S. Recording Company scandal, and initially frustrated the Justice Department's investigation into intelligence abuses. Is it really necessary for FBI Director William Webster to rely on senior officials whose decisions are predicated on perpetuating the myth of J. Edgar Hoover's infallibility? The same officials, in fact, who continue to insist they knew nothing of the illegal break-ins until 1976?

I think not.

If the FBI reflects the attitudes of a realistic cross section of American society, has a steady influx of new blood—young people with fresh ideas—and develops a leadership willing to admit past mistakes, accept criticism, and build public confidence from the present, then the organization, the country, and the citizenry will have benefited.